The Themed Space

HT
321
.T54
2007

The Themed Space

Locating Culture, Nation, and Self

Edited by Scott A. Lukas

LEXINGTON BOOKS

A division of
ROWMAN & LITTLEFIELD PUBLISHERS, INC.
Lanham • Boulder • New York • Toronto • Plymouth, UK

METROPOLITAN COLLEGE OF NY.
LIBRARY, 12TH FLOOR
431 CANAL STREET

LEXINGTON BOOKS

A division of Rowman & Littlefield Publishers, Inc.
A wholly owned subsidary of The Rowman & Littlefield Publishing Group, Inc.
4501 Forbes Boulevard, Suite 200
Lanham, MD 20706

Estover Road
Plymouth PL6 7PY
United Kingdom

Copyright © 2007 by Lexington Books

All rights reserved. No part of this publication may be reproduced, stored in a retrieval system, or transmitted in any form or by any means, electronic, mechanical, photocopying, recording, or otherwise, without the prior permission of the publisher.

British Library Cataloguing in Publication Information Available

Library of Congress Cataloging-in-Publication Data

The themed space : locating culture, nation, and self / edited by Scott A. Lukas.
   p. cm.
 Includes bibliographical references and index.
 ISBN–13: 978-0-7391-2141-2 (cloth : alk. paper)
 ISBN–10: 0-7391-2141-3 (cloth : alk. paper)
 1. Themed environments. 2. Urban economics. 3. Leisure. 4. Amusement parks. 5. Consumer behavior. 6. Consumption (Economics)—Social aspects. I. Lukas, Scott A., 1968–
 HT321.T54 2007
 330.9173'2—dc22   2007024363

Printed in the United States of America

Contents

Acknowledgments ix

1 The Themed Space: Locating Culture, Nation, and Self 1
  Scott A. Lukas

Theming as Authenticity

2 Torque: Dollywood, Pigeon Forge, and Authentic Feeling in the Smoky Mountains 23
  Melissa Jane Hardie

3 Luna Park's Fantasy World and Dreamland's White City: Fire Spectacles at Coney Island as Elemental Performativity 39
  Lynn Sally

4 From Downtown to Theme Town: Reinventing America's Smaller Historic Retail Districts 57
  Thomas W. Paradis

5 Theming as a Sensory Phenomenon: Discovering the Senses on the Las Vegas Strip 75
  Scott A. Lukas

Theming as Nation

6 The Landscape of Power: Imagineering Consumer Behavior at China's Theme Parks 97
   Hai Ren

7 Theming Mythical Africa at the Lost City 113
   Jeanne van Eeden

8 Leisure Space: Thematic Style and Cultural Exclusion in Casablanca 137
   Bahiyyih Maroon

Theming as Person

9 "Above Us Only Sky": Themes, Simulations, and Liverpool John Lennon Airport 153
   Peter Adey

10 Love Hotels: Sex and the Rhetoric of Themed Spaces 167
   Derek Foster

11 How the Theme Park Gets Its Power: Lived Theming, Social Control, and the Themed Worker Self 183
   Scott A. Lukas

Theming as Mind

12 Behind-the-Scenes Spaces: Promoting Production in a Landscape of Consumption 207
   Ann Brigham

13 The Experience of a Lifestyle 225
   Brian Lonsway

| 14 | Themed Environments and Virtual Spaces: Video Games, Violent Play, and Digital Enemies
Talmadge Wright | 247 |
| 15 | A Politics of Reverence and Irreverence: Social Discourse on Theming Controversies
Scott A. Lukas | 271 |

Key Terms	295
Bibliography	297
Index	311
Contributors	333

Acknowledgments

I owe special thanks to the many academics who helped nurture my development as an anthropologist, particularly professors of the anthropology departments at Indiana University, the University of Iowa, and Rice University. At Albion College and the University of Iowa, Dr. Allen F. Roberts sparked my initial interest in the discipline and helped suggest a mediation of aesthetics and anthropology. At Rice University, I owe special thanks to my dissertation committee who advised me on my research related to themed spaces—Stephen A. Tyler, George Marcus, James Faubion, and Katherine Milun. At Valparaiso University and Lake Tahoe College, I have enjoyed incredible collegial interactions with faculty, staff, and students. At Lexington Books, thanks are due to my editor T. J. MacDuff Stewart, editorial assistant Patrick Dillon, and production editor Lynda Phung.

At the "American Cities and Public Spaces" seminar at the Library of Congress (sponsored by the National Endowment for the Humanities, Community College Humanities Association, and the Library of Congress), I would like to acknowledge all of my wonderful seminar participants. In Valparaiso, Indiana, to Thad Donovan of Mindbend for his friendship and creative inspirations, including typographic advice on this book. I owe special thanks to my parents, Frank Lukas and Clara Lukas, for their unconditional support of my education and research efforts over the years. To them, I dedicate this work.

Chapter 1

The Themed Space: Locating Culture, Nation, and Self

Scott A. Lukas

Throughout the world the themed space has grown in ubiquity, popularity, and diversity. Themed spaces range from restaurants like Rainforest Cafe, where animal sounds and sights greet diners, to casinos like the Excalibur in Las Vegas, where Arthurian themes and knights are the norm, to hotels like the Fantasy Suite chain, where couples can stay in rooms that follow over twenty different themes, to theme parks like Six Flags Over Texas, where visitors can walk through and participate in theme lands like Spain, Mexico, Boomtown, Gotham City, France, and Old South. In many countries, including Japan, previously taboo subjects like prisons and disasters like the sinking of the Titanic are referenced in themed bars and restaurants. Theming involves the use of an overarching theme, such as western, to create a holistic and integrated spatial organization of a consumer venue. Owners and designers of themed spaces like the ones described above understand the powerful value that theming offers in the competitive world of retail, entertainment, and service. This volume focuses on the contemporary significance of theming as it is realized in numerous themed spaces throughout the world—from restaurants, to casinos, to theme parks, and surprising spaces like medical clinics. The contributors to this collection have focused on the many ways in which themed spaces are projections of authenticity, on the relationship of theming to the nation, on the ways in which theming relates to individuals and their lifeworlds, and on the extensions of theming to the realm of the mind.

Webster's 1913 dictionary defines a theme as "a unifying idea that is a recurrent element."[1] A corollary definition suggests that a theme is absolute, in the sense of a noun that remains unchanged or unmodified by other forms of language.[2] Both definitions emphasize the immutable and unifying nature that characterizes a theme. Themes pertain to a multitude of cultural realms, including music (in which a theme is a central idea carried throughout a composition), and literature (in which a theme is a central idea through which the plot develops, characters react, and on which moral or social lessons are based). In everyday life, people understand a theme as something consistent upon which someone can base an argument. The theme, as a central idea about literally anything, is the basis for the amalgamation known as a themed space. A themed space, whether a casino, theme park, or restaurant, employs a theme to establish a unifying and often immutable idea throughout its space.[3] The themes that are used to create space in various venues are often drawn from contrasting, contradictory, and unreliable sources. As Jeanne van Eeden offers in her chapter on the theme park the Lost City, the legend that is used to establish a mythical understanding of Africa is based on numerous movies from many decades, the political ideologies of colonialism, and popular layperson understandings. Theming is a motivated form of geographical representation in which meaningful connections are made among unifying ideas, symbols, or discourses.[4] Even when the sources of theming are suspicious and often felonious, the themed space can still be meaningful to people and significant to social researchers.

The term *themed space* is now a common one in intellectual circles and everyday life. As the authors discuss in this volume, because theming has become such a commonplace aspect of our everyday lives, we are often unwilling or unable to effectively understand the consequences of theming in our lives. As anthropologist Bronislaw Malinowski said many years ago, the most imponderable things in our world are often the most important and the items to which we should dedicate our greatest concern, analysis, and resolution. The contributors to this volume hope to not only emphasize the extent to which themed spaces have come to effect the lives of people throughout the world, but to chart their significance, from a variety of disciplinary perspectives, and to further awareness of their complexity, contradictions, and roles in the lives of people.

The synthesis of recognizable symbols with spatial forms is not limited to the contemporary experience of themed parks, restaurants, airports and interactive museums. Since *Homo sapiens* developed what anthropologists call culture over fifty thousand years ago, academics have maintained an interest in understanding how processes of ordering and symbolically marking environments have come to define the human condition. Like the symbolically-ordered caves and dwellings that characterized our species years ago, the themed spaces of the contemporary period reflect a fascination with the application of aesthetic, cognitive, and cultural frames to the natural environment. Unlike the archaic spaces of our ancestors, the themed spaces of the present function in primarily consumerist contexts. Though many people do enjoy the forms of entertainment that take place within themed venues, the primary purpose of these spaces is not to fulfill human needs but to play on human desires. Desires, of course, are conditioned by human needs that can be fulfilled by entertainment spaces, including sexuality, happiness, sociality, and autonomy. Abraham Maslow did not have Arthurian-themed shows, casino video poker, and S&M-themed hotels in mind when he established the hierarchy of human needs, nor did Walter Benjamin conceive of the types of themed spaces that, today, prove his theory of the loss of the aura of aesthetics.[5] What each might appreciate is how consumerism generally and theming specifically play integral roles in our lives. Some cultural critics have either downplayed these roles or have scoffed at them, suggesting that theming, like most forms of consumer culture, is characteristic of shoddy, cheap, simulated, unreal, mundane, and insignificant contexts and behavior.[6] What social theorist Mark Gottdiener identified in 1997 in *The Theming of America*, however, is that theming *is* culturally, politically, and cognitively significant.[7] In the years that have passed since Gottdiener's work, the theming industry has expanded. Theming is now present in cities across the world, even in small towns. Large Las Vegas casinos to small, traditional diners have embraced the technologies, forms of performance, and mentalities that are characteristic of theming. In some locales, businesses have no choice but to theme because theming has become *the* recognizable form of architecture and associated (performative) service that people have in their minds. Some corporations, such as Fry's Electronics, use theming in an eclectic and local way. Fry's features electronics stores that are themed in a variety of ways, including Wild West, science fiction, Mayan, the music industry, historic Las Vegas, the 1893 World's Exposition, and many others.[8]

Theming is now marked by a transformation—from bounded cultural object expressive of place, culture and the like to a more micro-focused dimension that is specific to groups of people, the individual, and modes of subjectivity. It is also marked by fluidity—no longer will one facade suffice over a long period of time. Designers must update their themed spaces frequently. Theming, reflective of cultural meaning, is often a connection of the individual to the modes of delivery and the context of theming than has been commonly assumed. This is obvious in the enthusiasm that has been associated with theming and everyday life with groups who actively assess the quality of rides, attractions, and entertainment at themed venues.[9] With this increase in the popular recognition of themed spaces, in part spurred by the ubiquity of the Internet and new media technologies, themed spaces have become the active subjects of cultural discourse, among both academics and laypersons. In some cases, themed spaces can provoke controversy because of their subject matter or approach to theming, as Scott A. Lukas relates in his chapter on theming controversies, and in other cases themed spaces can evoke a sense of contempt for a corporation, such as Planet Hollywood, resulting in boycotts or actions against the venue.[10] At a more practical level, some people feel that theming is risky, particularly in the restaurant industry.[11] Some restaurant owners go as far to state that their restaurants *are not* themed venues, while others complain that themes are gimmicky devices and that the thing that really matters is the quality of the food and the service.[12] In a competitive consumer market, new theming may emerge not as a result of the creative aesthetics of designers, but as a response to novelty and the need to be more shocking in a saturated consumer space.

Mundane work spaces, such as businesses and office complexes, have begun to theme their locales. A *Star Trek*-themed dentist office in Florida, discussed in chapter 15, utilizes the symbolic recognizability of *Star Trek* and its ubiquitous fandom to connect with customers. Playgrounds such as Centennial Park in Davenport, Iowa, Normandy Farms in Foxboro, Massachusetts, and the Department of Transportation's Child Development Center in Barrow, Florida use themes ranging from riverboats, farming and tractors, and dump trucks to create spaces for child entertainment.[13] As more corporations move from what Nike chairman Phil Knight calls the shift from a production-focused corporation to one based on marketing, the presence of new and previously unfamiliar themed venues will increase.[14] Some companies now specialize in creating themed displays for conventions or themed events for any number of purposes. One allows the customer to choose from a Hawg Heaven Biker Bar complete with temporary tattoo parlor, motorcycles, and pinball machines.[15]

Outside the corporate and consumer world, everyday people have reacted to the widespread nature of theming by using it as a means of personalizing their own home worlds. The housing industry is the subject of new forms of theming. Originally, homes reflected a prevailing design theme, such as the Southwest, but with urban sprawl similarity of design has become an architectural norm. Condominium projects like the Impala in Manhattan and retirement communities like the Villages, Florida have begun to reverse a trend of unthemed living spaces.[16] The Impala uses theming of impala sculptures, streams, fountains, and wildlife paintings to charge high prices for its units.[17] The defunct television show *Monster House*, in which ordinary homes are given extraordinary themes, illustrates a public fascination with the expansion of theming.[18] Many everyday homeowners organize their living spaces, such as bedrooms, offices and bathrooms, according to a particular theme. One person might incorporate Egyptian artifacts, consumer goods and color patterns in her bathroom because she is fascinated with the geography and culture of Egypt, while another might theme his bedroom with sports memorabilia because of his connection with a popular sports team. The theming of the home and of intimate spaces that are not used by the public or determined by a corporation suggests a movement of theming into a more personalized realm.

This volume seeks to analyze these multiple dimensions of theming in four senses. The first focuses on theming as a form of authenticity. The authors focus on the ways in which theming is constructed as an authentic or knowable form of popular culture. The second section emphasizes the connections of theming to constructions of the nation. The next section details theming as related to the individual, whether a famous corporate figure like Walt Disney or Dolly Parton or an anonymous individual who visits a theme park. The final section is an analysis of theming as a product of the mind, as a cognitive process that is beyond the material features that are commonly associated with themed spaces.

Theming as Authenticity

One of the most telling aspects of theming is its seeming naturalness. Theming appears organic to the consumer in part because of the recognizability of the symbols invoked by designers and in major part because of the willingness of consumers to accept the stories told in theming as real, meaningful, and intimate. Slavoj Žižek once suggested:

> Fantasy as a "make-believe" masking a flaw, an inconsistency in the symbolic order, is always particular—its particularity is absolute, it resists "mediation," it cannot be made part of a larger, universal, symbolic medium . . . the dignity of a fantasy consists in its very "illusionary," fragile, helpless character.[19]

In line with Žižek's understandings of the psychological structure of fantasy, theming is a projection of desire—the need to control imagination through recognizable illusions. The fantasy of architecture has begun to overwhelm the senses and the psyche, and a number of contemporary theorists have suggested that public spaces, however themed, have given way to corporatism and consumer ideology.[20] The success of the major theme park corporations like Disney and Premier Parks lies in the corporation's ability to psychically lure customers to their places. As a member of one of the major theming corporations (Gensler Entertainment, whose credits include the design of Universal's theme parks) said of themed spaces, "Our guests don't know what it is about these places that makes them so engaging—yet they find them very compelling."[21] Beyond the experiences of themed spaces, John Urry has described the general state of tourism as an ingestion of familiar signs and symbols on the part of the tourist.[22] A sense of sentimentality of the familiar is discovered in the organic nature of themed rustic, ethnic towns, such as Frankenmuth in Michigan, Solvang in California, and Leavenworth in Washington.[23]

Melissa Jane Hardie's chapter on the success of the Dollywood theme park in Pigeon Forge, Tennessee indicates that an authentic feel that is promoted in theme parks and restaurants, including the Cracker Barrel restaurant chain, is not simply a product of authentic material construction. In the case of Dollywood the persona of star Dolly Parton emerged from country music fame and numerous movies and television show appearances and it allowed for the creation of a star-based authenticity that connected with fans and theme park patrons. As Hardie writes, Dollywood is a place "where fantasy is collapsed with documentary," and Dolly Parton's biography and its use to construct an authentic order at the theme park bearing her name shares much in common with the Liverpool John Lennon Airport, described by Peter Adey. Parton's crossover success, like the similar phenomenon of branding and multiple marketing, creates a biographic self that is recognizable to wider audiences. Like the geographical constructions of Disney parks and their constant references to the life and history of Walt Disney, the various theme lands of Dollywood make allusions to Parton's life and thus lend a powerful form of authenticity to geography as it intersects with the life. As Hardie describes in her research, at Dollywood, authenticity is created as a feeling.

Authenticity may be tied to direct performative and corporeal realities of representation. Lynn Sally introduces in her considerations of fire and flames spectaculars of Coney Island amusement parks, that the elements can be utilized to create thematic associations between place, person, and performance, the sum of which reflects a disparate attempt at an authentic order. In the example of Coney Island, Sally illustrates that the emergence of themed spaces coincided with the growth of new architectural and social forms, including modern urban traditions, immigration, the development of the city, and rapid social change. The anxiety of the social and the architectural is exemplified in themed spaces in which elemental performativity is present. Many contemporary themed spaces, allegorical of Coney Island amusements, use the essence of the elements—including water, fire, and air—as a way to connect the viewer or patron to the themed space. The senses, as Lukas relates in his chapter on the Las Vegas Strip, follow a similar use—powerful stories are told through the sensory associations created by the design of themed spaces and their performances. Sally's article on Coney Island is informative for its indication of the influence that early forms of theming had on contemporary themed spaces.

Theming operates at multiple levels of the authentic. Individuals, like those inhabiting historic Coney Island and contemporary Las Vegas, are the personal subjects of the stories told in themed spaces. Theming can impact the nature of community, including its very survival. Thomas Paradis' work on the theming of Flagstaff, Arizona suggests such a connection of theming and community. As he relates, entire towns have used the varied principles of theming to establish local identity and simulate tourism. When applied to the dynamics of downtown development, the effects of theming stimulate a politics that impinges on the project of authenticity. Paradis illustrates that the postmodern inconsistencies of downtown theming—in which elements and associations of theming may reflect local issues, geographies, and people and other times not, and in which referents are sometimes clear and other times confusing—create political dynamics that rival those of traditional, unthemed communities. As more communities like Flagstaff struggle with identity and the ability to establish economic stability, the powerful sense of authenticity that is connected to theming will be seen as a solution. The expansion of theming into cities themselves is an indication of the corporate success tied to theming industries. Celebration, Florida, Seaside, Florida and many other planned communities use theming to provide an overarching framework that establishes both security and recognition.

In addition to its operation at the level of community, theming, as already stated, functions at intense interpersonal and phenomenological levels. One of the most common means of achieving authenticity is through the connection of themed space to the individual. Scott A. Lukas' chapter on the senses and the Las Vegas Strip argues that theming plays an inherently pedagogical role in consumer spaces. Theming exemplifies what he calls *consumer authenticity* as it creates "authentic" states of being that are left as naturalized or imponderable states in the consumer. Because the consumer market has been saturated with themed spaces, the senses are deployed to establish a distinctive character with the consumer. Buildings, often themed in minute ways through microtheming, the performances of workers in authentic dress and modes of acting, and the extent of sensory elaboration of theming, all combine as an overall ambiance of theming or theming complex. Theming is at its height when it achieves a consistent, varied, and overarching form. As customers move through the thematic spaces of casinos, the properties are naturalized through them, in corporeal and psychological ways, and social relations are created in the strive for authenticity. Authenticity, as a semiotic-sensory property, "is created when signs no longer draw attention to themselves." As Lukas suggests in the sexism of Las Vegas, a troubling result of consumer authenticity is the privileging of sexist essences or archethemes in many casino spaces. As much as it reflects the joys and hopes of people, theming also projects their demons.

One of the pioneers of early filmmaking special effects, Douglas Trumbull, is now one of the leading practitioners of special effects, motion-based and virtual reality rides in the world. Trumbull has been quoted in many theme park documentaries and in trade writing of desiring to create a physical and emotional intimacy with patrons in the rides that he designs.[24] It is not surprising that the immersive perspectives of virtual reality are often understood as authentic consumer forms. Theming has always relied on the senses to establish legitimacy as an entertainment philosophy. In its earlier manifestations reliance on visual sights provided patrons with a sense of the unreal, geographically and architecturally, but in its most current examples, theming relies on the use of immersive landscapes, technologies, and holistic/connected architectures. Talmadge Wright's contribution to this volume illustrates how the interactive nature of physical themed spaces has led to new, previously unknown spaces of virtual theming. In their use of total sensory experience, designers create what is essentially a form of experiential hypotyposis in which the customer's senses, social interaction, and physical body are drawn into vivid contact with a themed space. Much of this technology is not new, only expanded—Lynn Sally's chapter on fire-fighting spectacles at Coney Island makes this point clear. The so-called experience economy has led more business and cultural destinations to increase the scale and depth of immersion offered by their spaces.[25] It is an economy based on the immersion of the customer in experiences. One recent phenomenon of themed spaces is the behind-the-scenes tour. Ann Brigham's contribution to the volume addresses how such tours claim to immerse visitors in "hidden" spaces, including movie studios and automobile factories.

Scott A. Lukas's piece on theme park training at AstroWorld looks at how forms of worker and patron control produce what is a form of ultimate immersion or *lived theming*. Lived theming is a form of absolute integration in which customers and workers are unaware of their own participation in an experiential site that is not of their own making. As theming continues to expand in new spaces such as hospitals, schools, and public parks, it is the technology of immersion that makes theming possible as well as profitable. Immersion instigates the search for consumer authenticity.

Theming as Nation

As many of the contributors to this volume demonstrate, at the simplest level, theming is a form of simulation. Simulation operates through projection—to another place, time, world, or culture. In themed spaces the total fantasy of simulation is created through use of architecture, technology, and human performance, and one of the overall goals of theming is to highlight customers' sensory experiences. The simulated experiences of themed spaces are determined by the ever-expanding expectations of what Stephen Greenblatt calls the *resonance and wonder* of museal spaces.[26] Themed spaces create the effective associations of their originals and copies in the minds of patrons by playing on the symbolic power of the nation. Jeanne van Eeden's selection on the South African theme park the Lost City illustrates how the traditional hegemony of the nation is transported to the simulated and mythic space of the theme park. Simulation, whether occurring in a theme park, casino, or restaurant, is always a political project—one tied to varied dimensions of ethnicity, gender, and other master statuses.

Years ago, Jean Baudrillard related the story of a group of people who upon seeing the Matterhorn at Disneyland, added, "How did they get it here?" Baudrillard's playful example allows one to see that through the coalescing of symbols, language, and experience offered in myth, visitors to themed spaces will often accept the constructed realities of such spaces as authentic, even original. One of Baudrillard's premises is that simulation is a form of masking the real: "Disneyland is presented as imaginary in order to make us believe that the rest is real, whereas all of Los Angeles and the America that surrounds it are no longer real, but belong to the hyperreal order and to the order of simulation."[27] Baudrillard is correct that nations themselves, especially the United States, enact simulation for economic and political reasons. To contrast Baudrillard's philosophical reflections on simulation and the themed spaces of Disney, Jeanne van Eeden's portrayal of the Lost City theme park in South Africa offers a more specific glimpse at how theming displays simulation. Van Eeden's analysis of theming emphasizes that the managerial operation of a themed space is dependent on creating meaningful stories, or myths, that provide a foundation for the establishment of the simulated space. Yi-Fu Tuan also addressed the creation of the simulacrum in space. He noted the concept of mythic space to address the exclusions, contradictions, and semiotic inconsistencies of marked space.[28] In the application of his theory to themed spaces, it is understood that themed spaces, as they operate through myth, generally share qualities different than those of scientific and pragmatic spaces like laboratories, older shopping malls, grocery stores, and medical offices. In the themed space, such contradictions and exclusions can be left unresolved. In the contemporary world, simulation through myth is being applied in more and more of the spaces described by Tuan as pragmatic. Peter Adey's chapter in this collection relates the use of corporate symbolism—the visage of John Lennon—to construct the Liverpool John Lennon Airport. His analysis reflects the fact that theming has expanded into pragmatic spaces, and this airport is not unique in its use of techniques of simulation.

The nature of myth in the themed space has all but approached the allegory of the cave offered by Plato in the *Republic*. As David Lowenthal has said, "we crave imagined locales more than we do actual ones."[29] The spaces of EPCOT, like so many of Disney's attractions, combine ethnicity and technology to create an overarching simulation of Americana that is matched by few theme parks financially. As Terence Young has considered, "a theme park's landscape gives form and narrative to a myth, but it also gives it a place."[30] As many of the authors in this volume contend, it is not space alone that establishes a themed space. Experience and the construction of activity in a themed space has as much to do with the believability of myth as does architecture, signage, and attractions.

One of the primary means that themed spaces establish the believability of myth is through performative theming. In themed spaces like those described by Hai Ren in this volume, the use of specific modes of performance—including costumed actors, singing and speaking performers with accents, and people who replicate another place—creates an authentic sense of a theme. In the case of Ren's understandings of Chinese theme parks, the performances of actors in parks like the Chinese Ethnic Culture Park represent an extension of the nation through non-traditional political means. The principles of theming are simultaneously the products of nation and help construct nation. In the globalized and technological era of contemporary society, theming develops as a consumerist mediation of the self and nation. As Ren illustrates, theming is at once an incorporation of the narratives of nation in material forms, a decisive economic process, and a corporate order that is resultant from neoliberal globalization. Venues within Chinese theme parks, like the urban village, shape the behaviors of individuals, naturalizing them in spaces of consumption. Through a functionalist modality of control—including the coordination of scenic spots and attractions, daily schedules for entertainment, and tour routes—the Chinese theme park establishes a naturalization of the visitor's consciousness for consumption. Ren argues that the theme park, as a corporate form, acts as a de facto government, shaping the behaviors and consciousness of the citizen-patron through varied means of consumption and theming. As he states, the Chinese theme park "concretizes the abstract idea of the nation in the form of the commodity, encouraging a cooperation between the symbolic and the material."

Similar to Ren's work on Chinese theme parks, Jeanne van Eeden's research indicates that the thematic projects of the nation bring with them the traditional forms of colonialism, albeit in new consumerist ways. Her work analyzes the constructions of mythical Africa at the South African theme park the Lost City. Themed spaces, like the Lost City, develop nation through forms of the picturesque—now offered through simulated, technological and consumerist architecture and performance. Such landscapes simultaneously reference a fear of and a desire for the other, created from longstanding cultural stereotypes made possible by colonialism. At the Lost City, the project of nation is created on the repository of culture—the essence of Africa is formed by references to diffuse popular understandings of Africa. This essence, like that common to all themed spaces, is not based on one principle or one stable meaning, but on multiple styles and originals. Designers of the Lost City admit to creating their themed space through references to popular movies like *Tarzan, Indiana Jones,* and *The African Queen.* Like themed spaces of the United States, the venues of South Africa reflect an ideology of the nation that is enmeshed in the popular politics of film and other entertainment narratives. Van Eeden writes that the essentialized conception of a primitive, exotic Africa in the Lost City is formulated on age-old visions of raced, gendered, and classed discourse—the idea of a myth of harmony with nature, the timeless primitive, a place of endless wealth, and of unlimited erotic promise. Similar to traditional colonial forms of the gaze, themed spaces like the Lost City appropriate nature, race, and landscape for a new form of the gaze—a consuming one that reflects a nostalgia for a colonial past. Like the ideology that supports the simulations within the park, the architecture and material means by which theming is performed also reference essentialist political constructions of Africa. Various elements, including water, are utilized to create atmosphere within the park, and the Lost City's legend is written in accord with elements like water. Van Eeden's chapter illustrates how theming is a "dramatization of a few central ideas," albeit ones that are dangerously connected to the politics of nation and hegemony.[31]

Theming is only possible if the presence of familiar forms of social power and hierarchy are comfortably masked through the symbolism and activities of space. In the tradition of the world exposition, most notably in the midway at the 1893 Columbian Exposition, racialism extended the unlineal cultural evolutionary traditions of social thinkers and politicians to spatial realms. Today, the designers and operators of themed spaces claim to offer more democratic, inclusive, and multicultural entertainment in their venues. However, as Lukas indicates in his chapters on controversial theming and the theming at AstroWorld, some cotemporary spaces reflect racial politics worse than those of the historic world exposition midway. One themed space in Mumbai, India—Hitler's Cross—went so far as to theme its space with the associations of Adolf Hitler and Nazism. Unfortunately, because designers and managers understand that the politics of the nation are very powerful, they often resort to references to it in their theming that are offensive. In contemporary themed spaces, like Dollywood, ethnic segregation is used to emphasize specific forms of nativism. Segregation also occurs through social class. Many themed parks, hotels, and restaurants offer more visitors the opportunity to see more of the venues or to take a behind-the-scenes tour for a price. Segregation, as a method of constructing themed spaces, is, clearly, political, but on a more general level, segregation is present in the mechanisms and architecture—including signage, queue lines, forms of crowd control, and display technology—that are used to control the movement and activities of bodies within such environments. In this collection, Bahíyyih Maroon's focus on beachfront clubs in Casablanca makes a similar point that social access is a major factor in the construction and negotiation of themed spaces.

In Maroon's analysis of Casablanca's Ain Diab resort district, a global imaginary is constructed similar to that of the Las Vegas Strip or Disney theme parks. Architecture, the specific features of interior decor, the typeface of signs, and the palate of colors chosen to theme a space are all intimately connected to the politics of nation at Ain Diab. As Maroon suggests in her chapter, "the fact that Casablanca's resorts were constructed to provide consumers spaces of play should not tempt us to think of these spaces as socially or politically inconsequential." Like all themed spaces, the politics of Casablanca's resorts are embedded in the intersections of designers, their design choices, and the social relations, interactions and interpretations, that are reactions to the materiality of design. The nation, as Maroon's analyses suggest, operates at gendered and ideological levels. In the case of the Ain Diab resorts, men are afforded greater access to the public consumer spaces, while women, due to their social status inside and outside of the resorts, are allowed less participation in the forms of entertainment in Casablanca. This reality of Casablanca is similar to the gendered constructions along the Las Vegas Strip. As well, exclusion is felt at religious, ethnic, and social class levels. Maroon's analysis of the commercialized and entertainment venues at Ain Diab emphasizes the ways in which the nation mediates the architectural and experiential aspects of theming.

Theming as Person

Theming is often effective when it involves the incorporation of real and exaggerated life histories in space. Personal stories used in theme parks establish an effective anamnesis or recollection of the past, albeit in exaggerated ways. Two of the clearest examples of the life history narrative being incorporated into public space are found at Dollywood, where each theme land relates to a specific period in Dolly Parton's life, and Disneyland, where Walt Disney's childhood experience is reproduced in the space of Mainstreet U.S.A.[32] Just as themed spaces are expanding to more parts of the globe, the life narrative is finding increased prominence in such venues. In this volume, Peter Adey's focus on the Liverpool John Lennon Airport is one example of such prominence. As he illustrates, the familiarity of superstar musician John Lennon provided the airport with an immediate way to make their theming meaningful to travelers. In their consideration of the *experience economy*, Schmitt and Simonson suggest that one of the five key principles of theming involves an approach that "should fit the character of the enterprise staging the experience."[33] So powerful are the corporate narratives, and ever more so as corporate life narratives, that themed spaces utilize this technique to make powerful connections between customers and their own life histories. Personal narratives are often projected back onto visitors as they associate experiences from their own lives with memorable theme lands, attractions, or rides.[34] The overarching life narratives of celebrities are also used to further personalize and individualize the activities of patrons who upon leaving themed spaces will desire to return if not for the memory. Adey refers to *biographical simulation* as the means by which Liverpool individualized the experience for the traveler. Unlike some themes, which because of their generalized and seemingly depersonalized nature may not interest patrons, the life narrative as a theme is personalized. In the case of the John Lennon-themed airport, the customer's experience of the theme is internalized, sensed, and taken within. As Adey writes, not only is the customer made to feel a part of something larger than him or her by the connection to the life history theme, the airport itself and the community become part of a larger form of belonging. In an era of postmodern, abstract, and blatantly consumerist architecture, the person-themed space suggests a more intimate, personal, and expressive quality of dwelling.

As many authors in this collection emphasize, the life narrative is employed to include the everyday person as well as the celebrity or corporate mogul. In this volume, Derek Foster's chapter illustrates how the life narrative is realized in constructions of intimacy and the self in Japanese themed love hotels. Foster's analysis of the rhetorical intentions of themed love hotels is instructive. His research indicates how theming is importantly situated within the interpretive contexts of visitors to themed spaces, not simply within the obvious and often faux forms of the materiality of theming. Just as the life narrative is used to theme spaces like Liverpool John Lennon Airport, Japanese love hotels encourage visitors to explore the self. Though visitors to themed hotels often recognize the obvious mimicry at play, the spaces are made meaningful by their role in personal and social senses, particularly as visitors interpret and utilize hotels in ways unintended by designers. Spaces like the love hotel allow people to escape their everyday reality and the social constraints of kinship and sexuality. As the various themes of the love hotel are personalized by the patron, a secondary aspect of theming is instituted. Because the theme of love is inherently personal and social, in the case of Japan's love hotels, ideas, themselves, are themed. In this sense, abstract and culturally embedded ideas that are typically felt by people in interiorized or psychological senses are made "real," or materialized, through their portrayals as themed spaces.

Life narratives are also used in traumatic themed spaces, like the Museum of Tolerance in Los Angeles, Grūtas Statue Park ("Stalin World") in Lithuania, and the Occupation Museum in Estonia.[35] In the first case, visitors are brought into the narrative construction of the Holocaust by understanding the horrific life experiences of victims and survivors of the Nazi camps. As Lukas illustrates in his chapter on theming controversies, at the conclusion of the over two-hour guided tour of the museum's exhibitions, individuals are given pictorial laser printouts of both survivors and victims of the camps. As a political and ideological intervention of everyday life, themed spaces are increasingly identified with atrocities and difficult experiences of the past. Whereas traditional amusement spaces may have used theming and other entertainment technologies to idealize the past, or erase it completely, contemporary themed spaces reference the tragic past through memorialization.[36] Memory is inherently a personalized project, and some themed spaces cite the past through the life histories of the many nameless people who perished in genocides and tragedies. Life experiences of religious figures have even been themed at sites including the Holy Land Experience in Orlando, Florida, addressed in Scott A. Lukas' chapter on theming controversies. In the case of the controversial Holy Land Experience, visitors to the park are encouraged to make the themed space more meaningful by personally connecting to the religiosity exhibited in the park. Venues like the Holy Land may suggest that a future trend of theming is to establish connections between the material aspects of theming and the immaterial features of culture and self that are localized in the individual who visits these spaces. Just as consumer culture has shifted the location of the meaning of material culture from the utilitarian features of the product to the connection of the product to the personalized lifeworld of the consumer, the themed space now draws on the unique or boutique appeal of consumer space.[37] In the sphere of cultural politics, the emphasis on the uniqueness of the individual and the romantic spirit to stand out in the crowd is idealized in the material conditions of themed spaces.[38] As Ann Brigham relates in research on behind-the-scenes theming, the contemporary consumer is told powerful messages about the self as he or she is drawn into a world that appears to be mutable, personal, and meaningful.

In a further extension of the person, theming is increasingly tied to direct social relations and forms of interpersonal conduct. Scott A. Lukas analyzes this dimension in his contribution on theming at the defunct Six Flags theme park, AstroWorld. In his analysis, he suggests that theming is not merely a means of architectural order, but a form of immateriality that targets the subjectivities of workers and patrons of theme parks. As theming "acts at a distance" it is instilled in costumes, scripts, narratives, and forms of social interaction that resemble familiar cultural orders, like those displayed in popular films.[39] The most quotidian aspects of human life are controlled in the theme park—even personal things like emotions are deployed to provide cues to workers and patrons. Themes are made meaningful at this most personal level and can, in their extreme, become a form of what Lukas calls *lived theming*. Lived theming indicates the incorporation of the modalities of theming at the innermost psychological and existential realms of the individual. Ultimately, though managers of themed spaces like AstroWorld attempt to control behavior through the rigorous applications of theming, such as in scripts and proscribed performances, the improvisatory character of the theme park worker's job often results in irregular or ambiguous theming. As an ultimate form of consumer culture, theming may be the last refuge of the Tayloristic manager or designer who wishes to exhibit greater control in the increasingly liquid and postmodern world.[40]

Theming as Mind

For a themed space to resonate with the consciousness of a customer in a meaningful way, it must weave through the channels of the mind to register a semiotic effect that is palpable and personal. As David Lowenthal once said, "The antecedents of theme parks are not to be found in mundane landscapes; rather, they lie in wishful and willful geographies of the mind."[41] The chapters in the last selection of this volume illustrate how theming has moved beyond the material conditions of architecture to the immaterial domains of social and psychological space. Though theming is still wrapped up in space, including virtual space, it is now produced in the "geographies of the mind" suggested by Lowenthal. Spatial theming has consistently tied the realm of the physical with the immaterial, the symbolic and the cognitive. As the cave paintings of Lascaux offer us, associations of place to other places (past or present), other times, and organic or inorganic matter are of necessity in the epistemic and spiritual development of the human species. As Mark Gottdiener has written, in ancient times "everyday life consisted of fully themed spaces where every tree, stone, place, and or individual had a connotative symbol attached to it."[42] Though theming uses physical properties like architecture to establish the unique symbolic potentials of a venue, it is through the project of cognition that theming is manifested, understood, and realized as significant in the patron.

Symbolic anthropologists, like Victor Turner, mention the many properties common to symbols, including the feature of *multi-referentiality*—the attachment by people of multiple meanings to symbols.[43] Corporations have used this property of signs to their advantage in attracting diverse crowds for profit. As Gottdiener has written, "themed milieus are designed to allow polysemy."[44] For theming to be effective, it must be the case that it be structured along diverse conceptual and interpretive lines. The predecessors of themed spaces, such as the lavish gardens built for the nobility of Europe, rejected a singular explicit language in favor of a geographical discourse that drew on the symbols present in the minds of visitors.[45] In a similar respect, contemporary architecture responds to the varied taste cultures and differentiated consumer interests among people through the use of eclectic and multi-referential design.[46] As projections to the mind, themed spaces play on the multiple memes or units of information that are present in any patron's cognition. In part, designers of themed spaces recognize that the mind is bombarded or saturated with multiple types and modalities of information, and in part they are cognizant of the fact that there are multiple referents for any given theme, whether western, Polynesian, or Egyptian.[47]

One of the newest approaches of theming technologies is the promotion of behind-the-scenes experiences. Ann Brigham's work centers on the behind-the-scenes theming of tourist attractions, including Disney theme parks and the Ford Rogue Factory Tour. Brigham suggests that the growth of behind-the-scenes attractions is tied to changes in consumption patterns, notably the development of the consumer as an active as opposed to passive participant in the economy. As patrons move through themed automobile exhibitions and film-themed amusement venues like Universal Studios and Disney-MGM Studios, they are seeming witnesses to cultural production in the making. Theming, as a production within the mind of the patron, differs from earlier amusements that relied solely on architectural and material formations. In the new era of theming, like that identified in Brigham's chapter, individualism, free choice, and authentic or productive consumption are instilled as the positive values touted by Disney and Ford. Patrons are told that their experiences with the themed space are unique—that, contrary to the popular idea that experiences with popular culture are forms of conformity to the culture industry, patrons are a part of the production process itself. As Brigham connects to larger trends in television and media, such as shows like *American Idol*, contemporary themed spaces present the patron with opportunities to shape culture itself. Whether or not the consumer has an active role in the production that is purported to be occurring in these spaces is debatable, but as Brigham indicates, the trend of behind-the-scenes theming will continue to mount in contemporary entertainment.

Perhaps the most significant aspect of the themed space is its growing ubiquity. Spaces that formerly were austere architectural forms are now dynamic, themed venues. The immaterial conditions of such spaces, including the way in which the visitor interacts with the space, have also been altered by the new conditions of theming. Brian Lonsway's work with new themed entertainment venues demonstrates the way in which theming has moved beyond the materiality of architecture into the psychological spaces of the mind. In Lonsway's chapter there is an indication of the new eclecticism of themed spaces. He describes the shifts in the economy—notably the movement to an experience-based one—and the impacts on contemporary architecture and development. Groups like the Urban Land Institute advocate new entertainment-experience spaces, known as UEDs (Urban Entertainment Destinations). UEDs establish a spatiality that is based in a mixed-use model, fusing residential, hospitality, and retail spaces. Many of these spaces are heavily branded, including ESPN Zone, and Lonsway's writing indicates the ways in which contemporary themed spaces, as projections into the interpersonal and psychological dimensions of living, are branded realizations.[48] As new spaces are branded, customers are often left unaware of the intentions of corporate makers and designers, due heavily to the ways in which the narratives of the stage and screen are deployed in themed venues. Beyond individual venues like ESPN Zone, Lonsway discusses a growing trend of theming—the establishment of themed cities, including theme park offshoots like Universal Studios CityWalk and lifestyle villages like Santana Row in San Jose, California. Like the popular Celebration, Florida created by Disney, these new venues encourage multiple use of space where patrons can live, work, and play all in the same area. Lonsway's chapter concludes with what might be the most striking example of theming as a cognitive production—the theming of formerly unthemed spaces, including hospitals and Alzheimer's clinics. In both cases, the architectural, narrative, and performative approaches of theme parks are translated to medical and clinical spaces: "patients" become "guests," MRI machines are transformed into sand castles, and mammography areas become English tea rooms.

The most current expression of theming is the use of virtual reality and immersive technology. More museums and cultural centers—such as the Roman baths in Bath, England and the Jorvik Viking center in York, England—use a combination of traditional architectural and narrative approaches and contemporary technologies like computer animation and hands-on interactive displays. This trend suggests a fusing of educational and entertainment venues and a hybridization of spatial and virtual technologies.[49] Hybrid theming utilizes both traditional spatial and contemporary virtual means to theme space, but a new form of theming, virtual theming, seeks to transform the entertainment and theming industry. Today many computers are organized according to particular themes, including personalized desktops and thematic tableaus that can be personalized according to the computer user's entertainment and lifestyle preferences.[50] Online casinos are also becoming ubiquitous. One recent Las Vegas magazine advertises virtual casinos that mimic the variety of theming found in physical Las Vegas casinos. The virtual themes include science fiction, tropical, old west, Spanish, Egyptian, and Venetian.[51] Talmadge Wright's chapter in this collection expresses the movement of theming to the realm of the virtual. His research on popular online interactive games like *Counter-Strike* expresses how themed spaces are no longer traditionally reserved to the material spaces of theme parks, casinos, and restaurants. Now, gamers can go online and participate in immersive environments that, like their physical counterparts, are spaces in which people can move, interact, and respond. The freedom of movement and interaction, like the similar sense of production in Brigham's behind-the-scenes spaces, gives the gamer a sense of agency and identity. He or she can move in virtual spaces, respond to other plays in real time, and use both the virtual environment and the experiences of other players to strategically occupy themed space. In some cases, Wright indicates that game designers use real spaces, like a prison in *The Suffering: Ties that Bind*, to inspire the construction of virtual geographies. Wright's work on virtual theming does more than illustrate the blurring of the physical and the virtual architectural worlds, it helps clarify the sociality that characterizes these new spaces like their physical themed predecessors, and it puts Lowenthal's concept of the "wishful and willful geographies of the mind" into context.

Scott A. Lukas's selection on controversial theming closes the volume. Lukas focuses on a further virtualization of theming—namely, the movement of theming into the realm of social and political discourse. Theming is no longer a pure form of entertainment that is disconnected from the real world of politics and culture. Today, it is part of the same discursive struggles that characterize the non-themed, non-entertainment world. Lukas begins his chapter with a consideration of the controversial Hitler-themed restaurant in Mumbai, India—Hitler's Cross. Like any other themed venue, the restaurant uses exterior and interior architecture, photography, signage, and color schemes to create a venue that references other spaces, cultures, and people. Unlike most themed spaces, it does so in a way that attracts international outrage. Venues like Hitler's Cross, due to their offensive nature, are forced to undertake what Lukas calls *retheming* or the transformation of the venue to a new or altered theme, often as a result of political or social controversy. Like aesthetic productions and museum displays, contemporary theming reflects an embeddedness in culture and politics that necessitates social response, or what anthropologist Victor Turner cited as an instigation of social action.[52] In some cases social controversies over theming, like those at the Biblical Holy Land Experience in Orlando, Florida, do not result in retheming or alterations of the venue, but in others, like the Civil War theme park Disney's America in Manassas, Virginia and Dracula World in Sighisoara, Romania, the result is the failure to realize and build the themed project. Lukas identifies some projects—like Dracula World, and violence-themed restaurants like Crash Cafe and NRA SportsBlast—as examples of *dark theming*.

Dark theming draws on previously taboo themes like violence, death, and genocide to provocatively organize a space in a thematic way.[53] Some themed venues incite social controversy because of their postmodern or excessive approach to theming, and because of their strangeness, they are often unrealized. Though the mind is practically limitless in its expression of ideas, some themed spaces take representational and cultural modes too far. Lukas closes the chapter of the volume with a reflection on the future of theming. Ironically, he suggests that some controversial spaces that were never realized, including Disney's America, may have offered cultural and political opportunities for the society in which it was planned. Today's world is increasingly apolitical, and it is more and more a world of entertainment. As much as some people loathe them, the themed space may offer the mind an important opportunity to consider significant social and political issues that have been considered in other domains, like aesthetics. Whether it is a themed space or not, as Stephen Mills once said, "A sense of place is perhaps, the ultimate synthesis, the bringing together of all dimensions of environment, perception and experience into a vast whole."[54]

Theming will continue to play a prominent role in everyday consumer life. Previously unthemed restaurant chains like McDonalds are even moving to theming some of their venues.⁵⁵ As discussed earlier, some themed venues, including restaurants, face a risky market rife with finicky, entertainment-seeking customers, and some weakly-themed venues, like Applebee's, may remain the most popular with the public.⁵⁶ In Orlando, Florida, the Holiday Inn Family Suites Resort offers corporate-themed rooms, including the Minute Maid, Edy's Ice Cream, and Coca-Cola suites.⁵⁷ This trend of the creeping corporatization of theming illustrates that the theme industry is dominated by powerful corporate interests. As major parts of towns and entire cities become themed, a trend in theming is what insiders call *synergy*, or the marketing of product tie-ins across multiple markets and venues.⁵⁸

It is difficult to deny that theming does reference other cultures, places, and people that are unfamiliar to some patrons or viewers; as such, this could suggest an emergent multiculturalism within the theme industry. For example, there is a United States trend in "Buddhist"-themed venues.⁵⁹ Unfortunately, the places, people and cultures represented are often presented in essentialized and stereotypical manners—a trend that began with the world's exposition tradition.⁶⁰ As one author, speaking of Mayan-themed restaurants, suggested, "This is entertainment, not Ethnology 101 and authenticity isn't a requirement."⁶¹ Themed venues are opening throughout the world, but their ubiquity does not mean that workers and customers will necessarily benefit from any sort of emergent multiculturalism.⁶² At the same time, there is an indication that both industry members and customers have become more sophisticated and that the obvious and stereotypical forms of theming and their referents of the past may become obsolete.⁶³ Ultimately, theming will continue to transform the worlds in which we exist—both consumer and otherwise.

Notes

1. Webster's 1913 dictionary, <http://www.bibliomania.com/2/3/257/frameset.html> (10 November 2006).

2. Hyperdictionary, <http://www.hyperdictionary.com/> (5 October 2004).

3. Very recently, definitions of the specific term *theme park* have appeared in online dictionaries. One offers a theme park as "an amusement park with a unifying setting or idea." Judy Pearsall, ed., "Theme Park," in *The Concise Oxford Dictionary* (New York: Oxford University Press, 2001). A second defines the adjective *themed* as "of a leisure park, restaurant, event, etc., designed around a theme to unify ambience, decor, etc." Anon., "Theme n. & v.," in *The Oxford American Dictionary of Current English* (New York: Oxford University Press, 1999), <http://www.oxfordreference.com/>. Based on the definitions of the themed space, we can see various yet recognizable characteristics that apply to the abundance of examples in our world.

4. According to Bakhtin, "Theme is a complex, dynamic system of signs that attempts to be adequate to a given instant of generative process." Mikhail Bakhtin [as V.N. Volosinov], *Marxism and the Philosophy of Language* (Cambridge, Mass.: Harvard University Press, 1986), 100.

5. Abraham H. Maslow, "A Theory of Human Motivation," *Psychological Review* 50 (1943): 370–96. Walter Benjamin, "The Work of Art in the Age of Its Technological Reproducibility: Second Version," in *Walter Benjamin: Selected Writings, Volume 3: 1935–1938* (Cambridge, Mass.: Belknap/Harvard, 2002), 101–33. Theming is not necessarily new. Many world's fairs were themed spaces, as were the earlier amusement venues of Coney Island. Theming played a role in the restaurant industry as early as 1902 with the Native American-themed dining room at the Astor Hotel in New York City. Robert Klara, "Familiar Themes," *Restaurant Business* 100, no. 10. Another example is the Brown Derby and El Morocco restaurants, see Bill McDowell, "Bread and Circuses: The Theme Restaurant Revolution," *Restaurants and Institutions* 105, no. 11: 50–72.

6. Greil Marcus, "Forty Years of Overstatement: Criticism and the Disney Theme Parks," in *Designing Disney's Theme Parks: The Architecture of Reassurance*, ed. Karal Ann Marling (Paris: Flammarion, 1997), 201–07. For an anti-insider or anti-emic view of Las Vegas, see Bruce Bégout, *Zeropolis: The Experience of Las Vegas* (London: Reaktion Books, 2003).

7. Mark Gottdiener, *The Theming of America: Dreams, Visions, and Commercial Spaces* (Boulder, Colo.: Westview, 1997).

8. For all of the Fry's themes see <http://en.wikipedia.org/wiki/Fry's_Electronics>. Even the United States Army has seen the value of theming, see G.E. Willis, "Army Hits Hole in One with New Restaurant Concept," *Army Times* 57, no. 48: 24–25.

9. Most commonly, these groups focus on the quality of the experiences at a themed space, like a Disney theme park. There are numerous such groups on the Internet. See, Marla Dickerson, "Self-Styled Keepers of the Magic Kingdom," *Los Angeles Times*, 12 September 1996, A1, 24.

10. For more information on protests in themed environments see Mark Gottdiener, *The Theming of America*, 2nd ed. (Boulder, Colo.: Westview, 2001), 145–68.

11. For more on the risky nature of themed restaurants, see Bonnie Angelo and Stacy Perman, "Hungry for Theme Dining," *Time* 148, no. 5.

12. Nancy Brumback, "Theme Song," *Restaurant Business* 103, no. 13: 42–43. Brett Clanton, "Hollywood's Out, Carnival's In: Restaurant Gets New Theme," *New Orleans City Business* 21, no. 32: 7. For the topic as it relates to the closure of Fashion Cafe, see Andre Salvail, "Fashion Cafe Goes Out of Style in N.O." *New Orleans City Business* 19, no. 4: 1–3.

13. Lynn Pinoniemi, "Theme Parks: Creating Memorable Playgrounds by Building on a Theme," *Parks and Recreation*, November 2003.

14. Naomi Klein, *No Logo* (New York: Picador, 1999), 22.

15. For the company that produces themed events see <http://www.encoreentertainment.com/themed-events/index.html>.

16. For more on the villages see <http://www.thevillages.com/index2.htm>. See also Hugh Bartling, "Tourism as Everyday Life: An Inquiry into The Villages, Florida," *Tourism Geographies* 8, no. 4: 380–402.

17. Real Estate Weekly, "Impala Opens in the East 70's," *Real Estate Weekly*, 11 October 2000.

18. Sample homes from the *Monster House* show may be viewed at <http://www.monsterhouse.tv/>. The popularity of theming can also be seen in public culture. Recently, *New York Metro* ran a "Create a New York City Theme Restaurant" contest. "Create a New York City Theme Restaurant," *New York Metro* <http://www.newyorkmetro.com/nymetro/news/people/columns/intelligencer/thecompetition/10431/index.html>

(3 October 2006). See also, Jaspistos, "Competition: Themed Eating," *Spectator*, 13 November 2004, <http://www.spectator.co.uk>.

19. Slavoj Žižek, *Looking Awry: An Introduction to Jacques Lacan through Popular Culture* (Cambridge, Mass.: MIT Press, 1992), 156-57.

20. Rebecca Solnit and Susan Schwartzenberg, *Hollow City: The Siege of San Francisco and the Crisis of American Urbanism* (London: Verso, 2000).

21. Anthony Iannacci, ed., *Gensler Entertainment: The Art of* Placemaking (New York: Edizioni Press, 2001), 5. For a discussion of authenticity and its relationship to architecture see Bradley Joseph Beck, "From Brand to Architecture" (MA Thesis, University of Cincinnati, 2003).

22. John Urry, *The Tourist Gaze: Leisure and Travel in Contemporary Societies* (London: Sage, 1990).

23. Stephen Frenkel, Judy Walton and Dirk Andersen, "Bavarian Leavenworth and the Symbolic Economy of a Theme Town," *Geographical Review* 90, no. 4: 559-84.

24. Howard Rheingold, "Total Immersion: Douglas Trumbull's Big Budget VR Debuts (Where Else?) in Las Vegas," *Wired* 1.05 (November 1993).

25. Joseph B. Pine, II and James H. Gilmore, *The Experience Economy: Work Is Theatre and Every Business a Stage* (Boston: Harvard Business School Press, 1999).

26. Stephen Greenblatt, "Resonance and Wonder," in *Exhibiting Cultures: The Poetics and Politics of Museum Display*, ed. Ivan Karp and Steven D. Lavine (Washington, D.C.: Smithsonian Institution Press, 1991), 42.

27. Jean Baudrillard, "The Procession of Simulacra," in *Simulacra and Simulation* (Ann Arbor: University of Michigan Press, 1994), 12.

28. Yi-Fu Tuan, *Space and Place: The Perspective of* Experience (Minneapolis: University of Minnesota Press, 1977), 99-100.

29. David Lowenthal, "The Past as a Theme Park," in *Theme Park Landscapes: Antecedents and Variations*, ed. Terence Young and Robert Riley (Washington, D.C.: Dumbarton Oaks Research Library and Collection, 2002), 18.

30. Terence Young, "Grounding the Myth—Theme Park Landscapes in an Era of Commerce and Nationalism," in *Theme Park Landscapes: Antecedents and Variations*, ed. Terence Young and Robert Riley (Washington, D.C.: Dumbarton Oaks Research Library and Collection, 2002), 6.

31. Alexander Wilson, *The Culture of Nature* (Cambridge: Blackwell, 1992),182.

32. It is interesting to note that Walt Disney's memory of his hometown became an impetus for the development of the main street that greeted all customers at the Disney parks. For more on this topic, see Richard V. Francaviglia, *Main Street Revisited: Time, Space, and Image Building in Small-town America* (Iowa City: University of Iowa Press, 1996), 147.

33. Bernd H. Schmitt and Alex Simonson, *Marketing Aesthetics: The Strategic Marketing of Brands, Identity, and Image* (New York: Free Press, 1997), 51.

34. Scott A. Lukas, "Signal 3: Ethnographic Experiences in the American Theme Park Industry" (PhD diss., Rice University, 1998).

35. City Paper, "Stalin World," *City Paper*, 8 March 2004, <http://www.balticsww.com/stalin_world.htm> (10 November 2005). Michael Tarm, "The Gift: Olga Ritso and Estonia's New Occupation Museum," *City Paper*, 14 March 2004, <http://www.balticsww.com> (10 October 2005). Gediminas Lankauskas, "Sensuous (Re)Collections: The Sight and Taste of Socialism at Grūtas Statue Park, Lithuania," *Senses and Society* 1, no. 1: 27-52.

36. For more on memorialization and life history, see David Simpson, *9/11: The Culture of Commemoration* (Chicago: University of Chicago Press, 2006) and Andreas Huyssen, *Present Pasts: Urban Palimpsests and the Politics of Memory* (Stanford, Calif.: Stanford University Press, 2003).

37. Virginia Postrel, *The Substance of Style* (New York: Harper Collins, 2003). More themed venues are drawing on the local interests of people to establish their spaces. This suggests the more boutique or specialized focus of theming. Barbara Rattle, "Locals Plan Chain of Motor Sports Theme 'Fan Gear' Stores," *Enterprise/Salt Lake City*, 17 June 1996.

38. For a discussion of the spirit of individualism in U.S. society see Robert N. Bellah et al., *Habits of the Heart: Individualism and Commitment in American Life* (New York: Harper and Row, 1985).

39. Norman Klein, "Scripted Spaces: Navigating the Consumer Built City," in *Architectural Design: Consuming Architecture*, ed. Maggie Toy (West Sussex, UK: John Wiley and Sons, 1998), 80–83.

40. For more on the issue of liquidity and the self see the work of sociologist Zygmunt Bauman, including *Liquid Life* (Malden, Mass.: Polity, 2006), *Liquid Modernity* (Malden, Mass.: Polity, 2005), and *Liquid Love* (Malden, Mass.: Polity, 2003).

41. Lowenthal, "The Past as a Theme Park," 12.

42. Gottdiener, *The Theming of America*, 18.

43. Victor Turner, *The Forest of Symbols: Aspects of Ndembu Ritual* (Ithaca, N.Y.: Cornell University Press, 1986).

44. Gottdiener, *The Theming of America*, 127.

45. Young, "Grounding the Myth."

46. David Harvey, *The Condition of Postmodernity* (Cambridge: Blackwell, 1989), 77.

47. For more on the concept of saturation and cognition see Kenneth Gergen, *The Saturated Self* (New York: Basic Books, 1991), 15–16.

48. See Klein, *No Logo*.

49. For more on the fusing of education and entertainment see see Margaret J. King, "Theme Park Thesis," *Museum News* 69, no. 5: 60–62; Margaret J. King, "The Theme Park Experience: What Museums Can Learn from Mickey Mouse," *The Futurist* 25, no. 6: 24–31.

50. The popular online space MySpace is a example of the thematic organization of the Internet; see <http://www.myspace.com>. Another example is Second Life, which includes user-created themed spaces; see <http://www.secondlife.com/>.

51. *Gambling Online Magazine* (Kennesaw, Ga.: GAL Highbury House Communications, 2004). For an interesting discussion of the ideological components of theming in video game spaces, see Shoshana Magnet, "Playing at Colonization: Interpreting Imaginary Landscapes in the Video Game *Tropico*," *Journal of Communication Inquiry* 30, no. 2: 142–62.

52. Turner, *The Forest of Symbols*, 36.

53. The idea of dark theming pays homage to the work on dark tourism. John Lennon and Malcolm Foley, *Dark Tourism* (London: Continuum, 2000).

54. Stephen F. Mills, *The American Landscape* (Edinburgh, Scotland: Keele University Press, 1997), 1.

55. Alan Bryman, "McDonald's as a Disneyized Institution," *American Behavioral Scientist* 47, no. 2: 154–67.

56. Some consider Applebee's to be successful because it relies on low-key theming as well as locally-based theming, much like Fry's Electronics. Bill Carlino, "Applebee's

Takes Root, Bears Fruit in Neighborhoods across America," *Nation's Restaurant News* 30, no. 30.

57. Rafer Guzman, "Hotel Offers Kids a Room with a Logo," *Wall Street Journal*, 6 October 1999, F1.

58. Jerry Adler and Maggie Malone, "Theme Cities," *Newsweek*, 11 September 1995.

59. Alana B. Elias Kornfeld and Valerie Reiss, "WWBD?," *Newsweek*, 14 August 2006.

60. Robert B. Rydell, *World of Fairs: The Century-of-Progress Expositions* (Chicago: University of Chicago Press, 1993). Perhaps, in the future, themed spaces will move closer to more "reliable" forms of cultural portrayal. Arguably, these spaces will never be authentic, as cultural anthropology teaches us. Indeed, is any space ever authentic or reliable?

61. Elaine T. Cicora, "Your Place or Mayan?" *New Times*, Cleveland Scene, 25 October 2006.

62. As an example, on the topic of Eastern European-themed restaurants in New York City, see Katya Kazakina, "Eastern Bloc Party," *New York Times*, 25 June 2000.

63. As one insider stated, "You don't have to hit the customer over the head with cultural references like pagodas." John Forgetta, "Architect Brings Art to the Table," *Daily Variety* 270, no. 5. Additionally, some researchers are now beginning to focus on the patron's response to themed spaces. See Claus Ebster, "The Role of Authenticity in Ethnic Theme Restaurants," *Journal of Foodservice Business Research* 7, no. 2: 41–52.

Chapter 2

Torque: Dollywood, Pigeon Forge, and Authentic Feeling in the Smoky Mountains

Melissa Jane Hardie

> EXCUSE OUR PROGRESS
> *WE'RE BUILDING A BRIDGE TO THE PAST!*
> — Construction sign at Dollywood.

On the Dollywood Web site Dolly Parton writes that her "one wish for you during your visit to Dollywood is that the wonder of the Great Smoky Mountains will touch your heart."[1] In keeping with this wish, the centerpiece of the audiovisual attractions of Dollywood is a song called "Heartsong." The Heartsong video, which can be purchased at the park, represents Dollywood, and the Smokies, with hyperreal, *Blue Velvet*-like landscapes curiously juxtaposed with the lyrics of the song and its bittersweet refrain. In a landscape entirely denuded of its typical astringency, Parton's celebration of her life consists mostly of a representation of Mountain life in the forties, clusters of children and families, and Parton's reminiscing monologue. The heartsong metaphorizes the virtual space of Dollywood, a space in which an assemblage of attractions works to stir the heart. The heartsong also metaphorizes the park itself—a discrete themed space adjacent to the Smoky Mountains National Park—which "sings" its representations of the character of the district, past and present; though these temporal markers, like so much at Dollywood, are liable to blur. The park's purpose is to create an affective space where hearts are touched; in its evocation of the autobiographical narrative of Parton's life and career, of the history and vicissitudes of hillbilly life, and in its deliberations and calibrations of authenticity in the context of this conspicuously postmodern space, the experience of affective dislocation and relocation frames both the amusements of the park and narrative descriptions of its character. The park represents both a commercial space allied to the developing tourist sites, which its success has spawned, and a miniaturized and sequestered thematic virtualization of the "authentic," rustic past. This chapter explores its permutations of the possibilities of affect within these distinct yet interrelated precincts.

Since her crossover from country to pop in the 1970s, Dolly Parton has parlayed her idiomatic engagement with country music into a profitable empire. Crossover stages an allegorical journey from the authentic and naturalized interior of the country to its artificial and exploitative coastal fringes; what might otherwise be a transition over time is framed as spatial relocation. Parton's own Hollywood career replays this story of the country ingenue gone to town (*9 to 5*, *Rhinestone*, *Straight Talk*), extolling the entrepreneurial skills of the professional country woman (*The Best Little Whorehouse in Texas*). Named after Hollywood and herself, Dollywood, her theme park, is situated in Pigeon Forge, Tennessee, a town commonly seen as the tackier, "crossover" cousin of Parton's nearby hometown Sevierville, Tennessee.

Parton has turned the site of Dollywood into a simulation of the country way of life, employing numerous family members, and locals, and preserving country arts; Dollywood is Parton's prosthetic representation of both her personal past and the past of the Smoky Mountains. The surrounding Smoky Mountains National Park, cleared of inhabitants to become a national park, gives the tourist an interior and "authentic" space in which to experience uninhabited mountain life; expatriated mountain dwellers form part of the landscape instead of Dollywood's commercial precinct. Although Parton herself lives elsewhere, chimerical Dolly Parton residences stud the park. "Dolly's Tennessee Mountain Home," a "two-room replica of Dolly's childhood home," finds its latter-day companion in an apartment for Dolly when she is visiting the park—a residence that might mainly exist to mask the true location of Parton's Dollywood pied-à-terre.[2] Dolly's Tennessee Mountain Home contains relics of Parton's childhood, and features a narrative written by Dolly's sister, Willadeene, which opens, "The winter of 1946 is special in my memory," and continues to describe her anticipation of the birth of a sister who will become Dolly Rebecca Parton: "Don't ask Dolly what we had for Christmas that year. She would probably say nothing and just laugh—she doesn't remember for she was just a baby, not even born yet." Though the park can be understood as an autobiographical space, Parton as autobiographical subject is introduced well before her own birth, a Tristram Shandy figure entirely appropriate for the picaresque adventures the park recounts.[3]

The mission statement of Dollywood is "Create Memories Worth Repeating."[4] Since it opened in 1986, Dollywood has become both the most popular attraction in Tennessee, and the county's largest employer.[5] In purely economic terms, then, those memories are worth a great deal, and Dollywood's eminence was achieved with significant government support; according to Mark Gottdiener, the city spent $600,000 and the state $1.6 million for infrastructure to support the park, "including street and sewer lines."[6] In 1987, Dolly said that in her newly opened Dollywood "she wanted to build a fantasy world somewhere in the mountains for everybody to share with her" and to "show what her part of the country was really like, how her people really lived."[7] On the one hand Dolly imagines Dollywood as a place of imaginative projection, a "fantasy world" remote from the everyday and open to all. On the other she wishes for a simulation of life in the Smoky Mountain hollow, one whose value lies in its authenticity, that is, its closeness to the everyday. As distinct as these two ambitions may seem, this chapter argues that Dollywood represents an attempt to synthesize the two; one way to understand Dollywood is as a spatial resolution of these distinct aims. Dollywood becomes a venue where fantasy is collapsed with documentary, and located somewhere between the memories the park represents and those it creates.

Crossover

Michael Ann Williams and Larry Morrisey note that the development of the Great Smoky Mountains National Park was coeval with the emergence of a radio show broadcast nationally by John Lair from Kentucky:

> Unlike the largely uninhabited western lands that had earlier become parkland, the three eastern national parks authorized in the 1920s and created during the 1930s ... were inhabited. In the Smokies over a thousand families lost their homes, the largest park removal in U.S. history.[8]

As this pairing suggests, the creation of an environment such as the national park offered a form of authenticity that depended on its geographical anchoring and the arrest of human intervention in the natural landscape. At the same time, the facilities of broadcast radio promoted a certain geographical emancipation of local arts—an emancipation which represents at a technological level the hazard of late capitalism's technologies of commodification. The radio show—a staple of country music's commercialization as an industry—provided the means to do at an aural level what is otherwise denoted as a spatial transformation: to crossover, and television broadcast would extend that process as it became the principle venue for broadcasting country music, now audiovisual.

The historical record suggests that crossing over was always in Parton's future. As early as 1966, her recordings were pitched at a pop market, even against her will.[9] Parton was reportedly wary of a move to pop, but interested in complicating her role as country star by singing soul music.[10] Parton experienced her greatest exposure to the world of country as Porter Wagoner's "girl-singer," on his eponymous television show, but Wagoner scorned the very idea of soul on country television: "She would scream and holler—'Whaaaaa'—that type of thing ... and I wouldn't allow that on my show because I knew the people wouldn't buy that, with my audience."[11] Not surprisingly, Dolly's break with Porter Wagoner was the most decisive step she took as she crossed over, and her move to the mainstream, the first such break by a major female country star, was construed by her and others as "feminist"; crossover is read as both a mark of and inspiration for female "confidence."[12] Parton collected such unlikely fans as Andy Warhol and Patti Smith. Smith did a cover of Dolly's pre-crossover crossover hit "Jolene," while Warhol made her portrait. And for Parton, regular appearances on Johnny Carson's *Tonight Show* and astute management lead to personal wealth.[13] Parton's career epitomized a narrative of crossover success. Nonetheless, Parton was aware of the cost of crossing over—country fans are loyal to death, but pop fans are fickle, as Alanna Nash observes.[14]

Perhaps in an attempt to mitigate risk, Parton claimed that she was not leaving country but merely taking it wherever she went.[15] In her crossover, Parton did not simply lose or abandon her country roots. Instead, Parton complicated a formal account of country idiom, troping transcendence of parochial mannerisms and topoi as a parody of crossing. This complicated figure confounds the geographic delineation of a true or authentic country topography, suggesting that Parton replaces an understanding of topography as ground with a demonstration of country as figure. She meta-figuratively introduces her self as country, as coeval and coextensive with country, and a figure of country as the portable commodity she both possesses and materially instantiates. Rather than her following the country route, she herself becomes the route that country must follow.

Dolly Parton's plan to build a theme park appears to have been central to her conception of stardom, and significant as a way to mitigate the loss of authenticity entailed in crossover. Originally named Silver Dollar City, Dollywood's renaming concatenated the very local with the ultracommercial business of country music; Parton's neologism maps her own crossover and the practical shift of the operating center of her business empire to California—including her production company Sandollar—onto the landscape of Pigeon Forge, Tennessee. Dollywood's name plays on the phonological resemblance to Hollywood, rather than alluding to the more conceptually congruent name of Disneyland. However, the park mimics several aspects of Disneyland quite deliberately. Disneyland—a utopic rendition of a (Los Angelean) "Main Street U.S.A."—recreates the fantasized core of the American landscape on its entertainment coast. Dollywood features Dollywood Boulevard, and so replaying the pun of its name by relocating Hollywood Boulevard in the Smokies, a location that celebrates Parton's "memories worth repeating" as memories of the movies. Dollywood, in its address to the Hollywood Hills, reframes the Smoky Mountains as both the originating point of country culture and its logical place of retail and recreation: entertainment. Entertainment at Dollywood devoted to representing the travelling significatory possibilities of country music exemplifies the way in which its historicism can be understood in geographical or topographical forms. Transitions that characterize Dolly's past may be found in the show Back Where I Come From, "a spectacular multimedia experience that blends the beautiful imagery of the Smoky Mountains with today's most popular country hits."[16] The show features contemporary country but also showcases (now vintage) performers from the Grand Ole Opry, entertainers such as Charlie Louvin, Jean Shepherd and Jeanne Sealey. The idea of authenticity remains a critical factor for understanding Parton's permutation of "country style." Dolly's success as a country artist in the 1960s pivoted, in part, precisely on an appreciation of her authentic country roots and manners. Dolly claimed of herself: "I am so totally me that it would scare you to death."[17] Minnie Pearl, doyenne of the Grand Ole Opry and country legend claimed that: "She was so country. She was so authentically country.... The emphasis was on her singing then. They don't talk much about authenticity now because there's been so much crossover. But then it mattered a great deal. And she was authentic."[18]

Although debates over authenticity may have preceded its rise, it is the case that the development of "countrypolitan" music in the 1950s framed the debate as it touched Parton's own career. As Jensen notes, the "more pop-sounding" style of countrypolitan "sparked heated debates about whether country music had 'crossed over' and sold out."[19] The metaphor of crossover organizes the question of authenticity spatially. The concatenation of *country* and *politan* frames the question of genre in terms of a shifting or travelling location, from country to town. Williams and Morrisey note "the invention and mass production of the automobile made the widespread development of tourism possible."[20] Parton's crossover was also persistently metaphorized as a road trip. From *New Harvest* (1977) to *White Limozeen* (1989), Dolly traces her allegory of crossing through an intricate mix of country traditionalism and iconoclastic critique. The white "limozeen" figures the picaresque transformation of career through the figure of a transforming car. The cover of Dolly's crossover album, *New Harvest, First Gathering*, offers a representation of an allegory of the labor of journey involved in crossing. Parton, the passenger, sits in a pickup; a country metaphor of harvesting and gathering puts country behind her and puts herself behind country as a trope. Dolly remains a passenger, and so the vehicle becomes a figure for her as a witting manipulator of her own vehicular, figural status.[21]

The term *country* was first applied to regional American music in the eighteenth century, and histories of country music draw particular attention to the sourcing of country idiom, musical structure and topoi in British ballads and lyrics from at least the sixteenth century.[22] While the lyrical preoccupations of country music can be sourced in the transplanted archaism of a colonizing country, the construction of country music as an identifiable domain of artistic practice involved drawing on a wider set of sources, including the significant impact of Hawaiian guitar technique, and African American musical traditions. In other words, the colonial debt at evidence in the musical idiom of country is put to work with the lyrics of a colonizing culture. Whatever country music is, its sources demonstrate a complex colonial ideology—an account of which needs to include at least the colonizing of the American continent by Europeans, the colonizing of the Hawaiian islands by America, and the ubiquitous inscriptions of a slaving culture. British narratives of the frontier and of perils of liminality occult colonialism through figures of alien/supernatural invasion or retribution, as is seen most pertinently in the border ballads. These are redeployed in country music with precisely the same occlusions to do new work. Tropes of natural hazards, an unyielding nature, and of the brutality of the rustic are the ways in which a systematic oppression may be repressed and still memorialized. At Dollywood, many rides and attractions reflect this tension with nature and the rustic. White water rapids rides, mine rides and many other attractions point to the idea of a dangerous nature or frontier, but one that can be managed by human intervention. A discourse of regional authenticity similarly masks heterogenous origins. If country music is a generic and stylistic hotchpotch, which incorporates the rhetoric of colonization and displacement to produce a new idiom, one of the clearest effects of this etiology is provided by its discourse of purity. Similarly, at Dollywood attractions like an old country schoolhouse complete with a teacher who instructs students in spelling help focus the park narrative on the pure and innocent of culture. Though country was born from the accidental accumulation of diverse artistic practices through a series of colonial endeavors, country artists are carefully assessed according to their place of birth, their race, their accents and vocal technique:

> Since its commercial beginnings in the 1920s country music has been strongly self-referential, constantly making notes of its own authenticity. This referencing also takes place on the individual level; it is not enough to perform, write, or produce country music, one must authenticate one's own life experiences. Autobiography in a variety of forms is pervasive in country music. Despite the artifice of the genre and its show business roots in vaudeville and the travelling medicine show, "real" cowboys, cons, and coalminers' daughters abound.[23]

As Jensen notes, the question of authenticity in country music becomes a question related to genre: "country music uses authenticity as a generic marker, a way to define itself both as separate and worthy."[24] It is necessary to read this movement within country at least two ways, to recognize the multiple forms of historicism at work in the construction of authenticity. On the one hand, a concern with the preservation of country as a distinct and regional musical style acknowledges the impressive history of country music in the twentieth century, flagging this often maligned music as an impressive cultural contribution whose producers and consumers are drawn from some of the socially and culturally most marginal inhabitants of America. When country is understood as a rural and working class art, antagonism to crossover may be read as a response to the hegemonic globalizing of local practices that retreads regionalism according to the dictates of the marketplace, which takes a specific art form and turns it into a specialist's niche. Historically, country provides an account of contemporary internecine conflict, because in its rural idiom it describes the economic oppression of the "country" South by the North; crossover artists and strategies are denounced as "cultural carpetbaggers."[25]

Authenticity, according to Richard A. Peterson, is a conceptual cornerstone of country music: "[f]rom the outset, country music was seen as a rustic alternative to urban modernity."[26] Peterson's authenticity is fabricated; he notes that "authenticity is not inherent in the object or event that is designated authentic but is a socially agreed-upon construct in which the past is to a degree misremembered."[27] The authenticity of the country performance is both regional and related to pastness; authentic style has historical resonance as well as regional specificity. Parton's claim to authenticity was always represented as a fabrication. Nash explains: "Dolly comes across as being for real, the genuine article, despite the deliberate and obvious falseness of much of her exterior. Her ambivalences and contradictions seem somehow natural, normal, and almost totally uncontrived."[28] As Dolly herself sings:

> What difference does it make
> If I'm real or if I'm fake
> On the outside where it matters not at all.[29]

The term *countrypolitan* is heterglot in a fashion strikingly similar to *Dollywood*, mapping genre and location. Dollywood's themed environment organizes its own authenticity through similarly paradoxical markers of stasis and movement. Located so close to Parton's own birthplace and abutting the national park, Dollywood occupies its territory as a patch of ground devoted to the thematic representation of the aesthetics of both country music and county life. Throughout Dollywood's space, local craftspeople—advertised as "authentic"—portray the simple yet profoundly talented aspects of country life: soap makers, ironsmiths, and other trades are on display for the patron. At the same time the park features the usual assortment of amusements, and in particular a characteristic assemblage of rides which disorients its subjects: roller coasters and flume rides ("water excursions") work to destabilize any sense of physical stability. The Dizzy Disk, for instance, offers "a ride that glides back and forth while simultaneously spinning in circles."[30] Little about its experience assures a sense of belonging, let alone place; the simulated landscape of Dollywood is instead perceived through the rotations, convolutions, and sense deprivations of the ride. Similarly, the ride's progress is at best a form of transportational complexity rather than a transposition; like Parton's crossover, the ride glides back and forth.

Junk Jewels

> Every history that is not merely a chronicle or fable must presume to be intrinsically spatial, to be about spatiality, in much the same way that history is presumed to be intrinsically social, about the sociality of human life. But while the paren-

thetical (social) is normally taken for granted by historians, the parenthetical (spatial) must be insistently asserted—as geohistory or spatio-temporality, never history or temporality alone—as a consciousness-raising aide-mémoire.
—Edward W. Soja[31]

Roadside America's editors describe Pigeon Forge and the nearby town of Gatlinburg sparkling "like junk jewels on a necklace choking Great Smoky Mountains National Park," and note that Cherokee "applies torque from the North Carolina side."[32] Roadside America, "the online guide to offbeat attractions," is a self-consciously ironic Web site devoted to the seemingly infinite variousness of the American vernacular landscape. Part historical, part teratological, its catalog is framed as a virtual experience of the culture of automobile tourism. At Pigeon Forge it locates a sensation of engulfing asphyxiation, surely the antithesis both of the culture of ecological preservation *and* of the road trip, yet it describes Pigeon Forge as at once both exemplary and exceptional—"the standard by which all Tourist Traps must be benchmarked."[33] Circling the Smokies, the resort town's "junk jewels" fringe an authentic interior whose perimeter "neck" is defined as a state-sanctioned place of recreation and preservation.

Williams and Morrisey note that the National Park Service attempted to forestall commercial development close to the park:

> It appropriated land to create a buffer zone, denied leases of land to local people who wished to build tourist accommodations . . . [but by] the 1980s touristic development of Gatlinburg, wedged up against the park boundaries, had reached critical mass, and commercial growth spilled over into adjoining Pigeon Forge.[34]

Concern arises over the proximity of commercial activity to the park, and with the mobility of that activity which sharply distinguishes it from the park—whose contours are fixed and vulnerable to infraction. If the national park represents an aim to quarantine natural spaces and their authentic "history" from the vicissitudes of commodity commerce, these roadside attractions subject that park to torque: they "twist" or "rotate" it. The operations of torque resemble the nature of metaphors as tropes to "twist," and equally this vision of rotation must be metaphorical, a way of figuring the twisted or inauthentic version of the Smokies those towns render. At once, then, these attractions might offer genre "benchmarks"—"a standard or point of reference against which things may be compared or assessed"—and distortions or "twists" of their own locality.[35] Sixty years after its development, the pristine park, now archiving remnants of mountain life but evacuated of live inhabitants, is fringed or choked by the overpopulated and overly representative tourist towns.

In Pigeon Forge, Roadside America continues, a "hundred attractions crush your sense of proportion or dignity."[36] Benchmarking tourism produces another sense of loss, both physical and psychological—disorientations of scale produced by the indignity of sheer numerousness. Dignity—the prerogative, one presumes, of the natural landscape—isn't sensible to the tourist. The landscape itself loses its evocative potential (rendered as a pathetic fallacy at one remove) precisely as the tourist experiences the indignity of a man-made landscape. Like the "torque," or twisting that places the national park under stress, these tourist attractions crush: they suppress or overwhelm the visitor. The loss that might be attributed to residents—of home or semi-secluded locality, across the decades—is reassigned to the tourist.

The town disorients, above all, the knowing or witting spectator who became a key and prolific purveyor of the camp aesthetic in the 1980s. Roadside America salutes the "offbeat"—that which syncopates the landscape, drawing attention to what is unstressed; what abbreviates or punctuates that which is uniform and unremarkable. Roadside America's target reader is neither the ecologically minded park visitor nor the fan of the bungee jumping, miniature golf, Bible-themed memorabilia and taffy stands of Pigeon Forge and Gatlinburg, but rather the consumer of retro and camp. The interest and ubiquity of retro style in the 1990s was curiously buttressed by the development of the Internet as an archival and commercial space; Roadside America catalogs retro style, while Web sites like eBay sell it. Between these two distinct "authentic" spaces of the national park and Dollywood's "authenticity" as "misremembered past" is interposed a third zone—the citations and catalogs of the roadside connoisseur of vernacular culture.[37] Its characteristic mode is ironic, and its ambition is to place the affective effects of vernacular culture within the framework of a self-consciously parodic nostalgia for relics of a culture that typically rests outside the historical frame of the observer.

Offbeat attractions bear some of the characteristics of a market economy, and in particular they require at the very least a notional scarcity: the offbeat retro attraction of Roadside America is typically cataloged as a member of a dying species, as fallen into desuetude, as unappreciated and imperiled by virtue of that fact. The deployment of an Internet archive for these abandoned or forgotten relics narrates a story where what was once plentiful has become scarce. This representation of the vernacular landscape as a dwindling resource creates another form of historical narrative, one in which the past not the present figures plenty; it is not the "good old days, when things were bad" that Parton sings about, but the past as boom culture. It is no coincidence that the audience of the offbeat attraction is typically a baby boomer, and it is no wonder, then, that the "plenty" of Gatlinburg and Pigeon Forge is at odds with the ethos of the site.

Roadside America writes of Pigeon Forge that "[a] hundred attractions crush your sense of proportion and dignity."[38] The body in this landscape loses its capacity to feel oriented, and its disorientation is reminiscent of Fredric Jameson's postmodern hyperspace "transcending the capacities of the individual human body to locate itself, to organize its immediate surroundings perceptually, and cognitively to map its position in a mappable external world."[39] This space offers none of the soberness of the national park with its carefully delineated borders and buffer zone, but it reproduces instead the dizzying disorientation that constitutes the privileged experience of the theme park's dizzy disks. The park's play with temporalized space—"authentic" historical interiors that relocate temporal change as spatial distinction—continues in the commercial space of the strip mall and its serial attractions. In excess, the offbeat produces the sensation of syncope: "to swoon."[40] This loss of attention or cognitive arrest, displayed in an extravagant physical lapse, is perhaps what makes Pigeon Forge a benchmark for the tourist experience as it produces an offbeat or quotidian version of that sense of sublimity dubbed Stendhal's syndrome after that writer's description of the fainting fits occasioned by the spectacle of "real" artworks in sublime clusters.[41]

Whereas the "differentiation of product" defined the postmodern vernacular aesthetic of the Las Vegas Strip according to Robert Venturi, the attractions of Pigeon Forge and Gatlinburg—miniature golf courses, go-cart racing, bungee jumping, and souvenir shops—tend to resemble one another, and operate more as an assemblage of similar sites than a strip of singular variety.[42] They are not only wedged up against the park but against one another, providing little visual relief or variety. What is stranger, of course, is that these congeries of attractions can have the capacity to draw together essentially dissimilar signifiers to look the same: dinosaurs, giant skulls, rabbits and rebel flags tend to resemble one another in an aesthetic that ties the archaic to the transitory, and creates the new through the application of fluorescent paint, aging finishes and the simple suggestion of "attraction." Amusements which seem culturally and historically poles apart—Pigeon Forge offers both a bear pit and bungee jumping—coalesce in their shared space, producing abrupt and disorienting juxtapositions and incitements of interest. While the modest (though lurid) facades of the attractions might hide rambling spaces—the souvenir shops are warehouses of kitsch—it is a collection of sites that imparts the sense of "statistical density" largely through aesthetic continuity.[43] Precisely as Stendhal's syndrome depends on the experience of numerousness—the assemblage of artworks within the one locality or horizon—Pigeon Forge disorients through the power of numbers. This bricolage effect puts pressure on the senses; disorientation comes from the flow of forms and their encroachment on the senses.

The Bargain Store

Applying torque, or twist, to the spectator and the natural landscape alike, these towns introduce a way to think about the southern landscape, ironic tourism, and the retailing of authenticity. More specifically, Roadside America's apostrophe to the town of Pigeon Forge is remarkable for the attraction that it elusively names, merely to disdain: Dollywood. Ironically, given Parton's desire to demonstrate what that part of the country "was really like," the visitor from Roadside America chooses not to stop at Dollywood, describing it as looking "too corporate and too expensive."[44] If the offbeat attraction is one way to torque the notion of what may be aesthetically and culturally pleasing, another kind of disorientation is provided, in turn, by the attraction that fails to attract. Euro Disneyland, now Disneyland Paris, epitomized the unattractive attraction, as well as the ungainly transportation of a corporate aesthetic (read North American) to an "other" landscape; it is not much help in understanding the disdain evident in the comment at Roadside America.[45]

The commerce of Dollywood, like that of Pigeon Forge and Gatlinburg, is framed around the deployment of authenticity as a feeling. While the national park provides a venue in which to experience a romantic sublime, the postromantic allure of the commercial strip unsettles the sense of place ostensibly offered by Dollywood's "heartsong" of authentic time travel. The commercial strip is indebted to its location even in its disorienting variety; Dollywood cites a topography whose imaginary Southernism is historically and culturally specific. The traveler to the United States may find the delineation of the "South" and of "country" problematic precisely because they are not culturally indexed within these discourses, except as "outsider." Throughout the theme park, European American values and cultural histories are exhibited, to the exclusion of the life histories of other groups. Williams and Morrisey make the point that "in terms of visual imagery, the Wild West, Victoriana, and Appalachiana are largely interchangeable in the tourist world of the theme park."[46] Authenticity itself is supplanted by the citation of history *itself* as an act that holds authenticity as a characteristic. If the fringe of the roadside attraction, Pigeon Forge, trades on the irony of a commercialized authentic Smoky Mountains experience, Pigeon Forge itself is fringed, or cusped by the corporate site of Dollywood. These sites represent authenticity precisely as Parton characterizes her own authenticity—it is both self-evident and paradoxical. As Parton states herself:

> If I could get their attention long enough, I felt they would see beneath the boobs and find the heart, and that they would see beneath the wig and find the brains. I think one big part of whatever appeal I possess is the fact that I look totally one way and that I am totally another. I look artificial, but I'm not.[47]

In all these comments, the question of authenticity is relocated to the interior and mapped onto the physical and topographical "heart." This move is insistently antimodernist, in Gottdiener's sense that modernism entailed a desire to "eradicate all sentimentality and traditional symbols within the city."[48] The pattern of heart and fringe refigures the urban landscape as intensely sentimental, and what consistently characterizes the experience of it in this precinct is its capacity to create sensation, even if this sensory experience is typified by Roadside America as deleterious.

The roadside postmodern landscape of manufactured authenticity is demarcated by its affective appeal, its capacity to dis- and re-orient bodies in space as a way to experience the pastness of a style, a place, a life. Brian Massumi notes that the notion of positionality requires the conception of a still body, "the body in cultural freeze frame."[49] Yet such a representation of the body presupposes its place in systemic relations, not in lived, dynamic experience; "to the extent that it is dynamic and alive" the body is "in passage or in process."[50] The experience of sensation resembles the experience of authenticity Parton offers and metaphorizes it in her own body; it is an experience necessarily self-conscious and reflexive, because "sensation is never simple. It's always doubled by the feeling of having a feeling."[51] The sense of complexity is reminiscent of Dollywood's mission: "create memories worth repeating." Memory has that same self-consciousness as memories are always remembered *as* remembered, always already repetitious and doubled by the experience of remembering. It is perhaps with these experiences of numerousness that the origin of the fainting or swooning encounter with the commercial strip, and the "too commercial" Dollywood, might be best reframed—the experience of sensations that overwhelms a sense of positionality within the landscape. Parton's landscape simultaneously shows something of history and creates something to be remembered.

Parton's 1975 hit song "The Bargain Store" offers a similar analogy in its evocation of a seduction as another form of restitution of value:

> The bargain store is open, come inside
> You can easily afford the price
> If you don't mind the fact that all the merchandise is used
> With a little mending it can be as good as new[52]

Parton's song sustains a sometimes tenuous allegory between a woman's life and the commodity: "my life is likened to a bargain store." Ten years later Parton "likens" her life to a theme park. Secondhand goods remind us that something already owned is distinctively different to something "brand" new. Within the confines of the themed space—the bargain store—value is found in that which has already been used, but which can be fabricated to create fresh sensations, "memories worth repeating."

Williams and Morrisey write that:

> Dollywood, created in the 1980s, contain[s] compelling testimonies to the changes in the lives of individuals in the upper South during the early to mid-twentieth century and provide[s] alternative perspectives from those found in the "authentic" and official material representations of life during that period.[53]

The space of Dollywood is a miniaturized landscape that does not reproduce, but rather invents a lived, authentic experience of the district by which it is surrounded. That district, meanwhile, exhibits few of those features, either because of a state-sanctioned program to remove their traces (the clearing of the national park) or because of the encroaching quality of the commercial strips, built, ironically, on the success of the park they "choke" with their prosperity. As a miniaturized landscape, Dollywood shares those qualities of the miniature isolated by Susan Stewart, who writes that "[t]he miniature does not attach itself to lived historical time . . . the metaphoric world of the miniature makes everyday life perfectly anterior and exterior to itself."[54]

This miniature world may incorporate the kinds of testimonies Williams and Morrisey mention, but in doing so it frames an authentic recreation outside the everyday in a space whose authenticity is registered not by its historical accuracy but by its hyperbolic, affecting qualities. It is an invented landscape just as the "country" of country music is "both a real and imaginary landscape."[55] The aim is not to stir memory, but to *create* memories from the fabricated authenticity of the space, a process of recollection that recreates value from what is otherwise lost. Such recreation does not provide a sense of sure location; by contrast, the work of the park is augured by the disarranging sensations of the tourist traps, Pigeon Forge and Gatlinburg. These towns thwart the incorporation of the area into a catalog of the offbeat by virtue of their capacity to overwhelm—a capacity which shakes the body from its sure position and into an experience of its own motility. This work replicates the attractions of the theme park, a space devoted to the enhancement and exaggeration of sensation in the physical experience of the ride and the emotional experience of the heartsong in its nostalgic recreation. From the depopulated center of the national park, to its miniaturized remnant Dollywood, to the choking cluster of attractions that circle its perimeter, this district offers themed spaces as exercises in physical disorientation and historical invention.

Notes

1. See <http://www.dollywood.com>.
2. This comment was made to me by a staff member on a visit to Dollywood in summer, 1998.
3. *Tristam Shandy* was a novel published by Laurence Sterne in 1759.
4. From the official Dollywood Web site, <http://www.dollywood.com/general/ddays.html>.
5. Information taken from "Dollywood General Fact Sheet," available through the park's Web site, <http://www.dollywood.com>.
6. Mark Gottdiener, *The Theming of America* (Boulder, Colo.: Westview, 2001), 116.
7. Leonore Fleischer, *Dolly: Here I Come Again* (London: Star Books, 1987), 223.
8. Michael Ann Williams and Larry Morrisey, "Constructions of Tradition: Vernacular Architecture, Country Music, and Auto-Ethnography," in *People, Power, Places: Perspectives in Vernacular Architecture, VIII* (Knoxville: University of Tennessee Press, 2000), 167. See also Michael Ann Williams, "What Have they Done to the Old Homeplace?: The Uses of Traditional Architecture in the Country Music Industry," *Tourism Development: The Theming of Vernacular Settings* 104: 1–12, Center for Environmental Design Research, International Association for the Study of Traditional Environments, Traditional Dwellings and Settlements, Working Paper Series (Berkeley: University of California).
9. Alanna Nash, *Dolly* (Los Angeles: Reed Books, 1978), 64.
10. Nash, *Dolly*, 112.
11. Nash, *Dolly*, 112.

12. Nash, *Dolly*, 4, 211.

13. Nash, *Dolly*, 138.

14. Nash, *Dolly*, 36.

15. Nash, *Dolly*, 1.

16. <http://dollywood.com/shows/show_detail.aspx?AttractionID=336>.

17. Nash, *Dolly*, 187–88.

18. Nash, *Dolly*, 108–89.

19. Joli Jensen, *The Nashville Sound: Authenticity, Commercialization, and Country Music* (Nashville, Tenn.: The Country Music Foundation Press and Vanderbilt University Press, 1998), 3.

20. Williams and Morrisey, "Constructions of Tradition," 161.

21. At Dollywood, the car plays an important role in a number of the park's attractions. During some seasons, classic cars line the "main street" area of the park.

22. Nick Tosches, *Country: Living Legends and Dying Metaphors in America's Biggest Music* (New York: Charles Scribner's Sons, 1985).

23. Williams and Morrisey, "Constructions of Tradition," 162.

24. Jensen, *The Nashville Sound*, 7.

25. Nash, *Dolly*, 149.

26. Richard A. Peterson, *Creating Country Music: Fabricating Authenticity* (Chicago: University of Chicago Press, 1997), 55.

27. Peterson, *Creating Country Music*, 5.

28. Nash, *Dolly*, 2.

29. Nash, *Dolly*, 129.

30. From the description of rides on the park's Web site; see <http://dollywood.com/rides-attractions/ride-detail.aspx?AttractionID=103>.

31. Edward Soja, *Thirdspace: Expanding the Geographical Imagination* (Oxford: Blackwell, 1996), 171.

32. Roadside America's "Pigeon Forge and Gatlinburg" at <http://www.roadsideamerica.com/attract/TNPIGmecca.html>.

33. "Pigeon Forge and sister tourist town Gatlinburg sparkle like junk jewels on a necklace choking Great Smoky Mountains National Park (mini-mecca Cherokee applies torque from the North Carolina side). Statistical density hampers attempts to assess this Mecca cluster (as with super-stuffed Wisconsin Dells, Wisconsin or Branson, Missouri). A hundred attractions crush one's sense of proportion and dignity." See <http://www.roadsideamerica.com/attract/TNPIGmecca.html>.

34. Williams and Morrisey, "Constructions of Tradition," 170.

35. *The Oxford English Dictionary*, <http://www.oed.com>.

36. <http://www.roadsideamerica.com/attract/TNPIGmecca.html>.

37. Peterson, *Creating Country Music*.

38. <http://www.roadsideamerica.com/attract/TNPIGmecca.html>.

39. Fredric Jameson, *Postmodernism, or, the Cultural Logic of Late Capitalism* (Durham, N.C.: Duke University Press, 1991), 44.

40. *The Oxford English Dictionary*, <http://www.oed.com>.

41. The concept is associated with the author "Stendhal" in the book *Naples and Florence* and was also described by psychiatrist Graziella Magherini's 1989 book *La sindrome di Stendhal*. In 1996, the director Dario Argento offered a film that dealt with the syndrome and it was also considered, albeit as a psychological reaction to brands and consumer products, in William Gibson's novel *Pattern Recognition* (New York: G.P. Putnam's Sons, 2003).

42. Robert Venturi, Denise Scott Brown, and Steven Izenour, *Learning From Las Vegas: The Forgotten Symbolism of Architectural Form* (Cambridge, Mass.: MIT Press, 1993), 34.

43. There are of course a few exceptions to this rule, most particularly the Carbo Police Museum and the bear pit at the Three Bears Gift Shop which, at the time of my visit, confusingly exhorted the passer-by: "see five bears!" Both attractions are singled out for special mention by Roadside America.
<http://www.roadsideamerica.com/attract/TNPIGmecca.html>.

44. <http://www.roadsideamerica.com/attract/TNPIGmecca.html>.

45. For more on Euro Disneyland see Andrew Lainsbury, *Once Upon an American Dream: The Story of Euro Disneyland* (Lawrence: University Press of Kansas, 2000).

46. Williams and Morrisey, "Constructions of Tradition," 170.

47. Fleischer, *Dolly*, 223. For more on Dolly Parton's autobiographical details, see Dolly Parton, *My Life and Other Unfinished Business* (New York: Harper Collins, 1994).

48. Gottdiener, *The Theming of America*, 30.

49. Brian Massumi, *Parables for the Virtual: Movement, Affect, Sensation* (Durham, N.C.: Duke University Press, 2002), 3.

50. Massumi, *Parables for the Virtual*, 5.

51. Massumi, *Parables for the Virtual*, 13.

52. Dolly Parton, "The Bargain Store," *The Bargain Store*, © 1975 RCA.

53. Williams and Morrisey, "Constructions of Tradition," 162.

54. Susan Stewart, *On Longing: Narratives of the Miniature, the Gigantic, the Souvenir, the Collection* (Durham, N.C.: Duke University Press, 1993), 65.

55. Jensen, *The Nashville Sound*, 7.

Chapter 3

Luna Park's Fantasy World and Dreamland's White City: Fire Spectacles at Coney Island as Elemental Performativity

Lynn Sally

Here, seated in an outdoor auditorium, are thousands of people who have paid, some dearly, to watch a tenement-looking house erupt into flames, fire fighters rush onto the scene to fight the fire, and inmates of the inferno narrowly escape death as the flames are extinguished.[1] This scenario was featured in two exhibits at Coney Island in 1904: Fire and Flames and Fighting the Flames at Luna Park and Dreamland, respectively. Why turn-of-the-twentieth-century thrill seekers at Coney Island were willing to pay to watch such a scenario is somewhat understandable. There is an inherent fascination with watching the flames of a fire, and fire fighters had by this time solidified a place in the public imagination as urban folk heroes. The exhibit may serve as a precursor to the genres of disaster films (*The Towering Inferno, Backdraft*) and amusement rides (Backdraft and Earthquake rides), an early experiment that proved people enjoy watching (and experiencing) catastrophe and chaos slowly overtake order.

But why were these exhibits, in all their simultaneously mundane and spectacular glory, the most popular attractions at Coney Island's enclosed amusement parks during the 1904 and 1905 seasons? Thrill seekers could ride on camels, catapult through the air on roller coasters, take a trip to the moon with moving dioramas fabricating take off. They could experience catastrophic disasters—floods at Galveston and Johnstown, eruptions of Mount Pelée and Vesuvius—spectacularly presented as elaborate stage productions with beautifully painted backdrops and moving scenery and more electric illumination than could have possibly been imagined. They could see moving films, projected larger than life, and wander through acres and acres of architectural glory—a permanent world's fair affixed in a natural landscape in close proximity to yet worlds away from the metropolis. And among all this architectural and technological glory, a simple exhibit with a simple story became the hit show of Coney Island.

Though the story line was simple (fire erupts, fire fighters rescue victims and become heroes, flames are extinguished), and the set of the drama was familiar (a tenement-looking building on an urban street), the narrative that these exhibits put forth was anything but simplistic. Precisely why the Fire and Flames and Fighting the Flames exhibits became so hugely popular is unanswerable to some degree. Ultimately, I am less interested in finding a definitive answer to that question than I am in thinking through the exhibits' multiple and often contradictory production of meanings. Fighting the Flames and Fire and Flames staged the burning of a tenement-looking building, providing spectators with disaster that was thrilling yet benign. Examining this exhibit provides insight into urbanites' growing anxieties surrounding the influx of immigrants, the growth of the metropolis, and the advent of modernity. I am proposing the concept of *elemental performativity* to theorize what these exhibits "brought into being" in their historic and cultural specificity.

By examining performativity and how it has been adopted and developed by other theorists, elemental performativity seeks to theorize the thing done (the reiteration of the urban order and fire) and the doing (the multiple layers of meaning produced from these exhibits) as mutually constituting. Elemental performativity suggests a space of liminality—a space that, in the context of fire-based disaster spectacles at Coney Island, allowed pleasure seekers to celebrate the growth of the metropolis, the heroism of fire fighters, and the advent of modernity at the very same moment in which they were invited to succumb to their anxieties surrounding those same phenomena. While elemental performativity is dependent on the natural elements, namely fire, for its possibility of being, it is not reducible to nature and is, as I will argue, a distinct phenomenon of American mass culture.

Luna Park's Construction of a Fantasy World

At the turn of the twentieth century, cultural institutions such as amusement parks ordered subjects through their desire to suspend their social norms and participate, though purchasing power, in a fantasy world. In the case of Coney Island's enclosed amusement parks, such a fantasy world was fabricated through unimaginable displays of technological innovations, architecture, amusement rides, and exhibits that constructed another world.[2] The fantasy world of the amusement park allowed spectators to momentarily suspend expected social roles: grown-ups could act like children; courting couples could act as if they were married; working-class women could play the role of the genteel lady; genteel ladies could put themselves in compromising positions by riding on camels and mechanical amusements rides that may cause their skirts to fly suggestively above their ankles.[3]

The construction of a fantasy world that allowed for patrons' suspension of social norms had its most elaborate consolidation in Coney Island's second major amusement park, Luna Park, which was built in 1903. Luna Park was predicated on literally and conceptually taking spectators out of their everyday, urban experience and transporting them to another world. At the geographic and conceptual center of Luna Park was the Trip to the Moon exhibit that premiered at the Pan-American Exposition in 1901. George Tilyou, the creator of Coney Island's first major enclosed amusement park, Steeplechase Park, invited Frederic Thompson and Elmer Dundy to move the successful Trip to the Moon exhibit to Steeplechase in 1902. The success of the Trip to the Moon exhibit at Steeplechase propelled Thompson and Dundy to construct their own amusement park at Coney Island that was topically and architecturally conceived around the concept of an out-of-this-world fantasy land. Thompson and Dundy purchased the unsuccessful Sea Lion Park and, six months after construction began and one and a half million dollars later, opened Luna Park on May 16, 1903 at 8:00 p.m.

Luna Park strategically planned its opening at night, for the display of electricity thrilled spectators with its technology and helped catapult pleasure seekers into another world. Through its use of over "200,000 Electric Lights Used in the Colossal Electric Carnival," Luna Park designated itself in promotional materials as the "Electric City by the Sea." Electricity of this magnitude was still a novel concept at this time, and by exploiting the marvels of this technology, producers created worlds that were unimaginable to amusement spectators. A visitor to Luna Park confirmed this sentiment when, beholding the twinkling skyline produced from the park's electric illumination, he exclaimed: "Ah, God, what might the Prophet have written in Revelations, if only he had first beheld a spectacle like this!"[4] Part of Luna Park's construction of another world depended on spectatorial fascination with electric illumination of this magnitude. Rem Koolhaas presents Luna Park's use of electric illumination as the "essential ingredient of the new paraphernalia of illusion" constructed at that amusement park.[5]

Capitalizing on the technology of electric illumination, Luna Park introduced nighttime entertainment into the amusement park genre. Electricity at Luna Park was used not only to entertain and to edify but was characterized as an assurance of safety.[6] Electric illumination prevented Luna Park from becoming a repository for undesirables and illegal activity at night. The illumination at Luna Park was both symbolic and practical—there were no "dark shadows" in which questionable characters could hide.[7] The literal and figurative enclosure of a space and the display of new technologies allowed for the architectural construction of another world that promoted the safety of park patrons.

Patrons at Luna Park could leave their quotidian preoccupations at the gate's entrance and enter another world. The architecture, rides, and exhibits at Luna Park were meant to be specimens of the moon. Based on the concept that human emotions could be produced through architecture, Thompson wanted to fabricate the spectator's experience on every level. "Thompson believed the spirit of gaiety and emotional excitement in a park must be manufactured—via scenery, lights, shows, and buildings," Stephen Weisten points out, "An 'other world,' a fantastic fairy land or dream city, must be created."[8] Since Luna Park's innovative use of architecture and electricity to construct another world, the fabrication of a dream world has become the benchmark of amusement parks.[9]

Luna Park constructed a space that visually embodied the future and represented progress. Thompson claimed that the success of Luna Park depended on its ability to continuously change: "You see, this being the moon, it is always changing . . . stationary Luna Park would be an anomaly."[10] Executing his theory that progress is predicated on this continual cycle of creation and destruction, Thompson radically reconstructed Luna Park every new season.[11] "The equation of Luna Park with 'lunar change,'" argues Register, "provided a rich synthesis of the way the resort combined artifice with nature, the quest for novelty with premodern myth, systematic managed technology with the improprieties of carnivalesque dreams of plenty."[12] By appealing to the masses' desire for constantly reimagined displays of spectacle, Luna Park mirrored—albeit on a more spectacular and fabricated way—the constantly changing urban order.

Luna Park's display of the changing urban order was consolidated most aptly in its Fire and Flames exhibit. Fire and Flames presented a spatially and temporally contracted form of the ever-changing urban landscape. Though Luna Park was predicated on taking pleasure seekers out of their everyday lives, the Fire and Flames exhibit staged a phenomenon that Manhattanites were quite familiar with—urban fire, particularly in tenement buildings. Though spectators were familiar with urban fire, Fire and Flames abstracted any real danger that was implied in this image of urban destruction. Fire and Flames thrilled spectators with the benign presentation of disaster, the prowess of fire fighters, and spectacular images of the metropolis.

Fire and Flames was showcased in advertisements and print culture for Luna Park's upcoming 1904 season as a fantastic new exhibit, boasting that "[t]he great fire spectacle" would culminate in the "[a]ctual burning of a city block" under the protection of "[f]our complete fire companies under command of Chief Henry W. McAdams."[13] Spectators were seated in an auditorium across from a 520 × 250 feet stage that featured a four-story tenement-looking building and a cast composed of 657 men, women, and children.[14] Fire and Flames allowed pleasure seekers to watch, and vicariously experience, the spectacle that erupts from disaster: a building would be "set on fire"; a crowd of spectators would develop; firemen—who were supposedly stationed as permanent fixtures of the exhibit—responded to the alarm; fire trucks would arrive on the scene; actors caught in the burning house would be rescued by firemen or would leap into safety nets; firemen would "put out" the fire, save the day, and the show would be over. Within three weeks of opening, the new exhibit was touted by the press as a "sensational success."[15]

Fire and Flames proved to be the most popular attraction at Luna Park throughout the 1904 and 1905 seasons.[16] The popularity of the exhibit produced some interesting byproducts, such as firemen who visited from out-of-town to witness the spectacular display of their fellow fighters' prowess.[17] As a result of its huge popularity, in August, Thompson and Dundy declared the "mimic street" along Fire and Flames a "public thoroughfare" to allow "Coney Island policemen, whose presence is necessary to keep order," more direct access to the exhibit.[18] This architectural adaptation, though clearly enacted to ensure safety within and around the popular attraction, fits within the taxonomy of Luna Park's mission to create a continuously changing landscape. In addition to the practical changes to the park's architecture, producers claimed that Fire and Flames was constantly "improved every week."[19] Such improvements were largely about changing small details or rotating performers to fabricate novelty in the hopes that patrons would visit and return to the exhibit. Former Barnum and Bailey performer Miss Ernestine McCallum added to the acrobatic spectacle by sliding "down a rope from the roof of a burning four-story building."[20] More elaborate changes were also enacted to increase the spectacle, such as the addition of a water tower on the stage and other structural changes to the set.[21]

As the success of the Fire and Flames exhibit indicates, part of Luna Park's construction of a constantly changing lunar landscape was predicated on presenting the destruction of the urban order. The fabrication of a fantasy land at Luna Park seemed to suggest that tenement buildings and other icons of urban life be presented as ephemeral and fragile. Seeing images of chaos slowly overtaking order must have been simultaneously exhilarating and terrifying to turn-of-the-twentieth century pleasure seekers. The narrative of Fire and Flames within the themed landscape of Luna Park allowed pleasure seekers to witness a theatricalized version of the changing urban landscape at the very same moment they were allowed to succumb to their anxieties about the consequences of that same phenomenon. Though the Fire and Flames exhibit produced particular meanings within the context of Luna Park's constructed environment, interestingly it was not the only fire-based disaster spectacle at Coney Island.

Dreamland's White City

Across the way from Luna Park, Dreamland opened on May 14, 1904 to an estimated quarter of a million patrons with its own fire-based disaster spectacle, Fighting the Flames.[22] Though Dreamland replicated many of the innovations developed at its predecessors—Steeplechase Park (1897) and Luna Park (1903)—it explicitly divorced itself from the prior two amusement parks. While Steeplechase boasted inexpensive prices that could be had by all and Luna Park heralded its cacophony of sounds, sites, and architectural wonders, Dreamland advertised itself as clean, spacious, and devoid of chaos.

Conceived by politician and realtor William H. Reynolds who wanted to build a "higher class" amusement park, Dreamland was designed to be the antithesis of New York City's noise, crowds, and congestion. Reynolds employed many of the design principles he used when creating the suburban community of Borough Park, such as building detached private homes and wide streets that were meant to cater to the upwardly mobile middle class.[23] Influenced by the architecture of world's fairs and turn-of-the-century urban planning movements, Dreamland was designed as a more genteel amusement park meant to appeal to a higher class of patrons.[24]

Advertisements for Dreamland boasted a minimalist sentiment and aesthetic that visually embodied the starkness of Dreamland's White City. These ads simply read:

DREAMLAND
CONEY
ISLANDS [sic]
MYSTIC CITY
OF THE SEA
OPEN TO-DAY [sic]
CREATED AT A COST OF $3,500,000.[25]

In contradistinction to the crowded design of surrounding advertisements, the producers of Dreamland choose an advertising aesthetic that was simple and clean. Luna Park's advertisement—which appears directly next to Dreamland's—packs information into a small space including the description of three new exhibits (including Fire and Flames) and an extensive transportation schedule to the park. Dreamland uses the same advertising space to announce its opening in a majestic way through minimalist design. While Luna Park's advertisement for its opening day represented the "something for everyone" approach that popularized the beachside resort for many segments of the population, Dreamland's advertising aesthetic mirrored its architecture that was intended to be open, devoid of chaos and would, according to Reynolds, alleviate all congestion.

Producers claimed that such an objective had been met when, the day after Dreamland opened, the advertisement that had been used to publicize the park's opening once again graced the pages of newspapers but with the following addendum: "Such a place as 'Dreamland' solves largely the hardest of police problems—Commissioner McAdoo."[26] Depicting Dreamland as a safe haven that in fact could alleviate larger social orders—and that this claim was substantiated by New York City's Police Commissioner—discursively substantiated Dreamland's objective to create a clean and secure amusement park.

The construction of a safe, clean Dreamland was consolidated in its aesthetic sensibilities. Dreamland, like the White City at the Chicago World's Columbian Exposition of 1893, was completely white. Both Dreamland and the Chicago Exposition explicitly invoked the image of a utopian White City that symbolized purity and the purging of contaminating elements. At the Chicago Exposition, the White City was explicitly constructed to contrast with the colors of the Midway, the entertainment section of the fair. The construction of this American utopia through the pure, uncontaminated White City with its white walls and non-Western peoples relegated to the Midway, explicitly put forth a narrative of evolutionary and racial progress. This aesthetic choice was meant to construct a "great object lesson" to show white Americans that they were culturally and intellectually more advanced than non-Western people.[27] According to Robert Rydell, the White City at the Chicago Exposition was a "manifestation of what was good in American life" and served not only as a dreamlike getaway but also as a didactic model of how America, and Americans, should be.[28]

Dreamland's construction of a White City explicitly invoked the Chicago Exposition's aesthetic and ideological bifurcation between white (and whiteness) as pure and purifiers and non-white (and non-whiteness and immigrants) as non-pure or contaminants. As the safe, homogeneous White City at Dreamland was meant to appeal to a higher class of patrons, the park discursively and aesthetically equated whiteness with purity and with wealth. The White City's edifying objective to illustrate bourgeois sensibilities and instruct the middle and working classes about proper, clean, respectable entertainment did so through excluding those who were not members of this implied audience.

At the center of this all-white utopian city devoid of color and chaos, appeared the Fighting the Flames exhibit which explicitly staged the burning of a tenement-looking building. This exhibit directly referenced and in fact performed the elimination of the immigrant population that had come to symbolize the tainted image of a "pure" America. As Weinstein makes clear, "[ap]pealing to New Yorkers made uneasy by the influx of immigrants, Dreamland stressed the sharp physical contrast between its own spacious grounds and congested New York."[29] By invoking the cultural purity of a White City and staging the tenement-looking building in its Fighting the Flames exhibit, Dreamland staged growing anxieties about immigration and the future of the metropolis and the nation.

The building that housed the Fighting the Flames exhibit featured a figure of a fireman and emblematic symbols of fire fighting such as horses, helmets, and axes that were carved along the upper edge of the roofless structure.[30] Fighting the Flames was located on the lagoon that led to Dreamland's Beacon Tower that served as the architectural and symbolic center of the amusement park. Built explicitly to rival Luna Park's Electric Tower, the Beacon Tower at Dreamland, according to promoters, was adorned with one hundred thousand electric lights that could be seen thirty miles away.[31] Dreamland magnified the use of electricity as spectacle throughout the amusement park: while Luna Park touted its two hundred thousand lights, Dreamland advertised that over one million lights were used to amaze spectators.[32] The architectural centrality of the Fighting the Flames exhibit placed it in a position of visual and spatial primacy within Dreamland's construction of a pure, White City.

In the spirit of Dreamland's escalation of spectacle, the four-story building at the center of the Fire and Flames exhibit grew to six stories and the number of performers increased. Hyperbolic descriptions of two thousand characters—including Fire Chief Sweeney, fire fighters, actors, and stage hands—ensured that Fighting the Flames was entertaining, logistically sound, and safe for performers and spectators.[33] As Koolhaas argues, the "Fighting the Flames constitutes [Reynolds'] most convincing exposition of, and commentary on, the metropolitan condition itself," appealing to spectators' simultaneous fascination with and anxieties surrounding the changing urban landscape.[34]

Like Fire and Flames at Luna Park, Fighting the Flames became the most popular exhibit at Dreamland.[35] As a result of the success of Fighting the Flames, in 1904, the exhibit was expanded for the 1905 season. The "construction and recasting involving an expenditure of $40,000" included the addition of an "entire block of buildings" that would be "fire-ravaged at each performance."[36] The remodeling also occurred on the level of performance, such as actors who would jump "into life-saving nets" in the service of producing "additional excitement."[37] The expansion of Fighting the Flames proved successful and the exhibit maintained its status in 1905 as one of the most popular at the park.[38] Despite its successful season, Fire and Flames closed before the 1906 season and the park began to make room for the "dreadfully sensational" San Francisco Earthquake spectacular in which "350 persons, scenery, fire, smoke, and a quaking machine will represent the great city of the Pacific."[39] As one article lamented, "[s]ightseers found their favorite, 'Fighting the Flames,' closed and the old sign gone."[40] However, the new exhibit that inhabited the same space similarly capitalized on the spectacularization of the elements and urban disaster.

Placed within Dreamland's White City and its implied narrative of racial progress, the message put forth by the Fighting the Flames exhibit cannot be easily extracted from its historical and social context. The producers' decision to display a tenement-looking building at the center of these exhibits was not a random choice. This exhibit put forth a message about the status of these tenement-looking buildings—and the people who occupied them—as dispensable and simultaneously responsible for the problems associated with urban growth. The burning of the tenement-looking building as entertainment at Coney Island's enclosed amusement parks represented and perpetuated pleasure seekers' anxieties about the influx of immigration and what this influx meant for New York City—in terms of population, sanitation, and employment—and ideologically for the status of the nation. Anxieties surrounding immigration were bound up with fears of the changing concept of "America," and the burning of the tenement-looking building in these exhibits represented a desire to get rid of these unwanted elements of the social fabric.

Creative Destruction and Elemental Performativity

> By the turn of the century it is evident that *creation* and *destruction* are the poles defining the field of Manhattan's abrasive culture.
> —Rem Koolhaas [41]

The Fire and Flames and Fighting the Flames exhibits at Coney Island staged Manhattan's process of becoming, and attempted to control, contain, and put order to the inevitable chaos of fire and the unpredictability of the growing metropolis. By conceptually destroying and reconstructing the same tenement-looking building multiple times a day to entertain and edify amusement park patrons, Coney Island staged the poles of creation and destruction in its Fire and Flames and Fighting the Flames exhibits. The cycle of creation and destruction has been used by theorists to address the complexities and inherent contradictions of capitalism (Marx), modernity (Berman), the development of the metropolis (Koolhaas and Page), and, as this chapter suggests, spectatorial fascination with fire-based disaster spectacles. These thinkers all theorize through their objects of study by way of the seeming paradox that progress is predicated on the perpetual cycle of creation and destruction. In Marx's formulation, "all that is solid melts into air" in the bourgeois capitalist system—a metaphor that is prevalent throughout Marx's early work. The concrete and the tangible can easily be destroyed and, in fact, must be in order for progress to continue.

Berman uses Marx's phrase "all that is solid melts into air" as the central trope for his pivotal work on modernity. For Berman, "the heat that destroys is also superabundant energy, an overflow of life."[42] It is this abundance, this idea that heat is both destructive and energizing, that is a foundation for my concept of elemental performativity and, as Berman claims, serves as a "hallmark . . . of the modernist imagination."[43] For Berman, the permanency of commodities and modern life becomes understood as temporary, ephemeral, and fragile:

> From the clothes on our backs to the looms and mills that weave them, to the men and women who work the machines, to the houses and neighborhoods the workers live in, to the firms and corporations that exploit the workers, to the towns and cities and whole regions and even nations that embrace them all—all these are pulverized or dissolved, so they can be recycled or replaced next week, and the whole process can go on again and again, hopefully forever, in more profitable terms.[44]

In this formulation, the very processes of capitalism and modernism are predicated on commodities being created so that they can be "recycled or replaced next week." Destruction becomes a necessary stage in this process of making room for these new commodities.

Max Page uses the concept of *creative destruction* to understand the ways that the growth of the metropolis is predicated on a perpetual cycle of creation and destruction. According to Page, the "intentional destruction and rebuilding" of Manhattan made it a "city in the process of becoming."[45] While destruction is often couched in negative terms, Page rethinks destruction as intentional and in fact necessary for the growth of the city. Before Page, Rem Koolhaas also conceptualized the metropolis, aptly summarized in the epigraph to this section, through the cycle of creation and destruction.

The centrality of the concept of creative destruction in academic literature is prefigured by the central practical and conceptual subject of this study—fire-based disaster spectacles in popular amusement settings at the turn of the twentieth century. Fire and Flames and Fighting the Flames staged, in a temporally and spatially contracted way, this cycle of creation and destruction. In these exhibits, fire would "destroy" the buildings, fire fighters would become heroes and victims would be saved, the building would be "reconstructed," and the performance would begin again. But by fabricating this process of creative destruction within the controlled setting of an amusement park, these exhibits ensured that in fact nothing would change: the performance was predicated on the same fire burning and being extinguished in the same way by the same performers at the same times every day. The unpredictability of fire, modernity, and the growth of the metropolis is predicated on their inability to be contained. Though these exhibits staged the poles of creation and destruction, they ultimately were unable to truly embody the paradox of creative destruction. This conundrum will help us theorize the cultural meanings produced in these fire-based disaster spectacles, what I have come to term *elemental performativity*.

Before embarking on elemental performativity, I will take a short detour to explain the performative utterance, popularized by speech act theorist J.L. Austin. The purpose of this detour is to introduce the concept that has spurred scholars to adapt the performative—from Judith Butler's gender performativity, to Eve Sedgwick's queer performativity, to Vivian Patraka's Holocaust performativity—to understand one of the ways that meaning is produced in language.[46] The aim is to begin deciphering what the performative does and, by extension, how this helps contextualize what was brought into being in the fire-based disaster spectacles at Coney Island's enclosed amusement parks at the turn of the twentieth century.

J. L. Austin posited the notion of a performative—a statement that is neither descriptive nor true nor false but through its utterance brings that which it names into being. Austin conceptualizes moments in which language can, in particular circumstances, enact. Through the performative, Austin posits that "the issuing of the utterance is the performing of an action."[47] Examples abound but one of the most clearly demonstrative can be found at a wedding: at the moment the words "I do" are uttered, the couple is bounded by their vows and become married.[48] As this example begins to suggest, not all utterances of "I do" are necessarily performatives. Imagine if the couple getting married is composed of children playing a game; obviously the "I do" would not enact their union.

Austin would definitely discount the possibility that the children's "I do" could constitute a performative. Austin claims that performative utterances must be issued in "ordinary circumstances" and "other things have to be right" for the performative to enact what it names.[49] If the circumstances are "abnormal," then the performative fails; these are termed unhappy performatives or infelicities. Austin makes clear that often a number of other extenuating circumstances have to be in place for the performative to be enacted. For the "I do" to be a performative in the United States, it would be necessary that the people being married are not already married to other people, that they are of legal age, and that they have a marriage license, in addition to other prerequisites.[50] Children playing "grown-up" would undoubtedly constitute an Austinian "abnormal" circumstance on a number of levels.

Adding to his examples of unhappy performatives, Austin considers all utterances spoken in a theatrical context as abnormal or nonserious. In an often-cited passage, Austin argues that the performative utterance is "*in a peculiar way* hollow or void if said by an actor on the stage."[51] Austin excludes the utterance spoken on stage for the context of the theatre automatically discredits it as "nonserious." "Language in such circumstances is in special ways—intelligibly—used not seriously," Austin claims, "but in ways *parasitic* upon its normal uses—ways which fall under the doctrine of the *etiolation* of language."[52] While Austin excludes the very possibility of the intersection of the performative and performance, recent debates have opened up a space for the possibility that performance can be performative, that is, through the doing of the performance, something is brought into being.

Elin Diamond reconfigures the Austinian exclusion and suggests that performativity must in fact be "rooted in the materiality and historical density of performance."[53] In this sense, performance does not "void" the performative but rather is the very condition of its possibility of being. Diamond, borrowing from Butler's definition of performativity as reiteration, posits:

> When performativity materializes as performance in that risky and dangerous negotiation between a doing (a reiteration of norms) and a thing done (discursive conventions that frame our interpretations), between someone's body and the conventions of embodiment, we have access to cultural meanings and critique.[54]

Diamond suggests that the intersection of performance and performativity—as a doing and a thing done—is a real and fruitful space, a space that I will return to shortly to help elaborate the meanings of the Fire and Flames and Fighting the Flames exhibits.

Other scholars have highlighted that the context of performance does not render performative utterances non-serious or parasitic. Rather, the performative in performance is just as "serious" as it is in the context of what Barbara Johnson calls "the fiction we call real life."[55] Johnson reminds us that characters such as a judge or priest uttering performatives in "real life" may also be performing personas. The performative "fictionalizes its utterer when it makes him the mouthpiece of a conventionalized authority . . . [b]ecause behind the fiction of the subject stands the fiction of society."[56] Johnson is pinpointing the slippery division between the "real" and the "fictional," a distinction that Austin wants to make but that is, ultimately, impossible to maintain.

As it is able to cross disciplines, the performative is also capable of traversing topics from the serious to the trivial, from hate crimes to reality television's popularization of performatives such as Donald Trump's now infamous "You're Fired" on the television show *The Apprentice* and Paris Hilton's "That's Hot" phrase. However, this is not to purport that the performative is a magical term that means all things to all people. Rather, I want to invoke the conceptual complexities of the performative to further understand the ways that Fire and Flames and Fighting the Flames produced meaning in their cultural, historical, and social contexts. In the context of fire-based disaster spectacles at the turn of the twentieth century, the cultural meanings produced in such displays provide insight into pleasure seekers' fears and fascinations with the growth of the metropolis, the influx of new technologies, and the changing urban landscape.

If we adapt Diamond's understanding of gender performativity to elemental performativity, it "doesn't exist unless it's being done." This helps us understand that the version of the disaster spectacle studied here is in "quotes," that is, it is a citational repetition of earlier acts (both theatricalized and real world) and it also comes into being, like fire itself, at that moment of combustion, at that moment in which it is being "done."[57] Understanding the Fire and Flames and Fighting the Flames exhibits as elemental performativity, then, makes the reiterations (the thing done) and the doing (the multiple layers of meaning produced) mutually constituting.

I have developed this notion of elemental performativity to conceptualize the paradox of fire—that fire is simultaneously mundane and spectacular, generative and destructive, archaic and modern. As a property that can be defined and as one of the four natural elements, fire is tangible, something that can be measured and calculated. Fire is a chemical reaction that releases light and heat, a reaction that requires the correct balance of oxygen, fuel, and temperature. Yet that process is far from simple and its effects are often nothing short of spectacular. Fire is excessive and produces more than can be ascertained by a description of its physical properties. "Among all phenomena," writes Gaston Bachelard, "[fire] is really the only one to which there can be so definitely attributed the opposing values of good and evil. It shines in Paradise. It burns in Hell. It is gentleness and torture. It is cookery and it is apocalypse."[58] For to focus on one of fire's personalities—to herald the creative, life-sustaining attributes of fire without acknowledging its destructive capabilities—is to fallaciously reduce the inherent complexity of fire to a binary.

Fire embodies the very tenets of poststructuralism: it is irreducible to a binary structure as it is both creative and destructive; it is archaic and modern. Fire cannot be "overcome" as a result of modernization and technology. Fire constantly reinvents itself—literally and figuratively—and it comes into being through its own disappearance. Jacques Derrida illuminated on the poststructural tenants of fire in his ruminations on cinders: *il y a là cendre*.[59] The phrase *il y a là cendre* means both that there are cinders and that cinders there are. While saying what it is, "cinders there are" also says "what it was," that the cinder "remains in memory of the departed [*feu*]."[60] The cinder would not exist without fire and comes to stand in for what is no longer there, both the departed fire and the object reduced to ashes. The cinder, then, "remains *from* what is not, in order to recall at the delicate, charred bottom of itself only non-being or non-presence."[61] The process by which fire obliterates objects to ashes is not a singular, simple process, for the cinder contains within itself the possibility that the fire will return. For Derrida, the phrase "cinders there are," then, simultaneously represents both non-being and becoming. Through such vanishing acts, cinders paradoxically embody yet cannot possibly begin to contain within their bodies the fire that they represent.

Fire and Flames and Fighting the Flames capitalized on and theatricalized this tension that fire signifies far more than its signifier can contain. Like cinders that represent yet cannot contain the fire, fire-based disaster spectacles represented the modern, urban order in its display—from the tenement-looking building to the heroism of fire fighters and their modern equipment—but they were unable to contain those elements of the urban order that are uncontrollable, chaotic, or unexpected. The exhibits embodied and put on display this tenet that modernity is both dependent on, yet cannot overcome, fire.

Thrill seekers at turn-of-the-century Coney Island were familiar with the images (and consequences) of fire in an urban setting. Though the thrill of watching fire is always-already spectacular, the staging of this representation gave new meaning to both real fires and to the staged ones. One of the most salient features of the Fire and Flames and Fighting the Flames exhibits is that while thrill seekers flocked to Coney Island to get away from the metropolis, they were met with images of the destruction of the city that many of them considered home. With an increase in multifarious forms of transportation to Coney Island and the introduction of leisure time to the working class, it can be assumed that some portion of the audience who watched the burning tenement-looking building were tenement dwellers themselves. In short, tenement dwellers may have paid to watch images of their own demise. Though it is impossible to locate precisely what such spectators may have thought about these representations, it is clear from the immense popularity of these exhibits that the public was fascinated with the images of the destruction of the urban order, images that spectators were implicated by in often more ways than one.

It is the meanings produced from these theatricalized elaborations of real-world concerns that serve as a foundation for elemental performativity. Elemental performativity seeks to theorize the production of the meanings of the display of the excesses of the elements in theatricalized or performance settings. Staging the elements in theatrical or display settings ("elemental performance") is not equivalent to elemental performativity. By elemental performativity I mean to indicate that that which comes into being through the staging of the elements is in excess of the physical and chemical components of the object displayed. The excess of the staging of fire produces, among other things, spectatorial fascination with the quotidian and the commodification of disaster.

While in this employment of elemental performativity I emphasize the primacy of fire, this does not preclude the possibility of thinking through other displays of the elements as elemental performativity. Instead, I seek to propose that elemental performativity, like the very elements that are its conceptual base, is a framework that is open for interpretation, nonstatic, and constantly evolving. While elemental performativity seeks to elaborate the particularities of what was brought into being through the theatricalized display of fire in the Fire and Flames and Fighting the Flames exhibits at Coney Island at the turn of the twentieth century, I would like to invite others to apply the concept of elemental performativity to other cultural displays of the elements.

What was "brought into being" in these exhibits, then, was more than simply a recreation of the modern, urban order but rather a number of interconnected social phenomena that had real-world consequences. Heroes were constructed out of actors/fire fighters and victims were saved from tenement-looking buildings (thereby constructing a binary between those who help and those who need help). These exhibits staged the best (fire fighters as urban heroes) and the worst (tenement houses and by extension the immigrants that inhabited them) that modernity had to offer through the signifiers of fire. The elemental performativity of these exhibits brought into being an excess that allowed pleasure seekers to inhabit a liminal space between the mundane and the spectacular, between cutting-edge technologies and the natural elements. Elemental performativity's production of this liminal space allowed pleasure seekers to celebrate the growth of the metropolis, the heroism of fire fighters, and the advent of modernity at the very same moment in which they were invited to succumb to their anxieties surrounding these very same phenomena. Elemental performativity, while it is dependent on the natural elements, is not reducible to nature and is a distinct phenomenon of turn-of-the-century new American mass culture.[62]

Notes

1. For an extended discussion of the argument presented in this chapter, see Lynn Sally, *Fighting the Flames: The Spectacular Performance of Fire at Coney Island* (New York: Routledge, 2006).

2. For a discussion of the relationship between new technologies and the transformation of spectacle as sensorial experience in Coney Island's enclosed amusement parks, see Lynn Sally, "Fantasy Lands and Kinesthetic Thrills: Sensorial Consumption, the Shock of Modernity, and Spectacle as Total-Body Experience at Coney Island," *Senses & Society* 1, no. 3

(November 2006): 293–309.

3. For an excellent discussion of George Thompson's construction of a make-believe fantasy world that allowed grown-ups to act like children at Luna Park, see Woody Register, *The Kid of Coney Island: Fred Thompson and the Rise of American Amusements* (Oxford: Oxford University Press, 2001).

4. Judith A. Adams, *The American Amusement Park Industry: A History of Technology and Thrills* (Boston: Twayne Publishers, 1991), 48.

5. Rem Koolhaas, *Delirious New York* (New York: Montacelli Press, 1994), 41.

6. Advertisement, *New York Times*, 16 May 1903, 7.

7. Register, *The Kid of Coney Island*, 132 and 347n162.

8. Stephen Weinstein, "The Nickel Empire: Coney Island and the Creation of Urban Seaside Resorts in the United States" (PhD diss., Columbia University, 1984), 132.

9. Weinsten, "The Nickel Empire," 132.

10. Koolhaas, *Delirious New York*, 41.

11. For a detailed list of seasonal changes at Coney Island, see Jeffrey Stanton, *Coney Island* (1997), <http://naid.sppsr.ucla.edu/coneyisland/articles>.

12. Register, *The Kid of Coney Island*, 121.

13. Advertisement, *New York Evening Post*, 14 May 1904, 5.

14. Details of the stage dimensions come from "Coney's Opening in Luminous Mist," *The World*, 15 May 1904, 3 and of the cast from "Coney Island," *New York Times*, 5 June 1904, 13.

15. "Coney Island," *New York Times*, 5 June 1904, 13.

16. Fire and Flames was described as "without a doubt the most popular attraction in the Park." "This Week in the Theatres," *New York Times*, 28 August 1904, 13. Managers were reported as claiming the "'Fire and Flames' and the chute-shooting elephants are the big attractions" at Luna Park. *New York Times*, 28 July 1904, 7. The exhibits' popularity continued throughout the 1905 season, though, according to reports, Fire and Flames did not change substantially and was "about the same sort of exhibit." "Chilly Damp Spoils Coney Island's Bow," *New York Times*, 14 May 1905, 14. By August of 1905, Fire and Flames was still "the greatest drawing card" at Luna Park. "Midsummer Programmes Provided by Theatre Managers," *New York Times*, 6 August 1905, SM9.

17. "This Week at the Theatres," *New York Times*, 26 June 1904, 20; "Last Nights' Amusements," *New York Times*, 28 June 1904, 9.

18. "This Week's Amusements," *New York Times*, 7 August 1904, 10.

19. "This Week at the Theatres," *New York Times*, 12 June 1904, 10.

20. "This Week at the Theatres," *New York Times*, 12 June 1904, 10

21. "This Week at the Theatres," *New York Times*, 12 June 1904, 10

22. "New Coney Dazzles Its Record Multitude," *New York Times*, 15 May 1904, 3.

23. Weinstein, "The Nickel Empire," 248.

24. Weinstein, "The Nickel Empire," 249.

25. Advertisement, *New York Evening Post*, 14 May 1904, 5.

26. Advertisement, *The World*, 15 May 1904, Metropolitan Section, 4M.

27. Robert Rydell, *All the World's a Fair* (Chicago: University of Chicago Press, 1984), 40.

28. Rydell, *All the World's a Fair*, 40.

29. Weinstein, "The Nickel Empire," 249.

30. Koolhaas, *Delirious New York*, 56.

31. John F. Kasson, *Amusing the Million: Coney Island at the Turn of the Century*

(New York: Hill and Wang, 1978), 85.

32. Kasson, *Amusing the Million*, 85.

33. Statistic from Stanton, *Coney Island*. Koolhaas claims that four thousand performers graced the stage of the Fighting the Flames exhibit. Koolhaas, *Delirious New York*, 56.

34. Koolhaas, *Delirious New York*, 56.

35. Newspaper accounts throughout the 1904 and 1905 season substantiate this claim. Fighting the Flames was depicted as "the dominant feature" and as "one of the great shows of Dreamland. "Amusements of the Week," *New York Times*, 4 September 1904, 7 and "Amusements of the Week," *New York Times*, 18 September 1904, SMA3, respectively.

36. "Great New Dreamland at Coney this Year," *New York Times*, 23 April 1905, 18.

37. "May Day Revelers Overflow Park," *New York Times*, 7 May 1905, 22. Today's theme parks demonstrate a similar trend in their emphasis on high-energy stunt shows.

38. *New York Times*, May 21, 1905 and *New York Times*, 13 August 1905, SM9.

39. "Dreamland Reopens and Shows New Glories," *New York Times*, 20 May 1906, 9.

40. "Dreamland Reopens and Shows New Glories," 9.

41. Koolhaas, *Delirious New York*, 53.

42. Marshall Berman, *All That Is Solid Melts Into Air: The Experience of Modernity* (New York: Penguin Books, 1988), 89.

43. Berman, *All That Is Solid*, 89.

44. Berman, *All That Is Solid*, 99.

45. Max Page, *The Creative Destruction of Manhattan: 1900–1940* (Chicago: University of Chicago Press, 1999), 2 and 17.

46. Butler's concept of gender performativity as developed in Judith Butler, *Bodies that Matter: On the Discursive Limits of "Sex"* (New York: Routledge, 1993) is explicated most clearly in her essay, Judith Butler, "Performative Acts and Gender Constitution: An Essay in Phenomenology and Feminist Theory," in *Performing Feminisms: Feminist Critical Theory and Theatre*, ed. Sue-Ellen Case (Baltimore: Johns Hopkins University Press, 1990). For queer performativity, see Eve Kosofsky Sedgwick, "Queer Performativity: Henry James's The Art of the Novel," *GLQ* 1 (1993): 1–15. For Holocaust performativity, see Vivian M. Patraka, *Spectacular Suffering: Theatre, Fascism, and the Holocaust* (Bloomington: Indiana University Press, 1999).

47. J.L. Austin, *How to Do Things with Words*, eds. J. O. Urmson and Martina Sbisa (Cambridge, Mass.: Harvard University Press, 1962), 6.

48. Austin, *How to Do Things With Words*, 5.

49. Austin, *How to Do Things With Words*, 13–14.

50. The language used in this example is purposefully non-gendered to allow for an expansion of the definition of marriage beyond a heterosexual union between a man and a woman.

51. Austin, *How to Do Things With Words*, 22.

52. Austin, *How to Do Things With Words*, 22.

53. Elin Diamond, ed., *Performance and Cultural Politics* (London: Routledge, 1996), 5.

54. Diamond, *Performance and Cultural Politics*, 5.

55. Barbara Johnson, *Critical Difference: Essays in the Contemporary Rhetoric of Reading* (Baltimore: Johns Hopkins University Press, 1980), 60–61.

56. Johnson, *Critical Difference*, 60.

57. Diamond, *Performance and Cultural Politics*, 4–5.

58. Gaston Bachelard, *The Psychoanalysis of Fire* (Boston: Beacon Press, 1964), 7.

59. Derrida claims the phrase haunted him in his work, and traces of it can be found in *Dissemination* (Chicago: University of Chicago Press, 1981), *Glas* (Lincoln: University of Nebraska Press, 1986) and *The Postcard* (Chicago: University of Chicago Press, 1987). In 1991, he wrote an entire book, *Cinders* (Lincoln: University of Nebraska Press, 1991), dedicated to this phrase.

60. Derrida, *Cinders,* 35.

61. Derrida, *Cinders,* 39.

62. Today's contemporary themed spaces owe much to the elemental performativity of Coney Island attractions. Fire plays a key role in the thematic productions and performances at famous venues like the Mirage and Caesars casinos in Las Vegas.

Chapter 4

From Downtown to Theme Town: Reinventing America's Smaller Historic Retail Districts

Thomas W. Paradis

Throughout America, smaller towns and cities are reconstituting themselves as themed visitor attractions following decades of economic and social decline. Their main street retail districts are being transformed from traditional community trade centers to more postmodern specialty shopping districts designed to promote consumption of both product and place. Taking their cue from larger metropolitan themed environments that depend on the creation of urban entertainment destinations, smaller urban places rely more on local heritage and environmental appeal from which to theme their historic downtown spaces.

The creation of themed environments in smaller business districts is best understood within the context of downtown redevelopment initiatives common to both large and small cities. This chapter focuses on two intertwined processes that invoke cultural or economic rationales in the production of places. The first is the cultural discourse of the historic preservation movement.[1] The second of these processes is the political economic perspective of downtown growth coalitions.[2] The case of downtown redevelopment in Flagstaff, Arizona (population 52,894) discussed herein indicates that deeply entrenched place identities and small-town cultural values can affect local decision making within the redevelopment process, and in turn, the materialized landscape.

Reflecting the experience of cities nationwide, a growth coalition in Flagstaff has revitalized its compact, fifteen-block downtown core into a hub of postmodern consumption focused on social entertainment, mixed-use development, tourism, specialty retail, professional offices, and city and county government functions. Central to this redevelopment effort is the recent invention of a collective downtown image, resulting in the manifestation of numerous local identity themes. In characteristic postmodern form, Flagstaff's "new" downtown is comprised of a collage of seemingly unconnected images, architectures, symbols, artwork, and functions, all placed within the context of the conservation of older historic commercial buildings. This is Flagstaff's own emerging fantasy city found not in Las Vegas, Nevada, but in a more typical, and much smaller, growing American community.[3]

Cities and towns of all sizes have effectively revitalized their downtown centers (or main streets), though the metropolis has gained the most attention from scholars and practitioners.[4] A continued decline of manufacturing and other industrial activities has encouraged the rise of new urban landscapes catering more to professionals and middle-class visitors and oriented more to consumption than production activities.[5] Throughout the urban hierarchy, American cities and towns are being transformed as centers of postmodern consumption.[6] In them, "consumer goods and media images play a major role in the everyday life of urbanites."[7]

Investigations of the downtown redevelopment process have ranged from structure-based perspectives, in which cities respond to challenges brought about through external trends and circumstances to political economy perspectives that focus on the important role of local agency and the associated concept of growth coalitions.[8] The "growth machine," defined by John Logan and Harvey Molotch as "an apparatus of interlocking progrowth associations and governmental units," exemplifies this agency-based framework in which citywide coalitions of individuals, organizations, and interest groups work together on strategies to promote economic growth.[9] Though most often associated with larger metropolitan growth initiatives, the growth coalition concept is likewise relevant for understanding themed developments in smaller places.

The role-players in small-city growth coalitions can vary from one community or project to another, though I have found certain consistencies across the communities I have studied, including the cases of Pontiac and Galena, Illinois; Madison, Indiana; and Roswell, New Mexico.[10] It is common for downtown coalitions to include members of a downtown business organization such as the Main Street Program, local city government, a chamber of commerce, convention and visitors bureau (CVB), a local visitor center, and various local museums, universities, and other private and pubic entities that stand to benefit economically from downtown redevelopment. It is likewise common for elite property owners and other individual stakeholders to become involved, exerting their own interests for the purpose of cultural or economic improvements, or both. Encouraging public involvement is the omnipresent local media, which tends to follow the progress of changes downtown, making local TV and newspaper organizations pivotal players in coalition projects. Often providing impetus and guidance for downtown redevelopment projects is state-enabling legislation used strategically by local growth coalitions to affect change. Other external influences typically involve outside design consultants, architects, developers, and builders. Downtown agendas and projects may be conceptualized and promoted locally, though the entire redevelopment process can depend on a wide range of such external factors.

The Postmodern Downtown

Growth proponents in small and large cities alike are relying more on the production of landscapes designed for tourism, sports, culture, and entertainment, often associated with local heritage and the creative reuse of historic resources and identities.[11] These new consumption-oriented cityscapes are increasingly organized around a set of scripted themes extracted most often from professional sports, Hollywood icons, and popular culture.[12] In place of the traditional business district focused on local services and retail is something scholars now describe variously as tourism business districts, tourist-historic cities, or in smaller places, theme towns.[13]

Numerous authors have offered perspectives on the definition and character of the postmodern urban condition.[14] Despite much attention in the literature, the concept of postmodernism remains highly contested. Edward Soja even chose to title his recent volume *Postmetropolis* instead of *Postmodern Metropolis*, he explained, to avoid framing the book "around the most controversial and misunderstood of these *post*-prefixed terms."[15] As poorly defined the concept may remain, however, it is still possible to synthesize some relevant ideas of postmodernism into a practical perspective to better understand emerging urban patterns.

For instance, Mansfield highlighted the prevailing characteristics of postmodernism found within contemporary world metropolises.[16] Paraphrased here in part, these include a focus on difference, diversity, discontinuity and fragmentation as opposed to the modernist ideals of sameness and universalism; an emphasis on the consumption and reproduction of images, whereby social identity is formed in relation to the sphere of consumption (such as leisure) rather than production (like work); and an increasing acceptance (and encouragement) of pastiche, collage, spectacle and the associated promotion of commodities designed specifically for differentiated markets.

Consequently, in the postmodern metropolis described by John Hannigan as fantasy city, one of the six defining features of contemporary urban developments is its postmodern cultural qualities, "insomuch as it is constructed around technologies of simulation, virtual reality and the thrill of the spectacle."[17] For Mark Gottdiener, the central manifestation of this emerging postmodern culture is the themed environment.[18] While Hannigan views the process of theming as one of several components of the postmodern metropolis, Gottdiener focuses more specifically on the theoretical logic and material production of themed spaces. The intensifying importance of symbols in marketing has led to no less than *The Theming of America*, as Gottdiener titled his book on the subject. The proliferation of themed environments since the late twentieth century—including themed restaurants and shopping malls, theme parks, historic districts, airports, professional sports venues, festival marketplaces, and suburban neighborhoods—is rooted in the economic imperative to attach cultural symbols to otherwise ordinary products and places within a consumption-oriented, late-capitalist economy.

Within metropolitan areas, the redevelopment process predominantly reflects the interests of developers who collectively produce a consumption-oriented, postmodern downtown, increasingly focused on the privatization of city streets and urban venues.[19] This trend has produced a solipsistic quality within the postmodern metropolis, whereby new and shiny urban entertainment destinations are increasingly "isolated from surrounding neighborhoods physically, economically and culturally."[20] M. Christine Boyer, for one, has expressed concern for the future of American cities, in that "these gigantic urban regions are disintegrating into unrelated groupings of shopping centers, special zoning districts, and housing tracts, all carved up by highways and multilevel traffic interchanges."[21] Cities have increasingly turned to their remaining downtown historic areas and transformed them into festival marketplaces and specialty shopping districts.[22] The crafting of heritage themes and identities therefore plays a central role in the postmodern development of fantasy city. Boyer suggests, however, that these repackaged historic tableaux "are the true nonplaces, hollowed out urban remnants, without connection to the rest of the city or the past, waiting to be filled with contemporary fantasies, colonized by wishful projections, and turned into spectacles of consumption."[23] Smaller places, in contrast with Boyer's metropolitan "nonplaces," however, may be better poised to avoid such negative postmodern trends due to higher levels of community involvement and local senses of place that can influence decision making. This appears to be the consistent case with smaller downtown redevelopment agendas including those of Flagstaff, Arizona.

From a historic preservation perspective, America's focus on the past is "no longer an organized historical corpus but a potpourri of everything that ever happened, in which a 1930s cinema attracts the same degree and type of interest as the Parthenon."[24] Critics of postmodernism lament that the past is apparently being treated as a "spare-parts warehouse," as architects and their followers may be trivializing the past rather than adopting it carefully for purposeful meaning. Regardless of how history and heritage are being interpreted and used for contemporary purposes, however, it is clear that a redirected focus on the past, rather than on the future, remains a central component of postmodern theme development. This renewed interest in heritage and local sense of place is playing a fundamental role in the production of revitalized, smaller downtown commercial districts.

Themed Redevelopment in Flagstaff, Arizona

Located 140 miles north of Phoenix and 80 miles south of Grand Canyon National Park, Flagstaff's relative isolation on the Colorado Plateau did not prevent the decentralization of retail functions from its traditional downtown. By the early 1980s a local shopping mall and numerous roadside shopping plazas had encouraged many traditional retail functions to abandon downtown. With the city's approval and partial funding of the Main Street Flagstaff Foundation by the late 1980s, the groundwork for establishing an informal growth coalition had begun.[25] This encouraged downtown businesses, property owners, and local elites to strategize with the city on a downtown redevelopment initiative. As Main Street gained momentum with some initial small projects, the city contracted with a design consultant in Boulder, Colorado to create a master design plan for Flagstaff's downtown area. The consultant recommended a distinct theme to unify the downtown aesthetically and functionally, focused in this case on Flagstaff's recognized railroad heritage. This design plan has served more or less as a fifteen-year "road map" for achieving a downtown revival based on tourism, leisure, and consumption, all embedded with the scripted theme of railroad heritage.

All five projects described below were implemented during the height of Flagstaff's downtown redevelopment efforts in the 1990s, collectively adding to the district's emerging postmodern qualities. Not revealed through a quick read of the resulting human landscape, however, is the social process that enabled its creation, interpreted here as an ongoing negotiation between those fostering a sense of place through various cultural representations (use values), and those variously involved with a local growth coalition attempting to revitalize an ailing downtown economy (exchange values).

It should be noted, however, that this dichotomy risks becoming overly simplistic, given that cultural and economic imperatives of growth-coalition role-players are often intertwined in complex ways. A downtown business or property owner, for instance, may feel a strong, emotional attachment to place and support historic preservation initiatives to improve some subjective connection with the past, while at the same time becoming active with the local "growth machine" in pursuit of economic revitalization promised to benefit his or her investments in the downtown.

Flagstaff's own revitalized downtown displays a variety of local and regional identities and representations of place. Fifteen years of downtown redevelopment efforts are manifested in the form of a standard, "textbook" pedestrian streetscape, new and inviting public spaces, renovated historic buildings, several new structures exhibiting postmodern architectural styles, and a wealth of visitor-oriented businesses and restaurants. The downtown is once again attracting tourists on the way to the Grand Canyon and other regional destinations. Adding to the diversity are numerous county and city government functions that remained downtown, and a regular infusion of college students from nearby Northern Arizona University. The five separate though interrelated projects discussed below reveal the extent to which local growth coalitions were responsible in various ways for promoting and enabling this revival. I have selected these projects not as a comprehensive story of downtown redevelopment, but as representative cases demonstrating a broad array of approaches to theming and preservation commonly found in smaller cities. All projects variously involved the role of Flagstaff's informal growth coalition, though each revealed a unique set of place-based circumstances and external influences.

Pedestrian Streetscape

Uniting the entire north downtown was an extensive streetscape project completed during the middle 1990s. The final version mirrored similar pedestrian-friendly projects across the nation, including expanded brick sidewalks, planters, trees, benches, trashcans, pedestrian streetlights with interchangeable banners, and occasional way-finding stations with visitor information. Flagstaff's version required a monumental effort by its local downtown growth coalition. First, city leaders and planners created a new district, allowed by the state of Arizona through enabling legislation. Known officially in Arizona as a *Special Improvement District*, or SID, its purpose is to levy a special tax for property owners within the specified district boundaries. Following city council approval through a local ordinance, an additional property tax could be collected to fund the project. Each commercial property owner in the district—anyone who owns commercial buildings, parking lots, and so forth—would be required after 1995 to pay an additional annual tax for a period of ten years to pay for the streetscape improvements, totaling more than $2 million.

A uniform formula was devised to determine specific tax assessments for each downtown property. This process was contentious, in that numerous factors had to be considered. The formula first included a base rate for each property, with an additional rate calculated for the amount of square footage, street frontage, alley frontage, and perimeter frontage. Owning a property on the perimeter of the district actually lowered the rate; presumably, properties that were "landlocked" within the district boundaries would benefit the most from the downtown improvements. Further, several levels of enhancements were planned for different parts of the district, so three base rates were calculated for each of the three enhancement zones.

That various property owners viewed their assessments as unfair was no surprise. One Flagstaff realtor, for instance, owned four downtown properties, the assessments for which he viewed as far too high. The assessment for one property alone was calculated to be $40,000 over ten years for his 21,300-square-foot parking lot. His other parcels of land along Route 66 would cost him an additional $16,000. "They should have looked at the value of the buildings on the property," he claimed in the Flagstaff *Daily Sun*, because "if you look around, I'm paying the same tax as some of the most expensive buildings downtown, and I just don't have the same income that they have."

After adjusting the assessment formula to attract the greatest number of downtown property owners, the city council members voted unanimously in favor of "an intent to form a downtown improvement district" in the north downtown area. By this time the area south of the transcontinental line of the Atchison, Topeka and Santa Fe Railway (AT&SF) had been eliminated from the plan, where weak local support was deemed insufficient for success. Following the vote of those located north of the tracks, letters were sent to all property owners in the new district, explaining that they would be given fifteen working days to protest the SID in writing. This process was not to be decided by a regular "yes-no" vote; instead, a "no" vote could only be recorded with a "letter of protest" submitted to the city within fifteen working days. Any owner not submitting an opposition letter would be counted as a "yes" vote.

Additionally, the votes did not count equally. Those who owned multiple parcels of land were allowed to cast separate votes (of opposition) for each of them. The votes were also weighted proportionally according to a given property's amount of frontage within the district. According to these rules provided by state-enabling legislation, the district would not take effect if more than 49 percent of owners with street-front property opposed it. Stated in another way, if more than half of the district's 14,810 feet of property frontage was assigned a no vote by its collective owners, the district would be defeated. It was conceivable that a few large property owners could control much of the decision.

One longtime business and property owner wielded considerable influence. Through one investment at a time, Richard (a pseudonym) had become one of the larger property owners in the downtown area and a key role-player with the Main Street Flagstaff Foundation. Richard held approximately 13 percent of the total vote, given that voting would be weighted proportionally to a property owner's frontage. When asked to explain the passage of the SID in a personal interview, Richard commented that "without too much exaggeration, I could say they had me, and that helped them. I had 13 percent of the vote because of the property I owned. I mean, if you win with 63 percent and somebody has 13 percent of the vote."

In an attempt to promote the SID, the city and the Main Street Flagstaff Foundation lobbied heavily for support. Most significant, representatives of the city and Main Street together held a series of special meetings with property owners during the period between January and March 1993, leading up to the fifteen-day protest period. Rather than simply calling one large meeting for all owners, however, every affected property owner was scheduled to meet individually with five community leaders, namely the director of the Main Street Flagstaff Foundation, the president of Main Street's board of directors, the City Beautification coordinator, a city engineer, and the Flagstaff city manager. In this way, votes for the district were earned one owner at a time. By meeting with property owners prior to announcing the city council's planned intent to form the SID, Main Street's director claimed in the *Daily Sun* that the city would "fix the problems before we get to the vote."

The downtown coalition, embodied at this point by the five aforementioned role-players, met with no less than sixty-seven property owners in the proposed district. More than one meeting was held in certain cases. The city manager explained in a personal interview that his office served as the meeting place, and the meetings held three basic purposes: (1) to explain to property owners how their tax assessments were calculated, (2) to discuss the plans for changes in the "physical infrastructure" of the area and immediately outside their properties, and (3) to solicit questions and concerns of the property owners so that changes could be made if necessary.

Despite a last-minute effort by seventeen downtown property owners to protest the SID, the district passed by 63–37 percent. SID supporters were pleased, hoping for at least a 60 percent approval. The city council was still required to vote one more time to officially implement the SID. In all, the 37 percent opposition was represented by a total of twenty-eight protests, not a surprise for those monitoring the vote. The bulk of protests came from property owners not involved with retail sales. Several comments protested the plan's emphasis on foot traffic, from which professional businesses would benefit little. One opponent commented in the *Daily Sun* that "downtown Flagstaff could use a kick-start, however it should not come solely in the way of expensive window dressing."

That the SID had passed was certainly no accident. Some might attribute the success to strong, local pride for downtown and to individual cultural values that supported a perceived sense of place. Although these factors were important, it was more the result of a planned and calculated political effort by local actors who learned how to take advantage of state-enabling legislation. Large property owners enjoyed the advantage, given voting rules weighted proportionally to the amount of property frontage owned. No community referendum was required, though business owners in other parts of town would have favored a referendum. It stands to reason that the bulk of membership and leadership within the Main Street Flagstaff Foundation consisted of a mixture of small business owners and large property owners in the downtown area who desperately desired to see an economic rebound.

Further, not all property owners were interested in the downtown redevelopment efforts. An uncalculated number of institutions and larger businesses downtown, such as the branches of state banks, may have missed or neglected to study the downtown plans. In any event, apathy or lack of involvement was automatically converted into a "yes" vote for the SID. When asked to explain the factors leading to the passage of the SID, Richard replied in part, "I think the fact that there were a lot of institutions that didn't take a position, but their votes counted as 'yes.' You know . . . there are tactics that are used to build coalitions."

Having been approved by a comfortable majority of downtown business owners, the city council made the SID official with the passage of Resolution No. 1843 on April 26, 1993. The resolution defined once again the specific area of downtown to be included within the district and ordered the improvement of streets and rights-of-way within that district. The resolution specified a wide array of improvements, such as paving, curbs and gutters, landscaping, irrigation, street and pedestrian lighting, traffic signals and new signage, street furniture, water and sewer lines, storm drains, and "appurtenances related thereto." Because all of the improvements in the SID (completed by the end of 1996) ultimately cost more than $8 million, the city (and thus its tax-paying citizens) paid for approximately $6 million, causing no small amount of local controversy.

Heritage Square

The size of one-quarter city block in the heart of downtown, Heritage Square is a successful public space whose symbolic landscape celebrates a selective array of Flagstaff's local histories and regional characteristics. Initially purchased by a local developer aiming to install a parking lot, the city eventually bought the property to facilitate a public-private partnership with a developer of its own choice. The city envisioned a major redevelopment project including an underground parking garage and a pedestrian plaza of some kind, both of which were completed by 1997. In November of 1991 the city council voted 4–1 to purchase the 33,000-square-foot lot comprising the site of today's Heritage Square.

One councilmember objected to the purchase, arguing that the city did not yet have a plan or a recent appraisal for the land. The purchase was speculative, with the aim of developing the land at a future time. The mayor and other city council members disagreed, believing the purchase was wise because it would give "the council an opportunity to turn downtown into a beautiful area, something it hasn't been for the past twenty-five years," as one *Daily Sun* article reported in November 1991.

Quintessentially postmodern in its design, the Square in its final form includes a variety of historically unconnected images with multiple meanings that, in their totality, claim to represent the best of Flagstaff's past as well as its popular environmental setting. The "stage set" for the park consists of a large brick patio broken up by the inlaid images of a railroad track and a wandering stream channel—the former celebrating the town's beginnings along a transcontinental railway, the latter recognizing the innocuous Rio de Flag, the troublesome floodplain in which the downtown area is built. Embedded into this patio is a small amphitheater designed for various community productions, used heavily during the summer. To the credit of Flagstaff's Downtown Business Alliance—the successor to the Main Street Flagstaff Foundation—the amphitheater hosts a wide variety of community events including concerts, weekly summer movies, theatrical performances, public speakers, and other local offerings. The place's continuous activities and human-scaled landscape provide the essence of a typical urban European square.

Built within the park are numerous other themes and symbols invoking local heritage and environment, not the least being a series of creative railroad wheel benches, supported by authentic railroad axles. The eclectic imagery and cultural representations reach beyond the railroad. The backs of the benches include silhouettes of ancient Southwest Indian pictographs, local science themes including nearby Lowell Observatory, and various regional plants and animals. In the northwest corner of the Square is a feature representing the origin of the community's name, a flagpole carved out of ponderosa pine and flying the obligatory Stars and Stripes, at once connoting local and national pride. The base of the flagpole consists of a stone pedestal built with layers of rock representing the stratigraphic sequence of the Grand Canyon.

Completing the collage of postmodern eclecticism is the accompanying A. G. Edwards building, housing office and retail space built to provide revenue for the Square's construction. The brick, two-story structure is a historical replica of Flagstaff's old Victorian-era City Hall, demolished in the 1970s. Credit for the idea of replicating old City Hall goes to another longtime local businessman, John (a pseudonym), who became a willing participant in the design and funding of Heritage Square and its inclusive retail/office building. In a personal interview, John indicated the reasoning behind the design of the A. G. Edwards building:

> There was a private consortium of foundations—my family's foundation [and several others]—all went together and agreed with the city that they would help to fund the square, open space, improvements. . . . We had meetings over the course of a year, with the city and designers. We pretty much designed the square; we did the building based on Flagstaff's first city hall—it's almost an exact replica, on a grand, larger scale. . . . I don't want to take too much credit, but I think it was pretty much my idea, and then the Main Street Foundation picked it up. Everybody liked . . . using the heritage theme for the plaza.

The primary goal of this consortium was political, in that its elite members were concerned about losing control of the Square's design with the city's selection of an outside developer. The group therefore negotiated with the city to include some local influence in the park's design in return for contributing approximately one million dollars to the project. One example of the group's input consisted of the aforementioned railroad benches, credited to John's trip to New Zealand. As he explained:

> We saw these great old benches made out of railroad axles and thought, well, the railroad is kind of the key, it's the reason why Flagstaff is here at all. So we came back and designed the railroad benches with these little historic themes on the back: ranching, skiing, forestry, observatory, and all that stuff. It was just people around a table for many months thinking about heritage themes and how to execute those themes.

Flagstaff Visitor Center

When Heritage Square was still a parking lot owned by a local developer, community discussion focused on the need for a new visitor center. As interpreted here, its primary economic rationale was to streamline the tourism component of Flagstaff's local growth coalition. Initially, the goal of the Flagstaff Chamber of Commerce was to create a visitor center at one of the freeway interchanges on the edge of town. In a State of the Chamber address in early 1988, the chamber's president, Jack Duffy, promoted the idea of creating a new visitor center to increase tourist activity in and around Flagstaff. Tourism had become Flagstaff's leading industry ahead of lumber and logging, and Duffy commented in his address that, "there is a tremendous potential to develop it further." A *Daily Sun* editorial concurred, predicting that "restaurants and lodging establishments could advertise their businesses at the center," and tourists could be further directed to the "Museum of Northern Arizona, Lowell Observatory, Northern Arizona University, historic downtown Flagstaff and highways to Wuptaki, Sunset Crater and Walnut Canyon national monuments." From a political economy perspective, then, a new visitor center would contribute directly to the exchange value interests of Flagstaff's local and regional growth proponents. Presumably, the consumption of places and products would be stimulated through the process of directing and guiding visitors from a central location.

The planned location of the center kept changing. A tourism consultant recommended a site close to the I-40 and I-17 interchange south of town. "Pick a property 1 to 1.2 miles within the intersection of I-17 and I-40," she advised, adding that any other site outside that zone should not be considered. The community then learned of a historic preservation project beginning in the downtown area—that of the deteriorated 1926 AT&SF Railway depot. "Years of use and abuse have caused premature aging," read one *Daily Sun* article, "and passengers are now greeted with orange and green plastic chairs, a leaking roof and locked, antiquated restrooms." The building served Amtrak's twice-daily passenger train, as it still did in 2006.

In November 1988 the year-old Main Street Flagstaff Foundation provided its opinion—its director suggesting that the depot be renovated into the new visitor center. Not only did Main Street "urge the city council to find a suitable site within the downtown," but it also warned in the *Daily Sun* that "moving the visitor center and Chamber of Commerce from downtown puts the entire Main Street Program at risk." In early 1990 Main Street recommended four of its own potential sites, all within the downtown area. Letters to the editor appeared in the *Daily Sun*, several supporting a downtown site that would presumably contribute to the revival of the business district. One writer argued that "if you want the most gain for the dollar, establish a visitor center near the center of town, which will reflect Flagstaff, not Wal-Mart." About the proposed site near the interchange, the letter continued, "The day Flagstaff outdraws the Grand Canyon will be the time to build the Taj Mahal you envision." Thus, arguments for a downtown location invoked both use and exchange values, promoting a distinctive sense of place while encouraging economic gains.

It was the city council that enabled the project. At a work session in October 1991, five out of six city council members preferred the depot over other sites. From that meeting, the plan materialized rapidly. The AT&SF Railway owned the building and leased space to Amtrak for its ticket and waiting services. The remaining space, according to Amtrak officials, would include 600–700 square feet for a potential visitor center. Much smaller than envisioned, the council appointed the president of Main Street to negotiate with the railway for more floor space. Ultimately the city purchased the depot property from the railway for a price of $480,000, with an estimated additional cost of $390,000 for the depot's renovation and for an additional parking lot. The deal proved mutually beneficial, as the railway expressed interest in selling the depot as well. Once again, the city council and the Main Street Flagstaff Foundation had played a significant part in a substantial historic downtown project.

Original AT&SF Depot

Across the street from the Visitors Center is Flagstaff's original depot, constructed of locally quarried sandstone in 1889. Now a contributing, restored landmark in the historic downtown, the old depot was actually slated for removal by the AT&SF railway in the 1980s due to the company's reluctance to fund maintenance or personnel. A wholehearted effort was required of local individuals and organizations to save the building and find an appropriate adaptive use.

In 1994 the city was tentatively awarded a half-million dollar federal transportation (ISTEA) grant to purchase and renovate the old depot. Citing safety concerns, however, the AT&SF Railway preferred not to sell unless the building was moved elsewhere. However, the removal of the building would make the necessary federal grant null and void. In a more favorable twist of fate, the AT&SF merged with the Burlington Northern Railroad in 1995, creating the giant BNSF Railway Corporation. The merger led to a reversal of the railway's decision on the depot. In a 1997 *Daily Sun* article, the BNSF liaison for Flagstaff explained that "the merger came along and we [the BNSF] had the need to put more people in Flagstaff and no place to put them." The company thus became interested in the depot for office space.

Following an agreement between the city and the railway, the city sought and secured a $123,000 grant from Arizona's State Historic Preservation Office (SHPO) to aid with the building's restoration. The BNSF contributed $95,000 to renovate the interior for its own needs. Additionally, the city provided $152,000 in beautification funds from the city's bed, board, and beverage tax. Completing the renovation was the BNSF's investment of $160,000 for a depot parking lot and the reconfiguring of the railroad's downtown freight yard. The city could then obtain the $500,000 it expected earlier from the federal ISTEA grant to complete the bike path and streetscape. All of these projects were completed by 1997. The organization and funding for the entire project therefore came from a variety of local, state, and federal sources associated with a mutually beneficial public-private partnership.

Old Two Spot

At one end of the original depot sits Old Two Spot, one of numerous steam locomotives that served Flagstaff's lumber mills and peripheral logging railroads until replaced by trucks in 1966. For many local residents the locomotive and logging car that trails it serve as nostalgic reminders of Flagstaff's early extractive economy based on the logging industry, contributing to the overall railroad theme of downtown. The engine officially bore the number "25," painted on the cab. Water bags dangled outside the locomotive window for years and gradually wore away the "5," giving rise to the name "two spot."

When Stone Forest Industries planned to close Flagstaff's last lumber mill in 1993, the fate of the locomotive sitting on its property remained uncertain. Soon the local media and community took notice. The Northern Arizona division of the Arizona Historical Society expressed interest in saving the locomotive because, as the group's director explained in the *Daily Sun*, "it could help preserve a part of Flagstaff's lumber mill heritage." Letters to the editor of the *Daily Sun* began to appear, including one that read, "I think it would look great sitting next to Route 66. . . . It would be a shame to let something that represents Flagstaff so well be moved away from here. After all, aren't we trying to spruce up the downtown?" For this letter writer, downtown still represented the obvious display location for the locomotive.

The salvaging and restoration of this locomotive is owed mostly to the persistent efforts of seven local business owners with access to the capital required for its purchase. Stone Forest had just sold it to a California buyer who agreed to have the train off its property by February of 1995. These seven individuals then purchased Old Two Spot from the buyer in California. According to one of the purchasers, Stone Forest had refused to sell the locomotive to Flagstaff, given the city's support of federal environmental legislation against logging. The Flagstaff businessmen consequently asked the California party to purchase the engine, to be purchased back by the businessmen days later. Regardless of how the transaction took place, one purchaser made a presentation to Flagstaff's Tourism Commission, where he asked the city to reimburse the businessmen for the locomotive and to move it to an appropriate place for display. Another purchaser, John (from Heritage Square fame), promoted the locomotive as a potential centerpiece for a railroad theme park in downtown Flagstaff.

No money had been allocated in the city's fiscal-year budget to reimburse the businessmen. They had paid $61,500 to the California buyer and expected the city to cover the cost. Patience was running thin, however, and the businessmen announced that they would consider selling the locomotive elsewhere if necessary. This news spawned a flurry of letters and articles in the *Daily Sun* from residents and organizations urging the businessmen to be patient and to wait out the city's budget process. The locomotive's role in enhancing Flagstaff's sense of place was of utmost importance. The writers of one letter commented that "now it seems the train is about to be sold. Once bought, it could be transferred out of state, where the original historical association with Flagstaff would be lost forever." Another letter writer compared the significance of Old Two Spot with surrounding parks and monuments: "The old locomotive is as rare and precious to our community as Walnut Canyon, the Mount Elden Pueblo ruins or any of the other reminders of our past.... Please let us keep a part of Flagstaff's reason for existing—logging—from slipping away from us."

The *Daily Sun*'s editorial board agreed, pleading, "Keep the brakes on Flag's train." In part, the editorial read, "Nobody in Flagstaff wants to see Old Two Spot leave town.... The city needs to do whatever it can to quickly provide some sort of commitment to the train buyers." In the end, the editorial encouraged public participation to persuade the city to commit to purchasing the locomotive. The saga of Old Two Spot finally ended happily in June of 1995 when the city agreed to reimburse the businessmen. The engine now sits—aesthetically restored—next to the sandstone depot along old Route 66, at the heart of the "railroad historic district."

Themed Development in Small Urban Places

The projects above indicate a small-city redevelopment process that mirrors its metropolitan counterparts in important ways. Local growth proponents form fleeting coalitions to effect change for mutual economic benefit, not unlike metropolitan growth machines. In Flagstaff as in other communities, the city council and its staff become prominent role-players, working closely with local business alliances—in this case the Main Street Flagstaff Foundation, guided in turn by its own umbrella organization, the National Trust for Historic Preservation. Likewise, local chambers of commerce, tourism bureaus, elite downtown property and business owners, and other organizations often collaborate to transform downtown into a tourist-oriented, themed environment—often one project at a time—taking advantage of favorable enabling legislation. Funding for such projects can include private, local, county, state, and federal sources such as federal transportation grants, the foundations of prominent family members, and state-funded historic preservation grants.

Aside from the omnipresent growth coalitions, fundamental geographic differences of scale exist at opposite ends of the urban hierarchy. These differences are highlighted by Kent Robertson, who explains how spatial characteristics unique to smaller places present a different set of challenges and opportunities when planning for the revitalization of declining urban areas.[26] Smaller cities like Flagstaff, for instance, maintain central business districts that exist at a more human scale and are therefore plagued less by twenty-four-hour throngs of people and traffic congestion. Further, smaller places are less dominated by a corporate presence and rely more on independent local and regional business entrepreneurs, as exemplified above. Regional and national chains typically show less interest in small downtowns due to insufficient market size. Redevelopment efforts therefore rely much less on massive signature projects such as sports stadiums, convention venues, theaters and downtown shopping centers and more on the community's collective efforts rooted in a variety of state-enabling legislation. Perhaps most important, smaller places are likely to possess a much higher percentage of their historic building stock than metropolitan downtowns. This has generally occurred through decades of benign neglect in small business districts, whereby historic resources were largely ignored by major land clearance programs.

Likewise, Hannigan's six dominant characteristics of fantasy city apply to smaller places in important but sometimes limited ways.[27] Fantasy city's theme-o-centric quality, for instance, is typically based on scripted themes adopted from various sports, history, or popular entertainment identities. Similar attempts at scripted theming have also materialized in smaller places, typically within revitalized historic business districts. However, themes centered around sports and entertainment are less common, where aspects of local cultural and industrial heritage, historic preservation, natural environment, and rural "countryside" myths are favored in more fully developed theme towns.[28] Further, themes in smaller places are typically not divided into a series of disconnected zones as often occurs within larger metropolitan downtowns (Las Vegas, Nevada, for example), given the relatively compact and limited extent of smaller business districts.

Further, whereas fantasy city is aggressively branded, this is much less often the case in smaller places where large-scale corporate investment has simply not occurred. It is unlikely that one would find the corporate logos of Nike, Universal, Coca-Cola, or ViaCom, to use Hannigan's examples, lighting up Flagstaff's downtown Aspen Avenue.[29] The corporate branding of sports stadiums, union stations, and shopping malls will rarely occur in such settings. The imprint of globalization and the corporate marketplace is likewise subtler, found instead on various global products for sale within newer tourist-oriented shops and occasional international-themed eateries.

Some smaller downtown areas have experienced success with fantasy city's third quality, that of operating day and night. The installation of "White Way" pedestrian lampposts along downtown streets across America is indicative of a revived interest in encouraging nighttime commerce as well as pedestrian safety.[30]

It is more likely, however, that revitalized small-town business districts will focus on daytime activities of festivals, shopping, and entertainment-oriented consumption. Though various restaurants and bars, downtown theaters, and specialty shops may attract some scattered nightlife, smaller business districts typically do not attract the volume or diversity of visitors who might allow these places to remain lively throughout the day and night.

For similar reasons, smaller downtowns are less likely to demonstrate modular or solipsistic qualities more characteristic of fantasy city—qualities that have come under increasing scrutiny from those who lament the fragmentation and privatization of the urban realm. In smaller places, the sole downtown business district is often immediately adjacent to a variety of residential neighborhoods of various socioeconomic and ethnic compositions. Consequently, these neighborhoods can be active in downtown decision making. All downtown business activities are concentrated in a relatively small space, easily accessed by foot, bike, or car from nearby neighborhoods. The inward-focused and privately controlled urban entertainment destinations of fantasy city have not yet found their place on main street, except in unique circumstances (casino gaming, for one).

Granted, redevelopment agendas within smaller places are favoring middle-class, consumer-oriented functions of leisure, shopping, and entertainment, rather than traditional local services and retail. Most if not all city leaders nationwide understand that their downtowns will never again serve as the regional retail hubs they once were.[31] Still, the downtowns of smaller cities continue to be touted more as the hearts and souls of their respective communities and less as isolated and inaccessible tourist "bubbles" that unwittingly exclude non-Anglo, non-middle-class consumers.[32] For these reasons, smaller downtown spaces are more likely to demonstrate inclusive, rather than exclusive qualities. The case of Flagstaff suggests that postmodern development guided by informal small-city growth coalitions is not necessarily contradictory to the broader goals of downtown viability, enhanced public space, recognition of local heritage, and community participation.

Notes

1. For two interpretations of historic preservation as discourses materialized, see Richard Schein, "The Place of Landscape: A Conceptual Framework for Interpreting an American Scene," *Annals of the Association of American Geographers* 87 (1997): 660–80; and Thomas Paradis, "Updating the Small Town in Pennsylvania: Discourses Materialized on Main Street, Madison, Indiana," *North American Geographer* 3 (2002): 46–83.

2. Andrew E. Jonas and David Wilson, eds., *The Urban Growth Machine: Critical Perspectives Two Decades Later* (Albany: State University of New York Press, 1999); Andrew E. Jonas, "Urban Growth Coalitions and Urban Development Policy: Postwar Growth and the Politics of Annexation in Metropolitan Columbus," *Urban Geography* 12 (1991): 197–225.

3. John Hannigan, *Fantasy City: Pleasure and Profit in the Postmodern Metropolis* (London: Routledge, 1998).

4. Kent A. Robertson, "Can Small-city Downtowns Remain Viable?: A National Study of Development Issues and Strategies," *Journal of the American Planning Association* 61 (1999): 270–83; C.R. Bryant, "The Role of Local Actors in Transforming the Urban Fringe," *Journal of Rural Studies* 11 (1995): 255–67.

5. Robyne S. Turner, "The Politics of Design and Development in the Postmodern Downtown," *Journal of Urban Affairs* 24 (2002): 533–48.

6. Turner, "The Politics of Design"; Sharon Zukin, "Urban Lifestyles: Diversity and Standardization of Spaces of Consumption," *Urban Studies* 35 (1998): 825–40; John Urry, *Consuming Places* (London and New York: Routledge, 1995).

7. Stephen Page, *Managing Urban Tourism* (Harlow, England: Prentice Hall, 2003), 34.

8. For an example of a structural approach to understanding urban redevelopment, see Jon C. Teaford, *The Rough Road to Renaissance: Urban Revitalization in America, 1940–1985* (Baltimore: Johns Hopkins University Press, 1990). For a further discussion of three common theoretical approaches for understanding urban redevelopment, see Bernard Frieden and Lynne Sagalyn, *Downtown Inc.: How America Rebuilds Cities* (Cambridge, Mass.: MIT Press, 1989). On urban growth coalitions, see Jonas, "Urban Growth Coalitions"; Jonas and Wilson, *The Urban Growth Machine*.

9. John Logan and Harvey Molotch, *Urban Fortunes: The Political Economy of Place* (Berkeley: University of California Press, 1987).

10. For additional examples of my own case studies showcasing the role of growth coalitions in small towns: Paradis, "Updating the Small Town in Pennsylvania"; Thomas Paradis, "The Political Economy of Theme Development in Small Urban Places: The Case of Roswell, New Mexico," *Tourism Geographies* 4, no. 1 (2002): 24–43; Thomas Paradis, "Conceptualizing Small Towns as Urban Places: Downtown Redevelopment in Galena, Illinois," *Urban Geography* 21, no. 1 (2000): 61–82; Thomas Paradis, "The Small Town Growth Machine: Making the Commercial Strip Work for Downtown Redevelopment," *Small Town* 29, no. 2 (1998).

11. Hannigan, *Fantasy City*; Frieden and Sagalyn, *Downtown Inc.*

12. Mark Gottdiener, *The Theming of America* (Boulder, Colo.: Westview Press, 1997, 2001). See also, Norman Klein, "Scripted Spaces: Navigating the Consumer Built City" in *Architectural Design: Consuming Architecture*, ed. Maggie Toy (West Sussex, UK: John Wiley and Sons, 1998), 80–83.

13. Stephen J. Page, *Urban Tourism* (London: Routledge, 1995); Donald Getz, "Planning for Tourism Business Districts," *Annals of Tourism Research* 20 (1993): 583–600. G.J. Ashworth and J.E. Tunbridge, *The Tourist-Historic City: Retrospect and Prospect of Managing the Heritage City* (Amsterdam: Pergamon, 2000). See also: Paradis, "The Political Economy of Theme Development"; Stephen Frenkel, Judy Walton, and Dirk Andersen, "Bavarian Leavenworth and the Symbolic Economy of a Theme Town," *Geographical Review* 90, no. 4 (2001): 559–84; Steven D. Hoelscher, *Heritage on Stage: The Invention of Ethnic Place in America's Little Switzerland* (Madison: The University of Wisconsin Press, 1998); Thomas Paradis, *Theme Town: A Geography of Landscape and Community in Flagstaff, Arizona* (Lincoln, Neb.: iUniverse, 2003).

14. Some excellent examples of discussions on postmodern urbanism from various perspectives include: Page and Hall, *Managing Urban Tourism*; Michael J. Dear, *The Postmodern Urban Condition* (Oxford: Blackwell, 2000); Edward Soja, *Postmetropolis: Critical Studies of Cities and Regions* (Oxford: Blackwell, 2000); Eric Pawson, "Consuming

Spaces," in *Explorations in Human Geography: Encountering Place*, ed. Richard Le Heron, Laurence Murphy, and Pip Forer (Oxford: Oxford University Press, 1999); Setha M. Low, ed., *Theorizing the City: The New Urban Anthropology Reader* (New Brunswick, N.J.: Rutgers University Press, 1999); Brian Graham, G. J. Ashworth, and J. E. Tunbridge, *A Geography of Heritage* (London: Arnold, 2000).

15. Soja, *Postmetropolis*.
16. Mansfield cited in Pawson, "Consuming Spaces."
17. Hannigan, *Fantasy City*, 4.
18. Gottdiener, *The Theming of America*. Mark Gottdiener, "Consumption of Space and Spaces of Consumption," in *Architectural Design: Consuming Architecture*, ed. Maggie Toy (West Sussex, UK: John Wiley and Sons, 1998), 12–15.
19. Turner, "The Politics of Design and Development."
20. Hannigan, *Fantasy City*, 4.
21. M. Christine Boyer, "Cities for Sale: Merchandising History at South Street Seaport," in *Variations on a Theme Park*, ed. Michael Sorkin (New York: Hill and Wang, 1992, 181–204), 191.
22. Frieden and Sagalyn, *Downtown, Inc.*
23. Boyer, "Cities for Sale," 191.
24. David Lowenthal, *The Past Is a Foreign Country* (Cambridge: Cambridge University Press, 1985), 384.
25. The National Main Street Program, under the jurisdiction of the National Trust for Historic Preservation, is an approach to downtown revitalization in smaller communities that relies on four interrelated goals: organization (of downtown business owners), promotion (advertising downtown to the community and region), design (historic preservation and adaptive reuse), and economic restructuring (encouraging businesses to locate downtown).
26. Kent Robertson, "Downtown Development Principles for Small Cities," in *Downtowns: Revitalizing the Centers of Small Urban Communities*, ed. Michae Burayidi (London: Routledge, 2001), 9–22.
27. Hannigan, *Fantasy City*.
28. Hoelscher, *Heritage on Stage*; Kevin S. Blake, "Peaks of Identity in Colorado's San Juan Mountains," *Journal of Cultural Geography* 18, no. 2 (1999): 29–55; Frenkel and Walton, "Bavarian Leavenworth"; Paradis, "The Political Economy of Theme Development."
29. Hannigan, *Fantasy City*.
30. John A. Jakle, *City Lights: Illuminating the American Night* (Baltimore: Johns Hopkins University Press, 2001).
31. Carl Abbott, "Five Strategies for Downtown: Policy Discourse and Planning since 1943," *Journal of Policy History* 5 (1996): 5–27.
32. For more on the concept of "tourist bubbles," see Dennid Judd, "Constructing the Tourist Bubble," in *The Tourist City*, ed. Dennis Judd and Susan Fainstein (New Haven, Conn.: Yale University Press, 1999), 35–53.

Chapter 5

Theming as a Sensory Phenomenon: Discovering the Senses on the Las Vegas Strip

Scott A. Lukas

In this chapter I will address theming from a sensory perspective, with a specific emphasis on the way in which the senses—touch, sight, hearing, smell, and taste—operate to create and maintain theming on the Las Vegas Strip.[1] Theming has sometimes been understood only as a static phenomenon—as a combination of architecture, interior design, signage, and associated forms of performance that relate to the common theme. I hope to illustrate the flexible and lived nature of theming, particularly as the five senses are utilized in the maintenance of themed venues. On the main Strip and in surrounding environs, there is a multitude of themes—including western, tropical, Egyptian, Arabian, Irish, pirates, Italian, Mediterranean, New Orleans, Arthurian, circus/carnival, sports, French, space, music, and many others.[2] At the most immediate level, themes assail the senses. Whether it is a tropical waterfall mist, a massive light beam emanating from a pyramid, the smell of fresh pastries in a Parisian cafe, the roar of a crowd dancing to steel drums outside a carnival space, or a cold drink in a themed tumbler, the patron immediately knows that he or she is in Vegas—a deep familiarity is inculcated in him or her as each moment is a moment of the senses.

Over the last ten years, a significant trend has been the pronounced use of the senses in consumer space. Businesses have moved to sensory media to establish a closer connection with the consumer.[3] In an era of growing eclecticism of the market, expanding consumer media, and further embellishment of the service industry, businesses employ the senses as a means of both standing out among the clutter and noise of the market and of connecting intimately with consumers. In terms of the first area, themed spaces have typically been regarded as extraordinary spaces—as standing out in the crowd—but on the Las Vegas Strip, with its abundance of eclectic themed casinos, it is difficult to compete. To increase their notoriety, casinos have used theming in particular and idiosyncratic ways. At a simple level, the more sensory a themed space, the more it can communicate to the visitor and the more that it can demarcate itself from other themed or non-themed spaces. The sensory is that which signifies and thus what sells. Contrary to popular notions that the most popular Vegas casinos are those of scale, abundance and excess, based on my studies, I have identified that the most successful casinos are those of nuance, minuteness, and precision. In short, those that are sensed.[4] Like the anthropological concept of culture, these casinos represent a knowable order that is present but not overly present.

The two major ways in which casino designers and operators have drawn on sensory experiences are microtheming and performative theming. Microtheming refers to the specific and nuanced ways in which theming is developed on a minute level. In Las Vegas, microtheming, whether noticed by the customer or not, can distinguish one casino as opulent and grand and another as cheap and unrefined. In my research on the Strip, I have commonly noted that customers focus on the extent to which theming is developed in a casino. Though they do not call it this, they often critique casinos that do not microtheme and praise those that do. In trips to the Aladdin, I have heard some customers say that the scale of the interior architecture and decor, including inlaid gems on pillars, is "all wrong." I have heard others complain that the casino looks "cheap" and "shoddy."[5] Conversely, while at the Wynn and the Bellagio, I have witnessed customers react with awe at the levels of ornateness that are detected in features like floors, ceilings, and light fixtures. Microtheming is also present in mid-end casinos like the New York–New York where a recreation of a quaint New York village includes smoking manhole covers, trees, and authentic streets. At its most effective level, microtheming includes a bombardment of the five senses, ideally occurring in imperceptible levels to the customer. At Caesars' Forum Shops, for example, many customers stroll through the shops unaware of the changing hours of the day reflected on clouds and night sky on the ceiling. They are being effected, but in the most subtle ways.

Performative theming is a second way in which the senses are used as a motivated means in the themed casino. Like microtheming, performative theming is a sensory assault of the customer within the space. During my years as an employee trainer at a Six Flags theme park, I was familiar with the uses of performance as a means of employee control. We stressed the idea of "always being on stage" and that employees should always "play their part" while they were around customers. This recognition of the role of the employee in maintaining the themes of the park is now common in many themed service industry locales. In Vegas' casinos it is a common occurrence to note French-speaking workers in the Paris casino cafes or to hear Italian serenades by gondoliers in the Venetian. Not all of the Strip casinos engage in performative theming, for, like the requirements of microtheming, it is not easy to train employees to speak another language or to glean the cultural nuances of a culture not their own, and, it is certainly expensive. Performance employed as theming can include non-human elements, such as the dancing water fountains of the Bellagio and the erupting volcano of the Mirage.

As microtheming and performative theming are developed within a casino, an overall complex, a theming complex, is created. For unthemed casinos like Bally's there is no theming complex and visitors have to focus on other elements, like the quality of entertainment, the taste of food, and the excitement of slot machines and table gaming, rather than on a particular theme and its elaboration. For the themed casino, the theming complex is the sum of all efforts to carry out a theme in its space. Some writers have suggested that many of Vegas' casinos lack adequate theming, they "frequently jumble multiple conflicting themes, or stop and start themed areas without thinking about the edges or juxtaposition."[6] Indeed, there is a debate as to whether a casino should emphasize its theme versus other non-themed aspects, including architecture and layout, and the result of these aspects on higher slot and table game returns for the casino.[7] The theming complex recognizes that the senses are geographical and that customers at any retail or entertainment space expect more than the availability of products or entertainment; they expect a sense of discovery and sensory stimulation.[8] An effective theming complex will result in a seamless connection of spaces, decor, and performance—in short, it is ambiance.

Ambiance is an integrated use of the senses. In nature, an explorer may become awed with the features of the landscape. These features do not affect merely one or two of the senses, they impact all five, often simultaneously. The smell of clean mountain air, the taste of a plant, the sounds of chirping birds, the texture of a jagged rock, and the sight of an incredible vista simultaneously effect the explorer; the sum of all of the senses is a cybernetic relationship of the explorer and the environment. In nature this relationship is one of the sublime; unfortunately, in architecture and consumer built spaces, achieving this same ambiance and sense of the sublime is a major challenge.[9] One way of achieving the natural ambiance present in nature is to develop eclectic themed architecture. Like the monumentality of the medieval cathedral, the contemporary themed casino is an environment that "stimulates the simultaneous use of three or four sense receptors." In the case of the medieval cathedral, geographer Yi-Fu Tuan writes that each sense reinforces other senses and all "clarify the structure and substance of the entire building, revealing its essential character."[10] Visitors to the Strip's themed casinos often comment on their visual impact and they commonly remember their trips to Vegas through references to its themed spaces and the specific sensory ways in which these spaces play out in their minds and bodies.[11]

Theming the Senses and the Body

Some studies of the themed space have indicated the role that sensory phenomena play in the construction of theming. Visitors to the various theme lands of Disney and Six Flags parks are familiar with the use of theming as a deployment of the senses. In my work as a former theme park trainer, I consistently informed employees of the importance of creating effective sensory experiences for the customer. Vision was implicated as employees were told to maintain effective dress code and to convey positive image with gestures and body language. The auditory sense was stressed as we told employees to present a positive greeting to customers and to not discuss back-of-house matters in earshot of the guest. The other senses—olfactory, touch, and taste—were further referenced in general theme park mandates on delivering satisfying food, gaming, rides, and grounds control practices. Significantly, in our trainings we stressed that all of these uses of the senses must be connected to the theme related to the employee's work area.[12] In the Las Vegas casino there is a similar emphasis on the appropriate connections of theming and sensory stimulation. As I wrote earlier, the use of microtheming and performative theming indicates nuance and can establish both the uniqueness of the casino and the idea that the experiencing of it is a unique, personalized circumstance focused on the customer.

On the occasion of visiting the city for the first time, an individual may find the visual force of the Strip to be overwhelming. The incredible scale of major hotel casinos and eclectic themes like Egyptian, tropical, and Arthurian create a sense of visual amusement. The visual force of architecture, that in scale and theme looks nothings like architecture in one's hometown, produces an immediate effect in the visitor. Certain structures, including the Luxor, Caesars, and the Stratosphere, use architecture in an iconic sense—the building, itself, is emblematic of theme. In the case of the Luxor, the beam of light that emanates from the top of the pyramid is visible in space and it is a visual feature that unlike most other casinos' features can be seen from anywhere on the Strip.[13] Other casinos, like the Bellagio and Wynn, use architecture to draw the consumer inside, where there elaborate decor, lighting, furniture, and other features are used to visually embellish theme. Sight has been called the most expressive of the senses and, particularly in the age of the Internet, mass consumer media, and video games, the appeal of Vegas' iconic buildings, flashing lights, and distinctive billboards and signs is not surprising.[14] It would be difficult to call Las Vegas anything other than a visual city, but because there is such bombardment of the visual senses in the city, it is important for casinos to theme experiences in ways that reference multiple uses of *all* of the senses.

One of the most overlooked aspects of the themed space's relationship to culture and to humans is the way in which theming implicates the body. In Vegas, the senses are always connected to the body and the body is, in turn, used to create thematic space. At a general level, movement of the body constitutes an archetheme in the city. Everywhere one looks, there is a crowd, there are people bustling here and there, and there are spontaneous movements of bodies as people draw closer to the structured performances of pirate shows at the Treasure Island and water shows at the Bellagio. Yet, the body, as it is motivated to move among crowds on the Strip and within the casino, is not part of a conscious thematic operation. Certain bodies are—particularly those of women—and they are often unnoticed forms of theming due to their ideological nature. At the Riviera, a loosely themed casino at the north end of the Strip, the bronzed and patinated buttocks of the Crazy Girls (members of a topless review) encourage visitors to employ both vision and touch. I have seen many men and women, even families with young children, take their photos with the anonymous bronze women. Even more commonly I have witnessed Vegas visitors touch the buttocks, thus creating the patina that is a visual expression of the gendered politics of the Riviera and Vegas. At the new Hooters casino, occupying what used to be the San Remo, the female body is fully themed. Like the chain of Hooters restaurants, the casino in Vegas uses the mass sensory appeal of sexism to motivate its beach-themed interior. Signs near the casino restrooms—including, "Caution: Blonde Thinking"—further exemplify the visual construction of the theme.

Many themed casinos rely on the sexualization of women as part of the visual order. A form of beverage service at the topical Rio called *Bevertainment* involves scantily clad waitresses serving drinks to patrons and spontaneously dancing on techno stages throughout the casino.[15] The Paris casino uses a Parisian-style outfit to clad its female beverage servers, and numerous other casinos on the Strip use themed dress to simultaneously sexualize women and convey the theme of the casino. As an archetheme or overriding theme that cuts across all other specific casino themes, gender is connected to both the senses and the body. In these many cases what is significant is how the sexualized female body is a ready-made, capable of being deployed in any themed land—Parisian, tropical, Egyptian, and Italian. Male and female patrons are told the powerful gendered message that women's bodies are subject to the visual gaze and the unwelcomed touch.[16] The presence of archethemes like the gendered body suggests that certain cultural behaviors and ideologies crosscut the varied themes on the Strip.[17] Male workers also play significant parts in the thematic plays of casinos—such as the gondoliers who sell the theme of Italian charm at the Venetian—and they, along with customers, may represent an ultimate form of sensory deprivation that will be addressed at the conclusion of this chapter.

Patrons are most commonly drawn into the themes of the Strip's casinos through their bodies. By reducing the experience of Vegas to the sensory domain of the patron's body, the theming complex can function most effectively. As the themes are deployed in casinos, "the sensory structure of everyday life is experienced as neutralized, almost cosmic time over and against which eruptive, 'sensational events'... are profiled."[18] Many of Vegas' themes create a meaningful reality by directly connecting the senses and the body. Certain casinos create vistas that give the patron a sense of "I am there" as they move through the casino. The western theming of the Frontier is amplified by the visual appeal of vintage slot machines and decor, the touch of wooden floors against the feet, and, in its performances that include mud wrestling and bikini bull riding at Gilley's saloon, the raucous shouts of cowboy males who exhibit the male gaze.[19] Many tropical themed casinos use more sensuous approaches to convey their themes. Ambiance is created as customers focus on water—an archetheme on the Strip—and feel it hit their bodies in lazy rivers at the Mandalay Bay, splashes from waterfalls on their bodies at the Tropicana, the sound of water habitats (aquariums, waterfalls, ponds, and pools of all sorts), the taste of island cuisines at the Mandalay Bay and the Tropicana, and the smells of open air, island freshness of various sources that attempt to replicate the experience of being on an island paradise. All the time, the powerful visual sense of architecture supplements the other senses that are also being used to enact the given theme.

In themed casinos that purport to recreate an actual space, such as a city, the senses are used in a number of ways to connect the worker and patron to an economy of senses that, as simulated as it is, recreates the holistic tableaus of senses that are present in real cities. At the Paris casino, sounds of street performers speaking French mingle with street signs written in the same native language and various French goods in store windows. The smell of crepes and fresh baguettes permeate the Parisian-style street outside the casino space, while diners sample French wine on the boulevard that sits against the Strip, just under the recreation of the Eiffel Tower. The creation of multisensory ambiance is common at most place-focused themed casinos, including Bellagio, Caesars, and Venetian. The various senses that make up the thematic experiences found at casinos like Paris are interpreted by the viewer as distinct, seamless, and meaningful. Like the anthropological concept of culture, the theming complex that is created and maintained by the various senses is a holistic statement about the world. Similar to culture, theming often acts on the body in ways that are imperceptible but definitely felt, similar to what Bronislaw Malinowski noted as *imponderability*. Far from being a generalized impact within consumer society, theming is a specialized technology that directly acts on the self.

Theming and a Sense of the Self

The deployment of the senses as a means of connecting the worker and patron body to the theme relates to deeper aspects of the self. Themed spaces, as they are effectively designed to engage the customer's senses, are interactive, immersive geographies. One theming expert advising the industry recommended that theming "can't be two-dimensional. It's got to be three-dimensional. It's got to reach out, touch and envelop the people who are coming to whatever the attraction might be."[20] Often, themed casinos carry a narrative throughout the space to instill a sense of connection between the customer and the casino. Visual cues, like signs, pathways, lighting; olfactory ones, such as introduced scents or the smells of a buffet; touch cues, like the nuanced features of a wall or a combination of geometric angles; auditory effects, including machine sounds, artificial sounds of nature; and taste cues, with numerous emphases on eating and sexuality, are used as a sensory order of immersion.[21] The Arthurian-themed Excalibur uses references to knights, empire, and ideas of conquest to connect patrons to restaurants, shops, entertainment, and gaming throughout the casino. During one ethnographic visit I noted many references to meat and empire—exemplified in "You Rule!" billboards and visual depictions of turkey legs and roast beef—that playfully appealed to numerous sensory dimensions of patrons. Caesars has a similar approach, particularly in its use of thematic vistas that are placed throughout the structure. Patrons move from a shopping area that features pleasant smells of food and perfume to a casino that is visually themed with references to Caesar and Roman architecture; then, they move into another shopping area that includes a Roman pantheon show complete with smells, sights, and deafening sounds. Later, patrons can relax and shop as the skies above them change from night to day. What both the Excalibur and Caesars accomplish is the elaboration of theming throughout their casinos, and their primary means of achieving this is through the intense referencing of each of the senses.[22] By engaging the five senses and their combinations in synesthetic ways, the themed space creates an experiential ground for the consumer that appears to be individualistic. As the individual gains a scent of bloomed flowers in the Bellagio's Conservatory or is visually tantalized by the molten eruptions of the Mirage, she is told, essentially, that Vegas is about *her*.[23] The personalization of the themed space is perhaps the greatest advancement in thematic architecture. Virginia Postrel writes that in contemporary consumer society "sensory appeals are everywhere, they are increasingly personalized, and they are intensifying."[24]

In the theme park and the themed casino, a new form of consumer authenticity is created. Its primary means of conveying its message is not information—though content matters in some themed displays, signage and other aspects of design, it is not the primary focus. The emphasis in theming is representation, or how something is said, not what is said. As the patron picks up on sensory cues, he or she is taken with the performative dimensions of the theme and the sense that things seem real or authentic because *they are happening*. In some cases, authenticity is produced through the denial of one sense and the heightening of another. At the Hard Rock Hotel and Casino, glass cases feature the rock and roll memorabilia of Janis Joplin, Jimi Hendrix, and other celebrities. There, sight is museal and the patron is left unable to touch or closely interact with the museum pieces. In fact, many of the Strip's casinos have used the sensibilities of the museal to increase the notoriety of their casinos—some have opened mini museums, like the Bellagio, Wynn, and Venetian, while others have turned their attractions into museum-like spaces.[25] As I shall relate later in terms of its impact on social relations, the Bellagio utilizes a combination of an Italian-charm theme and a heavy emphasis on austere, sober elitism. Within the Bellagio there are no loud crowds or unruly dancers of the sort found in tropical casinos like Harrah's, instead the senses are kept to a certain minimum. The interior architecture, featuring many smooth surfaces and palatable color schemes, does not carry sound in the manner of other casinos, and the visual features are intended to lull the patron into a sense of refinement and respect. One of the clear markers of theming and its sensory project along the Strip is the different social orders that are connoted in the design and performance of theming.

The creation of authentic themed spaces is never left to one sense. The senses, in a combinatory manner, establish the reality of the unreal conceptions and values that are particular themes. To accept the pirate themes of the Treasure Island as something other than facade, the viewer must be given multiple channels of sensory information. Just as contemporary popular music is a holistic order composed of multiple tracks of sound, vocals, and effects, Treasure Island uses each of the five senses, and their overlap, to produce an order that is complete and believable. The Treasure Island's famous Siren Show uses most of the senses—including vision, hearing, and touch—to notify the patron of the reality of the pirate theme.[26] Performance is one of the most common sensory expressions on the Strip and, as an archetheme, it communicates to the viewer the legitimacy of what awaits him or her inside the casino. If the pirate show appears to the patron as an effective, multisensory experience, he or she will be more likely to enter the casino. Once inside, the multisensory bombardment continues where more of the senses, including olfactory cues provided by restaurants and food stands, are motivated. However, there must be sensory balance in a themed casino, particularly between the extreme highs of excitement and the considerable lows of solitude. Through its theming complex, the casino develops a range of sensory expressions that correlates to different themed areas of the venue. For example, the Luxor offers Ra, an Egyptian nightclub that features sensuality, techno music, and explorations of the body; it also features themed statues, walls, and other features of interior architecture that create womblike spaces in which gamblers can enjoy private time and the occasional interruption that occurs with a major win. Restaurants, like Isis (now defunct), offer theming and opulence that give diners an opportunity to escape the noisy confines of the craps table or Ra.

Wayne Curtis once described the authentic as "something that looks as you imagine it might"[27] The authentic as a recreated project puts the visitor at ease—though the patron is engaged in a scripted narrative, the narrative is ready-made. It is sensory available, and it must be not very difficult to connect to what is represented. At a semiotic level, authenticity is created when signs no longer draw attention to themselves. Even a space that references no original location or concept can have a lasting effect of authenticity on the patron. Starbucks is an example of an international coffee/retail chain that creates a distinctive look, feel, and sensory order that is incredibly popular with consumers. Its authenticity lies in its state of being immediately knowable to the patron. When backed by corporate capital, themed spaces create a particularity or distinctiveness that provides the corporation with a dominant product. Starbucks coffee houses use the company's recognizable logo, modern organic decor with a soothing color palate, and the aroma of coffee to dominate the coffee market.[28] Referencing Bloch, Allen Feldman suggests realism is "the culture of the immediately ascertainable fact."[29] For the patron, a given theme in a casino or restaurant acts as a fact for the reason that is immediately known to that person, an empiricism of the moment. The patron does not need to question the circumstance of the visual panorama of various Egyptian structures, statues, and features in front of his or her eyes; simply, these features are accepted as the theme expressed by the Luxor. At the Venetian, one day as I observed tourists snapping still shots and video clips of the visual spectacle of the Mirage volcano explosion, I noticed a family taking a moment of distraction from the visual feast—they began to rub their hands across the faux-patinated surface of one of the Venetian's outdoor columns. Their hands touched the bumpy surface and made their way to some depressions in the "stone," which have been fashioned to appear on sight and on touch as something old, as if from Venice itself.[30]

On numerous occasions I have been taken with the ambiance inside the Mandalay. In addition to the smell of fresh, clean air, there is an openness of Mandalay Bay's casino that allows my eyes to wander, and I have always preferred this open casino to the cramped ones like the Imperial Palace, Paris, or New York–New York. What I have noticed, like most other patrons, is that particular casinos put me at ease, and they do so by creating a holistic themed experience that connects with each of the senses. A Disney individual once stated, "What we are selling, is not escapism, but reassurance."[31] What this individual helps identify is the extent to which theming, if correctly executed through sensory elaboration, provides the patron with reassurance. Las Vegas' themed casinos are often viewed as places of fantasy, excitement, and excess. This interpretation does apply to many circumstances, but theming can also comfort, so much that one is lost in the self. For the casino, this sensory solitude serves an economic purpose. If the gambler enters a comfortable space, he or she is more likely to gamble and later visit restaurants and other venues that will give the casino greater revenue.[32] As a sensory structure, reassurance functions on a continuum from the total excitement of maximum sensory elaboration to the total low of sensory deprivation that is akin to a body in an anechoic chamber. This range is significant, for each casino, though often targeting different demographic markets, depends on the possibility of connecting with all visitors—old and young, male and female, gambler and non-gambler, and from all ethnic and personal backgrounds. The range of senses deployed in the themed casino guarantees an immersive experience as well as the availability of varied experiences, from the highs of major crowd excitement to the solitude of a quiet experience in front of a slot machine.

Touch offers the themed casino an opportunity to ask the patron to reconnect to nature, species, and places far removed from the artificiality of the Strip. The Mirage's tropical theme is complemented by references to living nature. The popular Siegfried and Roy white tiger show, though now closed due to a tiger attack, was a draw, and the casino makes a point of emphasizing its commitment to conservation efforts on indoor video screens. The same casino allows customers to experience live dolphins in an outdoor space near the pools. The MGM uses lions—a reference to the iconic MGM lion, not to the tropics—in a similar effort to create a nature spectacle within its casino. In a grotto that looks like something out of a large zoo, people gawk at lions while sounds of lion roars are pumped through speakers. The Mandalay Bay's aquarium features rare hammerhead sharks, while the Bellagio's popular Conservatory, though not featuring live animals, offers papier-mâché versions of them and the smells of real flowers. The now defunct Reserve casino, well off the Strip, was based on the theme of the safari and nature. For patrons, nature is associated with the sensory—it is the opposition to the cold, industrial, and inhuman world of the city. In theming, "the focus is on softer factors, on intangible feelings which architecture has always had trouble dealing with as soon as its ambition has nothing to do with monumentality, sanctity, or sheer power."[33] In the numerous examples of the simulation of the senses of nature, Las Vegas casinos play to the patron's sense of self by exhibiting what is meant to be a project counter to the sensory bombardments of much of the Strip. Whereas other casinos may use loud music, gyrating dancers, and other unintended sensory elements provided by patrons, like the stale air of cigars, the many casinos that rely on nature as a thematic emphasis seek to counter one form of sensory stimulation with another. As much as this example demonstrates the inherent focus of theming on the individual, theming and its sensory projections also impacts the nature of social behavior on the Strip.

Theming, Sociality and the Senses

During a 2005 research trip to the city, I spent an afternoon at the western-themed Frontier. The Frontier sits near the edge of the Strip at the northern end. The first thing that struck me about the place was the unambiguous sounds of coins hitting trays on the slot machines. Many Vegas casinos have moved to ticket-in/ticket-out systems that eliminate coinage entirely from slot transactions. After I won five bucks on a slot, I had to wait ten minutes for an attendant to pay the sum to me. During a conversation I asked him about the new ticket machines which he said he hated. He also narrated about a fellow who always plays at the Frontier, "He does so because he likes the *real* sounds of coins hitting metal," he told me. The discussion with the gentlemen struck me as interesting—it spoke of the transformations that are taking place in Vegas, many of which lie at the cusp of theming and sensory perceptions. Some critics have argued that the new Vegas is focused more on glitz, entertainment, and Disneyfied architecture.[34] I would add to this criticism that like the architecture and entertainment, the ways in which the senses are realized through themes have also been altered dramatically within the city. The stories of Vegas old invite nostalgia. Older Vegas casinos like the Castaways, Moulin Rouge, and the Dunes relied on theming, but a much more organic form of it. In newer casinos, there is more attention to the fickle nature of customers. Restaurants come and go, walls go down and new ones are erected, and entire casinos, like the Aladdin, are rethemed. Like the sensory moods that the patron travels through while in a casino and on the Strip, themed architecture is fleeting and temporary. An interesting dimension of Las Vegas is the effect of the transformations of the sensory order created by theming and its relationship to social relations occurring in and outside of casinos.

The senses act as a "collective medium of communication" and the means by which information about theming is conveyed by patrons, customers, and managers. Theming itself—as a sign vehicle that is transmitted through the senses, many of which are intimate ones—can induce sociality, albeit consumerist forms of it. Casinos rely on the multisensory aspects of kinetics to assist in theming.[35] Some, such as New York–New York, the Stratosphere, Circus Circus, and Bellagio—with roller coasters, rides, big top shows, and dancing fountains—utilize the spectacular aspect of movement to emphasize the excitement of their thematic apparatus. The popularity of the Cirque du Soleil shows at many Strip casinos illustrates how movement is tied back to corporeality.[36] The movement of crowds, however, can turn off Vegas visitors. Often what a customer desires is an escape from the bustle of crowds and their noisy appearances. Touch is often the escape from movement. Many casinos use the opportunity to touch patrons or to have them touch things as an inducement to pleasure and relaxation. Major spas in the casinos allow patrons to receive expensive but intimate treatments, and many malls, such as those inside Bally's and Excalibur, feature low-priced massage tables. Water is a tactile element that is used by a number of the tropical themed casinos along the Strip. In the case of Bellagio's fountains, vision is favored to touch and the effect is the customer watching the remarkable show but not being a part of it. In contrast, the Mandalay Bay's many interior water features, aquarium, and gigantic water park with lazy rivers, pools, and a massive wave pool, invite the patron to touch and to experience the casino's theme in a more intimate sense.[37] These varied uses of the senses reestablish the patron in opposition to the social—he or she is referenced by atavistic senses and very subtle uses of them.

Many of the most notable senses in Las Vegas are social. Taste is a highly social sense, and is on constant display in the casino.[38] In some obvious respects, taste plays on the social stage of the buffet and the performance restaurant. At the Excalibur's Tournament of Kings patrons watch jousting and other Arthurian events while they consume turkey legs and other food. In many buffets, like the Rio's Carnival World Buffet, a carnival atmosphere is promoted as food items are presented in various stations—each reflective of a different region of the cuisine world. In contrast, the buffet at Paris, though also utilizing different food stations, is presented in an architectural atmosphere of a quaint French small town. Though diners at each buffet partake in the olfactory and taste excesses that characterize the city in general, there is a difference in how the senses are used to present the food and, likewise, there is a different construction of sociality present at each casino that further reflects the overarching theme.[39] The smell and taste of food and drinks also connects back to the body, what I have argued is a major site of the themed casino's effect on the customer. A trend that began in the late 1990s is the promotion of ultra lounges—expensive, refined, and elaborate settings in which patrons can engage in dancing, drinking, smoking, and socializing.[40] Many of the ultra lounges reflect the theming complex of the casino, such as the MGM Grand's Studio 54, but others do not consistently reflect the theme, such as Tao at the Venetian. The interior of the Tao is themed, and it promotes an overall archetheme of sensuality, common to most of the ultra lounges. Scantily clad servers pour $200 bottles of Dom Perignon, and strike up conversations with the people at their tables. The movement towards table service at these venues has been a recent trend, and it suggests a connection back to the overriding focus on sensuality, intimacy, and interpersonal relations. Many have criticized Las Vegas' lack of intimacy, and it seems that the themed ultra lounges of the Strip promote a use of the senses that is counter to this claim.[41] They are intimate places, albeit with a price.

Theming, as it clarifies the roles of workers and offers meaning to customers, is pedagogical. Because it "instigates a displaced perception of the world and sense of reality," it is incumbent on casino designers and managers to motivate the relationship of person and place; this is done, primarily, through sensory elaboration.[42] In chapter 11 I address the specific ways in which theming acts as a means of social control, and it is interesting to note the similar ways in which theming, specific to the senses, maintains social order along the Strip. As a project of social control, it is often difficult to establish—after all, the senses that are promoted in casinos or resultant from the activities associated with them (such as the male gaze, overeating, flatulence, shouting and catcalls, groping of people) are not typically associated with sober sociality. In some cases, the dominant sense of physical restraint or a pronounced verbal threat is used by casino security guards to abate the least desirable examples of Vegas sensory excess, but in other cases, more subtle means are employed. Theming acts as a narrative that is played out in various ways throughout a casino. The specific ways in which the narrative develops over time and space are dictated by the casino and are geared at worker and customer alike. Depending on the location of the casino, certain extreme expressions of sound, like shouting, may be tolerated. Screaming at a craps table, for example, can provide cheap advertisement suggesting to the customer that people are lucky and winning. Obnoxious behavior at a high-end bar or in the high limits slot area, however, will not likely be tolerated. In some cases overly sensed customers may be brought in line by workers or even other customers, in others, certain cues are provided by architecture, decor, mood lighting, and color. Performances—like those of gondoliers at the Venetian and themed actors in the St. Mark's Square (part of what the casino dubs as *Streetmosphere*)—also inform patrons that certain moods are expected. Cher Krause Knight indicates that theming is now more commonly associated with public spectacle, not private space like gardens. Similarly, a designer of the famed Forum Shops at Caesars stated that "This isn't great architecture, it's great theater."[43]

The technologies of theming are directly tied to the ideological order of the State. Many theme parks, including Dollywood, portray distinctive narratives about race, patriotism, and gender, and all themed casinos, as I have argued, include gender as part of their narrative about the body and culture. Social class is also implicated in the themed casino's construction of culture, especially in its attention on social relationships that take place within casinos. In terms of the senses, David Howes has written that "the dominant group in society will be linked to esteemed senses and sensations while subordinate groups will be associated with less-valued or denigrated senses."[44] The casinos of Las Vegas help illustrate Howes' point relative to the senses and social class. Las Vegas' historic casinos lacked the sensory elaboration that dominates the large contemporary themed casinos. Many of the contemporary themed casinos develop theming through a specific class-based use of the senses. Prominent billion-dollar casinos like Bellagio, Venetian, and the Wynn rely on sensory elaboration to promote social class. The grandiose architecture of these casinos may, at first glance, cause some less wealthy consumers to avoid the casinos. Their theming may appear stuffy and proper and cause such customers to visit a less intense casino like Excalibur, Monte Carlo, or Imperial Palace. Walking inside the Bellagio the patron is immediately struck by a sensory palate of social class—the ornate decor looks nothing like the cheap interior of the Monte Carlo, a casino that feigns social class in name only. The sensory orders of high-end casinos like the Bellagio, Venetian, and Wynn, create an affective relationship between the consumer, other consumers and workers, and the narratives that are told in various forms of entertainment, dining, and forms of material culture. They form what Pierre Bourdieu denoted as *habitus*.[45] Of course, Vegas' sensations are also democratic in a number of respects. Smaller and less elaborate casinos feature references of the senses that also relate back to the self. Ultimately, the theming of casinos serves both the personal lifeworld of the individual (psychology and the body) and well as the social order that is noticeable along the Strip and within the casinos.

The Future of Vegas Sensations

> Sensory values not only frame a society's experience, they express its ideals, its hopes and its fears.
> —Constance Classen[46]

An interesting sign adorns an area in the Paris casino: "Caution: The cobblestone floor you are about to enter is a re-creation of an authentic Paris street. It is an uneven surface. Therefore, please watch your step." This sign illustrates the casino's attempt to create authenticity, in this case through the visual design of the street and the tactile impressions that it leaves in the customer.[47] Paris is a casino that attempts to create a multisensory themed experience. Efforts to attract more customers include a redesigned Eiffel Tower experience that is described on signs and brochures as "more sensual," and the prominence of many restaurants that approximate both upscale Parisian venues and small street stands. Yet, amidst all the sensuality and the attempts to create the sensual order of Paris, I am always struck at the lack of edginess that would, in my opinion, constitute more attention to the sensory details of Paris. Gone in the sanitized versions of the Paris casino are references to less desirable senses—the shout of a drunk outside Gare du Nord station, the smell of urine on the streets, the cacophony of a street musician inside the subway. Of course, many travelers describe the senses that they experience in their travels as a mixed bag. Some enjoy experiencing the new scents, sounds, vistas, and tactile aspects of their trips, while others bemoan the lack of familiarity that impacts them in the new sensory culture.[48] Under conditions of tourism, the senses produce culture shock, while under the conditions of theming the senses institutionalize culture shock. Themed casinos and other themed venues will continue to utilize the senses as a means of connecting with the consumer and as a strategy of making the goods and services that they offer appear to be personally connected to each person.

Throughout capitalist society, the use of the senses to sell products, exhibit services, and influence consumer decisions is a common occurrence. As David Howes has stated, multisensory marketing—ranging from the smooth tiles in a store, the music in a cafe, or the scents of a home products outlet—is now a predominant part of the consumer world.[49] C. Nadia Seremetakis suggests that under capitalism the senses have been mobilized, commodified, detached from one another, and employed by the State to serve utilitarian needs.[50] In no social space is this conclusion more evident than in a themed space. Female cocktail waitresses are often required to use the senses, including touch and visual display, to provide male patrons with service that is themed consistently with the casino's material and architectural foundations. Patrons are asked to accept the sensory decisions that have been produced by the casino, whether or not they feel a real connection between the sensory cues and their existential and personal states. Chapter 11 of this volume deals with the topic of the dehumanization of workers and patrons that may occur in themed spaces and their associated interpersonal dimensions.[51] In the final section it is worth considering the contexts of dehumanization, alienation, and rationalization that are connected to the deployment of the senses in themed casinos.

Karl Marx was concerned with the effects of work on the individual, particularly as interpersonal and personal dimensions of the worker were subject to alienation, dehumanization, and sensory deprivation.[52] For workers, especially female ones who are subject to the dehumanizing aspects of sexism that pervade most themed casinos in the city, the experience of dealing with customers in hectic service settings is enough—adding the element of "emotional labor" that is produced when workers act out themes for patrons makes work even more challenging.[53] Some Vegas workers with whom I have spoken enjoy both the gregarious tasks of service and the emotional requirements that are connected to the playing out of multiple senses for the customers. Others find the need to always be on stage and to give their senses to the customer freely as major challenges. For the patron, the idea is that the casino's theme, and the way in which it comes across through the senses, is presented, primarily, for him or her. Of course, patrons are also manipulated by theming. The forced perspective that is used to fool the eyes in both the exterior and interior architecture of the New York–New York, the ambient, piped-in forest sounds that are evident in the nature-themed Rainforest Cafe inside the MGM, and the real and simulated sounds of coins that are found throughout any casino, are all exemplifications of decisions that have been made not by the consumer, but by a corporation.[54]

The danger of the senses as they are realized through Vegas theming is that they invite unintended consequences that are, ironically, consequences of the senses. The sensory apparatus is too fickle for designers and managers of themed spaces to predetermine the behavior of patrons. For example, the retheming of the Aladdin into the Planet Hollywood may be a result of ineffective theming. The Desert Passage shops featured elaborate simulated effects that referenced most of the senses, including simulated thunderstorms that utilized sight, sound and touch, but many visitors with whom I have spoken did not find the theming, as involved as it was, to be convincing. Theming is a subjective realm of culture, as are the senses, and the combination of the two may result in an ambiguous situation for all. In terms of the concerns regarding dehumanization and rationalization, perhaps there is a more balanced possibility. Few people who would support the expression of free speech in diverse aesthetic modes and cultural contexts would also uphold the value of multisensory expressions in themed venues. Perhaps just as the new museum or heritage center deploys senses like smell to challenge the traditional means of cultural representation that limit the viewer's experience to sight and, sometimes, touch, the contemporary themed space utilizes the senses in new ways to create new opportunities.[55] Some authors have written that the deployment of the senses in the themed casino is a form of leading the consumer "by the nose instead of being addressed through the more legitimate (read 'rational') channels of visual and verbal communication."[56] At the same time, all forms and uses of the senses have a politics, and it is possible to read the way in which theming plays off the senses in a narrative manner. In another perspective, the consumer completes the text that has been laid out in a themed casino.[57]

In my studies of the theming of the Las Vegas Strip, I have sometimes found myself seduced, as any consumer is, by the overload of sensory information that greets me in any casino. As an individual, I have experienced joy in Las Vegas, and it concerns me that cultural critics disregard the role of pleasure in consumer spaces chiefly because they dismiss such pleasure as inauthentic and the result of rationalization in society.[58] At the same time, as an ethnographer I am concerned about the ills that are associated with the senses and themed casinos. As I discussed earlier, some of the most common sensory cues are deployed through incredibly sexist representations like those of the Riviera, Rio, and Palms. As well, the way that the senses are used to seduce people into slumbers of alcohol and to convince them to depart with the money in their pocketbooks is a major social issue. I have taught in Lake Tahoe, a community with a number of casinos, and I have witnessed people succumbing to the numbing effects of alcohol, violence, and gambling. The psychological self, as it is now more commonly produced under the semiotic, informational, technological, and architectural contexts that are exemplified by theming, is, like the theming, no longer bounded to traditional or holistic foundations.[59] Like the ironies of theming itself—a technology that confounds due to its shifting and deliberately playful relationships to originals—the ideological dimensions of how the senses are deployed to produce themed spaces will, no doubt, remain equally as ironic.[60]

Notes

1. This research is based on multiple years of ethnographic research in the city of Las Vegas. It is important to note that the five senses discussed in this article are not necessarily reflective of sensory orders of other cultures. Some taxonomic orders include up to nine senses. For more see Kathryn Linn Geurts, *Culture and the Senses: Bodily Ways of Knowing in an African Community* (Berkeley: University of California Press, 2002), 9.

2. In total, I have identified twenty-six extant and extinct themes on the Las Vegas Strip. The most common theme is tropical and New Orleans, followed by Italian and Mediterranean. For a "theme map" see <http://www.scotlukas.com/thememap.htm>.

3. Bernd Schmitt and Alex Simsonson, *Marketing Aesthetics: The Strategic Management of Brands, Identity, and Image* (New York: Free Press, 1997), 3, 15. See also Martin Lindstrom, *Brand Sense: Build Powerful Brands through Touch, Taste, Smell, Sight, and Sound* (New York: Free Press, 2005); and Kevin Roberts, *Lovemarks: The Future Beyond Brands* (New York: powerHouse Books, 2005). Special thanks to David Howes for bringing these references to my attention.

4. A similar concept emerged at the San Francisco Exposition of 1915. In response to a signage ordinance that forbade signs, developers used exotic architecture, including Blarney castles, Samoan villages and recreations of the Grand Canyon, to establish decidedly marked spaces. See Barbara Rubin, "Aesthetic Ideology and Urban Design," *Annals of the Association of American Geographers* 69, no. 3 (1979): 349.

5. In 2006, the Aladdin began transformation to the new movie-themed Planet Hollywood Hotel and Casino. Perhaps this retheming reflects the lack of customer interest in the old Arabian-themed casino.

6. Frances Anderton and John Chase, *Las Vegas: The Success of Excess* (London: Ellipsis, 1997), 52.

7. This argument is developed in depth in Bill Friedman, *Designing Casinos to Dominate the Competition* (Reno, Nev.: Institute for the Study of Gambling and Commercial Gaming, 2000). Friedman believes that theming distracts players and essentially hides the merchandise (gaming equipment). See also, Bill Friedman, "Casino Design and its Impact on Player Behavior," in *Stripping Las Vegas: A Contextual Review of Casino Resort Archi-*

tecture, ed. Karin Jaschke and Silke Ötsch (Germany: University of Weimar Press, 2003), 69–86.

8. See John Urry, "The Tourist City," in *The Tourist City*, ed. Dennis R. Judd and Susan S. Feinstein (New Haven, Conn.: Yale University Press, 1999), 71 and Paco Underhill, *Why We Buy: The Science of Shopping* (New York: Simon and Schuster, 1999), 158.

9. As one author states, "a consistent theme in engagement with the sublime is not to wholly identify oneself with a transcendent ideal power but to enjoy that as an abstract, exciting but unachievable possibility." This definition applies to the explorer's experience with nature but is more difficult to achieve in the case of themed spaces. Claudia Bell and John Lyall, *The Accelerated Sublime: Landscape, Tourism, and Identity* (Westport, Conn.: Praeger, 2002), 6.

10. Yi-Fu Tuan, *Topophilia: A Study of Environmental Perception, Attitudes, and Values* (New York: Columbia University Press, 1990), 11.

11. Stephen Greenblatt suggests that resonance is the "power of the displaced object to reach out beyond its formal boundaries to a larger world" and wonder is "the power of the displaced object to stop the viewer in his or her tracks." I would suggest that resonance and wonder are both significant elements in Las Vegas theming. Stephen Greenblatt, "Resonance and Wonder," in *Exhibiting Cultures: The Poetics and Politics of Museum Display*, ed. Ivan Karp and Steven D. Lavine (Washington, D.C.: Smithsonian Institution Press, 1991), 42.

12. As I suggest in chapter 11 of this collection, many employees were disciplined and ultimately fired for not creating sensory experiences consistent with theming.

13. A 2006 television ad for the Luxor stated, "It all begins with the brightest light in the world." Other Luxor advertisements focus on the pyramid as the defining visual feature of the Luxor, such as, "Luxor, the Shape of Escape."

14. See Martin Jay, *Downcast Eyes: The Denigration of Vision in Twentieth-Century Thought* (Berkeley: University of California Press, 1994), for a discussion of the dominance of the visual sense in culture.

15. For examples of this form of entertainment, see Dick Foster Productions, "Bevertainers," <http://www.dickfosterproductions.com/bevertainers.htm>.

16. In addition to the bronzed buttocks of the Riviera's Crazy Girls, there are many stories of female cocktail servers who have been physically groped by customers. As well, some have called the world of Strip cocktail waitresses a "Darwinian world" in which the most sexualized and beautiful women are preferred. Liz Bentson, "For Servers Strip Casinos Prefer Beauty Over Age," *Las Vegas Sun*, 21 May 2006, <www.shns.com> (24 October 2006).

17. The senses not only embody cultural categories, but make "into body certain cultural values or aspects of being that the particular cultural community has historically deemed precious and dear." Geurts, *Culture and the* Senses, 10.

18. C. Nadia Seremetakis, "Intersection: Benjamin, Bloch, Braudel, Beyond," in *The Senses Still: Perception and Memory and Material Cultures*, ed. C. Nadia Seremetakis (Chicago: University of Chicago Press, 1996), 19.

19. For more information see <http://www.gilleyslv.com/>.

20. Ronald P. Mendoza, "Themed Retail Design," *Where It's @*, <http://www.where-its-at.com/articles/spotlightarticles/spotlight4.html> (2 March 2004).

21. Michael Taussig writes of mimesis as a dual phenomenon—"a copying or imitation, and a palpable, sensuous, connection between the very body of the perceiver and the perceived." Michael Taussig, *Mimesis and Alterity: A Particular History of the Senses* (New

York: Routledge, 1993), 21. Theming has too often been understood only in its imitative function, not its sensuous qualities.

22. As some have written, theming is often produced as a story or narrative in which the customer provides the motivation to move through the story. See The Project on Disney, *Inside the Mouse: Work and Play at Disney World* (Durham, N.C.: Duke University Press, 1995), the specific chapter "Story Time," 79–97. As well, see Norman Klein, "Scripted Spaces: Navigating the Consumer Built City," in *Architectural Design: Consuming Architecture*, ed. Maggie Toy (West Sussex, UK: John Wiley and Sons, 1998), 80–83. For additional discussion of the theming vista as a form of the picturesque and "stations," see Jeanne van Eeden, "Theming Mythical Africa at the Lost City" in this volume.

23. As Baudrillard has written of consumer objects, "[they] no longer serve *a purpose*, first and foremost they serve *you*." Jean Baudrillard, *The Consumer Society: Myths and Structures* (London: Sage, 1998), 159. Additionally, Postrel writes that in contemporary, consumer society, "*I like that* merges into *I'm like that*. Identity prevails." Virginia Postrel, *The Substance of Style* (New York: Harper Collins, 2003), 101.

24. Postrel, *The Substance of Style*, 5.

25. For more on the traditions of museums in Las Vegas, see William L. Fox, *In the Desert of Desire: Las Vegas and the Culture of Spectacle* (Reno: University of Nevada Press, 2005). Also, some theme industry insiders have refered to some venues that offer memorabilia in their spaces, such as Planet Hollywood and Hard Rock, as "museum concepts." See Nancy Brumback, "Museum Piece?" *Restaurant Business* 99, no. 24.

26. For more on the show see <http://www.treasureisland.com/pages/ent_sirens.asp>.

27. Quoted in Giovanna Franci, *Dreaming of Italy: Las Vegas and the Virtual Grand Tour* (Reno: University of Nevada Press, 2005), 118.

28. See Postrel for a discussion of Starbuck's "distinctive look and feel." As she writes, it is not so much the objects or people within the spaces but "the evolution of the environments that surround them, and us." Postrel, *The Substance of Style*, 8, 19. Also, it is worth noting that the distinctive sensory order of a venue can lead to brand association. This association creates an almost intimate connection between the perception of the viewer and the sensory aspects of the venue. For more on the trend of branding in consumer spaces see Anna McCarthy, "Brand Identity at NikeTown," in *Signs of Life in the USA: Readings on Popular Culture for Writers*, 4th ed., ed. Sonia Maasik and Jack Solomon (Boston: Bedfords/St. Martin's, 2003), 410–14.

29. Allen Feldman, "From Desert Storm to Rodney King via Yugoslavia: On Cultural Anesthesia," in *The Senses Still: Perception and Memory and Material Cultures*, ed. C. Nadia Seremetakis (Chicago: University of Chicago Press, 1996), 91.

30. Walter Benjamin once wrote of the traveler as a naïve person who "passes through cities and countries with anamnesis . . . [and whose] senses respond to every nuance as truth." Walter Benjamin, "The Great Art of Making Things Seem Closer Together," *Walter Benjamin: Selected Writings, Volume 2, 1927–1934*, ed. Michael W. Jennings (Cambridge, Mass.: Harvard University Press, 2001), 248.

31. Friedman, *Designing Casinos*, 318.

32. For more discussion of the casino creating a private world for the gambler see, Friedman, *Designing Casinos*, 22.

33. Oliver Herwig and Florian Holzherr, *Dream Worlds: Architecture and Entertainment* (Munich: Prestel, 2006), 36.

34. See Sally Denton and Roger Morris, *The Money and the Power: The Making of Las Vegas and Its Hold on America, 1947–2000* (New York: Alfred A. Knopf, 2000).

35. C. Nadia Seremetakis, "The Memory of the Senses, Part I: Marks of the Transitory," in *The Senses Still: Perception and Memory and Material Cultures*, ed. C. Nadia Seremetakis (Chicago: University of Chicago Press, 1996), 6.

36. The upscale restaurant Aureole in the Mandalay Bay has been made famous in large part due to its use of kinetics. At Aureole, a wine tower is operated by wine angels—women clad in tight catwoman outfits. Aureole uses the movement of the angels as a visual spectacle, a means to denote incredibly personalized service, and an approach to connect the diner with sensuality in the restaurant.

37. For a detailed discussion of Las Vegas sociality and theming, see Scott A. Lukas, "The Theming of Everyday Life: Mapping the Self, Life Politics, and Cultural Hegemony on the Las Vegas Strip," forthcoming *Community College Humanities Association Journal* (2007).

38. As Classen writes, "Sensory relations are . . . social relations." Constance Classen, "McLuhan in the Rainforest: The Sensory Worlds of Oral Cultures," in *Empire of the Senses: The Sensual Culture Reader,* ed. David Howes (Oxford: Berg, 2005), 162. For more on taste as a social relation see Diane Ackerman, *A Natural History of the Senses* (New York: Vintage, 1991), 127. Lynn Sally also writes of the ways in which the senses act as "a mediator for social knowledge" in her study of the sensory aspects of the historic Coney Island parks. Lynn Sally, "Fantasy Lands and Kinesthetic Thrills: Sensorial Consumption, the Shock of Modernity, and Spectacle as Total-Body Experience at Coney Island," *Senses and Society Journal* 1, no. 3 (November 2006): 293–309

39. One of the most exciting ethnographic portrayals of the Las Vegas buffet is Natasha Schull's *Buffet: All You Can Eat Las Vegas*. The film was screened at the American Anthropological Association 2006 Annual Meeting. For more information: buffetmovie@yahoo.com.

40. For more on this trend of the Ultra Lounge see Geoff Schumacher, *Sun, Sin and Suburbia: An Essential History of Modern Las Vegas* (Las Vegas: Stephens Press LLC, 2004), 82–83.

41. The Tao emphasizes a mystical approach to the senses. Much like the Tantra in Miami, Florida. According to their Web site, "Miami Beach's hottest dining destination, Tantra features an exotic Middle Eastern decor, including a live grass floor and waterwall, sensual music and the acclaimed aphrodisiac cuisine." The Tantra creates "an ancient Middle Eastern philosophy focusing on spiritual enlightenment through the appeasement of the six senses." <http://www.tantrarestaurant.com> Overall, "Buddhist"-themed venues are becoming more poplar throughout the United States. Alana B. Elias Kornfeld and Valerie Reiss, "WWBD?" *Newsweek*, 14 August 2006.

42. Herwig and Holzherr, *Dream* Worlds, 37.

43. Cher Krause Knight, "Beyond the Neon Billboard: Sidewalk Spectacle and Public Art in Las Vegas," *Journal of American and Comparative Cultures* 25, no. 1/2 (Spring 2002): 10, 11.

44. David Howes, "Introduction: Empire of the Senses," in *Empire of the Senses: The Sensual Culture Reader*, ed. David Howes (Oxford: Berg, 2005), 10.

45. Pierre Bourdieu, *Distinction: A Social Critique of the Judgement of Taste* (Cambridge, Mass.: Harvard University Press, 2002). See also Marcel Mauss, "Les Techniques du corps," *Journal de Psychologie* 32 (3–4), on "body techniques."

46. Classen, "McLuhan in the Rainforest," 161–62.

47. A number of other casinos also employ realistic floors as a form of sensory theming, including New York–New York, Frontier, and Hooters.

48. One issue that is worthy of future ethnographic study is the circumstance in which the sensory order, established by the cues of the themed casino, breaks down as the result of patron intervention. I have noted that flatulence is a common occurrence inside casinos. Farting breaks down both the olfactory and aural order of the casino. A second issue is the possibility of breaking down the sensory order in a meaningful way, such as in the example of experimental tourism. "Experimental Tourism Catches On," *CNN.com*, 1 September 2003, <http://www.cnn.com/2003/TRAVEL/09/01/experimental.tourism.reut/> (16 October 2006); and Stephen Hodge et. al., *An Exeter Mis-Guide* (Exeter, England: Wrights and Sites, 2003).

49. David Howes, "Hyperesthesia, or, the Sensual Logic of Late Capitalism," in *Empire of the Senses: The Sensual Culture Reader*, ed. David Howes (Oxford: Berg, 2005), 288. See also J. Hornik, "Tactile Stimulation and Consumer Response," *Journal of Consumer Research* 19: 449–55.

50. C. Nadia Seremetakis, "The Memory of the Senses," 9–10.

51. In his study of McDonaldization, George Ritzer remarks, "Dehumanization occurs when prefabricated interactions take the place of authentic human relationships." George Ritzer, *The McDonaldization of Society*, rev. ed. (Thousand Oaks, Calif: Pine Forge, 1996), 131.

52. David Howes writes that capitalism acts to seduce "the senses of the consumer in the interest of valorizing capital." "Hyperesthesia," 289–90. For more on the relationship of the senses and leisure spaces, see John Urry, "Sensing Leisure Spaces," in *Leisure/Tourism Geographies: Practices and Geographical Knowledge*, ed. David Crouch (London: Routledge, 1999), 34–45.

53. Arlie Hochschild, *The Managed Heart: Commercialization of Human Feelings* (Berkeley: University of California Press, 1983).

54. David Howes writes that "it is difficult to contest a sensory order that is backed up by science or religion." David Howes, "Introduction: Empire of the Senses," in *Empire of the Senses: The Sensual Culture Reader*, ed. David Howes (Oxford: Berg, 2005), 1–17. To Howes' suggestion, I would add capitalist consumerism and maintain that it is equally difficult to contest the ways in which the senses are deployed under the magical system of capitalism. Within the themed casino, the viewer is at the mercy of the specific decisions that have been made by designers in the planning of casinos, managers in the day-to-day operations of them, and workers who execute the desires of both designers and managers in the quotidian interactions with patrons. In a similar tone, Stephen Fjellman suggests in his study of theming at Walt Disney World that theming is an envelopment of the patron. According to Fjellman, themes are subdivided with the hierarchy of them serving purposes of appealing to customers' desire for varied entertainment and sights, structuring the traffic and flow of the park, and engaging individuals in the corporate vision of Disney. Stephen M. Fjellman, *Vinyl Leaves: Walt Disney World and America* (Boulder, Colo.: Westview, 1992), 23.

55. Jim Drobnick, "Volatile Effects: Olfactory Dimensions of Art and Architecture," in *Empire of the Senses: The Sensual Culture Reader*, ed. David Howes (Oxford: Berg, 2005), 270.

56. Howes, "Hyperesthesia," 291. The specific quote references the use of smell in consumer spaces discussed in Constance Classen, David Howes, and Anthony Synnott, *Aroma* (New York: Routledge, 1994).

57. I take this idea from C. Nadia Seremetakis who states that, "The surround of material culture is neither stable nor fixed but inherently intransitive, demanding connection

and completion by the perceiver." Seremetakis, "The Memory of the Senses," 7. See also Norman Klein, "Scripted Spaces: Navigating the Consumer Built City," in *Architectural Design: Consuming Architecture*, ed. Maggie Toy (West Sussex, UK: John Wiley and Sons, 1998), 80–83.

58. For a discussion of how anti-Disney discourse has negatively impacted cultural criticism see, Greil Marcus, "Forty Years of Overstatement: Criticism and the Disney Theme Parks," in *Designing Disney's Theme Parks: The Architecture of Reassurance*, ed. Karal Ann Marling (Paris: Flammarion, 1997), 201–207. For a similar discussion in terms of the discourse related to the Hummer and its impact on considerations of automobiles and ecology see Scott A. Lukas, "The Hummer as Cultural and Political Myth: A Multi-Sited Ethnographic Analysis," in *The Hummer: Myths and Consumer Culture*, ed. Elaine Cardenas and Ellen Gorman (Lanham, Md.: Lexington Books, 2007), 115–34

59. In his work *The Saturated Self*, psychologist Kenneth Gergen argues that the contemporary self, bombarded with multiple and contradictory images, messages, and memes, is no longer secure or bounded. Kenneth Gergen, *The Saturated Self* (New York: Basic Books, 1991), 15–16.

60. The sensory technologies exhibited in Las Vegas' casinos are expanding to more mundane locales, including mid-size American cities. As John Hannigan writes in *Fantasy City*, "the fantasy city is one that a dependent on a recognizable and marketable theme." John Hannigan, *Fantasy City: Pleasure and Profit in the Postmodern Metropolis* (London: Routledge, 1998), 1. It is clear that this issue of ideology, the senses, and theming is now relevant to cities beyond Las Vegas.

Chapter 6

The Landscape of Power: Imagineering Consumer Behavior at China's Theme Parks

Hai Ren

As the development of theme parks has become a global phenomenon, theming has been incorporated into many areas of everyday life.[1] The Walt Disney Company refers to theming as *imagineering* and uses it to revitalize urban environments, such as New York's Times Square, and to create planned communities, including Celebration, Florida.[2] Theming has become a dominant business practice in the leisure and service sectors such as themed restaurants, like the Hard Rock Cafe and Planet Hollywood; shopping malls, such as the Mall of America and West Edmonton Mall; sports stadiums like Seattle's Safeco Field; and airports, like Phoenix Sky Harbor International Airport and McCarran International Airport in Las Vegas. Currently, theming, as a technology for building and operating an environment for the sake of consumption, is common among many spaces such as theme parks, shopping malls, festival markets, themed restaurants, and planned communities.

To understand theming as spatial technology, a clarification of the notion of space is necessary. Conventionally, space is narrowly viewed as built environment, a resulting product of human building activity, which may include building type (dwelling, temple, or meeting hall), defined or bounded territory (square, plaza, or street), landmark or site (shrine), specific building elements (doors, windows, roofs, or walls), and building subdivisions (living room, kitchen, or bathroom). When considering human interactions that deploy the technology of theming, space is necessarily viewed not only as a product of human building activity but also as a medium of social action.[3] Thus, themed space, as a *product* of building activity, refers to both the material ground of labor and the result of the operations and inscriptions of capital in the form of land value and the property regime. Meanwhile, as a *medium* of social action, consumer space structures social interactions in a particular way through technologies of theming.

Theming—the production of an environment as a themed space—is a technology for incorporating a narrative or story into a controlled movement in a built environment.[4] This spatial technology includes three components. First, an environment is built both as a medium for integrating a story or theme into the controlled movement and as the message of the medium—what is communicated by the medium itself. Here, the storyteller is an engineer rather than a conventional counselor who, according to Walter Benjamin, offers "less an answer to a question than a proposal concerning the continuation of a story which is just unfolding."[5] Second, theming is an economic process that operates on the basis of separating the stage (consumption and the performance of work) from the backstage (production and surveillance). A key principle of operation is synergy, a mode of capital accumulation based on convergence or cross-promotion within and among media (such as print media, broadcast media, theme parks, and the Internet), entertainment, retail, real estate development, and other aspects such as education.[6] Finally, the producer or/and the manager of the built environment is a corporation or an organization, usually a private company or its division.

The significance of theming as a spatial technology is historically situated within the context of neoliberal globalization, the reconfiguration of the global political and economic systems at least since the 1970s.[7] The nation-state system is under significant transformation as national and local governments have systematically withdrawn from various areas traditionally associated with governmental responsibilities—social welfare, education, communications, and even national security. While alternative political systems like socialism appear to fail, civil society gains more ground—instead of counterbalancing the government's control, civic associations begin to replace the government in controlling the daily lives of individuals, including homeowner associations. In the realm of the economy, consumption has been transformed as a privileged site for the fabrication of self and society, and of culture and identity.[8] Consequently, class has become a less plausible basis for self-recognition and action when growing disparities of wealth and power would point to the inverse. Meanwhile, such categories as gender, race, ethnicity, and generation have become compelling idioms of identification, mobilizing people, both within and across nation-states, in ways often opposed to reigning hegemonies.

Both linking together and explicitly facilitating private controls and consumption-based economy, the technology of spatial thematic production normalizes the development of a particular kind of built environment, which is characterized by security (clear, safe, and orderly), excitement (alternative, diverse, and entertaining), and control (limited access and private management). This normative space is fundamentally paradoxical. On the one hand, it is used to manage fears and uncertainties, and control terrors, crimes, and threats. Their diverse sources may include job insecurity, everyday boredom, racial and ethnic differences, illegal immigration, and mass media crime dramas. On the other hand, the normative space also offers excitement that security and control do not offer. Sources of excitement may include encountering others (marked by gender, ethnicity, citizenship, and class), physical challenges, role-playing, and survival games. Thus, a theme park like Disneyland is not simply a tourist attraction, it also embodies the normative space—an effective themed built environment for managing the contradiction between the desire for experience and the parallel reluctance to take risks.

To address the relationship between theming and the development of this normative space, I turn to China's theme parks, where spatial theming has been clearly appropriated as a powerful tool for inscribing and legitimating a new social relationship in China's neoliberalization since 1978, when the country began its "economic reforms." During this period China witnessed the incorporation of the market as a regulative logic in the economy and the gradual rise of private controls that performed governmental functions. Focusing on the Chinese Ethnic Culture Park in Beijing, a major theme park opened in 1994 to represent China's ethnic minority cultures, I examine the park's construction of an "urban village" (a middle-class ideal of suburban lifestyle), its application of a particular mode of capital accumulation, and its use of consumption to shape visitors' behavior.[9] Through this example, I will illustrate the way in which spatial theming is deployed as a technology for structuring economic, social, and cultural organization of everyday life in China, especially at the historical moment when the Chinese Government shifts its orientation of social development policies towards consumption and leisure.

China's Themed Spaces in a Historical Context

The theme park is often viewed as a recent phenomenon in China because the country's first modern theme park, Splendid China in Shenzhen, was only established in 1989. However, the theme park as a cultural form has a long history in China. The Old Summer Palace—or the imperial garden of Yuanming Yuan—built from 1709 to 1774 and destroyed by British and French soldiers during the second opium war in 1860, may be viewed as a prototype of the modern theme park. It has been used as an excellent model not only for building an ideal garden but also for combing both entertainment and consumption in a built environment. The pre-1860 garden contained architecture (both traditional Chinese and European styles), gardens with pools and fountains, and displays of artifacts from China and other countries, and a wall painting about life in an European town.[10] The garden was built for Qing emperors and their families. A make-believe market town was set up to entertain the emperor and his guests. The town included built streets, squares, temples, halls, markets, shops, courtrooms, palaces, and even a harbor. Eunuchs ran the market and assumed the roles of shop owners, teahouse keepers, and vendors who sold antiques, books, furniture, silk clothes, porcelain, varnish works, and the like. In order to make them look exactly like merchants in downtown Beijing so as to maximize amusement, the eunuchs loudly shouted the vendors' cries (*jiaomai*), while busily emulating aggressive salesmen to catch customers by the sleeves to press for sales. To make the common street scene come alive, they even pretended to quarrel and fight among themselves and wait for arrest by security guards, as often happened on the real streets. This market normally lasted for nine days as part of the celebration of the New Year.[11]

In the ordinary lives of urban residents, traditional forms of entertainment and amusement were often combined with shopping. The New World and South City Amusement Parks in Beijing offered entertainment, performances, and games in connection with market days and temple fairs.[12] In Shanghai, the Great World (1916–1949) was the most influential and popular amusement center that included variety shows, food shops, and cinemas.[13] The four major department stores in the International Settlement of Shanghai—Xianshi (Sincere), Yong'an (Wing On), Xinxin (Sun Sun) and Daxin (Sun)—were also entertainment centers that included not only merchandise on different floors but also recreational facilities such as dance halls, rooftop bars, coffeehouses, restaurants, hotels, and playgrounds.[14] The practices of combining entertainment and shopping were not systematic and thus limited in their scale and influence in the lives of urban residents in the early part of the twentieth century. From 1949 to the end of the 1970s (the period of socialism), entertainment was disconnected from consumption and was oriented toward political education. Popular theater and performance, for example, only served the purpose of socialism, aiming at representing life as "typical," "idealized," and "universal." Leisure was not differentiated from work, and material enjoyment was not distinguished from spiritual enjoyment.[15]

Although leisure and consumption have become marked as separate categories since the 1980s, they still maintain governmental purposes in shaping everyday life in China. The development of themed spaces clearly illustrates this point. Since 1989, China has witnessed a "theme park" (*zhuti gongyuan*) fever. Hundreds of theme parks have been constructed around major urban centers, and billions of dollars have been spent. The most well-known and most successful theme parks are those focusing on cultural themes.[16] The "world" (*shijie*), for example, is a major theme. Some world parks tend to be smaller and more focused. Chengdu's Wild West Cowboy Street, for example, draws on Hollywood's western genre to recreate the scene of a U.S. frontier town: a ranch-style country house, a cowboy bar, a sheriff's office, a carriage, a corral, and bone-buried desert diorama. However, China's well-known world parks tend to be much bigger and most of them provide a grand overview of countries around the world. Parks like Shenzhen's Window of the World, the Beijing World Park, and the Chengdu World Park typically divide the whole environment into five continents, each of which includes replicas of famous sites, architecture, and urban and natural scenes. From the perspective of cultural representation, all of these parks tend to provoke a strong sense of Westerncentrism. Europe is usually located at the center of a park. For example, the Hungarian Hero Plaza is placed as the center square at the Chengdu World Park, where the most elaborate and extravagant performances are staged on a daily basis. In the Beijing World Park, Europe occupies the park's center and is the largest space. Two countries are always highlighted—France and the United States. The Eiffel Tower becomes a landmark sign. In Shenzhen's Window of the World, the tower is one-third of the original size, but it is one of the most visible structures both in the park and in the Overseas Chinese Town in the city. A visitor can ride the elevator to the top of the tower.

In recent years, China has witnessed a stunning development of mega-shopping malls, as income per person in China has reached the equivalent of about $1,100 a year, up 50 percent since the year 2000. Chinese developers have traveled around the world to learn from famous shopping malls and from Las Vegas, and many of the world's visionary architects have been hired to design the malls.[17] More than four hundred large malls have been built in China in the last six years. Currently, China is home to the world's five largest shopping malls.[18] Golden Resources Mall in Beijing (opened in October 2004), the world's third largest mall (7.32 million square feet), cost $1.3 billion to build. It spans the length of six football fields and easily exceeds the floor space of the Pentagon, the world's largest office building, at 3.7 million square feet. It is a single, colossal five-story building—with rows and rows of shops stacked on top of more rows and rows of shops—so large that is hard to navigate among the one thousand stores, 230 escalators, and the thousands of shoppers. According to Fu Yuehong, the mall's manager, an average of forty thousand people visited on weekdays, and more than eighty thousand on weekends in 2005.

Many mega-malls are explicitly created as themed spaces. South China Mall in Dongguan, the world's largest mall (9.58 million square feet), was built after its developers traveled around the world for two years in search of the right model. This $400 million fantasyland includes 150 acres of palm-tree-lined shopping plazas, themed venues, hotels, water fountains, pyramids, bridges and giant windmills. Trying to exceed even some of the over-the-top casino extravaganzas in Las Vegas, it has a 1.3-mile artificial river circling the complex, which includes districts modeled on the world's seven "famous water cities." The southern California section, marked by a reproduced Hollywood sign, is a giant Imax theater complex that partially encircles this area of the mall. The Paris section is a recreation of the Champs-Élysées with a full-size (85-foot) reproduction of the Arc de Triomphe at its center. And the Venice section highlights Gondola rides on a canal under bridges with a new Shangri-La Hotel on one bank.

Whether theme parks or shopping malls, these themed spaces follow the global trend in the development of hybrid forms of consumption—shopping is intertwined with entertainment (through cinema, games, and amusement rides), education (through stories and themes), merchandising (through copyrighted images, brands, and logos), performative labor (of front-stage employees), and control and surveillance (of both employees and consumers).[19] Meanwhile, they are also part of the neoliberal trend of globalization in which conventional social relations are uprooted and reconfigured through private means of control. To elaborate how the technology of spatial theming is deployed in a way linking both consumption and private control in China's neoliberalization, I turn to my ethnographic example, the Chinese Ethnic Culture Park in Beijing, which I have studied since 1996.

The Chinese Ethnic Culture Park as a Landscape of Power

The Chinese Ethnic Culture Park, located to the west of the National Olympic Center in Beijing, occupies a total of forty-five hectares of land. It consists of two parts—the south site and the north site. The construction of the south site has been completed. The north site, about twenty hectares, was opened to the public in June 1994. The construction cost of this site was approximately $36.1 million, and 85 percent of the capital for this site came from Taiwan and Hong Kong. The park, as described in the park's brochure, "blends architecture and cultures of Chinese minorities to provide visitors with a unique place to experience the life of the minorities in the metropolitan capital."

The north section includes a group of sixteen life-sized villages, each representing houses and dwelling environments of a "national ethnic group" (*minzu*). The sixteen national ethnic groups are the Zang ("Tibetan"), the Qiang, the Jingpo, the Hani, the Wa, the Miao, the Yi, the Buyi, the Dong, the Hezhe, the Dauer, the Ewenke, the Elunchuan, the Korean, the Taiwan Aborigines, and the Dai. Each village includes displays of daily artifacts, furniture and houses, ethnic performers who may belong to the ethnic group the village represents, and cultural objects such as ethnic food, tea, and souvenirs.

The visitors to the park are mainly Chinese citizens. Although the visitors include those from outside mainland China—such as foreign tourists, overseas Chinese, the Hongkongese, and the Taiwanese—the majority of the visitors are from mainland Chinese cities. They are "middle-class" (*zhongchan*) or "leisure-class" (*xiaofei jiecheng*) consumers whose income level permits them to pursue "leisure" (*xiuxian*) activities such as dining in restaurants, entertaining at nightclubs, driving their own automobiles, owning their own apartments or homes, and conducting other activities distinguishing them from the rest of mass consumers (*gongxin jiecheng*) who calculate, on a daily basis, to make ends meet and pursue their pastime in activities such as watching television or movies.[20] This group of visitors is capable of spending their own money on the high admission charge of $7.25.

Building a Themed Space

Within the urban context of Beijing, the park renders itself as a triumphant site of interest by juxtaposing itself with Beijing's most famous national cultural and historical sites. In the park's brochure, one reads: "The park stands by the city's axis: Beichen Road, a northern section of the axis. This road connects the park to a series of national sites: the National Olympic Center (across Beichen Road), Tiananmen Square, and the Forbidden City (only about five kilometers away from the park)." This spatial presentation associates the park with Beijing's triumphant images—the most prominent national sports center that exhibits the physical strength of the nation and the most well-known monumental sites that display the nation's essence.[21]

Three gigantic billboards outside the park link the park to the Great Wall and the Palace Museum, and highlight the important role the park sees itself playing in the national context. One billboard portrays a group of flower-holding ethnic minorities standing in a line and welcoming the visitors. Two lines of Chinese characters are written above the image. The top line reads: "Go to the Great Wall, Go to the Forbidden City, and Go to the Ethnic Park; You'll See History, See Culture, and See the Chinese People." The lower line reads: "The Chinese Ethnic Culture Park Welcomes You." Another billboard portrays a group of ethnic minorities dancing and celebrating "Long Live the Great Unity of All Peoples in the Country." The third billboard reads: "Let the World Understand China; Let Us Understand Ourselves." Following the billboards, messages, history, culture, and people are inseparable. Visiting the Great Wall and the Palace Museum means viewing history and culture correspondingly; and visiting the park means viewing ethnic minority peoples. The phrase "Let Us Understand Ourselves" suggests that not only some Chinese—Han Chinese in the cities in particular—should "understand" ethnic minority Chinese because they do not understand ethnic minorities, but they also may discover and define a clearer sense of the self through understanding ethnic minorities.

In addition to juxtaposing itself with Beijing's most triumphant sites, the park also presents itself as "a village in the urban setting," providing a space of "nature" in Beijing's urban setting.[22] Contrasted with "the urban jungle" marked by "jammed streets," "dashing crowds," and "noisy markets," the park is "a land of peace" or "the countryside of harmonies." There, one can view "rice fields," "ponds and streams," "wooden buildings," and "stone houses." In conveying the pastoral idea, the park covers 85 percent of its grounds with exotic grass, trees, flowers, and crops. Whether inside or outside the park, one is always able to see the striking differences between the outside "urban" environment and the inside "natural" pastoral setting—a contrast between gray and green, and between concrete structures and wooden buildings.[23]

What this so-called countryside of harmonies constructs is an "ethnic minority region" (*minzu diqu*). The term *ethnic minority region* originally refers to an area where the ethnic minorities live and which is usually separated from where the Han people live. Here, the ethnic minority region is integrated into the lives of the Han people in the urban setting. One visitor recognized:

> The most attractive aspect of the ethnic park [is related to the experience provided by the park]. In visiting the ethnic villages, a tourist has a sensational understanding of these ethnic peoples in a short period of time; [he/she] watches and participates in performances, festivals and games, tastes ethnic food, and buys stuff. During such a visit, one can transcend a sensational understanding to a rational understanding. Because those ethnic minorities working in a village are those represented by the village, visiting the village almost allows one to have an experience of touring the ethnic minority region represented by the village [my translation].

According to a park manager, the planning principle for constructing the "ethnic minority region" is that of "respecting the natural and re-presenting reality." In accordance with this principle, all major construction materials for a building were imported from the area represented by the building; and construction for each village was carried out by construction companies employing experienced craftsmen from the area represented by the village. Like the construction of Disney's Animal Kingdom and the Venetian in Las Vegas—both of which employed workers indigenous of the places being simulated in theming—the park developed what can be called an authenticity of construction. For instance, a dark purple plant used for architectural decoration in the Zang village was transported from Tibet and the village was constructed by a company from Lhasa and was overseen by a Tibetan architect. Everything Tibetan (the design, materials, construction) guarantees "the original flavor" of the Zang buildings. The general manger said that the construction of the ethnic minority villages by local ethnic minority craftsmen was a "rescuing" project because these villages (in the park) will become "the last ones" when "the old ethnic minority craftsmen die and all of the old stuff gradually disappear after ten to twenty years." Therefore, what the park constructs is not only a "countryside of harmonies" but also an "ethnic minority region" in the urban lives of the Han people.

Maintaining "harmonies" and "ethnic" flavor, however, has to confront the adaptability of reconstructed landscapes, connecting to ongoing environmental changes. For example, because many construction and decorative materials as well as artifacts are from a mild and moist environment in southwestern China, the park finds it difficult to maintain the original condition of these materials in Beijing's cold, windy, dusty, and dry environment. From late autumn to early spring, most of the plants in the park, like other plants outside the park, lose their peaceful green color. Many artifacts on display have been damaged as a result of being directly exposed to Beijing's natural environment. The park regularly replaces these old materials with new ones in order to maintain their original appearance.

Consumption-Oriented Economy

In reinforcing the park's image as a landscape of China's ethnic minorities or establishing the new nature as a continuation of the old nature, the park's operations hide most of the "un-natural" facilities such as restaurants, stores, restrooms, offices, and ethnic performers' dormitories underneath individual village sites, or operates them as part of the villages.[24] Hiding "manmade" facilities intends to maintain the "natural" or "ethnic minority" flavor of the reconstruction, but more importantly, it is directly related to the way in which the company accumulates capital through arranging signs such as artifacts, buildings, corporate logos, souvenirs, food, staged shows, and performers on the basis of selected themes in the built environment. This economic operation of using signs and space follows what sociologists Scott Lash and John Urry call *reflexive accumulation*, which is characterized by the central role of knowledge in capital accumulation—by the reflexivity of both production and consumption, and by the increasing importance of non-material products such as services, communications, and information.[25]

Although the park projects its image as an urban village or city garden for middle-class consumers, it is operated on the basis of consumption. Consumption-orientation drives the park to conceal the production process in the eyes of the public—that is, the unnatural aspects of the park. The park's backstage, including planning, operations, management, negotiating, training, and delivery is never exposed to visitors' eyes. The sociologist Anthony Giddens argues that the distinction between the front stage and back stage in professional operations is a strategy to reduce the impact of imperfect skills and human fallibility in order to make laypersons trust an expert system like the air travel or the hospital system.[26] In this case, however, making the backstage invisible to the public does not intend to reduce the impact of imperfect skills or human fallibility; rather, it deliberately separates the sphere of consumption from that of production so that acts of consuming are not seen as productive, or labor intensive.

At the park, the process of consumption is intimately connected to the knowledge of and about ethnic minorities in China and non-material products such as service and information. This information- or knowledge-based economic practice displays "cultural markers" (*wenhua fuhao*). "Ethnic costumes" (*minzu fuzhuang*), the park's most important "coded stuff" (*fuhao xing dongxi*), for example, are presented to the public continually by the ethnic minority performers. Wearing them to be identifiable as ethnic minorities, ethnic performers embody positions as code-tellers.[27] The meaning of ethnic costumes is based on existing knowledge of and about the ethnic minorities, a knowledge that has been accumulated by Chinese ethnologists and historians since the beginning of the 1950s when the Chinese state began to systematically classify ethnic minorities.[28] At all stages of planning and operation, the park maintains a close relationship with experts such as ethnologists, folklorists, and museum professionals; and it consults them for ideas and even hires them as managerial staff. In doing so, the park ensures that it presents authentic and authoritative meanings of displayed objects. Thus, the park's capacity for reconstructing exhibits is determined by an instrumental rationality that guarantees a way of reasoning that depends no longer on a transcendental relationship between the knowing subject and the object of knowing, but on an immanent relationship between the knowing subject and a set of structural interconnections interior to the object of knowing. In other words, all the park's exhibits that are used to illustrate ethnic minorities are subjected to the knowledge system of Chinese ethnology.

Ethnic costumes are not simply markers of ethnic minority groups; more importantly, they function as commodity packaging, what Susan Willis calls "a device for hailing the consumer and cueing his or her attention . . . to a particular brand-name commodity."[29] Ethnic costumes connote ethnic performers as the "ethnic minority" brand. Ethnic minorities representing the performers are incorporated into the process of reflexive accumulation not as an object of knowledge but as a means for capital accumulation. After all, visitors interviewed consider interactions with ethnic performers as their favorite consuming activities. In addition, ethnic costumes as a technical means for packaging ethnic minorities also function to maintain their purity—ethnic performers in costumes are required to be "clean" and "neat." The hygienic and neat costumes ensure contacts between ethnic performers and visitors that are safe and secure. Thus, the park provides an enclaved space for Han Chinese visitors to maintain their own sense of the self while consuming the exotic peoples and their materialized cultures. The hygienic and neat commodity packaging is part of the role the park plays in directing and changing social experience in an ordered way during China's incorporation of capitalism.

Consumption as a Mechanism of Behavior Modification

In his study of Disneyland, the historian John Findlay demonstrates that Disney offers a functional space—clean, safe, and orderly—that contrasts with the outside malfunctioning and chaotic urban spaces in Southern California.[30] Similarly, the Chinese Ethnic Culture Park also offers a successful model for managing social order in a crowded place like Beijing where urban residents are anxious about the potential disorder caused by the influx of people, particularly migrant workers from the countryside.[31] All the park's service employees, including security guards, salespeople, and sanitary workers, are required to wear uniforms. Their physical appearance ensures that visitors will be aware of the park as a functional space—orderly, safe, clean, and friendly.[32] More importantly, the park deliberately appropriates the built environment to discipline the visitors to behave properly according to a social norm predetermined by the park—a norm of orderly consumption.

The park regulates the flow of the visitors in a prescribed route in order to naturalize the visitors' consciousness for consumption. This naturalization controls the speed of visiting to direct the visitors to pursue time (schedules for shows) rather than forms (objects on display).[33] The park carefully coordinates the following three elements: locations of scenic spots, shops, restaurants and performance sites; daily schedules for performances; and tour routes. In doing so, the park constructs a social order of consumption, manipulating visitors to spend their money at an appropriate site and an appropriate time, determined by the park.[34]

For example, a forty-minute show is scheduled at one performance site (the Dai village) at 9:30, hailing visitors to move to and stay there for about forty minutes; another show is scheduled at a different site (the Miao village) around 10:30, directing visitors to move there after a twenty-minute walk. The purpose of this controlling technique is to direct visitors to move naturally to the park's restaurant site (the Buyi village) where they may spend their money. After watching the second forty- to sixty-minute show, visitors naturally move on to new scenic spots. As they begin to feel hungry at lunch time around 12:00, they find themselves already at the restaurant site. According to my observation in 1996 (from March to August), many visitors stayed to consume the food at the restaurant, although some either carried their own food or chose to continue their visit without having lunch. In addition, this strategy of flow control is also caused by competition between the park and another company that leases a space within the park. Due to the park's management of the flow of the visitors, more visitors consumed food in the park's own restaurant than in the restaurant operated by the other company.

Besides directing visitors to arrive at the park's own restaurant around lunch time, the park also employs a few ethnic minorities in costumes to receive visitors outside the restaurant. In early 1996, park managers hired a few Qiang from Sichuan Province and trained them how to receive guests. At lunch time, female Qiang employees regularly sang and danced outside the restaurant to attract visitors' attention while a male Qiang employee also regularly toasted guests at their lunch tables. Thus, ethnic minorities in costumes are employed to guide tourists not only to visit the Han's nationalist representation of ethnic minority peoples but also to behave according to a capitalist order of consumption.

In sum, the Chinese Ethnic Culture Park as a landscape of capital accumulation and social order is shown by three important aspects of spatial practice. First, the park is a themed built environment. The building of a "natural" environment in the urban context of Beijing involves both constructing a landscape of the ethnic minorities and associating it with Beijing's most well-known national sites such as the Palace Museum and the Great Wall. In this way, the socially reconstructed "ethnic minority region or space" is closely tied to wider social forces. This leads to the second aspect of spatial practice. The park appropriates the built environment as an important resource for capital accumulation. This mode of accumulation is mainly characterized both by separating consumption from production and by incorporating existing knowledge of and about the ethnic minorities into systems of consumption. Finally, the process of accumulation is also a process of disciplining visitors to follow a social order structured by spatial and temporal arrangements of exhibits and performances. In the process, tourists are guided not only to visit the exhibitions of the ethnic objects but also to behave properly according to the spatial order of these objects. In this sense, the spatial, the temporal, the performative, and the material are intertwined in a disciplining process.

Theme Parks and the Imagineering of Government

Chinese theme parks function as an institution of social engineering in the broader context of China's social transformation in the past two decades. They represent an efficient and flexible economic system in which the production of cultural commodities, moving between economic and cultural circuits, increases the economic value of investment capital.[35] As illustrated in my ethnographic example, representing the Chinese nation through displaying ethnic minority objects and ethnic minorities themselves is an economic process in which cultural symbols and commodities are made to float in relation to one another. An ethnic costume, for example, is not only an ethnic marker for the nation but is also a commodity. The Chinese Ethnic Culture Park concretizes the abstract idea of the nation in the form of the commodity, encouraging a cooperation between the symbolic and the material.

In making economic calculation cooperate with the construction of social norms, the theme park also ensures its representation of China's ethnic minorities will have concrete social effects. The themed environment is built as a highly efficient space for managing behavior and manners. The company that operates the space exercises as a de facto governmental authority, making visitors become citizens by guiding them to consume properly. The visitors become subjects of the authority as soon as they enter the theme park—they are guided to plan their visit around the schedules of performances and to purchase food and drink, souvenirs, and costumes according to a prescribed order. As Chinese citizens, their obligation to the institution is logically anterior to their own rights. Meanwhile, the theme park provides an enclaved space for preventing the social experience associated with China's "marketization" (*shichanghua*) in the 1990s from being out of order. In drawing a sociocultural boundary between the Han and the ethnic minorities in China, the park highlights the cultural difference as an important factor in the establishment of a proper social order necessary for China's social transformation.

Although I focus on China, my argument about the social engineering function of theme parks has broad implications. Built as a landscape that combines a thematically coordinated environment, knowledge available after the completion of the technical work of collecting and classifying, and an ideology of consumption, the theme park provides theming as an "imagineering" technology, a spatialized signifying practice of institutionalized knowledge in the form of images of social engineering.[36] This technology draws from expert systems of knowledge (such as ethnology, archaeology, folklore, and history) and deploys various media and objects (such as artifacts, clothing, and architecture). Not only does it construct a coherent meaning for a themed space, but it also guides activities within this themed space to follow a prescribed speed. Thus, in producing social experience associated with a themed space, theming is fundamentally a technology of speed control through private means.

Notes

1. On Europe, see Miles Orvell, *After the Machine: Visual Arts and the Erasing of Cultural Boundaries* (Jackson: University Press of Mississippi, 1995), 147–59, 181–83; and Andrew Lainsburg, *Once Upon An American Dream: The Story of Euro Disneyland* (Lawrence: University Press of Kansas, 2000). On South Africa, see Jean Comaroff and John L. Comaroff, *Of Revelation and Revolution, Volume Two, The Dialectics of Modernity on a South African Frontier* (Chicago: University of Chicago Press, 1997). On Japan, see Aviad E. Raz, *Riding the Black Ship: Japan and Tokyo Disneyland* (Cambridge, Mass.: Harvard University Asia Center, 1999); and Joy Hendry, *The Orient Strikes Back: A Global View of Cultural Display* (Oxford: Berg, 2000). On Indonesia, see John Pemberton, "Recollections from 'Beautiful Indonesia' (Somewhere Beyond the Postmodern)," *Public Culture* 6 (1994): 241–62. And on China, see Ann Anagnost, "The Nationscape: Movement in the Field of Vision," *Positions: East Asia Cultures Critique* 1, no. 3 (1993): 585–606; and Hai Ren, "Economies of Culture: Theme Parks, Museums and Capital Accumulation in China, Hong Kong and Taiwan" (PhD diss., The University of Washington, 1998).

2. For a systematic explanation of Disney's conception of imagineering, see Karal Ann Marling, ed., *Designing Disney's Theme Parks: The Architecture of Reassurance* (Paris: Flammarion, 1997). On urban revitalization, see Charles Rutheiser, "Making Place in the Nonplace Urban Realm: Notes on the Revitalization of Downtown Atlanta," in *Theorizing the City: The New Urban Anthropology Reader*, ed. Setha M. Low (New Brunswick, N.J.: Rutgers University Press, 1999), 317–41. On an ethnographic study of Disney's Celebration, see Andrew Ross, *The Celebration Chronicles: Life, Liberty, and the Pursuit of Property Value in Disney's New Town* (New York: Ballantine Books, 1999), and Douglas Frantz and Catherine Collins, *Celebration, U.S.A.: Living in Disney's Brave New Town* (New York: Owl Books, 2000).

3. This understanding draws on the French philosopher Henri Lefebvre's work on the social production of space, which considers three elements: land as a territorial formation, built environment as a resource, and space as a medium of human interaction. See, Rob Shields, *Places on the Margin: Alternative Geographies of Modernity* (London: Routledge, 1991), 50–51.

4. Current understanding of theming is not only narrow but only focuses on the effects of theming. Mark Gottdiener, for example, regards theming as an effective technique for "the transfer of value from the commodity to its realization in sales." *The Theming of America: Dreams, Visions, and Commercial Spaces* (Boulder, Colo: Westview, 1997), 45. My use of theming is broadly defined as I illustrate below.

5. Walter Benjamin, "The Storyteller," in *Illuminations* (New York: Schocken Books, 1968), 86.

6. John Hannigan, *Fantasy City:Pleasure and Profit in the Postmodern Metropolis* (London: Routledge 1998); Constance Balides, "Jurassic Post-Fordism: Tall Tales of Economics in the Theme Park," *Screen* 41, no. 2 (2000): 139–60; and Janet Wasko,

Understanding Disney (Cambridge: Polity, 2001).

7. David Harvey, *A History of Neoliberalism* (Oxford: Oxford University Press, 2005).

8. Consumption, as Jean Comaroff and John L. Comaroff point out, has replaced production to become "the moving spirit of the late twentieth century." See "Millennial Capitalism: First Thoughts on a Second Coming," *Public Culture* 12, no. 2 (Spring 2000): 291–343.

9. This essay is part of a book-length study of China's themed spaces. I focus on this park for three reasons. First, it is one of the largest theme parks in China that is devoted to the representation of ethnic minority cultures. While ethnic diversity is represented, ethnic minority workers—mainly young women from poor rural areas in Western China—are incorporated into three interrelated processes: making the cultural identity of the Han majority, transforming cultural representation as capital accumulation, and shaping the behaviors of consumers. Second, this park has been developed as a result of China's neoliberalization, especially in the real estate sector where privatization of land is tied to commercialization in the name of development. Third, although the park operates as a commercial institution, it is treated as a nonprofit organization and is registered officially as a museum. The park represents the dilemma of balancing between the commercial form of operation and the nonprofit form of organization. This dilemma is faced by the majority of China's museums that are in the process of transforming themselves to incorporate market mechanisms in their operations.

10. Carroll B. Malone, *History of the Peking Summer Palaces under the Ch'ing Dynasty* (Urbana: University of Illinois Press, 1934).

11. Malone, *History of the Peking Summer Palaces under the Ch'ing Dynasty*, 136; and Young-Tsu Wong, *A Paradise Lost: The Imperial Garden Yuanming Yuan* (Honolulu: University of Hawaii Press, 2001), 126–27.

12. Yue Dong, "Memories of the Present: The Vicissitudes of Transition in Republican Beijing, 1911-1937" (PhD diss., The University of California, San Diego, 1996), 328.

13. Frederic Wakeman, *Policing Shanghai 1927–1737* (Berkeley: University of California Press, 1995), 105–106.

14. Leo Ou-fan Lee, *Shanghai Modern: The Flowering of a New Urban Culture in China, 1930–1945* (Cambridge, Mass.: Harvard University Press, 1999), 13.

15. Shaoguang Wang, "The Politics of Private Time: Changing Leisure Patterns in Urban China," in *Urban Spaces in Contemporary China: The Potential for Autonomy and Community in Post-Mao China*, ed. D. S. Davis, R. Kraus, B. Naughton, and E. J. Perry (Washington, D. C.: Woodrow Wilson Center Press, 1995), 152–56.

16. Examples include Splendid China, China Folk Culture Villages and Window of the World in Shenzhen, the World Park and the Chinese Ethnic Culture Park in Beijing, the World Landscape Park and the Wonderland of the Southwest in Chengdu, and Yunnan Nationalities Villages in Kunming.

17. Jon Jerde (based in Venice Beach, California), for example, has designed Minnesota's Mall of America, the Las Vegas Bellagio Hotel, a Disneyland-like CityWalk in California, Fukuoka's Canal City Hakata, Kawasaki's La Cittadella, Osaka's Namba Parks, and Tokyo's Caretta Shiodome, among others. In China, his projects include Guangzhou's Tianhe Plaza, Shanghai's JointBuy City Plaza, and Concord World Mall. For more information, see Jerde Partnership International, *The Jerde Partnership International* (L'Arcaedizioni, 1999). Also, see Jon Jerde, "Capturing the Leisure Zeitgeist: Creating Places to Be," in *Architectural Design: Consuming Architecture*, ed. Maggie Toy (West Sussex, UK: John Wiley and Sons, 1998), 69–71; and, Michael Hong, "Interview with Michael Hong from The

Jerde Partnership," in *Stripping Las Vegas: A Contextual Review of Casino Resort Architecture*, ed. Karin Jaschke and Silke Ötsch (Germany: University of Weimar Press, 2003), 91–96.

18. See David Barboza, "The Great Malls of China," *New York Times*, 25 May 2005.

19. For a systematic study, see Alan Bryman, *The Disneyization of Society* (London: Sage, 2004) and George Ritzer, *The McDonaldization of Society*, rev. ed. (Thousand Oaks, Calif: Pine Forge, 1996).

20. For a study of how the Chinese spend their private time, see Wang, "The Politics of Private Time," 149–72.

21. For a systematic anthropological study of sports in China, see Susan Brownell, *Training the Body for China: Sports in the Moral Order of the People's Republic* (Chicago: University of Chicago Press, 1995). On the monuments on Tiananmen Square, see Hung Wu, "The Tiananmen Square: A Political History of Monuments," *Representations* 35, Summer (1991): 84–117. On the Hong Kong clock, see Hung Wu, "The Hong Kong Clock: Public Time-Telling and Political Time/Space," *Public Culture* 9, no. 3 (1997): 329–54.

22. The quotes are from the park's guidebook (printed in 1995). Unless specified, the quotes below are also from the guidebook.

23. Some Beijing residents told me that they went to the park because they found a sense of relaxation there.

24. For theoretical background on this issue, see Susan Buck-Morss, *The Dialectics of Seeing: Walter Benjamin and the Arcades Project* (Cambridge, Mass.: MIT Press, 1989), 110–116.

25. Scott Lash and John Urry, *Economies of Signs and Space* (London: Sage, 1994), 60–61.

26. Anthony Giddens, *The Consequences of Modernity* (Stanford, Calif.: Stanford University Press, 1990), 86. See also Erving Goffman, *The Presentation of Self in Everyday Life* (New York: Anchor, 1959).

27. According to a chief consultant of the park, although a performer may not voluntarily tell what ethnic group the costume he or she wears signifies, he or she is often asked by tourists to do so.

28. For detailed discussions of this process, see Dru Gladney, *Muslim Chinese: Ethnic Nationalism in the People's Republic* (Cambridge, Mass.: Council on East Asian Studies, Harvard University, 1991); Gregory Eliyu Guldin, *The Saga of Anthropology in China: From Malinowski to Moscow to Mao* (Armonk, N.Y.: M. E. Sharpe, 1994); and Stevan Harrell, *Cultural Encounters on China's Ethnic Frontiers* (Seattle: University of Washington Press, 1995).

29. Susan Willis, *A Primer for Daily Life* (London: Routledge, 1991), 1.

30. John Findlay, *Magic Lands: Western Cityscapes and American Culture after 1940* (Berkeley: the University of California Press, 1992), 52–116.

31. Local newspapers such as *Beijing Youth Daily* and *Beijing Evening News*, for example, often linked urban problems to rural migrant workers.

32. For more on the control of workers, see Scott A. Lukas, chapter 11 of this volume.

33. By examining the aesthetics of disappearance, Paul Virilio establishes a link between the control of speed and the development of consciousness. He suggests that the development and the disappearance of consciousness results from the control of speed for recognizing what he refers to as *picnolepsy* or frequent absences. For instance, the rationalization of the real or the establishment of its laws and its models (in cinema) "redistribute[s] methodically the occasional eliminations of picnolepsy." In other words,

rationalization of the real can be regarded as "a trick whose purpose is to deny particular absences any active value." Paul Virilio, *The Aesthetics of Disappearance* (New York: Semiotext(e), 1991), 31.

34. The same feature is found in the Orlando, Florida theme park known as the Holy Land Experience. For the connection, see Scott A. Lukas, chapter 15 of this volume.

35. Sharon Zukin, *Landscapes of Power: From Detroit to Disney World* (Berkeley: University of California Press, 1991), 260.

36. By "knowledge available after the completion" I am referring to the body of ethnographic knowledge that is used to produce the representations in theme parks.

Chapter 7

Theming Mythical Africa at the Lost City

Jeanne van Eeden

Theming is a mode of spatial practice, and consequently intersects with discursive formations and implicates power, ideology, myth, identity, capitalism, the representation of the past, and entertainment. Henri Lefebvre maintains that all socially produced spaces can be read as systems of signification that are linked to modes of production and historical circumstances.[1] This chapter examines aspects of the theming of mythical Africa at the South African theme park, the Lost City. It suggests that tropes such as the exotic and the picturesque—which serve both aesthetic and ideological ends—are embedded in the spatial practice and theming of this entertainment landscape. Because landscape, like theming, is a textual system, it "can be linked with generic and narrative typologies such as . . . the exotic, the sublime, and the picturesque."[2] I am consequently interested in the manner in which the picturesque in particular informs the theming, conceptualization, and instrumentalization of space at the Lost City. The fact that the picturesque landscape is generally reconstructed, "improved" and commodified in order to serve ideologies (such as imperialism or entertainment) is one of the main points of departure of this chapter.

I first suggest that the geographic simulation of a picturesque landscape that is essentially alien to Africa at the Lost City resonates with the colonial inscription of foreign lands; colonial narratives required that landscapes be re-presented as "readable" texts, and this control, manipulation, and staging of land was frequently enacted according to familiar aesthetic codes such as the picturesque. Quite simply, as the expansion of culture into physical space, colonialism required other lands "to look more like Europe."[3] My second point is that this extension of ideology by means of the restructuring of space is reminiscent of the manner in which theme park landscapes are themed in order to give form to narrative, myth, and ideology. Theme parks rely on easily understood narrative structures that tap into the myths and visual imagery generated and sustained by popular culture. The picturesque resonates with distant memories of pristine nature and extinct civilizations, and because the "picturesque landscape is one that one walks into like a picture," it coincides with the manner in which space is thematically enframed at the Lost City.[4] The picturesque is a narrative mode based on artifice that lends itself to mystification and the ideological manipulation of scenery attendant upon discursive practices such as imperialism and theme park entertainment.[5]

I start this chapter with an overview of the Lost City before turning my attention to how a vision of mythical Africa is constructed by means of stereotypical thematic devices at the Lost City. The topic may be tackled by any number of interpretative frameworks, but I have chosen to focus on a postcolonialist form of cultural analysis. My point of departure is therefore that the strategies used by imperialist discourse to imbue colonial spaces with new identities that often concealed their real past and culture is analogous to the ways in which the Lost City creates an escapist theme in a fictionalized space. The simulacrum of Africa that results from this fabrication is a raced, gendered, and classed discourse that perpetuates asymmetrical power relations under the guise of entertainment.

Sun City and the Lost City

The Lost City opened in 1992 and "Africa's kingdom of pleasure" immediately assumed a unique position in the South African entertainment industry. The Lost City forms part of the larger destination resort Sun City and was the first fully thematized entertainment landscape that was built from scratch. The South African leisure entrepreneur, Sol Kerzner, visualized the Sun City hotel, casino, and entertainment complex in 1978. Sun City was built in a neighboring homeland of apartheid South Africa, Bophuthatswana, because it centered on gambling and adult entertainment, then illegal in South Africa.[6] The Nationalist apartheid government divided black people into their ethnic groups and allocated separate Bantu homelands or *bantustans*, which was inscribed in Act No. 68 of 1951, the infamous Bantu Authorities Act introduced by H. F. Verwoerd. The ten designated homelands were Bophuthatswana, Ciskei, Gazankulu, KaNgwane, KwaNdebele, KwaZulu, Lebowa, Qwaqwa, Transkei, and Venda. Believing that the homelands should be allowed to develop independent of white capitalism, white-owned industries sprang up in the areas bordering on the homelands. In effect this policy, while claiming to encourage the future independence of the homelands, as enacted in the 1959 Promotion of Bantu Self-Government Act, led to the homelands being politically and economically dependent on South Africa, and this situation was exploited by many business enterprises. Self-governing status was given to the homelands Bophuthatswana, Ciskei, Gazankulu, KwaNdebele, KwaZulu, Lebowa, Qwaqwa, and Venda between 1971 and 1977, and full independence was granted to Transkei (1976), Bophuthatswana (1977), Venda (1979), and Ciskei (1981). The six other homelands were not granted independence as the political situation was changing in the 1980s, and with the first majority rule government in 1994, the homelands were incorporated into the nine newly designated provinces of South Africa.

Sun City was opened in 1979 to fulfill the entertainment and leisure needs of white South Africans in the Witwatersrand region, the industrial and financial hub of South Africa. *Sin City*, as it was fondly called, rapidly gained iconic status in South African popular culture. The journalist Andrew Donaldson remarks that Sun City was "an anaesthetised Sodom for suburbia, a glitzy getaway for middle South Africa seeking respite from the Puritanism of Christian nationalism; a place just 90 minutes' drive from Johannesburg [and Pretoria] where they could indulge in otherwise illegal activities like gambling, topless revues and arty soft-porn movies."[7] The Lost City theme park and Palace Hotel were added to the Sun City destination resort in 1992 and represented a shift from Las Vegas entertainment to family oriented Disney theme park leisure space. Sun City had already started to alter its profile by the late 1980s, indicating a modification from a "sinful gambling mecca . . . [to a] new position as an imperative African experience destination for international travelers."[8] Kerzner started planning the Lost City early in 1990 when the then President of South Africa, F. W. de Klerk, announced radical changes to the country's politics—the African National Congress was unbanned and the symbol of resistance to apartheid, Nelson Mandela, was freed. With the changing political dispensation, Kerzner saw the potential to attract global tourists, and used the Lost City as a tempting representation of the so-called essence of Africa.[9]

Kerzner selected the architect Gerald Allison of the American firm Wimberly Allison Tong and Goo (WATG)—celebrated for their contribution to the hospitality, leisure, and entertainment industries—to realize his idea of mythical Africa. The use of a foreign architect already implicates a formulaic and stereotypical vision of Africa that underscores Kerzner's wish to render a "vision of Africa that is all happiness and light."[10] The true history of Africa, and in particular the history of the Shona people of the region in which Sun City was built, was simply not considered glamorous enough to constitute a thematic device for the Lost City.[11] Allison was responsible for the design concept, schematic design, and design development of the luxurious Palace Hotel and the Lost City Day Visitors Centre. The latter comprises the mock "ruins" of the village, a themed waterpark, and a simulated tropical beach known as the Valley of Waves. The South African landscape designer Patrick Watson was responsible for the design concept of the Palace Gardens and the Lost City jungle, which transformed the original dry bushveld into a tropical fantasy forest. WATG was in charge of the overall cohesion of the theming of the Lost City and thus had to organize all the interior and exterior designers "to assure [*sic*] that the architectural and interior design [was] well coordinated and consistent in character."[12]

Kerzner and Allison based their unifying theme for the Lost City on the notion of "a lost civilisation, an African Atlantis being discovered."[13] They envisioned a scene that "would appear as if a jungle had parted to reveal a mystery, whose origins are hidden in the mists of time. It would be a palace and an adventureland of water and rocks, which once had been the proud boast of a highly developed civilization, and a homage to the natural [sic] gods it worshipped."[14] Allison accordingly formulated the fictional Legend of the Lost City that tells the story of how an ancient civilization, originally from Northern Africa, flourished until it was annihilated by an earthquake some three thousand years ago. All that remained were the village ruins and the remarkably intact Palace that were subsequently "discovered" and "restored" by the intrepid explorer, Sol Kerzner. The Legend is a picturesque story that evokes a lost arcadia and the age-old myth of a rural golden age based on harmony with nature. The Legend appears in print form for visitors to the Lost City and is replicated on plaques throughout the site. An abridged version of the Legend relates that:

> Centuries before tall ships were ever dreamed about, long before the dawn of a western civilisation, a nomadic tribe from northern Africa set out to seek a new world, a land of peace and plenty. The tribe wandered for many years in search of such a magical place, and at last their quest was rewarded. The land they discovered to the south became the legendary valley of the sun, known today as the Valley of Waves. Not only did they bring with them a rich culture, but also architectural skills which were exceptional even by today's standards. Something special was created: from the jungle rose an amazing city with a magnificent Palace, a world richer and more splendid than any they had ever known. Then a violent earthquake struck this idyllic valley, the survivors fled, never to return and left it to be found and restored by archaeologists centuries later.[15]

Allison, who had previously been involved with architectural projects for the Disney Corporation, summed up his brief for the Lost City in the following way:

> The Lost City [is] a fantasy world in the heart of South Africa. The client specified a luxury hotel of unprecedented opulence and originality. The 68-acre site, in the midst of a volcanic crater 100 miles from the nearest urban center, was unremarkable and the area technologically primitive. The challenge sparked a literary blueprint: a fictional narrative of a mythical lost kingdom became the basis of design, and all public areas and guestrooms carry out this theme.[16]

Allison admitted that when formulating the theme and Legend of the Lost City, he had been inspired by Tarzan, films such as *The African Queen*, and the Indiana Jones epics.[17] When asked whether he was not perpetuating stereotypes about Africa, Allison remarked that nothing comparable to the Lost City had ever been depicted in films; furthermore, he stated that he had tried to develop an architecture that would capture Africa for the visitor, but not insult the African.[18] The archaeologist Martin Hall considers that people believe the Lost City themed fantasy to be real precisely because it "rests on a deep and wide foundation of popular mythology."[19] WATG pride themselves on the fact that their projects embrace "cultural authenticity" and culturally sensitive design that creates architecture with a sense of place.[20] This begs the question: how can a "fictional narrative of a mythical lost kingdom," a contrived confection, be culturally authentic? It is apparent that this design philosophy, at least as far as the Lost City is concerned, cites essentialist perceptions that construct an(other) Africa of the Euro-American imagination. Many critics have felt that a more authentic or "essentially African theme" could have been deployed. Hall, for example, suggests that there are other thematic possibilities, such as the ruins of Great Zimbabwe, which could have been designed with more "sensitivity to the cultural heritage of the host community."[21] The next sections of this chapter focus on aspects of the practice of theming and the picturesque aesthetic that form the foundation for the subsequent discussion of the theming of the Lost City.

Theming and Spatial Practice

Theming is a cultural device that relies on the "dramatization of a few central ideas" that creates an overall narrative or identity in an entertainment landscape.[22] The notion of consistent theming is a relatively recent idea, but has had an immense influence on all manner of architecture and entertainment spaces.[23] Themes generally strive to appear more exciting than real life and to convey a pleasurable leisure experience. Margaret King argues that by using theming's "shorthand stylizations of person, place and thing, an archive of collective memory and belief, symbol and archetype has emerged. This is the 'bank' of popular culture."[24] This statement indicates that themes are gleaned from popular history or memory, and that they find cultural resonance because of their familiarity. Themes are expedient form-givers that establish product identity by means of one idea, such as "Paris" or "Africa." Themes do not have to be specific or based on fact, and something as intangible as the "exotic" may function as a thematic structure.[25] Geographic, cultural, or mythical locations, whether fictional or historical, may serve as inspiration for themes.[26] The architect Arata Isozaki concurs that almost anything can be fabricated as a theme: "'Fantasy', 'Caribbean', 'typhoon', 'cinema', 'space', and 'utopia' [or in the case of the Lost City, 'mythical Africa'] become . . . equally possible themes."[27] John Urry concludes that themes do not necessarily recount "actual historical or geographical processes" and this confirms that theme parks commonly deploy pasts that are deliberately vague and generalized merely in order to fabricate an "aura of pastness."[28] Themes consequently both displace and conflate real time, place, truth, and fiction, creating landscapes that are eternally locked in an unspecific timelessness. In this sense, the Lost City becomes a romanticized marker for all lost cities and lost civilizations.

It does not appear to be important whether a theme is accepted as true or real by audiences; the only requirement is that it ought to have a core of plausibility and be appropriate to the demands for spectacle and entertainment. Waldrep comments that theming should not be too explicit in terms of place or time, since it only needs to convey the "imagined essence" of a place or period.[29] The fictionalized mystique must thus be vague enough to manipulate memories and conjure up associations, but need not have specific referentiality. This idea echoes in the theming of the Lost City, which strives to evoke the imaginary *essence of Africa* without referring to any one specific style, period, or culture. Most tourists visiting the Lost City probably have only a vague conception of what African architecture or culture look like, and seem to be satisfied that their experience has been "totally African."[30] Indeed, the proprietors of the Lost City, Sun International, seem to be convinced that the "visitors are captivated by the living proof of the lost tribe legend . . . [and] come to Sun City for the total African experience."[31] In the same way that "English scenery need not even be in England to be archetypal," the theme of Africa at the Lost City presents a metonymic geographic simulacrum that sits comfortably with visitors' preconceived ideas of Africa received from other inscriptions in popular culture.[32] The vast store of stories produced by popular culture is brought into play in theming, but the success or authenticity of a theme always depends on consumers' prior knowledge of an "absent genuine."[33]

Architects are eager to point out that themes are often deliberately imaginary: "the more they seem unrealisable, the better."[34] In defending themed architecture, WATG stated that it "requires discipline and forethought to translate ideas into realities—ideas that are borrowed from the past or created from our own imaginations."[35] Accordingly, WATG explain that it is sometimes necessary for architects to:

> create [their] own legends—in the same way that a screenplay writer invents a storyline—and these "scripts" form the backbone for our architecture. Themes are woven throughout every detail of our projects, influencing the artwork (sets), the uniforms (costumes), and even the menus. Guests are invited to immerse themselves in our creative vision and, thereby, enrich their experiences.[36]

Scripted or themed environments are generally created to guarantee consumer pleasure, and the potentials of this merchandised experience fascinate both the audiences for whom they are created and the multinational corporations that engineer them.[37] Theming has become a ubiquitous part of the entertainment and leisure landscape and spending itself has become thematized.[38] Places such as Las Vegas are almost nothing more than themed re-creations of other places, and Paul Steelman, the "[g]uru architect of the gambling world . . . admits that theming is out of control."[39] Nonetheless, theming is crucial in creating distinctions between similar places of consumption.[40] The theming of the Lost City as an African fantasy and exotic utopia conferred a unique spatial experience that was indispensable in luring foreign tourists to South Africa throughout the period of political transformation during the early 1990s.

As a design strategy, theming instrumentalizes space in a specific manner. This comprises the structuring of the physical environment (the layout, landscaping, and architecture); the sensory environment (the rides, attractions, sounds, textures, and light); and related commodities offered for sale (crafts, food, and costumes).[41] Theming is closely linked to the way in which visitors to theme parks are motivated to move through space in order to experience the narrative. Hence, at most theme parks the visual and auditory effects are placed in space and are experienced with the unfolding of time to produce the preferred or definitive narrative.[42] The total visual impact of theme parks—which to a great extent determines the success of the immersive entertainment experience—is principally the product of theming and the narrativization of space. This implies that the whole environment is customized to involve all the senses and to sustain a specific story line.

Miodrag Mitrasinovic is of the opinion that theme parks present chains of "themescapes" that operate on the principle of framing or "the displacement of visitors by the force of an alien visual and spatial ordering system and the impact of an exotic visual/narrative theme."[43] Simulated pseudo-events are then enacted in a strictly determined temporal/spatial axis within each themescape. I shall suggest later in this chapter that many of the themescapes at the Lost City are structured around picturesque narrative fragments that both constitute atmosphere and drive the narrative of the Legend. The eighteenth-century picturesque aesthetic was originally "envisioned" as a series of planned and composed static pictures or as a sequence of scenes that were designed to be seen from specific viewpoints.[44] I believe this is comparable to how themescapes can enframe space and imbue it with narrative and identity. Picturesque tourism customarily directed discerning travelers to the best views, which they gazed at from the vantage point of "stations" situated on elevated outcrops, and themescapes at the Lost City operate according to the same kind of principle.[45]

The origins of contemporary theme parks have been located in European pleasure gardens of the sixteenth to nineteenth centuries. These gardens included various forms of entertainment, and like later theme parks, were spaces that resonated with visual allusions and associations. Of particular significance for the Lost City is that a common trope in many of these gardens was nostalgia for "[t]he lost village" that romanticizes the non-industrial past.[46] Also of relevance to the Lost City is the fact that many picturesque gardens of the same period meditated on the "lost world evoked by classical ruins."[47] Much has been written about the spurious nature of theme parks and their cavalier attitude towards the past, but as typical postmodern spaces, they can accommodate contradictory narratives with ease.[48] Like colonial landscapes, theme parks are liminal spaces, bounded, controlled, and staged for the consuming gaze. Furthermore, just as colonial landscapes were manipulated to approximate another vision of nature, theme parks frequently undermine local topography and identity and transform landscapes for the purposes of entertainment.[49] The pursuit of the colonial picturesque frequently deprived landscapes of their "natural" ambiance, and this is similar to the general aura of pastness that predominates at generic theme parks, as previously mentioned. The ways in which the picturesque makes possible the virtual eradication of spatial and cultural specificity are examined in the next section, which focuses on those aspects of the picturesque that are pertinent to the Lost City.

The Picturesque Aesthetic

The picturesque was identified as an aesthetic category in late eighteenth century England. At that time, the most important aesthetic category was the beautiful, but its hegemony was dismantled with the burgeoning late eighteenth century romantic taste for roughness, irregularity, mountains, and ruins. The sublime and the picturesque reflected the new appreciation for nature, with the picturesque designating a somewhat tamed or elegiac form of the sublime.[50] European romantics recognized that the sublime or picturesque attribute did not necessarily reside in the object itself, but rather in the spectator's subjective or imaginative way of perceiving it.[51] Picturesque means "like a picture" or "suitable for a picture," which indicates that the appreciation of natural scenery was influenced by contemporary landscape painting that familiarized people with the idea of seeing nature "improved"; pictorial models therefore showed people how to "look" at nature.[52] Many notions of what constituted the picturesque developed out of a specific genre of topographical painting that often used a bird's-eye panoramic view to capture nature.

The theory of the picturesque was expounded in William Gilpin's *Observations Relative Chiefly to Picturesque Beauty* (1789) and *Three Essays on Picturesque Beauty* (1794), and Uvedale Price's *Essay on the Picturesque* (1794). The picturesque was initially most influential in landscape gardening, particularly in the English "natural" garden popularized by William Kent and Lancelot "Capability" Brown. The typical picturesque "garden of ideas" evoked melancholic and nostalgic longing in the viewer through the careful staging of uneven ground, hills, rocks, pools, cascades, trees, broken tree limbs, diagonal lines, natural groupings of plants, serpentine paths, avenues, glades, temples, grottos, statuary, mock overgrown ruins, and weather-beaten structures. The picturesque ideal rapidly spread from gardening to painting, architecture, poetry, travel, and literature, and became important precisely when urbanization and nostalgia for unspoiled nature placed a new value on wild, untamed areas distant from cities.[53]

Trees, mountain peaks, ruins, lakes, streams, and pools were particularly potent images in the lexicon of the picturesque, and became the locus of metaphorical meanings. Water, for example, was associated with infinity, reflection, and contemplation.[54] Ruins were commonly associated with transience and solitude, and induced nostalgia and melancholic thoughts.[55] They became prime exemplars of the picturesque because of their irregularity of form and possibility of imminent decay, and because they represented the "triumph of nature over the transience of artifice."[56] In keeping with the taste for "pleasing decay" in the eighteenth century, sham ruins were often fabricated to enhance the picturesque quality of gardens.[57] Moldering ruins, particularly (mock) classical ruins, became the primary markers of the passage of time, and exemplified the *memento mori* that induced reflections on extinct civilizations.[58] At the Lost City, the "ruins" overgrown by ivy at the Royal Arena and the Royal Baths are evocatively Greco-Roman in style and arouse memories of previously seen archaeological sites, whether real (Delphi) or fictional (Atlantis).

Picturesque vistas were constructed to comprise a "series of prospects representing scenes from nature . . . [including] large bodies of water, wooded islands, [and] a few carefully chosen architectural accents."[59] Gilpin divided landscapes into "readable" progressions from dark foreground to a lighter middle-distance and a shimmering, light background. This planar recession was often combined with "a dark coulisse on one side shadowing the foreground; a middle plane with a large central feature such as a clump of trees, [and] a plane of luminous distance," as perfected in the paintings of Claude Lorrain.[60] As previously indicated, the picturesque was deliberately visualized as a sequence of arranged scenes that were intended to be seen from specific stations. Many picturesque gardens had plaques with inscriptions that helped establish the narrative, and similar devices are found at the Lost City. Whereas eighteenth-century visitors were understood to have the formal education to grasp the classical allusions, today's textual and visual references stem from the bank of popular culture.[61] As a narrative and textual system that intended to make landscapes "readable," the picturesque clearly functioned as a type of punctuation in the landscape because it caused viewers to stop and reflect at particular predetermined sites.[62]

Because the picturesque embraced abrupt variation, irregularity, contrast, asymmetry, roughness, disorder, and rusticity, it was essentially predicated on formalist principles of visual appeal located in the effects of form, color, shape, light, shade, and modulation on the viewer.[63] By means of the picturesque, selected, ordered or "fixed" parts of nature were reduced to aesthetic experience and were appraised in terms of abstract pictorial values and painterly qualities. The picturesque relied on the creation of visual effect rather than the faithful rendition of space, and because it was primarily evocative, nostalgic, sentimental, and suggestive, it was able to associate states of mind and exotic ideas with specific landscape design.[64] The picturesque was encoded to privilege the quiet, and often solitary, contemplation of nature and this is invoked in the Lost City Garden where people are encouraged to linger in the magnificence of (constructed) nature.

Picturesque naturalism is inherently paradoxical because it represents escapism and retreat from anthropocentricism in a "nature nearly devoid of human presence," yet also epitomizes human control over nature. This control sought a preconceived, abstracted version of nature, reducing it to a "managed wilderness."[65] The picturesque is symptomatic of the possession and transformation of landscape, a kind of "place-making" or inscription that mediates nature into a graspable frame or theme.[66] This form of so-called picturesque improvement denotes restriction, forced design, and manipulation of nature to make it conform to picturesque expectations. Because this type of picturesque intervention manifested once fear of nature abated and control thereof was rendered possible, it corresponds to the management of nature at the Lost City, where "Africa" is tamed for consumption.[67] The picturesque is therefore an ideal vehicle for the Lost City, as it has become an empty signifier that engenders a simulacrum of nature that is easy to commodify. Because the picturesque embraces the sentimental, it can moreover be considered an example of kitsch, which supports its alignment with the generalized feminization that manifests in the discourses of colonialism, taste, tourism, leisure, and entertainment from the nineteenth century onwards. Some of the parallels between imperialist expansionism and the picturesque as a trope of possession are indicated in the next section.

The Imperial Picturesque and the Domestication of Difference

The picturesque can be associated with the ideological framework of colonialism since both functioned as modes of knowing and control founded on visuality and spatial practice; both are discursive formations based on mediation, confinement, possession, and transformation. The picturesque is indeed so prevalent in colonial rhetoric that this signals an intimate relationship between "colonial presence and the articulations of space which attend it."[68] The picturesque aesthetic was frequently invoked to construct a new sense of place in a colony. Like naming and mapping, the picturesque was an important enframing mechanism whereby colonial space was rendered familiar and manageable according to western schemas of representation. As a colony, South Africa experienced continual colonial intervention in its territory and otherness and ethnicity were positioned as sites of spectacle and entertainment. This legacy was perpetuated by apartheid that located power relations in the landscape, leading to racial and gender segregation in South African work and leisure spaces. Because Sun City is situated in an area fraught with colonial and postcolonial conflicts and contested histories that are endemic to South Africa—including the forced removal of people from the land—it automatically bears the ideological traces of colonialism. Early travelers to South Africa attempted to apply the category of the picturesque to the landscape, but found that it did not lend itself to this description, possibly because the land was too vast, "unstaged" or "natural," in contrast with the pictorial terms with which Europeans were familiar.[69]

Elizabeth Delmont and Jessica Dubow suggest that the constitutive power of the picturesque was precisely that it afforded "visualization for someone: a foreign landscape brought into 'being-for-the-gaze.'"[70] The imperial picturesque was a form of spatial organization that created bounded spaces that echoed the process of colonial settlement and the self-assured gestures of entitlement were played out in these enclosed spaces of power.[71] The picturesque vista recreated in a colonial setting thus symbolized both place making as the social production of space, and the subsequent possession thereof.[72] The European panoramic and topographic style of picturesque representation visualized colonial landscapes laid out like a map, across which the perceiving eye of the imperial subject could wander and consume at will. However, more importantly, the picturesque code that represented nature virtually free of human presence proposed a free and promising future for the colony, a *terra nullius* without so-called natives, endorsing colonial ideology that propagated the supposed unpeopled state of South Africa before colonial intervention.[73]

The picturesque consistently naturalized western hierarchies of race, class, and gender and functioned as a hegemonic aesthetic that implicated the domestication of difference born from the simultaneous desire and fear of otherness. The colonial mentality detested the backwardness of others, yet also desired to preserve selected picturesque aspects thereof.[74] Linda Nochlin explains that the colonial picturesque was a form of Orientalism that proposed that aspects of the dominated other that were *seen* as picturesque were deemed worthy of preserving in "imagery in which exotic human beings are integrated with a presumably defining and overtly limiting decor."[75] Picturesque tourism, dating from the late eighteenth century, was appropriated by mass tourism in the twentieth century and commodified the picturesque for touristic experience.[76] Modern tourism embraced the spectacle of difference "refracted though the fictions of the picturesque, the exotic and the primitive," and structured the manner in which places such as South Africa are perceived.[77] The fact that the picturesque was invariably "staged" is important in the contexts of colonialism, tourism, and theme parks, since in these discourses landscape is rendered as theater, spectacle, and performance, forming a pleasing backdrop for human desires. Spatial extension, but also the framing and setting apart thereof, is integral to representing myths and essentialist ideas, and is enacted in colonial settings and theme parks by means of mechanisms such as the picturesque and theming.[78] The last section of this chapter consolidates the ideas discussed above and applies them to an investigation of aspects of the theming of the Lost City.

Theming the Lost City

The Lost City represents mythical Africa by referring to received ideas about ancient royalty, nature, the exotic, the colonial romance, and the picturesque that resonate in the architecture, iconographic program, and landscaping. The overarching theme of the Lost City is based on time-honored stereotypes that position Africa as an exotic paradise that is timeless, primitive, the site of legendary wealth, and full of unlimited erotic promise. According to Stuart Hall, primitivism and the tropics are still the privileged signifiers of the erotic and pleasure in popular media, and the Lost City perpetuates this ideological construct that reveals nostalgia for the colonial romance.[79] The neoimperialist discourse that is reenacted at the Lost City taps into the myth of the archaeologist/explorer, and creates a fictionalized, escapist version of history that reflects ideological and hegemonic strategies. So, for example, the patriarchal and regal overtones of the Lost City are anachronistic and look to the romanticized past to offer a vision of an essentially "invented" Africa.

Wilson asks whether "[Native American] cultures [can] now be the theme of a hotel because they're thought to be extinct?" in relation to the theming of Disney World hotels and raises important issues regarding authenticity and cultural sensitivity.[80] Gerald Allison remarked that the Lost City was meant to "convey authenticity and a genuine atmosphere about the *two legends*: the Lost City and Africa itself . . . [and was planned with] as much ethnic authenticity as was possible. The Palace was to be a living re-creation of folk-memory and culture."[81] This reveals that Africa was reduced to a "legend," an invented simulacrum that carries only vague referentiality. In explaining his concept for the Lost City, Allison observed that:

> The "Legend of the Lost City" is based purely on fantasy, but colored by the heritage of Africa. As is consistent with the legend, we have tried to create a totally new architecture developed by a people completely isolated from any outside human influences. The architecture is the result of several centuries of such isolated development. The greatest influences were the weather, materials available, the skills of the craftsmen, and most importantly the flora and fauna of the region that existed during the time that the Palace was supposedly built. Some of the architectural forms were influenced by the legends and stories that the ancient ones passed on from generation to generation. These stories, both true and mythological, told of their forefather's life in northern Africa where great cities dominated by soaring, domed spires and high arched facades were common. As we developed this "new architecture," we tried very hard to recall in a mystical manner a conglomeration of historical influences instead of a specific north African heritage.[82]

"Both true and mythological" in the statement above signals that the Lost City bears interesting traces of the "imagined archaeology" identified by Jeffrey Cass and Dion Dennis at the Luxor Hotel in Las Vegas.[83] The Lost City mythology is also based on references to the romance associated with the archaeological dig; after the violent earthquake struck the idyllic valley, "the city was lost, and only a whispered legend of ancient grandeur remained to tantalise explorers. Almost three millennia after the earthquake . . . an archaeological expedition stumbled upon the ruins . . . The archaeological team set about the task of restoring the ruins to their original splendour."[84] Travel, exploration, and archaeological excavations were conflated during the nineteenth century and were symbolic of the extension of the colonial enterprise of discovery and control of spatiality. The heroic age of archaeology, from the late nineteenth century to the 1930s, led to the discovery of "real" lost cities in southern Africa, including Great Zimbabwe and Mapungubwe. Sol Kerzner tapped into this and assumed the persona of "Indiana Sol of the Lost City of Bop[huthatswana]," mythologizing himself as the "archaeologist and custodian . . . the creator, discoverer and interpreter of this Enchanted Ruin."[85] Like the Luxor Hotel, the Lost City is a capitalist gesture that commodifies exoticism and similarly reduces Africa to "simulated fragments that have been exhumed, recombined, displayed, and marketed because they are easily digestible, portable, and chic."[86]

Kerzner was adamant that the Lost City, although clearly mediated by Hollywood, had to carry unambiguous references to Africa: "We took a long time to get the architecture right. First it looked too much like a mosque . . . Moroccan. I wanted it to be unique. I said, 'Where's Africa? I don't see it. Do something to those domes, put elephant tusks on them or something. I want to see Africa in the design. Put animals on them. Put proteas on the pillars.'"[87] The final product—an eclectic appropriation of the Taj Mahal, Versailles, Turkey, North Africa, and Indiana Jones—met the approval of Kerzner: "'This,' says Sol . . . 'is Africa. Not Disneyland, not Hawaii.'"[88] The splendor of the architecture conveys the theme of royalty that forms an integral part of the Legend; a vision of "the blessed land" appeared to the king and the people of the Lost City built the "magnificent city of grand proportions as a tribute to the king who had led them to their Utopia."[89] The romance of an extinct kingdom bears within it signifiers of privilege, power, and patriarchy that are encoded in the Royal Staircase, Royal Baths, King's Suite, Cheetah Fountain, Sun Lion gong, elephant guard of honor on the Bridge of Time, leopard guardian of the Temple of Creation, and Mighty Kong Gates. The notion of the Lost City as "Africa's pleasure dome" resonates with the privileges of empire; it is probably not coincidental that tourists from former colonial powers such as the United Kingdom, Germany, France, and Italy have been specifically targeted by the Lost City.[90]

As previously mentioned, Gerald Allison explained that the "flora and fauna of the region that existed during the time that the Palace was supposedly built" influenced the concept of the Lost City.[91] Wimberly Allison Tong and Goo clarified their use of plant and animal motifs:

> The lore of Africa provided concept and decorative motifs, with no use of animal trophies. A constant sense of movement is captured in sculpted animal forms and in the lines of arches incised with native flora. Over 100 forms of natural vegetation and wildlife are represented in the ornament of towers and ceilings.[92]

Although plants are part of the lexicon of the picturesque, animals are not, and are used at the Lost City for their exotic value and to illustrate the peaceful interaction between the Ancients and a bountiful, animistic nature. The fact that the iconography of the Lost City is based on Africa's flora and fauna circumvents the problematic issue of representing its races.[93] This strategy can be linked to the older colonial tradition of essentializing Africa as the site of exotic animals and jungle scenes with negligible human presence.[94] David Lowenthal furthermore alerts us to the fact that in "new" places such as America and Australia (and arguably South Africa), the natural, as opposed to the cultural past, is habitually venerated.[95]

The Lost City Garden fulfils an important function because it amalgamates two ideas—namely the exoticism of the African jungle and the European picturesque garden. The notion of a jungle in the dry African bushveld in which Sun City is situated is inconsistent with reality and is characteristic of the stereotypical view of Africa as being populated by "lions in the jungle."[96] The tropical jungle fantasy theme predominates in a great deal of the interior decorating at Sun City and the Lost City and features in the twenty-five-hectare constructed jungle. According to Mda:

> The designer jungle, an ode to the flora and fauna of Africa, encompasses . . . rainforests to swamps, baobab trees and bamboo thickets. Everywhere you look there are elephants, leopards, monkeys, snakes, birds . . . palm leaves and the crowns of protea . . . immortalised in every nook and cranny of the city, both inside and out. And from the midst of the exotic jungle soars the Palace Hotel.[97]

Moreover, the Garden can be read as a romantic "garden of ideas" that is structured around typical picturesque iconography that creates a visual, atmospheric, and thematic backdrop for the Lost City, and specifically for the Palace Hotel. Patrick Watson accordingly transformed or "improved" the original dry bushveld into a fantasy forest. He designed the Garden around a series of artificial lakes, pools, fountains, waterfalls, ruins, and constructed paths to make it a picturesque, romantic landscape. The different sections in the Garden include an ornamental forest with palms and exotic fruit trees, a wet tropical forest, a dry indigenous forest and a royal palm forest. Only about 30 percent of the plants are indigenous to the region, whereas the other 70 percent are indigenous to Africa. Watson was aware of the need for an almost cinematic, picturesque panorama, stating that "the view 100 kilometres away is . . . important. The vista has to fade out, from tropical at the centre to indigenous mountainside at the edges."[98]

The Garden is structured to afford "endless opportunities for leisurely walks and scenic views" that may be compared to the picturesque "stations" and themescapes referred to previously.[99] Moldering, overgrown ruins and crumbling bridges, water and lush plants combine with plaques with extracts from the Legend to drive the narrative and sustain the thematic cohesion of the site. The iconography in the Garden is Africanized—instead of statues of Apollo and Venus, exotic animal and bird sculptures peek out between the foliage. Carter states that there are two kinds of picturesque, the one impenetrable and uninhabited—where one gets lost—and the other of openness and habitation.[100] Both of these forms of the picturesque are found in the Garden; the latter is particularly evident in the areas closest to the Palace Hotel where all the paths are paved, signposted, and meticulously maintained. This confirms, as previously suggested, that the picturesque does not necessarily reside in the object of contemplation but rather in the manner in which it is perceived and integrated in preconceived notions, in this case regarding the supposed "untamed wildness" of Africa.

Paths from the Garden lead past the sites of the ancient Gold and Diamond Mines and the ruins of the Village Wall and end up in the waterpark. Important sites are explained by means of plaques that sustain the theme and narrative. Water assumes importance at the Lost City as part of the thematic structure and as a device that creates atmosphere, with aptly named places such as the Monkey Spring Plaza, Valley of Waves, Waterpark, Sacred River, and Wishing Well. The artificial lakes, pools, fountains, and waterfalls in the Garden create the space for introspection and meditation required by the picturesque and convey the sense of lushness associated with African jungles. The waterpark is devoted to immersive adventure and includes the ninety-seven-meter drop of the water slide at the Temple of Courage, supposedly formed when water entered the old gold mine shafts. The Sacred River and Lazy River Rides offer glimpses of a stalactite cave and rapids, showers from a stone elephant, water tunnels and a misting rain forest, an ancient hunter's lair, and an old aqueduct. The main feature of the Valley of Waves is the scallop-shaped Wave Pool or Roaring Lagoon that was ostensibly formerly the village swimming pool: "Legend says that the earthquake which forced the original inhabitants of this valley to flee, altered the watercourses and reshaped the lakes."[101] This is a typical Caribbean-style beach with blue water, white sands, thatched umbrellas, and palm trees that serve as signifiers for exotic paradise and utopian space.

Because the primary theme of the Lost City centers on the notion of a defunct civilization, ruin imagery assumes mythic weight and serves to anchor the aesthetic of the picturesque. The picturesque is enunciated by means of the fake ruins, cracked masonry and weathering; the foregrounding of picturesque ruin and decay makes it eminently believable that the Lost City originated thousands of years ago.[102] Ruins were an integral part of picturesque tourism because they invoked an aesthetic experience based on the pleasures of the imagination, and at the Lost City they signify nostalgia, historical exoticism, sublime delight in pleasing decay, and picturesque romanticism.[103] The appreciation of ruins was located in a western mode of thought, and was underpinned by the notions of travel, exploration, and archaeological excavations referred to previously. Martin Hall observes that the attraction of the Lost City resides in its "picturesque decay and patina, cracked and crumbling icons of the archaeological site."[104] Picturesque decay is particularly evident at the Bridge of Time, a sixty-six-meter long pedestrian bridge that links the Lost City with the Entertainment Centre at Sun City. The bridge plays an important part in the narrative, as it is equipped with special effects that mimic the effects of the volcanic eruption and earthquake that destroyed the Lost City. Every hour, on-the-hour, "forces unleashed deep in the earth explode out of the Temple, the leopard's eyes grow fiery red, and smoke and steam pour out of fissures in the rock. There are sounds of lava hissing and bubbling as it flows beneath the Bridge of Time, which shakes slightly with this eruption of power."[105] This is a good example of the alliance between picturesque imagery and sublime effects in order to render an immersive and thrilling experience for visitors to the Lost City.

Ruin lore was firmly entrenched in the western Romantic and picturesque tradition, but by the late nineteenth century, it was also located in the legends of the Queen of Sheba and Prester John, archaeological discoveries in Africa such as Great Zimbabwe, and the adventure stories of Rider Haggard. In Haggard's *King Solomon's Mines*, for example, the British discover a black race living among the ruins of a supposed great white civilization. David Bunn believes that these ruins served the imperial capitalist drive by "reminding only of a *suitably distant epic past*" that posed no threat to colonial hegemony.[106] The ruins at the Lost City resonate with many texts that situate them in the trope of the picturesque. First, as "mass manufactured" mock ruins deliberately arranged in a landscape to create picturesque effects, they appeal to the so-called kitsch tourist.[107] Second, the Lost City ruins represent the capacity to fabricate the past in order to create a generalized sense of pastness; because they are devoid of original context or meaning, they merely become decor that stimulates touristic consumption. Furthermore, the "time-worn magnificence of The Palace" and the ruins depict a "suitably distant epic past" at the Lost City, and more importantly, naturalize and legitimate the Legend regarding contact from North Africa whereby local history and culture are rendered negligible.[108]

The theme of the Lost City is also conveyed by a number of maps that operate in accordance with the demands of the trope of the picturesque and that echo the mechanisms of colonial mapping. So, for example, one of the colorful pictorial maps presents a typical picturesque view from a designated "station" that looks out with a commanding gaze over the suggestively empty terrain. The image is framed by two proscenium-like columns analogous to the framing devices found in picturesque landscape paintings. The westernized perspective directs the possessing gaze over the land, which unfolds like a panorama and fades into a pleasing "luminous distance." All the details on this map exaggerate the picturesque depiction of ageing and ruination, and demonstrate how the picturesque operates across genres and in disparate parts to inscribe ideological and mythical intent.

In evaluating the theming of the Lost City, it is clear that there are two issues at stake. First, the theme itself is derived from a cultural stereotype that conforms to popular narratives that situate Africa as the seat of long lost civilizations. But together with the allusions to Africa as a paradise of immense wealth, symbolized by Solomon's lost mines, the mythical Legend of the Lost City also resonates with the dark eroticism of the Queen of Sheba and romanticizes the destructive natural forces of the continent. Martin Hall concludes that the Legend perpetuates ideas regarding the "inevitability of inspiration from the north, and of the shallowness, poverty and violence of Africa's own history."[109] It is interesting that there are no visual depictions of the "Ancients" at the Lost City; although this possibly avoids the essentialist trap of ethnic theming that commodifies cultural difference, choosing a narrative rooted in a recognizable South African cultural context could have afforded more successful theming.[110] Chris Buchanan has criticized the postmodern pastiches of Georgian, Roman, and Tuscan imagery that seem to prevail at South African casinos.[111] He believes that it is important for South Africa to develop a visual identity that is more attuned to an African ethos and context. It is a pity that the Lost City did not engage with this challenge since its imposed theme in effect prevents the reflection of an authentic national identity.

The second point according to which the theming of the Lost City ought to be judged is its consistency and sustainability. Again, there are points of criticism, mainly because the theme is not always linked to the narrative of the Legend and does not generate a consistent style or iconography. The theme appears essentially to produce a visual background or atmosphere, which corresponds with the idea of picturesque place making referred to previously. The theming of the Lost City conceives limited themescapes or picturesque narrative fragments that could have been developed into a cohesive narrative more successfully. Plaques bearing extracts from the Legend or other explanatory material are found throughout the site, but their physical condition is quite bad and they are generally difficult to read. The theming of the physical and sensory environment, although disappointing in parts, is more or less consistent, but the theming of the crafts, foods, and costumes is arbitrary and inadequate. For example, only the black staff at the Lost City wears vaguely "ethnic" dress, and some of the buildings in the Lost Village are used as fast-food outlets that bear no thematic relation to the overall identity of the landscape.

The main conclusion that can be drawn from the foregoing is that the theming of the Lost City constructs a simulacrum of Africa—but what is remarkable is that this simulacrum is not situated in Las Vegas or in a Disney theme park, but in Africa. Themed landscapes are generally created to afford pleasurable experiences and do not necessarily establish an active or authentic engagement with the past. Fantasy and imagination are not in themselves suspect or problematic, but the fact that people experience a constructed past at the Lost City is an issue that needs interrogation because the erasure of the "real" past bears the traces of ideological manipulation of memory, place, culture, and identity. Lowenthal reasons that it is precisely because the past is inaccessible that it is mystified, distorted, and recreated to suggest fake, benign pasts devoid of conflict.[112] He points out that the past as represented in contemporary landscapes—such as history theme parks that celebrate both factual and fictional pasts—is generally artificial, invented, constructed, and illusive.[113] South Africa has embraced the seductive commercial forces that selectively package the past as entertainment, not only at the Lost City but also at places such as Gold Reef City in Johannesburg, the Victoria and Alfred Waterfront and Robben Island in Cape Town, and Shakaland theme park near the KwaZulu homeland.[114]

Critics have pointed out that theme parks have the capacity to destabilize local and regional identities by conflating, jumbling, and commingling mythic essences, cultures, contexts, and epochs.[115] In the process, local identity is typically lost and it becomes possible to thematize the exotic/Africa and reduce it to harmless and familiar terms. Entertainment and tourism landscapes are designed to look as consumers expect them to look, leading Sarah Chaplin to conclude that what people want "is a planned series of edited highlights as a preferred substitute for the so-called real thing."[116] In this chapter, I suggested that the picturesque aesthetic is ideal for the ideological manipulation of spatiality found in both colonial and entertainment spaces. The imperial picturesque combined beauty with the imposition of stability and operated as an appropriation of territory, either by "improving" or colonizing it. The picturesque at the Lost City disingenuously offers visitors the supposed charm of the past, preserved and packaged as the vehicle for nostalgic escapism. Despite the fact that the ancient inhabitants are never explicitly represented, because they are enframed by the picturesque, we assume them to be primitive or, in other words, picturesque Africans. Whereas the eighteenth-century picturesque sought connections between nature and art, today's picturesque seeks associations between popular culture and landscapes as narrated in media constructions by Disney, Indiana Jones, *Gladiator, Relic Hunter*, Lara Croft, and Tarzan. Africa as experienced through the prism of the theming of mythical Africa at the Lost City is therefore the continent desired by the colonial imagination—constructed, tamed, familiarized, and commodified in a hyperreal simulacrum in which the imitation supersedes the original.[117]

Notes

1. Henri Lefebvre, *The Production of Space* (Oxford: Blackwell, 1991), 17.

2. W. J. T. Mitchell, ed., *Landscape and Power* (Chicago: University of Chicago Press, 1994), 1. The sublime can also be identified at the Lost City but is not so pertinent and is therefore not discussed in this essay.

3. Peter Childs and R.J. Patrick Williams, eds., *An Introduction to Post-colonial Theory* (Hemel Hempstead, UK: Harvester Wheatsheaf, 1997), 103.

4. Jessica Dubow, "'Bringing the Country into View': Baines and the Making of the Colonial Picturesque," (lecture, University of Cape Town, January 1997), 4.

5. Roland Barthes, "The *Blue Guide*," in *Mythologies* (London: Paladin, 1972), 81–84.

6. Gambling was illegal in South Africa under the rule of the National Party between 1948 and 1994, and was deregulated in 1996 in the new South African Constitution.

7. Andrew Donaldson, "The Chips Are Down," *Sunday Times Insight*, 30 July 2000, 1.

8. "Foreign Markets Targeted for Future Growth," *Pretoria News Business Report*, 28 June 1999, 9.

9. Martin Hall, "The Legend of the Lost City; or, the Man with Golden Balls," *Journal of Southern African Studies* 21, no. 2, (June 1995), 197. As Andrew Unsworth remarks, "In how many places can you experience Africa, play golf, view game, surf, lie in the sun or just live in opulent luxury and then walk in a man-made jungle?" "Prospero's Kingdom in the Bush," *Sunday Times Lifestyle*, 28 March 1999, 5. For a detailed discussion of the Lost City, see Jeanne van Eeden, "The Representation of Mythical Africa at The Lost City: a Critical

Analysis," (DLitt et Phil thesis, University of South Africa, 2000).

10. M. Silverman, "Sun King's Lost City, Walts and All," *The Weekly Mail*, 4–10 September 1992, 30.

11. Hall, "The Legend of the Lost City," 198.

12. Sun International, "Who's Who in Development at the Lost City," unpublished press release (Sun City: Public Relations Department, March 1992), 14.

13. L. Mda, "Lost City Splendour," *Femina* (September 1992): 88. Kerzner acquired Paradise Island Resorts in the Bahamas in 1994 and rethemed and relaunched its Atlantis resort in 1999. The themed architecture deals with Atlantian civilization and Mayan culture and was designed by WATG. Another ambitious Kerzner project centered on theming was the Mohegan Sun gaming resort in Connecticut, which opened in 1996.

14. Sun International, "Sculpting an Architectural Tribute at the Lost City," unpublished press release (Sun City: Public Relations Department, December 1993), 1. For visual material of the Lost City, see the WATG Web site <http://www.watg.com> or the Sun International Web site <http://www.sun-international.com>.

15. Sun International, "The Lost City and the Valley of Waves at Sun City," <http://www.sun-international.com/lostcity2.html> (23 September 1997).

16. "Hotels and Resorts. The Palace of the Lost City," <http://www.watg/lostcity.html> (19 November 1999).

17. Henry Louis Gates, "Into Africa with Henry Louis Gates: Lost Cities of the South," (television program broadcast on South African television, August 1999). It is interesting that the Lost City was used as the setting for the American television series *Tarzan: the Epic Adventure* (1998). For a fuller discussion of the Legend of the Lost City, see van Eeden, "The Representation of Mythical Africa."

18. Gates, "Into Africa."

19. Hall, "The Legend of the Lost City," 196.

20. "About Us," <http://www.watg.com/html/aboutus.html> (23 February 2000).

21. Hall, "The Legend of the Lost City," 198.

22. Alexander Wilson, *The Culture of Nature* (Cambridge: Blackwell, 1992), 182.

23. Mark Gottdiener, "Consumption of Space and Spaces of Consumption," in *Consuming Architecture,* ed. Sarah Chaplin and Eric Holding (Chichester, UK: Wiley, 1998), 13.

24. Margaret J. King, "'Disneyfication'? Some Pros and Cons of Theme Parks. 'Never Land' or Tomorrowland?" *Museum* 43, no. 1 (1991): 6.

25. John Urry, *The Tourist Gaze: Leisure and Travel in Contemporary Societies* (London: Sage, 1990), 144.

26. Margaret Crawford, "The World in a Shopping Mall," in *Variations on a Theme Park,* ed. Michael Sorkin (New York: Noonday, 1992), 16.

27. Arata Isozaki, "Theme Park," *The South Atlantic Quarterly* 92, no. 1 (1993): 181.

28. Urry, *Tourist Gaze*, 145. David Lowenthal, "The Past as a Theme Park," in *Theme Park Landscapes: Antecedents and Variations,* ed. Terence Young and Robert Riley (Washington, D.C.: Dumbarton Oaks Research Library and Collection, 2002), 17.

29. Shelton Waldrep, "Monuments to Walt," in *Inside the Mouse: Work and Play at Disney World,* ed. The Project on Disney (Durham, N.C.: Duke University Press, 1999), 204–205.

30. Gates, "Into Africa."

31. Sun International, *The Lost City at Sun City* (Johannesburg: Art Publishers, 2000), 1.

32. Lowenthal, "Past as a Theme Park," 13.

33. Michael Sorkin, "See you in Disneyland," in *Variations on a Theme Park*, ed. Michael Sorkin (New York: Noonday, 1992), 216.

34. Isozaki, "Theme Park," 182.

35. M. R. Paneri, "Is Themed Architecture Legitimate?" <http://www.watg.com/> (23 February 2000).

36. Paneri, "Themed Architecture."

37. Sarah Chaplin and Eric Holding, "Consuming Architecture," in *Consuming Architecture*, ed. Sarah Chaplin and Eric Holding (Chichester, UK: Wiley, 1998), 9; Charles Jencks, "Post-modernism: Between Kitsch and Culture," in *Post-Modernism on Trial*, ed. A. C. Papadakis (London: Academy, 1990), 25.

38. Alan Tomlinson, "Introduction: Consumer Culture and the Aura of the Commodity," in *Consumption, Identity, and Style: Marketing, Meanings, and the Packaging of Pleasure*, ed. Alan Tomlinson (London: Routledge, 1990), 28.

39. Chris Buchanan, "The Long Road to Riches," *Mail & Guardian Friday*, 30 June - 6 July 2000, 3.

40. Alan Beardsworth and Alan Bryman, "Late Modernity and the Dynamics of Quasification: the Case of the Themed Restaurant," *The Sociological Review* 47, no 2 (1999): 247.

41. Miodrag Mitrasinovic, "Theme Parks," <http://web.new.ufl.edu/~wtilson/miodrag.html> (29 March 2000); H. J. Hildebrandt, "Cedar Point: a Park in Progress," *Journal of Popular Culture* 15, no. 1 (Summer 1981): 98. See also, Miodrag Mitrasinovic, *Total Landscape, Theme Parks, Public Space* (Burlington, Vt.: Ashgate, 2006).

42. Waldrep, "Monuments to Walt," 187, 199.

43. Mitrasinovic, "Theme Parks."

44. Michael Sullivan, *The Meeting of Eastern and Western Art from the Sixteenth Century to the Present Day* (London: Thames and Hudson, 1973), 112.

45. Jonathan Bate, "Reshaping the Landscape/Rethinking the Land," RSA lecture, 31 January 2002, <http://www.thersa.org/acrobat/bate_31jan02.pdf> (26 June 2004): 4.

46. Terence Young, "Grounding the Myth—Theme Park Landscapes in an Era of Commerce and Nationalism," in *Theme Park Landscapes: Antecedents and Variations*, ed. Terence Young and Robert Riley (Washington, D.C.: Dumbarton Oaks Research Library and Collection, 2002), 2–3.

47. Robert Rosenblum, *Transformations in Late Eighteenth Century Art* (Princeton, N.J.: Princeton University Press, 1974), 114.

48. Young, "Grounding the Myth," 5.

49. Young, "Grounding the Myth," 6–8.

50. Susan Stewart, *On Longing. Narratives of the Miniature, the Gigantic, the Souvenir, the Collection* (Baltimore: Johns Hopkins University Press, 1984), 75.

51. Paul Carter, *The Road to Botany Bay: An Essay in Spatial History* (London: Faber, 1987), 239–40.

52. Christopher Hussey, *The Picturesque: Studies in a Point of View* (London: Cass, 1967), 4, 9; Rochelle Gurstein, "Pleasing Decay," Book review of *In Ruins* by Christopher Woodward, *The New Republic Online*, 23 February 2004, <https://ssl.tnr.com/p/docsub.mhtml?i=20040223&s=gurstein022304> (26 June 2004).

53. Hussey, *The Picturesque*, 5, 18; Bate, "Reshaping the Landscape," 3.

54. J. M. Coetzee, *White Writing: On the Culture of Letters in South Africa* (Sandton, South Africa: Radix, 1988), 44.

55. Hussey, *The Picturesque*, 152; Coetzee *White Writing*, 44, 46; David Lowenthal, *The Past Is a Foreign Country* (Cambridge: Cambridge University Press, 1985), 175.

56. Lowenthal, *The Past Is a Foreign Country*, 140, 156.

57. Lowenthal, *The Past Is a Foreign Country*, 148–49.

58. Rosenblum, *Transformations*, 114.

59. Heath Schenker, "Pleasure Gardens, Theme Parks, and the Picturesque," in *Theme Park Landscapes: Antecedents and Variations,* ed. Terence Young and Robert Riley (Washington, D.C.: Dumbarton Oaks Research Library and Collection, 2002), 85.

60. Coetzee, *White Writing*, 39.

61. Young, "Grounding the Myth," 4.

62. Carter, *Botany Bay*, 254.

63. Herb Gottfried, "Review of *Designed Landscape Forum I. Land Forum,"* The Critical Review of Landscape Art and Garden Design* Spring/Summer 1998: 2 <htttt://www.spacemakerpress.com/lfjune98/lfpage03.htm> (10 June 2004); Stewart, *On Longing*, 75; Hussey, *The Picturesque*, 16.

64. Young, "Grounding the Myth," 2.

65. Schenker, "Pleasure Gardens," 86.

66. Stewart, *On Longing*, 75; Hussey, *The Picturesque*, 2; Dubow "Bringing the Country," 6.

67. Hussey, *The Picturesque*, 5–7.

68. Dubow "Bringing the Country," 2, 4.

69. Coetzee, *White Writing*, 60.

70. Elizabeth Delmont and Jessica Dubow, "Thinking Through Landscape: Colonial Spaces and their Legacies," in *Panoramas of Passage: Changing Landscapes of South Africa,* ed. Elizabeth Delmont and Jessica Dubow (Johannesburg: University Art Galleries, University of the Witwatersrand, 1995), 7, 11.

71. Delmont and Dubow, "Thinking Through Landscape," 14–15; Carter, *Botany Bay,* 147.

72. Delmont and Dubow, "Thinking Through Landscape," 14; Carter, *Botany Bay,* 250.

73. Schenker, "Pleasure Gardens," 86; Coetzee, *White Writing*, 177.

74. Timothy Mitchell, *Colonising Egypt* (Cambridge: Cambridge University Press, 1988), 163.

75. Linda Nochlin, "The Imaginary Orient," in *The Politics of Vision: Essays on Nineteenth-century Art and Society* (London: Thames and Hudson, 1991), 50–51.

76. Schenker, "Pleasure Gardens," 87.

77. Griselda Pollock, *Avant-garde Gambits 1888–1893: Gender and the Colour of Art History* (London: Thames & Hudson, 1992), 60.

78. Young, "Grounding the Myth," 6.

79. Stuart Hall, "Race, Culture, and Communications: Looking Backward and Forward at Cultural Studies," in *What is Cultural Studies?*, ed. John Storey (London: Arnold, 1996), 342. On the nostalgia for the colonial romance see Deborah Root, *Cannibal Culture: Art, Appropriation, and the Commodification of Difference* (Boulder, Colo.: Westview, 1996); and Renato Rosaldo, "Imperialist Nostalgia," *Representations* 26 (Spring 1989): 107–122.

80. Wilson, *The Culture of Nature*, 181.

81. Gerald Allison, "Works of Wonder," *Habitat* 114 (February/March 1993): 40.

82. In Hall, "The Legend of the Lost City," 180.

83. Jeffrey Cass and Dion Dennis, "Ground Zero: Las Vegas' Luxor. An Imagined Archaeology of American Post-civilization," *CTHEORY* (1996): 1, 4

<http://www.ctheory.net/printer.asp?id=165> (12 October 2004). See also, Jeffrey Cass, "Egypt on Steroids: Luxor Las Vegas and Postmodern Orientalism," in *Architecture and Tourism: Perception, Performance, and Place*, ed. D. Medina Lasansky (Oxford: Berg, 2004), 241-64.

84. Sun International, "Fact Sheet: The Palace," unpublished press release (Sun City: Public Relations Department, May 1997).

85. D. Barkhuizen, "All's Not Lost! Sol's Dream of a City will Be Open on Time," *Sunday Times*, 4 October 1992, 1. Hall, "The Legend of the Lost City," 181.

86. Cass and Dennis, "Ground Zero," 2.

87. L. Burton, "Prophet of the City," *Cosmopolitan* (November 1992): 224.

88. Silverman, "Sun King's Lost City," 30.

89. Sun International, *The Lost City*, 3.

90. Tracey Hawthorne, *Lost City: Africa's Kingdom of Pleasure* (Cape Town: Struik, 1996), 61.

91. In Hall, "The Legend of the Lost City," 180.

92. "Hotels and Resorts: The Palace of the Lost City," <http://www.watg/lostcity.html> (19 November 1999).

93. Silverman, "Sun King's Lost City," 30.

94. Jan Nederven Pieterse, *White on Black: Images of Africa and Blacks in Western Popular Culture* (New Haven, Conn.: Yale University Press, 1992), 35.

95. Lowenthal, *The Past Is a Foreign Country*, 54.

96. Robert Stam and Louise Spence, "Colonialism, Racism and Representation," *Screen* 24, no. 2 (March/April 1983): 6.

97. Mda, "Lost City Splendour," 88.

98. Allison, "Works of Wonder," 50.

99. Sun International, *The Lost City*, 16.

100. Carter, *Botany Bay*, 232-33.

101. Marilyn Poole, *The Palace of the Lost City at Sun City, Republic of Bophuthatswana, Southern Africa* (Cape Town: Struik, 1993), 10.

102. Silverman, "Sun King's Lost City," 30.

103. Gurstein, "Pleasing Decay," 4.

104. Hall, "The Legend of the Lost City," 181.

105. Mda, "Lost City Splendour," 89.

106. David Bunn, "Embodying Africa: Woman and Romance in Colonial Fiction," *English in Africa* 15, no. 1 (May 1988): 18.

107. Ludwig Giesz, "Kitsch-man as Tourist," in *Kitsch: An Anthology of Bad Taste*, ed. Gillo Dorfles (London: Studio Vista, 1969), 172, 167.

108. Hawthorne, *Lost City*, 23.

109. Hall, "The Legend of the Lost City," 188, 193, 198.

110. Beardsworth and Bryman, "Dynamics of Quasification," 242.

111. Buchanan, "The Long Road to Riches," 2.

112. Lowenthal, *The Past Is a Foreign Country*, 53, 345, 356.

113. Lowenthal, "Past as a Theme Park," 13-14; David Lowenthal, *The Heritage Crusade and the Spoils of History* (Harmondsworth: Penguin, 1996), ix.

114. On Shakaland, see Carolyn Hamilton, *Terrific Majesty: The Powers of Shaka Zulu and the Limits of Historical Invention* (Cambridge, Mass.: Harvard University Press, 1998), 168-205.

115. Young, "Grounding the Myth," 8-9; Lowenthal, "Past as a Theme Park," 16.

116. Sarah Chaplin, "Authenticity and Otherness: the New Japanese Theme Park," in *Consuming Architecture,* ed. Sarah Chaplin and Eric Holding (Chichester, UK: Wiley, 1998), 79.

117. It is beyond the scope of this essay to explore all the implications inherent in the creation of a hyperreal world at the Lost City that seems to be grounded in reality but that actually depicts a fictional reality. Beardsworth and Bryman's ideas regarding theming and quasification also afford a point that deserves further elaboration, particularly the notion that parodic theming employs devices that are explicitly fake but experienced as real by consumers ("Dynamics of Quasification," 241); see also Umberto Eco, "Travels in Hyperreality," in *Travels in Hyperreality: Essays* (London: Pan, 1986) and Jean Baudrillard, *Simulations* (New York: Semiotext(e), 1983).

Chapter 8

Leisure Space: Thematic Style and Cultural Exclusion in Casablanca

Bahíyyih Maroon

In this essay I engage the dynamic of exclusivity produced through spatial interpretations of international cultures rendered in a local context. I will explore the significance of Casablanca's thematic space of beachside consumer leisure by layering ethnographic material and architectural data. Following the development of the resort district from its inception in the 1930s to its contemporary moment, demonstrates an intriguing relationship between the district's architectural style and the social life it contains. Historicizing the resort district reveals the central role of exclusion in defining Ain Diab's hierarchical social space. From era to era though, there is a marked shift in the grounds on which forms of exclusion are played out. Modalities of stratification present under colonialism—including class, ethnic, and religious divides—have been augmented in the contemporary period. In the contemporary moment, determinants of exclusion are informed by additional essential indicators of social status and gender. In the following pages, I will trace the forms and alterations of exclusionary practices that are at work in the architecturally thematic spaces of Casablanca's resort district.

At the Atlantic Ocean's edge in metropolitan Casablanca, one has only to walk a few kilometers to see the world over. Along the southern shoreline of Casablanca's Ain Diab resort district, international place names prominently mark the streets and the architecture. In a manner similar to the Las Vegas Strip or Euro Disney, the resort district provocatively localizes a global imaginary of style as national identity. The resort district beckons in an architecturally thematic invitation to take in disparate national experiences within one centralized locale. The architectural style of resorts on Casablanca's southern shore displays structural artifacts from around the world. The buildings are a celebration of the notion that national tastes can be interpreted as cultural truths and demonstrated by reproductions of architectural structure. Place as the cultural experience of shaping, building, and occupying spaces is taken to be reproducible and, critically, transportable. In the economic capital of Casablanca, Polynesian thatched roof huts sprinkle the sand of Tahiti Beach, while just a few meters over one can visit an American playground in Miami. At Club Miami there are poolside platforms and standard lounge chairs popularized by the Floridian pop school of American architecture. The thing which poet Audre Lorde declared as "the marvelous arithmetic of distance" is conquered in these local constructions of an international scene.[1] Relaxing on the beach in Tahiti, Miami, or Acapulco can be accomplished without stepping foot outside of the Muslim North African nation of Morocco. The thematic content of Casablanca's resort architecture richly demonstrates the process of what is, in Lefebvrian terms, the production of consumable leisure space.

Casablanca's resort district, Ain Diab, has been produced by historic sediments of strategic planning and the spontaneous combustions of a culture at once traditional and transformative. In the decades since Casablanca's planners and developers first broke ground on Ain Diab's beachfront district, the city looming behind the modern resorts has undergone dramatic transformations. Casablanca has experienced Moroccan national independence, severe economic ebbs, and intense demographic upheavals. Not surprisingly throughout its over seventy years of existence, the Ain Diab resort district has seen many of its smaller establishments come and go. The district's enduring resorts, however, are remarkably preserved icons of modernism's consumer architecture, circa the mid-twentieth century. Tahiti Plage, Sun Beach, Club Miami, and C.C.C. ("Club of Clubs") dominate the resort district today, just as they did when their doors first opened. These opulent and remarkably grand-scale resorts have provided generations of elite and upper-middle-class Casablancans with spaces of leisure and play. The fact that Casablanca's resorts were constructed to provide consumers spaces of play should not tempt us to think of these spaces as socially or politically inconsequential. Leisure spaces and the peculiar thematic content they produce are critical nodes in the social apparatus that circumscribes the ways and means of class and social formation.

Modern Leisure in the Shadow of Port

Historical and geopolitical power formations are inscribed in the character of Casablanca's buildings as much as in its overall urban plan. While this chapter focuses primarily on the development of Casablanca's resort district, it will be helpful to briefly elaborate on the city's unique birth as a modern urban center. Designated as the economic capital of Morocco's French protectorate, Casablanca grew dramatically during the first half of the twentieth century. By the eve of the 1930s, the "once sleepy port town" had awakened and begun to eat up enough land to triple its incorporated territory.[2] Indeed, the city's buildings and sprawling streets gobbled up so much land that it began to merge into the once distant agricultural hinterlands of Chaouia. The rapid population growth in Casablanca owed to the development of a modern industrial port capable of handling high volumes of commercial goods. The progressive expansion of land use in Casablanca is indicated in historic city plans by the successive coloring-in of emergent districts and quarters. Despite its massive land acquisition during the first three decades of its life, Casablanca's borders shifted almost solely north and eastward.

The direction of Casablanca's early spread on the land belies the industrial port's centrality in generating the conditions of possibility for the exponential expansion of the city. Urban planner and architect Michel Ecochard drew a tripartite historic map of Casablanca's first half century showing its transition by juxtaposing black populated space, gray mildly populated space, and white unoccupied space. Ecochard's map emphasized population domains to the exclusion of mapping streets or building blocks. It is thus significant that the only structural representation on the map enabling viewers to orient themselves is the rectangular jetty system at port. Parcel lots on early city plans also indicate the importance of the port. These maps reveal buildings formed between the tendril of streets shooting off from the prominent avenues and boulevards connected to the port. Built as a modernist temple for what David Harvey refers to as spaces of capital, Casablanca's twentieth century birth was effectively the architectural installation of financial capital in the port's shadow.[3]

Casablanca's first site for beachfront leisure was cultivated on the sand north of the port. Running adjacent to the industrial quarters of Roche Noire and Sidi Belyout, the first locations for play, sport, and rest at the shoreline grew up in immediate proximity to the port's unpleasant monumental structures and the sooty air of nearby shipping lanes. Despite the obvious shortcomings, the Roche Noire and Sidi Belyout beaches were popular locations for the city's European working- and middle-class residents. Beachgoers could rent parasols, visit cafes, play in designated sports areas, lay out towels and ground coverings on the beach, or enjoy "dance halls and restaurants."[4] The European population's dominating definitions of the early style of beachfront leisure is evident in the types of social establishments and the forms they took on the landscape. One example is the Roche Noire cafe. A photo of the cafe from 1928 captures the happy faces of beachgoers lounging on the terrace and the sand in front. The absolute absence of any Moroccan faces in the crowd reveals the ethnically based exclusions at work in the colonial beachfront scene. The cafe's architecture also suggests the hierarchy of exclusion. Shooting up squarely from the cafe's rooftop was an approximately two-story-high clock tower. Whereas the city's European residents kept time according to minutes and hours, the Muslim Moroccan population kept time according to the solar intervals between the Islamic call to prayer. Before French occupation, the civic architecture of time was constructed in the form of minarets—towers adjoining mosques from which Muzzein (prayer callers) signaled the hour of worship.

As the post-war boom of the 1920s raged on, Casablanca's European middle class and elites began to move southward, taking up residence in newly built apartment blocks and villas. Development of the city's shoreline followed swiftly. By the time the renowned La Reserve opened in 1933, the land around it had sprouted dramatically from once uncultivated earth. Ain Diab had grown into a field of streets, a boulevard, clusters of residences, some shops, and a flourish of cafes. Casablanca's resident city planner and favored architect during the 1930s, Albert Laprade, sketched a plan for the district that would have effectively superimposed the style and design vocabulary of the French Riviera on the African sand. In the area of land development though, it is often the case that dozens of schematic visions for a project are put forth, often over lengthy periods of time—years and sometimes even decades—while only a few projects make it to construction. The African Riviera that Laprade envisioned taking shape in Ain Diab was eclipsed by an altogether different spatial theme characterized by a collage of Americanized tropical motifs and international consumer architecture.

Styling Leisure at the Shoreline

For the first few years of its existence, Ain Diab's style was dominated by neo-cosmopolitanism. Constituting an international wave of industrial modernism in architecture, neo-cosmopolitanism turned to pure geometry and the triumph of engineering to shape space. The private restaurant and resort club La Reserve, built in 1933, showed off the subtler curves and decorated finishes of neo-cosmopolitanism's appreciation for geometric simplicity. The style was also represented in two prominent public pools, but through a more brutalist form of engineering. The Lido, which opened in 1930, offered Casablancans a public pool on the edge of Ain Diab. "The color scheme was distinctly south Moroccan—red ocher walls, ivory columns, and blue pergolas—and the exposed brick bar was wittily named Brik's Bar."[5] The Lido's central attraction was a concrete swimming pool whose engineered quality was an aesthetic statement in and of itself. The unadorned concrete and steel that made possible previously unimaginably large swimming pools, was also found in the George Orthlieb pool. Though situated just outside of Ain Diab in the slightly older quarter of TSF, the Orthlieb pool was close enough and certainly grand enough to be included in the locus of beachfront activity at the time. At nearly six hectares in size, the pool was the largest swimming structure in all of Africa and indeed rivaled by only a few other pools in the world at the time. A structural feat that effectively contained the ocean for safe swimming, the Orthlieb pool provided thousands of city dwellers with an enormous concrete deck bound by steel and exposed horizontal support beams.[6] Like the Lido though much bigger, Orthlieb was a hugely popular and unabashedly engineered site of water play and oceanside leisure.

The moment in which neo-cosmopolitanism's thrall of modern engineering provided a mix of public and private leisure sites along the spreading shoreline was notably brief. The Orthlieb pool, owing to numerous structural flaws, was prone to lengthy periods of closure and ultimately fell out of use altogether. The Lido, on the other hand, underwent a transformation in which it shed its largely public middle-class constituency in favor of a privatized existence for an elite consumer base. The changeover was pointedly announced by an exorbitant entrance fee as well as an expansion-driven makeover. Lido expanded its grounds with a new restaurant and pool. The design scheme shifted from the localized glow of Moroccan red to the marching flag color of modernism, pristine white. The Lido's changeover was symptomatic of Ain Diab's increasing absence of public leisure space and the rising dominance of wholly private resort clubs. The privatization wave in Ain Diab's development coincided with the emergence of a distinctly Americanized architecture of modern consumption. The central theme of the resort district became indelibly linked with the expansive aura of Hollywood's golden age dreams, which stylistically cannibalized everything from cars to palm trees to produce leisure lifestyle as a qualified aesthetic experience.[7]

As structural monuments to what members of the Frankfurt School termed the *culture industry*, the American brand of consumer architecture performed a perfect theft of modernism's universal tendencies.[8] The pristine edges and enforced structural simplicity of modern design was in many ways an ideal tableau on which to splash branded signage and hang thematic signifiers of consumable leisure. Consumer architecture overloaded the reproducible components of universal ideals promoted by early modernism with oddly complimentary structures bearing strategically placed neon lighting, Bauhaus-informed bold kinder colors like red and yellow or blue and white, and resurrections of art deco shaded in admixtures of pastel.[9] Though contrary by nature to the ideals of utilitarianism, consumer architecture borrowed directly from utilitarianism's toolkit of style repetition, economies of scale, and spatial programming. In Casablanca, consumer architecture increasingly claimed the city's post-World War II buildings. From parking garages and gas stations, to movie houses and private villas, the golden age of Hollywood movies and its characterizations of the American dream swept through the French-occupied African city, heralding a unique form of class desire encapsulated as the leisure lifestyle. The good life was suddenly distinctly defined by culture industry standards—access to entertainment, automobiles, luxury goods, and the infinite enjoyment of play and relaxation.

From the 1940s until independence, Ain Diab's resorts offered Europeans and a small number of wealthy Moroccan Jews access to exotic leisure spaces conceived as a fantasy land and branded in an Americanized design vocabulary. America's role in the theming of Ain Diab's resort district is in the form of a filter. The Americana style vocabulary articulated recognizable interpretations of yet other kinds of "foreign," including Mexico and the Pacific Islands. While the demand for independence and freedom from French subjugation was growing among Casablanca's thousands of economically disenfranchised Moroccans, the city's European elites further privatized access to leisure spaces and, to a degree, furthered the ethnic divides threatening the stability of the protectorate nation. The construction of new resorts in Ain Diab between 1945-1956—including Tahiti Plage, Kon Tiki, Miami Beach, and Sun Beach—effectively relandscaped the southern shoreline into the aesthetic afterglow of a Technicolor movie set. Like the racially segregated America from which their style was imported, the new resorts produced fully privatized, ethnically segregated spaces for class elites.

We can only imagine what the social scene was like in Ain Diab during the first decade of independence. The record gives us a few clues and certain facts, but no first-person narratives. After 1956, the population of French residents shrank radically. The Moroccan population, on the other hand, grew. It is unclear exactly how long it took for the resorts of Ain Diab to reflect, as they do today, the ethnic dominance of Moroccans—largely Muslim but also Jewish and Christian. While accurate social data on life in the resorts are missing, the architectural record bears provocative indications. In the 1960s existing clubs underwent "extension programs" and two altogether new additions were made in Ain Diab.[10] These additions, Acapulco and Tropicana, took up the few remaining swaths of open land on the beachfront. While closing off public access—by erecting fences, gateways, and doors—these resorts reconstructed interpretations of a Floridian fused with Mexicana modernism. Independence may have brought freedom from the tyranny of French rule, but it did not alter the tyranny of wealth and consumerism.

It is important to clarify that many of the construction developments in other recently independent African and Middle Eastern nations were clear efforts to redefine social space and re-engineer master plans in an attempt to reorganize and efface the imprint of colonial rule. In Casablanca, Morocco, by contrast, there was no movement toward a critical break with the inherited forms of colonial architects and planners. This is very evident in Casablanca's post-independence development projects—from housing works to villas, office buildings, shopping places and of course, resort spaces. The opening of Acapulco and Tropicana succeeded in extending rather than altering the aesthetic of international modernism and the privatized nature of Casablanca's beachfront construction. The ethnic composition of the resort district's elite class was changing, but the architectural gesture and exclusive character remained intact. As a result, the only sand ultimately left open to public use in Ain Diab is at either scraggly edge of long beachfronts. These public areas mark the points at which the rocky undercurrent of the Atlantic could not be drilled into, or exploded, carted away and replaced by reliable retainer walls.

In some senses the forms of construction that took place in post-independence Casablanca closely mimicked the process that Jean Baudrillard describes as an emptying out of the signifier. This process is the destabilizing loss, subsequent adoption, and synthesizing hybridization of signs in postmodern times. The signifier—the thing containing the meaning of the sign, undergoes a dialectic fold (Deleuze) or an "emptying of the thing itself," in Heideggerian terms.[11] Its double entendre is a reduction on the one hand—an absence of a specific presence within the container—and an expansion on the other; a transformation of the container into content. Throughout history there are evocative examples of this emptying and filling-up of architectural containers during post-revolutionary moments. The turn over of Casablanca's beachfront from European to Moroccan residents has, however, a twist. The spaces being occupied by the once-excluded were not signatures of their former occupants' national aesthetic identity. Instead, the ethnically reallocated spaces were aesthetic statements of a third-party cultural hegemony—Americanism. The triumph of Americanism rendered as tropical Googie style gone mad is best exemplified by the style consistency of Ain Diab's signage.[12] In signage we find a sly reproduction of the American imaginary's take on the global native. The signs are welcome posts, twenty- and thirty-foot declarations of twice-folded exotic space. The signage speaks an ethnographic language of many tongues, and yet all of it is shaped in a distinguishably American style. The names are international—Tahiti, Acapulco, Miami—but the construction of aesthetic ideals is not. From one exotic locale to another, the typeface school of Ain Diab's oversized architectural signage remains anchored in 1950s Americana. The American consumer modernism glossed into the district's signs was initially created to cater to the preferred tastes of Casablanca's European elite. After independence, the resort district's dialectic of aesthetic exoticism has continued to be reproduced and maintained, but by a privileged membership made up overwhelmingly of local Moroccans.

Ain Diab: A District of Exclusions

Casablanca's resort district has entered the twenty-first century as a sensual architectural testament to late modernism's global tango with consumer space. All along the city's southern beachfront, the buildings testify to the post-World War II convergence of Fordist industrialization and an expanding culture industry. The district is a rare pocket of architectural preservation in a city whose landmarks are elsewhere regularly demolished due to deterioration and the lack of financially backed interests in saving them. In the postindustrial age of color, though, it is easy to see how Ain Diab's "preserved" buildings and structural signage have been worn by time. Rust, chipped paint, and sun-bleached straw are common sights along the boulevard. Nonetheless, Ain Diab retains an aura of theatricality and surfside fantasy. The district's main artery, Boulevard Corniche, is still a terrifically popular thoroughfare for slow gazing auto drivers and leisurely pedestrians along the promenade. Ain Diab, in its twenty-first century lifecycle, retains its role as Casablanca's most popular destination for a taste of the leisure life.

From Friday afternoon to Sunday evening, the promenade along Boulevard Corniche is filled with underemployed and working-class families, some individual men, and groups of young men and women. Husbands and wives are often accompanied by their children. There are also small groups of women in mixed generations out with a gaggle of children. These are groups of grandmothers, mothers, sisters, and daughters. Women strolling the paved and asphalt stretch of promenade wear traditional headscarves as often as not. Notably though, it is rare to see an intergenerational group of women in which the elders, if not all of the women, wear head coverings. Out on the promenade, the traditional body dress of Moroccans, the *dhjellaba*, is worn by both men and women. Still, contemporary European clothing generally outnumbers the Moroccan *dhjellabas*. Jeans, T-shirts, button-down cotton shirts, sports jerseys, and tracksuits are all vibrantly worn by those who walk the promenade. It should also be said that the wearing of traditional headscarves by women strollers does not automatically correspond to wearing of the traditional *dhjellaba*. Often, the last silk or cotton ripple of a headscarf adorned by a strolling woman falls upon the shoulders of her track jacket worn along with Levis jeans. These details suggest the intimate forms of cross-cultural signification at work on the surface of public life's social fabric. The promenade's crowd wears signatures of style and taste in wonderfully mundane performances of what Erving Goffman, termed "presentations of self in everyday life"—which are in this context rich and complex acts of cultural métissage.[13]

In many ways the stretch of promenade is its own scene in the resort district. The social plurality of the Moroccan city is demonstrated in the streams of pedestrians in all manner of dress and groupings, brushing by each other with the greatest of casualness. On the promenade, people of different classes and statuses stroll by one another unaffected. Walking along the promenade can feel at times like participating in a critical mass of pluralism and civil society at play. Ice-cream vendors and kiosks selling everything from soda to toys, dot the street side of the promenade's walkway, giving it something of a Coney Island festive air. There is a sense that the only purpose in life is, if only momentarily, to stroll with pleasure and take in the sights. In Ain Diab the public is given access to a tripartite spectacle—the distant ocean, the immediate kinetic crowd of the promenade, and the observable, but railed-off, beachfront occupied by resort goers.

A space of public foot traffic and crowd gazers, the promenade is literally and symbolically set apart from the scenes playing out in the beach clubs. For promenade walkers who cannot afford membership in the beachfront clubs, the railing and concrete interface with sand that runs the walkway is more than a path marker, it is an active barrier. The guardrail acts further as a framing device setting the window scene before the strolling onlooker. The symmetrical borders of one club to the next serve to amplify the unnaturalness of the spatial arrangement and declare the modern triumph of linear style. The system of retaining walls, rock-girded wading pools, and property walls levels the beachfront's natural continuity. Instead, the civilized urban grid itself has been etched into the cordoned sand at the ocean's edge. The development grid of the beach resorts gestures evocatively to the orthogonal drawings of the city's defunct public pools. Public pools though, left the design of the interior and exterior spaces to the aesthetic bluntness of engineering as style. Resorts, by contrast, have for the most part attempted to landscape and decorate (out of sight) the engineering feats underlying the construction of spaces capable of holding the demanding tides of the Atlantic at bay. The land grid made by resorts declares orderliness, but subsumes the engineered foundations beneath a flurry of adornment. Well-positioned palm trees are abundant and strategically placed throughout the beachfront grid. Seas of cabanas are neatly partitioned between stylized resort borders. White cloth, beige cloth, and striped cotton are fabrics of choice for outdoor furnishings and temporary structures like the cabana—a freestanding tent. Despite the fact that Moroccans have used tents as an essential building type for over five hundred years, there is not a single beach changing tent in any of the resorts with indigenous Moroccan prints or patterns. The particular eras that the resorts gesture to are certainly varied from those of the 1930s through the 1950s and 1960s, but among the nuances and specificities, remains a well diffused gloss of Americanized tropics style.

An outing along the promenade in Ain Diab is akin to an unticketed visual encounter with the commercialized theater of a foreign world. A great deal has been written about the use of exotic cultures in ethnographic statements of amusement parks and resorts.[14] Less attention has been paid to how social actors in perceived exotic locales likewise make use of the foreign other by creating and maintaining spaces steeped in the cultural signifiers of distant nations. On the vibrant promenade, the locals constitute a kind of tourist class. The expanse of the beach provides a gracious contrast to the dense neighborhoods of the city. A family might come to the promenade after midday prayer and after lunch on a Friday late afternoon. They can picnic at the edges of the beachfront, though children need to be carefully watched because the tide has not been tamed in these sites. There are also some terrace enclaves offering coffee, pastries, and light fare for a tourist price of fifty percent more than an ordinary cafe in a city neighborhood. For less than ten dollars (110DH), a family can take their children to the amusement park at the southern tip of the resort district. Whichever modest amusements day visitors participate in, the promenade stroll is an essential part of the local tourist experience. What makes Ain Diab enticing and exotic as a local tourist attraction is mediated by the scopic lens. Those in the crowds along Boulevard Corniche who are excluded from entering the beachfront resorts, effectively become audience members watching the landscape as one would a film on the screen or on television. In Moroccan households, television is often watched while people are going about other activities, having conversations, perhaps not even able to hear the sound coming from the projected sets of life elsewhere. Such a habitus of audiovisual engagement makes the analogy to film all the more compelling.[15]

Looking west from the promenade, the Atlantic brims prominently against the last evidence of the horizon. Closer into the shore, its tide attracts the eye with movements, the materialization of foam, and the presentation of differentiated colors less dense and ominous than the dark blue of its reach in the distance. The African shoreline is transposed into a mere background, beaten out for center stage by the sprawling designed spaces of exclusive resorts. The thematic aura of Hollywood tropics upstages the natural wonder of the African shoreline. But it is more than the view of nature that is blocked by the resorts. For the many who are not members, the ability to experience the beach's sand and the ocean's water is also foreclosed. When considered in its role as a tourist attraction for the locals, Ain Diab's turn through the magical third is produced by the critical maintenance of exclusions.[16] These exclusions function on multiple levels and suggest the complex overlaps and distinctions between class and status as indictors of either the right to, or the negation of, inclusion.

Social Order in Leisure Space

In a thoughtful ethnographic essay on Casablanca's beachfront, Andre Levy details the different ways in which Muslim and Jewish Moroccans occupy club space.[17] Looking specifically at the activities and spatial arrangements at work in the Tahiti Club, Levy argues convincingly that the tensions between Muslim and Jewish members are negotiated through forms of play, conversation, and "staking out place" within the club's boundaries. While access to the club denotes entry in an American-designed ideal of the good life, social practices within the club indicate strong attachments to localized religious identities that engender forms of segregation and heavily negotiated means of social exchange. Levy provides several ethnographic examples of segregation. Muslim and Jewish children, for instance, are discouraged in obvious and subtle ways from playing with one another. The rental of cabanas, bungalows, and beach chairs are all clearly defined by religious affiliation. This has resulted in the distinctive naming of two areas of the club, one predominantly occupied by Jewish members, *Tel-Avi*, and the other occupied by Muslims, *Al Quds*.[18] The two religious groups meet at the table, albeit in a symbolic and real sense through the popular pastime of card games. The ethnographic lens that Levy focuses on Ain Diab's Club Tahiti gives us an important insight into the role of religion in shaping cultural exclusions within a resort club.

In addition to religious affiliation, grounds of exclusion and prohibition within the resort clubs are staked out in terms of gender. Indeed, gender segregation plays a defining role in shaping the social landscape of Ain Diab's resort clubs. Culturally validated interpretations of gender roles shape the dynamics of participation inherent in activities and social practices within the resort clubs in a number of tangible ways. The most obvious form of enacted prohibition is the clear absence of lone women. In American resort clubs, for example—which likewise cater to a local elite population—the daytime scene is often dotted with individual women, from housewives to teenage girls and single women, swimming or taking in the sun. No such population of unaccompanied women is found in Casablanca's resort clubs. On the one hand we can say that this is due partially to the value Moroccans place on group sociality. The individual's triumph over everyday life, which makes eating alone, living alone or strolling alone socially normative, is absent in Moroccan culture. To that end, one sees relatively few women or men in resort clubs engaging in leisure by themselves. Nonetheless, there is a critical difference in that men who choose to override the cultural norm of group activity run no risk of harming the status of themselves or their families. Women alone in public by contrast are subject to a backlash of gossip, rumors, and social judgments. The result is the practical absence of lone women in the resort clubs. When one does occasionally come upon a lone woman in the resort clubs, she is almost always a foreigner, whether tourist or expatriate. In essence one only encounters sole women whose nationality overrides the threat of social censure posed to Moroccan women who behave out of accordance with Moroccan cultural norms.

The substance of moral prohibitions that prevents Moroccan women from going to resorts alone also informs the exclusions at work in the activities of men and women. Women, to wit, are essentially excluded from most of the sports activities. Although sports—including swimming, soccer, volleyball, running, and martial arts—are central to the social scene in resorts, women's sports activities are almost wholly limited to well-mannered water play. The uneven division of playtime rights is as well reflected in the division of labor at the resorts. The absence of men in the performance of domestic tasks is as apparent in resort clubs as it is in Moroccan homes. Children can be seen sitting at the sides of their fathers and participating with them in casual sand sports or swimming, but the caretaking of children remains clearly the task of women and girls. Arranging the family cabana or bungalow, packing and unpacking beach clothes and accoutrements, setting out food and cleaning up, are all tasks which one will only see performed by female beachgoers. Women do participate in leisure activities like sunbathing and sipping tea under table umbrellas, but the fantasy of a suspension of everyday life's mundane activities that is supposed to underlie participation in the leisurely life does not entirely cohere in the experience of adult women in the clubs. Membership in a resort club is not enough to guarantee individuals full access to the experience of leisure as a state of nonproductive relaxation and enjoyment.

During my time visiting the Ain Diab's resorts, I found that unequal access to leisure is negotiated by women through a second layer of status distinction formed along generational lines. The success of women's ability to distribute responsibility for domestic duties is tied to the fact that women come to the resorts most commonly as members of a family—rather than alone, the reasons for which I have just explored. Younger women in a group can be assigned duties even when they are not mothers themselves. Older daughters, nieces, and younger cousins of matriarchs who come to the clubs with their family members can generally expect to be assigned responsibility for some of the ongoing domestic duties, including watching children, housekeeping in bungalows, light cleaning in cabanas, and helping to set out and clean up meals. This means that none of the women or older girls in a group can expect to fully engage in an extended period of leisure at the beachside without the interruption of domestic tasks. The right to assign tasks to younger women is determined by the hierarchy of age within a group, thus embedding generational status in the formation of social practices. This status-bound distribution of tasks, though hierarchical, ensures that there is less of a burden on any one woman. While it takes time away from women who are themselves not yet mothers or wives, it provides more time to women with age status to do what they ostensibly come to the club to do—which is nothing except to enjoy the ocean and the sun.

Men do not participate in most of the domestic work that punctuates the leisure of the clubs and women do not take part in the exhaustive display of business networking that goes on in the clubs. In some respects the clubs are luxurious open-air offices in which the city's businessmen pitch deals, negotiate contracts and celebrate partnerships. A Belgian acquaintance of mine, struggling to be a successful entrepreneur, remarked ruefully on the ability of established Moroccan businessmen to run their operations from poolside chairs. In addition to conducting an array of informal and often impromptu face-to-face business at resorts, members of the business class also use the recently popularized communication tool of mobile phones. To a degree, the practice of business networking among the male business class of club members undermines the fantasy of absolute leisure that the resorts are intended to provide. The productivity of work life invades the space of play and threatens its significance as an exclusive zone of sandy restfulness. In the larger context of Casablancan society, however, the role of business networking actually amplifies the significance of the clubs' exclusivity. One who does not have access to the resorts is not only excluded from the material enjoyments of life that money brings, they are also excluded from accessing essential means of generating money.

The American Dream is vested in the belief that individuals have the power to create fortunes regardless of one's standing at birth. In Morocco, the would-be actors of the American Dream are strikingly limited in number. There is, in fact, only a handful of multimillionaires and a sprinkling of millionaires. It was with one of these rarefied social actors, a self-made millionaire named Ahmad, with whom I made my forays into the most elitist of resorts shaping club life of Ain Diab. The first time I tried to enter the seemingly innocuous gates of the club, it was early on in fieldwork and I had not yet fully grasped the implications of my own gender (female) and appearance in determining spaces from which I might be excluded. As a light complected [sic] Black American woman, I was often taken for Moroccan and treated by the same standards as an individual Moroccan woman. It took some time and testing to learn that there were many places from which I would be excluded without a male escort. That early on spontaneous decision to visit the inside of the resort club by myself met with complete failure. The door matron regarded my entry request with contempt of startling magnitude. My reasoning—that I was an expatriate who might be interested in a membership—was sharply rebuffed.

Members I was told, "are voted in." "Guests," she informed me, entered "only with established members." I did not attempt to enter the club again until several months later. This time, I arrived as an "American researcher" listed as the guest of Ahmad.

The son of a frequently out-of-work civil servant, Ahmad won a scholarship at age fourteen to a prominent engineering high school. After graduation, he received an undergraduate degree from a prestigious university and went on to found a lucrative monopoly based on satellite technology. His ownership in a satellite allows him to sell signal distribution rights that are sought after by companies throughout Morocco and around the world. His lifestyle is a stereotypically opulent expression of entrepreneurial luxury. Sitting in his preferred poolside location, Ahmad often took business calls during our interviews. Speaking in French, Arabic, and English depending on his caller's preferred language, Ahmad casually discussed multimillion dollar deals while sipping on iced mint tea. The only element missing in Ahmad's presentation of the good life was a female companion. While every Hollywood hero has a heroine and the role of well-adorned women in filmic and socially reproduced sketches of the America dream is ubiquitous, Ahmad's public self at the clubs was decidedly single and unattached. What makes this significant is that outside of the club scene, Ahmad in fact has nearly a dozen "girlfriends." On the occasions that I interviewed Ahmad at other locations, including his home, his office, and cafes, one of his many female companions was always present. I asked Ahmad if he ever brought his girlfriends to the club and his answer was a pointed no. He went on to explain that it would not, "be right to bring a woman here that way. You know I have many women friends, okay? If I bring them all to the club, I mean at different times," he laughs and shakes his head, "then this doesn't look right. It's not good for me, you know this?" Ahmad's self-disciplining is yet another provocative expression of the ways in which the leisure space of Ain Diab's resort clubs is produced through the social construction of cultural values.

Casablanca's resort scene occurs in spaces aesthetically dominated by American themes, but the action in these spaces is steeped in Moroccan ideals and cultural evaluations. Taken together as objects on the landscape, Ain Diab's resort clubs remain enticing articulations of an idealized leisure lifestyle. Ain Diab's leisure style is hammered, nailed, and painted inside a neo-international frame that is brimming with what are now retro-American signs and signifiers. All the Americanized signifiers of exotic locales do not, however, turn the social spaces of resort clubs into sites of likewise cogently American cultural practices. Instead, this stylization of leisurely tropical modernity for sale generates a folding narrative. The lifeworld of Ain Diab suggests that having access to spaces of consumer leisure designed in clearly imported aesthetic forms does not inherently alter the local cultural boundaries circumscribing acceptable social behaviors and forms of prohibition. Ain Diab's success as a local tourist attraction and its prominence as the playground of Casablanca's elites indicates the work of style in generating the aura of consumer leisure space. The aura of leisure space is illuminated by architecture, but it is upheld by everyday local interpretations and practices of exclusivity and belonging. The prevalence of class exclusion that forecloses the possibility of participation for the lower classes shifts inside of the leisure clubs. Inside of the resort clubs, the imported forms of architecture and interior design are theatrical props and vast backdrops for the performance of yet more finely nuanced exclusions based on local notions of status and gender. Casablanca's resort district shows off the limitations as well as the malleability of style in determining the social order of culturally defined leisure space. The highly stylized resort scene in Ain Diab is thus simultaneously a dynamic architectural display of cultural métissage and a coherently organized social space shaped by localized expressions of Moroccan culture.

Notes

1. Audre Lorde, *The Marvelous Arithmetics of Distance: Poems 1987–1992* (New York: W. W. Norton and Company, 1994).
2. Douglas Porch, *The Conquest of Morocco* (New York: Alfred A. Knopf, 1982), 24.
3. David Harvey, *Spaces of Hope* (Berkeley: University of California Press, 2000).
4. Jean-Louis Cohen and Monique Eleb, *Casablanca: Colonial Myths and Architectural Ventures* (New York: Monacelli Press, 2001), 262.
5. Cohen and Eleb, *Casablanca*, 266.
6. Cohen and Eleb, *Casablanca*, 266.
7. Richard Longstreth, *The Drive-in, the Supermarket, and the Transformation of Commercial Space in Los Angeles, 1914–1941* (Cambridge, Mass.: MIT Press, 1999). See also Mike Davis, *City of Quartz* (New York: Vintage, 1992).
8. Max Horkheimer and Theodor Adorno, *Dialectic of Enlightenment* (New York: Continuum, 1976).
9. "Kinder" colors are basic or primary colors.
10. Cohen and Eleb, *Casablanca*, 418.
11. Gilles Deleuze, *The Fold: Leibniz and the Baroque* (Minneapolis: University of Minnesota Press, 1992). Martin Heidegger, *The Question Concerning Technology, and Other Essays* (New York: Harper Perennial, 1982).
12. Alan Hess, *Googie: Fifties Coffee Shop Architecture* (San Francisco: Chronicle Books, 1985).
13. Erving Goffman, *The Presentation of Self in Everyday Life* (New York: Doubleday, 1959).
14. See Hai Ren, "The Landscape of Power: Imagineering Consumer Behavior at China's Theme Parks," in this volume.
15. Pierre Bourdieu, *Distinction: A Social Critique of the Judgement of Taste* (Cambridge, Mass.: Harvard University Press, 2002).
16. The "magical third" is a term used by Marx and Hegel to indicate the practical role of people's esoteric nature as cultural beings. Karl Marx, *Capital* (New York: Verso, 1999). G.W.F. Hegel, *Phenomenology of Spirit* (New York: Galaxy Books, 1979).

17. Andre Levy, "Playing for Control of Distance: Card Games between Jews and Muslims on a Casablancan Beach," *American Ethnologist* 26, no. 3 (1999): 632–53.
18. Levy, "Playing for Control of Distance," 641.

Chapter 9

"Above Us Only Sky": Themes, Simulations, and Liverpool John Lennon Airport

Peter Adey

Like themes, simulations are generally understood to be copies. Addressed by philosophers and thinkers including Paul Virilio and Jean Baudrillard, a simulation is understood to be a counterfeit, a reproduction of an original.[1] As spaces that seem to borrow and collect forms, shapes, and meanings from other times and places, themed spaces have been said to be simulated spaces.[2] Recent developments in fields such as the history of science and science and technology studies suggest, however, that simulations do a bit more than this. According to such studies, simulations and models can be comprehended not merely as copies or referents, but mediators.[3] Models and simulators are used to connect theory with empirical reality by applying imagination to the real.[4] By way of modeling simulations, distant and obscure relations impart significance upon one another. It is in this sense that the simulation is a kind of bridge that blurs Euclidian spatiality with a topological relationality.[5]

In this essay I suggest that airports, so often described as themed spaces, actually share some of these bridging characteristics. This might seem blatantly obvious for we know that airports are excellent conduits and mediators by their very purpose; they facilitate movement between the ground and the air with efficiency, albeit some of the time! And yet, I want to argue that the theming of airports permits the mediation of time and distance in a social way. While airports tend to be characterized as placeless non-places, what Marc Augé has defined to be without identity or context, there is a sense that people find it difficult to belong in these sites.[6] I suggest that the art of theming airports marks a double attempt to not only make people belong in them, but to make the airport belong itself.

Part of the chapter focuses on how the theming of airports is, in fact, a rather old thing. The "conceptual framework" of shipping, railway industries, and even the cinema has so often formed the "wish image" of airport development.[7] Theming airports on these lines has made them act and resemble other places and spaces. I focus on the Liverpool Airport—which was built in the 1930s and is located just outside Liverpool in the Northwest of England—as a simulation, as a copy based on the model of Hamburg Fuhlsbüttel. The chapter moves on to look at the redevelopment and rebranding corporate strategy of the modern-day Liverpool Airport. In 2001 the airport was reopened after undergoing a £35 million makeover and name change. With the help of Yoko Ono, the airport officially changed its name to Liverpool John Lennon Airport, becoming the first airport in the United Kingdom to be named after an individual. The words "Above Us Only Sky," taken from the John Lennon song "Imagine," became the airport's slogan. The paper discusses the politics of this brand change. The shift in the airport's identity is understood as an attempt to bring the airport closer to its local societal context and as a ploy to connect with the international and global audience of the Beatles' popularity and fame.

I go on to explore how the theming of John Lennon has become much more than a discursive conveyor of meaning, but the theme is both materialized and performed within the terminal itself. The section investigates how the theme helps visitors form more kinesthetic and sensual connections with the terminal building. In the final section I discuss how even as airports have become remarkably thematized spaces—simulating other times and places—airports like Liverpool's are becoming themes in themselves.

The Airport as a Themed Space

The first airports were undoubtedly simulated spaces. Their designers and planners had little knowledge of what they should and could be. Indeed, the eventual form of the first airports could not hide their makers' confusion as they took on the characteristics of sites as diverse as a railway station to a seaport, from a racetrack to a park. For Smith and Toulier, these were building types "uncertain of their architectural identity."[8] While some initial projects employed the newest technologies and design techniques, their structure and use resembled quite different times and places. It is in this sense that we might understand the first airports as "wish images" as they aspired to belong by repeating the past and emulating other times and spaces.

In the United States, Janet Daly Bednarek tells us how the first American airports were inextricably bound up with the idea of a recreational space or a park.[9] Because of the wide-open space necessary for an airfield, airports were tied to the construction of municipal facilities for the public's enjoyment and use. The way they were used and conceived also reflected their ownership. At this stage, as well as in Europe, many airports were built and belonged to local municipalities. Airports were symbols of civic pride and prestige. Because many people could not afford to fly, airports had to work for the people in quite different ways compared to how they function today. Somewhat ironically, in today's concerns of climate change and environmental impacts, the airport was considered a "lung" for city life, often intercepting parklands, golf courses, and playing fields.

While airports were themed as parkland/green spaces, they took on the recreational typology to an even greater extent in the construction of the first major administrative public buildings. Airports would often construct bleachers, viewing stands, fenced-off areas for spectators to attend aviation galas, air shows and pageants. Hugh Pearman notes how early airports tended to resemble racecourses in their borrowing of the familiar white fencing, and, of course, the circular course layout. Grandstands were also built. As Pearman writes, the resemblance with a racecourse is not so surprising: "They resorted to the facilities and general layout familiar to them from permanent racing circuits and also from fairgrounds, circuses and, to an extent, industrial expositions."[10]

This quite temporary architecture soon became permanent as airports built the design of the temporary air show into the material form of the airport terminal buildings. Many airports constructed staggered viewing terraces that resembled the form of the theater or the cinema on top of the terminal buildings. People could visit the airport, pay a small fee to access the top balconies, and spend the day watching the everyday activities of the airport. Often these designs copied the cinema with their democratic architecture; some airports such as Berlin, Hamburg, and Speke featured a curved form which encased the apron area. In fact, Liverpool's design was a modified simulation of successful examples such as Hamburg Fuhlsbüttel.[11] From almost every point on the balcony, one's view would remain unobstructed. The balcony's proximity to the apron meant that spectators could almost reach out and touch the aircraft. Denis Cosgrove has even compared the airport to the Palladium country mansion with its sweeping vistas of open space.[12]

The theatrics of the stage or the cinema were most clearly repeated in the nightscapes of the airport. Enormous lights not only focused one's attention on the activities below, but the "machinic complex" of electricity, wiring, and bulbs, granted the airport a new special atmosphere as a place that never slept.[13] Floodlights permitted many airports an almost twenty-four hour operation, letting planes land in previously difficult circumstances, colonizing the previously empty spaces of the night. Moreover, the effect of the light reminds one of Wolfgang Schivelbusch's examination of the illumination that displayed the Parisian arcades and shops as spectacle.[14] "No commercial use of projected lights was quite as impressive as airport lighting," according to John A. Jakle.[15] Powerful floodlights constructed the apron and airfield as the illuminated stage, the terminal the darkened theater, and the spectators and passengers became the audience. Indeed, the limits of the floodlights gave the airport a sense of interiority. Where the light ended, darkness provided a wall-like veil that surrounded the airport.

The early airports even resembled other transportation interchanges. This must be attributed to the fact that city surveyors and engineers had very little to go on apart from their own experiences of train stations or even port designs. Municipal authorities tried experimenting with various attempts to merge the airport with the skyscraper, or in Liverpool's instance, the seaport. It was thought that seaplanes offered the future for transatlantic travel as they could stop and potentially replenish reserves at transatlantic refueling points. The initial plans for a Liverpool Airport therefore included the digging out and filling of a lake so that seaplanes could land and take off, even though the idea was eventually dropped.[16]

Maritime and sea themes continued in the developments at Liverpool and a few other airports as the control tower at Speke was designed to resemble a lighthouse. Octagonal in form, the eighty-foot tower was initially built as an iconic structure, later surrounded by the terminal and administration buildings in 1939. The tower, just like a lighthouse, could see all while it was able to project. It had to afford views of the airport and its surrounding airspace, as it needed to be able to transmit information and instructions to aircraft and pilots waiting to land or takeoff. Building airports to resemble older, historical and perhaps local structures could be seen as an attempt to embed the airport in spite of its embodiment of technological modernity. In Liverpool's case, the airport harked back to the prominence of the city's docks and port industry. Alastair Gordon describes how the much maligned pseudo-Moorish architecture used for Boeing Airport in Burbank California, "evoked an aura of the past in a part of the country that was self-conscious about its lack of history."[17]

Other airports resembled the form of transport technologies. Jersey airport, in particular, was thought to closely mimic the shape of a ship. Like many airports of its time, Jersey contained stacked modeling similar to that of the bridge of a ship. Neil Bingham writes how "the buildings' white render imparts the illusion of a liner afloat at sea." Moreover, this comparison found its culmination in "the addition of promenades, deck chairs and a snack bar for holiday makers who drifted over from the beach as the summer sun waned."[18]

In many cases the aircraft itself provided the greatest inspiration to the theming of the airport terminal.[19] The 1930s art deco-style airports celebrated the principles of speed and modernity by paying homage to "the very machine around which the building revolved—[the] aeroplane."[20] Smooth clean lines were wrought in plaster, metal work, and brick as the airport terminal became "an extension of the flying machine aesthetic that, as Le Corbusier proclaimed, was the 'exemplification of the new machine civilization.'"[21] Terminals such as Liverpool's were further decorated with winged creatures gesturing towards the flight the buildings made possible. Today, the aerofoil cross section of the aircraft wing permeates airport building design, usually finding its way into the shape of the roof. At other airports the aircraft itself has been reproduced through the layout of recent terminals such as

Norman Foster's Hong Kong International.

The theming of the early airports and aerodromes helped them build successful terminals with familiar built architectural geographies that echoed the machine age; and they may have helped the airports to belong. They diverged from the functional utility we might associate with the terminals of today and acted as recreational centers where one could enjoy a day out, become inspired by the open-air surroundings, or enthuse in the aircraft that passed by on the apron below. In belonging, these airports acted as social destinations, perhaps rendezvous for an evening dinner and a dance. People could not necessarily afford to pass through these sites by aircraft, but they could certainly travel to them.[22] Thus, despite aviation being the pursuit of a privileged few, through its use the airport became a site of collective and public engagement.

In today's airports the focus and theme is now quite different as airports have become palaces of consumption. Mark Gottdiener tells us how today's airports emulate other geographies in an attempt to become places in themselves.[23] Although I will discuss this in more detail later, airports are using their role as simulations in a way to encourage consumer spending through the consumption of the airport's simulated geographies. Criticisms have been leveled that they lack a sense of identity, reveling in their international nature by featuring the latest homogenizing global brands. Starbucks, Burger King, McDonalds can be found in almost any airport. At the same time, themed airports almost paradoxically appropriate elements of their local cultures. Perhaps here they have taken on the role of the railway station which acted as a suitable gateway to the city. The focus, however, tends to be always one of consumption.[24] Shops, restaurants, and stores are themed according to the airport's host culture; passengers are told where they are by the product being offered to them. Other airports express this through their architectural symbolism, often through the use of synecdoche. Denver's Jeppensen terminal is a case in point as the white fabric roof design is meant to resemble the snowcapped peaks of the nearby Rockies.

In short, the theming of the airport has occurred for a number of different reasons and in a number of different ways. What unites these themes is the way geography is deployed. The themed spaces of the airport connect to other spaces and other times. In the following section, I focus on the newly redeveloped Liverpool John Lennon Airport to explore how these geographies have become routed through the biographical theme of John Lennon.

The Airport as a Biographical Simulation

Liverpool Airport was reopened and rebranded Liverpool John Lennon Airport on March 15, 2002. John Lennon's widow, Yoko Ono, and the British Prime Minister's wife Cherie Blair opened the proceedings by celebrating the announced rebranding of the airport. Some months later the redeveloped terminal was reopened by the Queen. The words "Above Us Only Sky" from the John Lennon hit "Imagine" were attached to the airport's frontage. Trinkets such as mugs, keyrings, posters, and T-shirts could be bought from the tourist information center featuring Lennon's sketched self-portrait. On their way through the terminal, passengers were confronted by a bronze statue of Lennon sculpted by Liverpool artist Tom Murphy. The terminal had been transformed from what was known colloquially as a cattle shed—a term owing to its rather utilitarian construction—to a contemporary design featuring polished limestone surfaces and a light atmosphere facilitated by a glass curtain frontage.

Of course, Liverpool is not the only airport to be named after a person. While it was the first in the United Kingdom, airports across the globe have been named after various dignified individuals, politicians and celebrities. Rome's Leonardo Da Vinci, Paris's Charles De Gaulle, New York's JFK, Orange County California's John Wayne, George Bush Houston Intercontinental Airport, and Washington's Ronald Reagan National are among the most famous of these examples. Liverpool's renaming has stimulated this trend within the United Kingdom as several other airports have now been rebranded. Cases in point are Doncaster's Finningley renamed Doncaster Robin Hood Airport, and Belfast's City becoming George Best Belfast City Airport, named after the late Manchester United star.

News of Liverpool's rebranding became a global story overnight. Vectors of media communication in print, sound, and vision transmitted the airport's fortunes worldwide. From national news updates and news channels, to aviation industry mailing lists and online magazines, to Internet musical discussion groups, and even *Rolling Stone*, the renaming projected the airport into the local and global consciousness. As a corporate marketing exercise the rebranding enabled the airport to mediate between and collapse geographical scales and distances. The airport was able to force its way into the global audience that John Lennon and the Beatles had fostered and entertained. At a local level, the airport raised its awareness within the local Merseyside region and the rest of the country, who were unaware of the airport's existence as a fairly small operation hosted by a provincial city. But by connecting these scales the airport did not only raise awareness but it helped stimulate a sense of belonging and ownership.

I discussed the strategy behind the rebranding with an airport spokesperson who stated, "It's giving them something—like the name John Lennon Airport—giving them something slightly different that they can relate to, they can be proud of. I think this is what it comes down to."[25] Indeed, it was seen that only by having the newly built terminal would Lennon's widow, Yoko Ono, ever agree to the rebranding:

> Now is the right time. No point in taking the decision if it was the wrong time, if we've got nothing to sell. But we've grown and Yoko Ono has allowed us to use the name and use the lyrics. She might have not if it had been simply the same corrugated iron terminal; it had to be something good which she could be proud of.[26]

The renaming and rebranding of the airport helped connect the terminal to local interests and issues in a way that was intended to make people feel that the airport was their own. The idea was to allow people to relate to the airport. Again, this strategy was definitely not original. At several times in the airport's history, the local authority management had attempted to make people feel at home in the airport. The airport had been constructed as something that the citizens of Liverpool owned and had an obligation to use. Poorly supported air shows and pageants did their best to promote this. Rerouting this strategy through the John Lennon theme—the simulation of one of Liverpool's favorite sons—reinforced the sense that the airport was something owned by the locality.

"Why fly from Manchester" (Liverpool's nearest rival airport) "when you can from your own airport." Such phrases proliferated local billboards and the media. Within the terminal building, the theme of John Lennon was supplemented with themes of a local character. The airport's conference room was designated the Cavern Suite. Surrounded by photos of the Beatles, the room was named after the Fab Four's famous haunt the Cavern Club. Similarly, the estuary bar labeled the bar that looked over the Mersey Estuary it was named after, the Aintree food village after the nearby racecourse, just as a new pub was named the Argosy, one of the first aircraft to serve the airport in an experimental Imperial Airways service in the late 1920s. Marketing strategies similarly use the feelings of pride, attachment and ownership associated with the city and John Lennon. Even airline advertising played upon the celebrated football rivalry between Liverpool and Manchester's famous club Manchester United.

Embodying the Theme

As the themed environment of the airport is displayed and communicated at a symbolic and representational level, there are also ways in which the biographical theming of the airport was embodied and performed in a manner that stimulated passenger engagement with the new building. As Katherine N. Hayles tells us, simulations share their bases not just in the imagined and codified but also in the materially real world.[27] It is therefore necessary to consider how the airport, as a simulation of John Lennon, has come to inflect specific social practices and material and affective geographies.

The statue of John Lennon must be considered here for its placement and design is important as people engage with the statue on a frequent basis—it has become an important part of the airport landscape. In opposition to the sculpture *Vagamundo* that sits immobile in Madrid Barajas airport, the sculpture of John Lennon is far from immobilized but acts as an active participant in the airport building.[28] The sculpture is cast in bronze and, similarly to *Vagamundo*, appears static relative to the passengers that pass by it. Indeed, materially the sculpture is just as immobile as *Vagamundo*. However, looking beyond the corporeal, the artist who designed and sculpted it—originally out of clay before it was molded as bronze—attempted to infuse some kind of latent energy or potential into the sculpture. When I interviewed the sculptor he described how he was trying to give the sculpture a feeling that it was almost moving, that it was almost mobile:

> I definitely wanted that energy into it. You know that big striding pace . . . big strides . . . there's a name for it; that sort of John Lennon charisma if you like, that "enigmafying" and also there's also other aspect[s] to it . . . it's got that sort of, what do they call? They used to call it the "Liverpool swagger" which used to come from the docks and the navy influence. . . . You know the head's sort of ahead, the chest forward and that naval sort of walk . . . with the twists of the body, the jacket is sort of flowing off, so it's going through as if he's moving through space.[29]

According to the artist, he was attempting to create something which he likened to the potential of a coiled spring, a potential that could give life to the sculpture: "There's a kind of tension in them. I often say like a coiled spring, where the thing is ready to liftoff . . . because of stability problems and you know vandalism and the rest of it, sculptures are often . . . they look bolted down and the figures look heavy and dead."[30]

Given this very mobile form, the sculpture was placed on the bridge and was intended as a landmark not only for press interviews to be conducted, but its placement was intended to draw people through the building. Moreover, the sculpture had specific implications for the way the terminal was inhabited. The artist recalled how he would have preferred it to be in another area of the building where it could provide more of a focal point, yet, according to the artist, "It sort of grabs people . . . it jars slightly, in places. And which is the nature of John Lennon I guess . . . and it is a statue that greets people I think, that wait in the airport for the plane that doesn't arrive, or when they are leaving."[31]

Perhaps because of the animation or the motion of the figure, the sculpture also provides a site of engagement between people and the building. The artist recalled how people tend to take photos of the statue as they walk past it: "Yeah, you go up the stairs and go past it, and . . . it's a surprise to people who haven't been to the airport. Because years ago upstairs it was the cafeteria or something, and the bar, and I think the nice thing is that people have got their camera handy, they're always going to take photos of it."[32] In this sense the theme enables the appropriation of the airport by passengers who literally capture and take more than an image of the airport "but pieces of it, or even miniature slices of reality" away with them—just as postcards, mugs, and keyrings with Lennon's image can also be bought from the airport information center.[33]

Furthermore, many passengers do not merely react to the statue with a passive and distanciated gaze, but many become kinaesthetically involved in the sculpture. More often than not, passengers having their photo taken put their arm around it, or they sit at its base. Others pose with the statue by emulating Lennon's flowing walk or by acting with it; some pretend to strike up a conversation with the inanimate form. In many instances, Lennon's statue affects laughter and smiles, for others it is curiosity as they study the intricacies of the artwork. For some young children, the statue is frightening, which they express through tears or aversion. In short, passengers internalize and embody the theming of Liverpool John Lennon Airport. The theme is not just something to be seen, or comprehended, but it is sensed, felt, and taken within—it is internalized.

The Airport as Theme

Within contemporary social theory a proliferating body of work has used the airport to exemplify the globalized world in which we live.[34] The airport, it seems, is the epitome of placeless places.[35] Airports provide useful analogies for the sorts of connections and interstices that run across the globe.[36] Elsewhere, it has been used as a metaphor to explain nomadic theory.[37] Similarly, there are ways that airports, such as Liverpool John Lennon, are becoming themes in and of themselves. The branding of the airport has become such a success that the airport is being simulated and deployed in other situations and other geographies. The most obvious example of this theming of the theme can be found in the simultaneous rebranding of the airport's host, the City of Liverpool.

Yet again, this is not necessarily a new thing. The development of the original airport was the jewel in the crown of a set of projects aimed at rejuvenating Liverpool's interwar economy. The airport's development was tied up in the construction of a new Speke housing estate which was intended to alleviate the poor housing conditions of the nineteenth-century inner city slums. The Speke area was intended as a whole package of redevelopment for Liverpool. The airport, according to Lord Woolton (a trained sociologist committed to solving the problems of Liverpool's unemployment), could help stimulate discussion, publicity, and hopefully encourage inward investment to the area.[38] By building an airport, the city could align itself with the coming of an aerial age, and, thereby, advance its association with progress, speed and efficiency.

Even more so today, the airport is being used as a way to sell the city. Several rebranding exercises have been aimed at regenerating the economic and social fortunes of postindustrial Liverpool and the Merseyside region. Groups such as the Mersey Partnership, which promote Liverpool for inward investment, theme their promotional literature of the city with the airport. The airport's success as one of the fastest-growing airports in the world means that it acts as a good news story which the partnership uses to promote the city. The continual change and dynamism of the airport are employed as themes with which the city may be associated.

A respondent from the partnership expressed how the airport is used "as a kind of metaphor as it illustrates the continual dynamics. The fact that we always use about the airport is the rate of growth, over the years."[39] In other words, the fast growth of the terminal themes the city of Liverpool as a suitable site for investment. For the respondent it acts as "a kind of sign of the dynamic growth of the economy."[40] Billboards, mailings, and Web site advertisements feature images of the airport—perhaps at night—where the lit-up terminal affords an image of spectacle and technology; in others, time-lapse photos demonstrate the continual motion of the site.

The incessant movement of the airport's progression is partnered with the mobility it affords as an important theme for the city. Liverpool's status as a city about to become the European Capital of Culture for 2008 was founded upon the principal of the city's both historic and contemporary cosmopolitanism. The central theme of the city's bid for this status was given the name "The World in One City," representing the diverse communities that make up the locality.[41] Part of the bid included a range of events aimed at Liverpool's diversity and its international connections. The airport featured as both facilitator and theme in this bid. The airport's growing connections to various international destinations was publicized as a way to progress the city's branding. The airport could afford quick and efficient links with several of the cities Liverpool had twinned with and shared roots with historically.[42] In this sense, the airport—as a nexus of links, communications, and flows—was a driving theme in the proposal that celebrated how the city "bridges continents and cultures." The airport could physically and metaphorically help the city "explore the creative and historic threads that connect Liverpool with some of Europe's other most culturally vibrant and edgy port cities."[43]

The airport also sells the city through its previous incarnation. If one looks a few miles down the road from the John Lennon terminal, they will come across the original art deco Speke airport. Except now, people cannot fly from the site; they still pass through it, but they usually do so while spending a night there. The old terminal building has become a four-star Marriott hotel, sympathetically extended, refurbished, and restored to its original art deco style. The hotel successfully mediates between the past and the present by capturing the glamor and spectacle of the dawning aerial age, a considerable attraction for guests. Faux walnut walls and vintage carpets line the corridors, meanwhile the bar areas are designed like first-class airport lounges. Staff, dressed as in-flight stewards from the 1930s, perform the theme by serving patrons in the Starways restaurant that overlooks the apron while they peruse the airline-styled menus. If hotel patrons fancy a swim or a workout in the gym, they are pointed to the nearby leisure facility housed in the elaborately decorated building next door that was once one of the main aircraft hangars.

The Future of the Themed Airport

Many themed environments are marked by the way they compress the near and the far, the local and the global, into some kind of random and incoherent pastiche. Such sites can become decontextualized by emphasizing the superficial aesthetics of the far-off and exotic while severing ties and connections to the local and nearby.[44] This kind of "splintering glocalism" may serve to alienate local communities through its attempt to lure investments, tourists, and business people from valued far-off places.[45] At the same time, theming can do quite the opposite by celebrating local connections. Local identities, values, and civic pride can be stimulated by fostering more communal links. In this essay I have suggested that we might think of the themed environment of Liverpool John Lennon Airport as a means of connecting, not through its facilitation of aircraft and passenger mobilities, but as a simulation that draws upon various meanings and narratives in order to mediate social and material geographies. It connects to the far-off, the distant and the valued, while it simultaneously mediates relationships between the airport and the locality, or to the personal, embodied, and the affective. Echoing Justine Lloyd, the airport is a kind of "global-national-local" and, I might add bodily, "junctural zone."[46]

Why might it do this? The answer lies in the airport's need to belong for several different reasons. The first airports needed to be used very differently in order to sustain their financial solvency and the responsibility of citizens to visit them. Today, with private ownership and commercial pressures, an airport is a business that must make a profit. Creating a brand that can project the airport globally and also locally means the possibilities of increased passenger throughput and increased revenue for the airport

We might conclude that this process of connection and mediation is increasingly one of expansion and, perhaps, saturation. Scholars have suggested that themed spaces may encompass the sites and delights of the world, what Margaret Crawford has argued may be exemplified as "The World in a Shopping Mall."[47] Yet, as the airport terminal becomes a theme in itself—combined with creeping surveillance technologies normally associated with the spaces of airport security—there is a sense that the airport is exceeding its boundaries. The airport may be fulfilling Reyner Banham's derogatory metaphor by acting like a "demented amoeba" that cannot help but escape its own confines, destined to endless fabrication and Baudrillardian simulation.[48] Indeed, the whole world is an airport.

Notes

1. Jean Baudrillard, *Simulations* (New York City: Semiotext(e), 1983); Paul Virilio, *War and Cinema: The Logistics of Perception* (London: Verso, 1989).

2. Michael Sorkin, "See You in Disneyland," in *Variations on a Theme Park*, ed. Michael Sorkin (New York: Hill and Wang, 1992), 205–32; Edward W. Soja, *Postmodern Geographies: The Reassertion of Space in Critical Social Theory* (London: Verso, 1989).

3. Mary S. Morgan and Margaret Morrison, *Models as Mediators: Perspectives on Natural and Social Science, Ideas in Context 52* (Cambridge: Cambridge University Press, 1999).

4. Sergio Sismondo, Snait Gissis, and Arthur C. Peterson, "Modeling and Simulation," *Social Studies of Science* 30, no. 5 (2000): 793–99.

5. John Law and Anne-Marie Mol, "Situating Technoscience: An Inquiry into Spatialities," *Environment and Planning D-Society & Space* 19, no. 5 (2001): 609–21.

6. Marc Augé, *Non-Places: Introduction to an Anthropology of Supermodernity* (London: Verso, 1995).

7. Susan Buck-Morss, *The Dialectics of Seeing: Walter Benjamin and the Arcades Project* (Cambridge, Mass.: MIT Press, 1989).

8. Paul Smith and Bernard Toulier, "Introduction," in *Berlin, Liverpool, Paris: Airport Architecture of the Thirties*, ed. P. Smith and B. Toulier (London: Gingko Press, 2000), 16.

9. Janet R. Daly Bednarek, *America's Airports: Airfield Development, 1918–1947* (College Station: Texas A&M University Press, 2001); Janet R. Daly Bednarek, "The Flying Machine in the Garden—Parks and Airports, 1918–1938," *Technology and Culture* 46, no. 2 (2005): 350–73.

10. Hugh Pearman, *Airports: A Century of Architecture* (London: Laurence King, 2004), 38.

11. Roger Bowdler, "Liverpool Speke," in *Berlin, Liverpool, Paris: Airport Architecture of the Thirties*, ed. P. Smith and B. Toulier (Paris: Ginko Press, 2003); Peter Adey, "'May I Have Your Attention': Airport Geographies of Spectatorship, Position and (Im)Mobility," *Environment and Planning D-Society & Space* 25, no. 3: 515–36.

12. Denis E. Cosgrove, "Airport/Landscape," in *Recovering Landscape: Essays in Contemporary Landscape Architecture*, ed. James Corner (New York: Princeton Architectural Press, 1999), 221–32.

13. Nigel Thrift. "Inhuman Geographies: Landscapes of Speed, Light and Power," in *Spatial Formations*, ed. Nigel Thrift (London: Sage, 1996).

14. Wolfgang Schivelbusch, *Disenchanted Night: The Industrialisation of Light in the Nineteenth Century* (New York: Berg, 1988).

15. John A. Jakle, *City Lights: Illuminating the American Night, Landscapes of the Night* (Baltimore: Johns Hopkins University Press, 2001), 189.

16. Phil H. Butler, *Liverpool Airport: An Illustrated History* (London: Tempus Publishing, 2004).

17. Alastair Gordon, *Naked Airport: A Cultural History of the World's Most Revolutionary Structure* (New York: Metropolitan Books, 2004), 60.

18. Neil Bingham, "Arrivals and Departures: Civil Airport Architecture in Britain During the Inter-War Period," in *The Architecture of British Transport in the Twentieth Century*, ed. Julian Holder and Steven Parissien (New Haven, Conn.: Yale University Press, 2004), 106–32.

19. Pearman, *Airports*.
20. Bingham, "Arrivals and Departures," 107.
21. Bingham, "Arrivals and Departures," 107.
22. Peter Adey, "Airports and Air-Mindedness: Spacing, Timing and Using Liverpool Airport 1929-39," *Social and Cultural Geography* 7, no. 3 (2006): 343-63.
23. Mark Gottdiener, *Life in the Air: Surviving the New Culture of Air Travel* (Lanham, Md.: Rowman and Littlefield, 2000).
24. Jennifer Rowley, and Francis Slack, "The Retail Experience in Airport Departure Lounges: Reaching for Timelessness and Placelessness," *International Marketing Review* 16 (1999): 363-75.
25. Interview with author, Airport Spokesperson, 2004.
26. Interview with author, Airport Spokesperson, 2004.
27. N. Katherine Hayles, *Writing Machines, A Mediawork Pamphlet* (Cambridge, Mass.: MIT Press, 2002). The Beatles are a popular source of thematic inspiration. Plans have been announced for a Beatles-themed hotel. Tony McDonough, "Why He's Working Like a Dog to Launch Beatles-Theme Hotel," *Daily Post* (Liverpool), 19 July 2006.
28. David Pascoe, *Airspaces* (London: Reaktion, 2001).
29. Interview with author, Liverpool Artist, 2004.
30. Interview with author, Liverpool Artist, 2004.
31. Interview with author, Liverpool Artist, 2004.
32. Interview with author, Liverpool Artist, 2004.
33. John Urry, *The Tourist Gaze : Leisure and Travel in Contemporary Societies* (London: Sage, 1990).
34. Peter Adey, "Surveillance at the Airport: Surveilling Mobility/Mobilising Surveillance," *Environment and Planning A* 36, no. 8 (2004): 1365-80.
35. Hans Ibelings, *Supermodernism: Architecture in the Age of Globalization* (Rotterdam: NAI, 1998).
36. Michel Serres, *Angels, a Modern Myth* (Paris: Flammarion, 1995).
37. Rosi Braidotti, *Nomadic Subjects: Embodiment and Sexual Difference in Contemporary Feminist Theory, Gender and Culture* (New York: Columbia University Press, 1994).
38. 1st Marquis, Frederick James Earl of Woolton, *The Memoirs of the Rt. Hon. The Earl of Woolton* (London: Cassell, 1959).
39. Interview with author, Mersey Partnership Spokesperson, 2004.
40. Interview with author, Mersey Partnership Spokesperson, 2004.
41. Department for Culture Media and Sport, "Report on the Short-Listed Applications for the UK Nomination for European Capital of Culture 2008," 2003.
42. Quentin Hughes, *Seaport: Architecture and Townscape in Liverpool* (Liverpool, UK: Bluecoat Press, 1993).
43. The Liverpool Culture Company, "The Story Unfolds," Liverpool, 2003.
44. Michael Dear and Steven Flusty, "Postmodern Urbanism," *Annals of the Association of American Geographers* 88, no. 1 (1998): 50-72.
45. Steve Graham and Simon Marvin, *Splintering Urbanism: Networked Infrastructures, Technological Mobilities and the Urban Condition* (London: Routledge, 2001).
46. Justine Lloyd, "Dwelltime: Airport Technology, Travel, and Consumption," *Space and Culture* 6, no. 2 (2003): 106.
47. Margaret Crawford, "The World in a Shopping Mall," in *Variations on a Theme Park: The New American City and the End of Public Space*, ed. Michael Sorkin (New York: Hill and Wang, 1994), 3-30. Crawford's multifaceted discussion of the shopping mall in-

cludes considerations of the mall as a utopian space of consumption, as a form of magic, as a space for public life, and as a global phenomenon.

48. Reyner Banham, "The Obsolescent Airport," *Architectural Review* October (1962): 250–60.

Chapter 10

Love Hotels: Sex and the Rhetoric of Themed Spaces

Derek Foster

The hotel, like any other element of our contemporary landscape, can be themed. Indeed, in Japan, there is a unique variant of the themed hotel known broadly as *rabu hoteru*. These "love hotels" offer rooms as simulations or artificially re-created milieus designed to connote disparate fantasy spaces, "not in the interest of historical or everyday accuracy, but for the purposes of entertainment and commerce."[1] These are especially interesting social spaces because sex is the specific entertainment purpose that defines these hotel rooms. Consequently, much can be learned from an examination of how love hotels thematize sex. It will become clear that these themed hotels are overdetermined sites of amusement, consumption, relaxation, and titillation. They are coded as alternative, proscribed spaces insofar as their themes (and indeed the structures themselves) connote sex and licentious behavior in general. At the same time, love hotels operate as bastions of freedom from the mundane routines of everyday life. This tension defines love hotels in Japanese society, a tension that can be understood by approaching these themed landscapes as material instances of visual rhetoric. I will demonstrate how the themed environment of the love hotel provides a landscape constituted out of symbolic and material resources that are consciously chosen to allow people to escape their quotidian existences. As individuals use these as antidotes to their day-to-day reality, the wider Japanese culture uses them to redefine notions of propriety and excess. Therefore, love hotels demonstrate how themed spaces both employ and can be employed as symbolic inducements that help define marginality and normality. They are themed spaces whose fakery is understood as both threat and necessity.

Describing the Love Hotel

As one travel guide asserted, these establishments are "perfectly fine, if a little twee, for overnight accommodation."[2] This describes the dominant mode of love hotels' operation and motifs (regardless of theme); they are consciously distinct in an overdone or affected way. Rooms in love hotels are made available to visitors for two or three hour "rest" periods during the day but also for an overnight "stay" at special rates usually following 10 p.m. It is assumed that while these hotels are not generally sites for the procurement of sex, the rooms in these establishments are to be used for sexual escapades. The rationale for such hotels comes from typical Japanese living conditions in which close proximity with other family members makes unrestrained sexual freedom or even spontaneous sexuality a rare occurrence. With almost paper-thin walls between apartments and sliding doors between rooms that are more symbolic than real partitions, it has been reported that significant numbers of Japanese wives and husbands are "always" or "usually" bothered by the thought that children or others living with them might be aware of their intercourse. Thus, "with little privacy from growing children and/or the husband's widowed mother, the love hotel is for many Japanese virtually the only haven of sexual intimacy there is."[3]

The theming of these establishments is a crucial component of their popularity: "There are an estimated 35,000 such love hotels in Japan, often gaudy affairs shaped like ocean liners or castles and offering such extras as rotating beds, mirrored walls, video-cameras [sic], and fantasy-provoking decor."[4] Though notoriously difficult to accurately document how popular love hotels are, a common statistic suggests nearly five hundred million couples visit them each year. This equates to nearly 1.4 million couples using a love hotel per day, which reportedly is more than double the annual number of combined visitors to Tokyo Disneyland and Tokyo Disney Sea.[5] They are unlike other hotels in that their function is coded through an obvious symbolization and materialization of sex. This can be seen through comparison with other hotels. For instance, apart from the standard, western-style accommodation offered by luxury and resort style hotels, other Japanese options include "business hotels," "capsule hotels," and *ryokan*. Generally less accommodating to foreigners, business hotels typically offer futons and tatami mat floors for sleeping and Japanese style baths. Capsule hotels, meanwhile, are even more impersonal, typically $3\ 1/2 \times 3\ 1/2 \times 7\ 1/4$ feet long holes in the wall with only an alarm clock, a TV, and phone as amenities, and a very flimsy barrier separating you from other sleepers. Because of the setting, these are divided along gender lines and often exclusively for male patrons. Finally, another distinctive form of Japanese hotel is the *ryokan* whose motif is "traditional Japanese culture." In a sense, *ryokan* are also themed environments meant to entertain whose meanings are conveyed characteristically through symbols and allusion. They communicate meanings through traditional architecture, interior design, apparel, and rituals of greeting and eating— all invoke a Japan that is sincere, courteous, time-honored, and conventional.

While all these hotels offer distinct motifs that thematize escape in different fashions, the love hotel is unique in that its theming of escape is inextricably tied to sex. How is sex themed? For the most part, love hotels depend on somewhat gaudy exteriors and a typical bricolage of libertine interior facades and spaces. The symbolic and the material landscapes upon which love hotels traditionally depend are wide-ranging. "Traditional" accoutrements may include gilt or silvered splendor and royal red velveteen backdrops, colored spotlights, and twinkling chrome and glass chandeliers. Rococo vinyl, pinball gothic, and automotive chinoiserie might exist alongside S&M paraphernalia, sing-along karaoke, Jacuzzis, and palatial sunken baths. Plusher love hotels can feature beds modeled like Venetian gondolas, hearts, pineapples, jet planes, and assorted space craft.[6] Indeed, the buildings themselves are sign vehicles declaring their social function. One travel guide describes them as a "wonderful hybrid which can be a source of cheap accommodation for the adventurous. . . . They are immediately recognizable from their ornate exteriors, incorporating cupids, crenellations, or, most incongruously, the Statue of Liberty. . . . They're not as sleazy as they sound."[7] Another guide speaks to the artifice that is central to the love hotel's symbolic regime: "To find a love hotel on the street, just look for flamboyant facades with rococo architecture, turrets, battlements and imitation statuary."[8]

Situating the Love Hotel among other Themed Spaces

Mark Gottdiener's analysis of the Mall of America might easily apply to the love hotel: "The simulated environment is simply a cartoonish facade. . . . Apart from the skillful deployment of images it has no relation to any real places or cultures around the globe."[9] In a sense, love hotels also are like Orvar Löfgren's description of Las Vegas attractions. Both "combine the burlesque and the baroque in a totally uninhibited mix of styles, images, and effects" and both immerse visitors in "constant sensual bombardment."[10] And, though some might perceive love hotels to be uniformly tacky or even seedy, Nicholas Bornoff also notes "the oft-heard analogy with Disneyland is more than superficially apt [as] the love hotel has about it an air of childishness, of innocence, which not even a strong undercurrent of rapacious commercialism can wholly belie."[11] Like these other themed landscapes, a love hotel "cannot be judged on its historical authenticity. It creates a new world, mining history for a few building blocks but elaborating on the facts."[12] Love hotel rooms conjure the spirits of times and places that never were, reproducing just enough of a theme to make it recognizable and then stretching it to serve the purposes of the profit-driven facility and the pleasure-driven clientele.

Nothing in a love hotel is a concrete fragment of the past; the decorations are not meant as representations but as creative embodiments of such times and places. Indeed, more than just references to the past or far-off times and/or places, they provide spaces of and for the imagination, as the hybridized kink of Hello Kitty/S&M-themed rooms demonstrates.[13] With the omnipresent sexual paraphernalia and decorations, the themed landscape becomes imbued with pleasure and sexual gratification while the aesthetics and the material embodiment of the themed space becomes almost secondary to the experience of play and leisure that presumably motivated one to visit the hotel in the first place. After all, there is also the consideration that some venture to a love hotel just for the pleasure of another's company and/or the experience of unrestricted sex, quite apart from the theme. So, far from critiquing such establishments for their patent artificiality, we ought to recognize that the love hotel "isn't the mimicry of a thing; it's a thing."[14] Everything in the environment is self-consciously fabricated and obviously fake. The themed spaces of love hotels are not meant to be something else but exist simply to connote it, to allude to it so that the essence of such far-off (or far-out) places might attach itself to patrons, corporeally, for the duration of their short stay.

It is important to note, however, that love hotels are not simply quixotic examples of hotels that combine the opulent and the outrageously kitsch. Many other hotels are decorated both inside and out with evocative signs and symbols. And many other hotels—especially "no-tell motels"—are used for secretive rendezvous. But whereas the former are flamboyant and the latter are meant for discrete trysts, love hotels are both. Because of this association with sex and the audacious symbolization of this function, love hotels are typically thought of as something akin to a brothel, though, "like the restaurant, the coffee shop or the public toilet, the love hotel is a purely pragmatic answer to a basic physical need."[15] However, love hotels differ from themed restaurants such as the Hard Rock Cafe and the Planet Hollywood franchises where, "other than their themed environments, there is little to differentiate them from any other local American diner in nearly every town in the United States."[16] Love hotels are different from other hotels in three distinctive ways. First, they offer "stays" and "rests." Also, love hotels are wild departures from the hotel norm of standardized rooms that are clean, sanitary, and safe. While this can depend on the theme of the individual room, it is not the overall themed environment of the hotel that usually makes all the difference. Themed franchises like the Hard Rock, Planet Hollywood, or Rainforest Cafe are like the Holiday Inn or McDonalds in that visitors experience a comforting rhetoric of familiarity when one encounters similar if not highly uniform symbolic regimes. For most love hotels, this is not the case and one can reasonably expect nothing other than an environment that facilitates indulgence in sexual pleasure (which can take on many forms). Unless one is a repeat visitor to the same room, part of the thrill of visiting a love hotel is that one never knows exactly what to expect. Finally, perhaps the most distinguishing characteristic of love hotels is their provision of privacy, inextricably tied to patrons' need to escape.

Beyond the need for short-term accommodation to which all hotels cater, love hotels are places where one's stay should be pleasurable, where that pleasure is made to coincide with sex, and where sex is themed as an escape. They are, thus, action places in which the individual can let off steam and engage in licensed revelry. These are places of controlled excitement—escape centers in which the rules of everyday life are relaxed and the boundaries of social behaviors are rolled back.[17] It is this theme of sex as pleasure-filled escape that defines the love hotel. Love hotels do more than merely symbolize the need for a momentary escape from the constraints of everyday life—they materially embody this need.

Love Hotels as Escapist Fantasy

After a brief description of love hotels, *Eyewitness Travel Guides Japan* states, "the most entertaining offer thematic decor as an additional turn-on."[18] This is a very important note, for it is not the theming of the accommodation that distinguishes the love hotel—it is the theming of sex. Indeed, the moniker *love hotel* has always seemed somewhat of a euphemism to describe the main reason for patronizing such establishments. In the public imagination they are, ultimately, closer to other sex-related establishments than hotels meant strictly for short-term stays. They are paragons of pleasure-zone architecture with their explicit semiotics promising fantasies of exotic times and places or, at the very least, pleasure for pleasure's sake. Some love hotel themes are explicit with rooms sharing a consistent motif. These tend to be higher-end hotels. Establishments fashioned after Alcatraz, Peter Mayle's best-selling French-themed novel *A Year in Provence*, and ocean liners are obvious examples. But sometimes the baser qualities of peddling pleasure mean that the theme is sex itself. Or, the theme is pleasure, which demands privacy since it depends on base carnality. The theme, in these cases, is not pleasure through fantasy, per se, but simply pleasure through escape. Ultimately, this is the theme that ties together all love hotels.

Of course, there are specific motifs to which love hotels resort in their quest to provide escapist fantasies for their customers. Rooms in love hotels have traditionally followed the same pattern that Gottdiener notes: "Despite the wide availability of fantasies produced by the media, only a select number of themes are materialized in space."[19] The usual suspects in love hotels include motifs of the tropical paradise, the American Wild West, and especially classical civilizations of Greece and Rome. Other themes are meant to tap into codes that reflect some desirable fantasy aspect of Japanese culture. These other symbolic regimes have no apparent unifying base—some represent contemporary American phenomena (such as NASCAR racing), others are built around cartoon characters such as Hello Kitty, Winnie the Pooh, and Mickey Mouse. Still others depend on vaguely exotic but non-specific locales such as UFOs, jungles, and pirate adventures. However, it seems significant that, unlike many other themed spaces, nostalgia plays a very marginal role here. Love hotels are not places in which contemporary landscapes rearticulate the past in a way that makes the old new (or even more familiar to one's current life, or even "knowable" in any concrete sense). Love hotels "queer" landscapes of the past—they deliver exotic landscapes that are part of our present but which are far removed from the typical Japanese experience, and they invent spaces of the imagination that problematize aspects of popular culture in order to provide new and exciting fantasy places. When cartoon characters become an opportunity for bondage play, it should be clear that, far from a desire for community, love hotels are defined by their provision of a "much-needed holiday from the normal routines of everyday life."[20]

Thus, it is not a search for meaning and connections to fantasies and symbols that best characterize the themed spaces of the love hotel. Rather, it is the retreat from the meanings and commitments of everyday life and its quotidian routines that define love hotels. Love hotels offer an antidote to any environment whose allure is based on an attachment to time or place. Unlike Starbucks stores that "provide the rhetorical resources for creating coherency in the context of the seeming cultural chaos that is constitutive of postmodernity," Japanese love hotels are an oasis in a world of traditional family constraints and obligations.[21] Instead of being a comforting place of recognizable and soothing familiarity to counteract the abstractions of postmodernism, love hotels strive for these abstractions—a place whose materiality consciously disconnects from the concreteness of time and space, whose clearly artificial environs never achieve a sense of naturalness or home but provide an escape from these. Rather than serving as an anchor in a mediatized, postmodern field of vision and over-stimulation, love hotels present simulacra as a respite from the "real" and the material experiences of the everyday.

Love Hotels Versus Other Themed Hotels

In some ways, love hotels are exactly like the Las Vegas that Robert Venturi and his associates described—a pleasure zone whose imagery depends on "heightened symbolism, and the ability to engulf the visitor in a new role: vacation from everyday reality."[22] This is the motif from which love hotels derive their signifying power. They attract both visitors and controversy because of the way in which love hotels' facades literally and imaginatively advertise sex. Outside of Japan, however, other hotels gain renown for theming hotel rooms and providing fantasy stays that are tied to these themes, quite separate from the thematic of sex that defines love hotels. Take, for instance, the Fantasyland hotel in the West Edmonton Mall in Edmonton Canada.[23] Here, 120 fantasy themed rooms range from a truck theme (in which a bed is in the back of a pick-up truck), to localized themes such as Igloo and Canadian Rail styled-rooms, to more "traditional" exotic motifs of Hollywood, Roman, Polynesian, Arabian, and African themed rooms. Like love hotels, the notoriety of the Fantasyland hotel stems from the fact that its rooms are not ordinary and it offers an exclusive service. However, whereas the Fantasyland hotel's mixture of fun and fantasy merits the label, "hotel of distinction," love hotels bear the stigma of fantasies that are explicitly tied to sex.[24] Partially because of this, love hotels typically offer the cheapest overnight stays in Japan. Compared to these economical options, an overnight stay in the Fantasyland hotel will cost you hundreds of dollars.

Moving to yet another level, the even more indulgent fantasy spaces of Las Vegas arguably serve yet another social function. For instance, the fantasy suites at the Palms hotel in Las Vegas defer the "traditionally" exotic motifs and instead encourage guests to ensconce themselves in such themed spaces as the erotic, the celebrity, the hot pink, the director's, the MTV *Real World,* the kingpin, and the hardwood (basketball) suite.[25] Far more exclusive than even the Fantasyland hotel (room rates here start at thousands of dollars), these suites provide spaces of the imagination for large-scale entertainment where one can indulge with thousands of square feet and, in some cases, hundreds of guests. These suites are marketed with the slogan, "Stop Dreaming. Start Living." Even an overnight stay in such a fantasy space is a privilege reserved for a select few who can afford it. On the other hand, love hotels in Japan seem to suggest that patrons can "Stop living and start dreaming." As I have indicated, though, not all sex in love hotels is fantastically themed. For some, the destination simply is meant as an escape into the ludic, into a space of guilt-free sexuality. Still, given the variety of motifs, it seems reasonable to suggest that everyone who patronizes a love hotel does so to transgress the bounds of a normal hotel stay and to seek escape, whether it be from the typical hotel experience or escape from the confines of one's own house in the same city. Though sex is certainly part of the appeal of the Palms' fantasy suites, indulgence in these themes, as well as Fantasyland's, seems more celebratory and capitalistic than transgressive. Consequently, we should consider a visit to a love hotel as a moral holiday—an activity that may not involve actual travel but which replicates the sensation of escape and is an occasional foray into deviance undertaken by everybody.[26] Moral holidays are usually undertaken when one is away from one's home turf. We can see, then, how the experience of the love hotel promises this sense of escape and its themes encourage the accompanying temporary suspension of morality and responsibility that accompany it. This capacity for explicitly sex-oriented moral holidays differentiates love hotels from other themed hotels. It is also the source of their controversy and the rationale for studying them as visual rhetoric.

Love Hotels as Visual Rhetoric

When trying to understand the implications of theming a space such as a hotel and individual rooms within it, we should analyze both the space and the theme and how they function together as visual rhetoric. As Sonja Foss notes, since the 1970s, the study of rhetoric has been broadened to include the non-discursive and the non-verbal as well as the discursive and the verbal, and now any object, including architecture and the built environment, can be interrogated as rhetoric if it is intended to modify attention, perceptions, attitudes, or behavior.[27] Love hotels serve to teach their visitors—not about the era or place in which they are immersing themselves—but about rituals in Japan and what it means to be Japanese. They offer "constructed and thus structured invitations to meaning."[28] The point, then, is to explore the ways in which love hotels create these invitations and what these mean both for visitors and the wider culture in which these structures are located. Studied as rhetoric, one focuses on how these hotels make claims to audiences—how, by structuring these invitations as themes, the hotels affect our understandings of sex and pleasure and experience in Japan.

Themed environments certainly should be studied as visual rhetoric as "rhetoric is an action humans perform when they use symbols for the purpose of communicating with one another."[29] Love hotels, like any themed space, are the products of conscious decisions to purposively communicate something through the use of particular symbolic mechanisms in order to affect a particular change, whether this is to influence a certain action or induce a desired attitude in one's audience. In the case of love hotels, proprietors seek to metaphorically transport patrons to a temporary play space in which pleasure and fantasy interweave to create a sensation of escape. As rhetorical places or loci, landscapes draw together a wide range of cultural and historical resources.[30] It follows that themed landscapes do this in an even more accentuated manner. Consequently, when viewing these themed landscapes through the lens of visual rhetoric—wherein claims are made on audiences and change is affected through visual means—we ought to focus our attention on three important factors: (1) The materiality of the landscape, (2) audience responses to the themed milieu, and (3) the function of the theming.

As Carole Blair points out, too often, rhetorical analysis focuses on the symbolic and elides the materiality of rhetorical practices.[31] Love hotels' rhetorical appeals are not only located in their symbolic inducements of particular pasts or far-off or exotic locales, even though these are the themed motifs featured in their rooms. Instead these themes are used to induce a sense of pleasure, escape, and sex without constraints (other than one's imagination and pocketbook). And the rhetorical power of these themes is vested in their materiality as well as their symbolic nature. In other words, if, as Berger believes, "it is the symbolic aspects of these businesses that is important, then it is the image that counts."[32] But while images are necessary, they are not sufficient to fully ensconce visitors in a pleasurable, sex-filled escapist fantasy. Symbolism only goes so far. A Roman-themed motif on the walls is one thing, but the illusion is made all the more real with an approximation of a Roman bath. So, just as Gottdiener notes, "culture today takes the form of material environments," we should recognize that the materials used to convey symbolic themes are crucial.[33] A room meant to connote a mountain lodge is much more successful if it is designed using bricks, wood, and other natural material instead of chrome and leather. However, materiality refers both to the design features and to the material performances of visual artifacts.[34] Therefore, attending to the materiality of themed landscapes means looking beyond how such spaces of the imagination are constructed; one also should examine the precise ways that visitors experience and interact with these tangible but imaginary environments. While love hotels engage visitors on a symbolic level though the themed elements, they also engage them on "a material level by locating visitors' bodies in particular spaces."[35] For instance, as visitors move through the space and play with things in it—watch the free pornographic videos on the TV sets, lounge in the bath area, purchase sex toys from vending machines, use the provided condoms—they assent, even if incompletely or momentarily, to the narratives of the place.[36] In this way, a themed landscape "engages the body, shifts its attention, and does its work visually, aurally, and haptically," just as any experiential landscape.[37] One can argue, however, that the symbolic and material aspects of themed spaces combine to interpellate visitors as concrete subjects and reinforce the experience of the place in a way that ordinary environments cannot.

When it comes to interpretations of these landscapes, it is useful to note how audiences can experience a themed space on an aesthetic level—appreciating it for its color, sensing its form, enjoying its sounds, or valuing its texture. But there is no purpose here beyond simply having the experience. A rhetorical response, on the other hand, means attributing meaning to the experience. Here, colors, textures, sounds, and form all provide a basis for the viewer to infer meanings from the experience. Emotions and ideas are associated with the space.[38] So, when someone declares that the exterior of a love hotel with its neon signage and ship-styled architecture is garish, it is merely an aesthetic reading. To note, however, that such decoration invokes the Queen Mary ocean liner and that this signifies sophistication and worldly class is to suggest that it is a rhetorical artifact because its aesthetic elements are processed as symbolically significant. When viewing love hotels as visual rhetoric, it is clear that audiences play an active role in the construction of their meanings. However, meaning is not located in the objective construction of love hotel rooms nor in the subjective interpretation of these structures. Rather, meaning derives from the interplay of both these elements.

The point, however, is not to ask how audiences ought to interpret love hotels—that is, ask what they "mean?" Rather, we ought to examine their material dimension and ask what they do, what difference do they make? What are the social ramifications of these interpretations? To answer this question, and to fully understand the import of themed places such as love hotels, we should note Foss's distinction between the nature and the function of visual imagery. The nature of something is comprised of both its presented elements (the material out of which it is constituted) and its suggested elements (the concepts, ideas, themes, and allusions that a viewer is likely to infer from the presented elements). Meanwhile, to speak of an artifact's function is to analyze how it operates for its viewers. This is quite distinct from an artifact's purpose, which is the effect that is intended or desired by the creator of the artifact.[39] Thus, while love hotels ostensibly are built to fulfill a social need and to make money for their owners, people who view and who stay in these love hotels might have interpretations far from those of the creators.

To address the function of the love hotels' rhetoric, it is important to note that, when visiting one, the rhetorical situation in which people find themselves is not simply the themed room or even the themed hotel. Rather, it is the intersection between the themed space and the wider field of meanings out of which the space arises that provides the context for it to be meaningful. The rooms should not be viewed as discrete texts. Even though they may appear to have clear boundaries in time and space—we check in and out of a particular room and we stay for a clearly delimited time—they are more properly seen as diffuse texts, "with a perimeter that is not so clear, one that is mixed up with other signs."[40] For visitors experience more than just the room; they also undergo an association with the time/place invoked by the theme as well as the experience of going to the hotel in the first place. The experience of the themed space spills over into other sites. For instance, *Anne of Green Gables* takes on a new meaning after staying in a love hotel modeled after the novels. In the same fashion, Hello Kitty products will always be viewed differently after having checked into a room whose bondage theme is tied to the popular Sanrio character. Thus, we cannot interpret love hotels without situating them in the wider cityscapes in which they operate and the larger social and cultural landscape of Japanese society.

As diffuse texts, love hotels' rhetorical invitations are affected by the larger sociocultural milieu surrounding them. Interestingly, while themed experiences increasingly characterize other aspects of daily life, the number of these themed hotels is decreasing. This is occurring even as love hotels that do continue evolve into more elaborately themed environments. Since theming requires facilities not required for the basic purposes of guest lodging, love hotels find themselves regulated as "sex-related" businesses in the wake of legislation that targets businesses deemed to have a negative effect on public morals. Consequently, since love hotels seem to confirm the statement, "A walk down a street of any large Japanese city offers little more than a chain of visual insults," politicians in some areas are cracking down on these establishments.[41] New operations are forced either outside of cities or into specific areas zoned for sex-related businesses. When newer hotels are built or older ones refurbished, they are increasingly being marketed as "leisure," "boutique," or "fashion hotels." This is an attempt to distance the industry from its shame-ridden association with sex and the vice industries that spring up around it. Consequently, sex-oriented motifs are disappearing as interiors are designed to be more tasteful and the extravagance that is associated with love hotels is being made more ordinary. In part, there is a feminization of themes as a shift towards gentler decor replaces more traditionally masculine themes involving outer space and cars. This reflects a move towards hotels catering to female clientele with increasing social and financial power.[42] It also corresponds to laws that are forcing what might be termed the *gentrification of sex*. These newer love hotels downplay the sleaze and emphasize the fun that can be had in themed rooms that are more relaxation than sex-oriented. Taking the "love" out of love hotels destroys some of their uniqueness, but though the scene has changed, they still are designed to offer fully immersive private amusement zones. So, it does not matter what euphemism describes this type of hotel; whether people patronize these establishments for love/sex or for leisure of a different sort, they still will find a pleasure space into which they can escape—a landscape "between fantasy and desire."[43]

Interestingly, even as some attempt to make love hotels less gauche, some aspects of their ridiculously over-the-top tacky features are replicated in western themed establishments that tie together sin, commerce, and entertainment. For instance, huge neon coconut trees are often used to signal one's arrival at a Hooters restaurant. In all of these themed spaces, the purpose of themes and motifs is to make the owners money and make the customers happy. The function of these themed spaces, however, comes out of the significance of love hotels' material existence. To address this, one must also query how these themed spaces act on people. This goes beyond individual effects to involve a wider social function within Japanese society.

Social Consequences of Love Hotels

As garish eyesores that violate conventional building forms, love hotels disrupt the cityspace. As lascivious getaways, they violate conventional social norms. Read as rhetorical provocations, however, love hotels do not produce immediate persuasion. Rather, they function as inventive resources because it is through their material existence that they invent opportunities for future arguments and deliberation. Their function, then, is to cause audiences to (re)evaluate how they think of sex in Japanese society. As unique themed spaces, love hotels serve to thematize love and sex and play for all prospective audiences—both Japanese and foreigners alike. While Japanese citizens get to experience exotic themed landscapes while escaping the confines and the surveillance of their private environments, foreigners get to experience a sliver of exotic Japanese culture by staying in these hotels. Consequently, as a distinctive experiential landscape, the themed love hotel forms an important part of a wider geographical and cultural and cognitive landscape or dreamscape.[44] It functions as an escape valve in everyday Japanese life—an outlandish alternative to conditions of constant conformity in which it is difficult to express, much less act out, individual fantasies.

For visitors, the self-conscious artificiality of love hotel themes bespeaks the unreal, which Jean Bauldrillard suggested "is no longer that of dream or fantasy, of a beyond or within, it is that of a hallucinatory resemblance of the real with itself."[45] Here, the unreality of one's experience is precisely the point; one's stay, an escape from the real world, is an end in itself. The means to this end are the thematic elements in love hotels that facilitate simulation (of something exotic) and stimulation alike. One might think, then, that love hotels "confirm the postmodern idea that we live in a society in which the 'completely real' is identified with the 'completely fake.'"[46] But love hotels do not depend on the success of false representations or of ideological effects. It is not even a question of the real no longer being real. After all, love hotels offer temporary respite from the tedium and the confines of the real. They offer a diversion, a distraction, and a momentary thrill. They provide excitement and escape for its own sake and not as part of a wider mission to educate or inform. And, when visitors leave, there is always the shock of the real as they emerge from the parking garage or enter back into the streets, often acting stealthily in order to avoid the disapproving or simply curious gazes of others.

Thus, even as they appeal to some, love hotels offend others. While some find them simply titillating and use them as amusing distractions, others are troubled by the way in which they drape sex and love in inauthentic themes. Still, these mixed responses can be used as a source of creative tension insofar as they reveal a culture's wider values and suggest boundaries of the permissible. Themed spaces such as love hotels, then, can be symptomatic of what a wider culture thematizes as "good" and "bad," "appropriate" and "improper." Consequently, we can learn something from a careful investigation of them. As Robert Venturi, Denise Scott Brown, and Steven Izenour state, "It is often preferable to accept and glorify in the pluralism of the Good, the Bad, and the Ugly than to enforce the white bread dullness of good taste all over the landscape."[47] The types of themes in love hotels—and indeed, the need to thematize sex and the escape from the everyday—can be good, bad, and ugly, but they also sensitize us "to see the commonplace through new eyes."[48] As Charles Jencks asserted, "Since you can't escape bad taste any more, the only thing you can do is apply standards to it and discover when it is really subversive and enjoyable. Today, most man-made things are horribly mediocre, but happily, a few of them are really awful."[49] Themed love hotels have traditionally cultivated the pleasure that exists in these testaments to bad taste, and, even as standards of tastefulness change, they continue "to keep the lovably ridiculous from slipping into the merely no-account."[50]

Like the airports that Gottdiener describes, love hotels "are interesting themed environments not because they overwhelm us with highly coordinated themes . . . but because they are overendowed with sign systems."[51] I have used this over-endowment to prove the dictum that "rhetoric is everywhere."[52] I have also demonstrated that love hotels are unique themed landscapes in that they are both popular and marginal sites within Japanese culture. Thus, love hotels are not just quixotic expressions of this culture. As individuals negotiate what love hotels mean and what they accomplish, they become outposts of rhetorical activity that help constitute the wider social and political collectivity. Ultimately, even though one of their (unintended) functions is to generate controversy, love hotels are not simply spectacles that ought to be critiqued. Instead, we ought to view them (and all themed spaces, for that matter) as rhetorical artifacts that generate discussion and invite consideration of exactly what is being themed. Through this negotiation, love hotels instead advance the project of "critique through spectacle."[53] Their outrageous symbolic regimes put pleasure on display. They celebrate the artificial and the ludic and, viewed as rhetoric, they help constitute the identities of those producing and consuming (and debating) their curious spectacle. Love hotels are rhetorical invitations that encourage rituals both of national and personal identity formation. They are part of a theming milieu in which pleasure is pursued for pleasure's sake and in which inauthenticity and escape are crucial supplements to everyday life.

Notes

1. Mark Gottdiener, *The Theming of America: Dreams, Visions, and Commercial Spaces* (Boulder, Colo.: Westview Press, 1997), 121.
2. *Lonely Planet Japan* (Hong Kong: Lonely Planet Publications, 2005), 725.
3. Nicholas Bornoff, *Pink Samurai: The Pursuit and Politics of Sex in Japan* (London: Grafton Books, 1991), 18; Iwao Hoshii, *The World of Sex. Vol. 2: Sex and Marriage* (Woodchurch, UK: Paul Norbury Publications Limited, 1986), 182, 188.
4. Beth Reiber, *Frommer's Tokyo* (Hoboken, N.J.: Wiley Publishing, 2006), 71.
5. Tim Kelly, "Love for Sale," *Forbes*, <http://www.forbes.com/business/forbes/2006 /0605/106.html> (1 October 2006).
6. Bornoff, *Pink Samurai*, 18–21.
7. Jann Dodd and Simon Richmond, *The Rough Guide to Tokyo* (New York: Rough Guides, 2005), 145.
8. *Lonely Planet Japan*, 725.
9. Mark Gottdiener, "Themed Environments of Everyday Life: Restaurants and Malls," in *The Postmodern Presence*, ed. Arthur Asa Berger (Walnut Creek, Calif.: AltaMira, 1998), 85.
10. Orvar Löfgren, *On Holiday: A History of Vacationing* (Berkeley: University of California Press, 1999), 257.
11. Bornoff, *Pink Samurai*, 21.
12. Alan Hess, *Viva Las Vegas: After-hours Architecture* (San Francisco: Chronicle Books, 1993), 105.
13. See examples at <http://www.quirkyjapan.or.tv/hotels.html>. This also provides a sampling of pictures of some "typical" love hotels, as does the online article "Between a Rock and a Soft Place," available at <http://www.tokyo.to/backissues/apr00/tj0400p6-10>.
14. Gottdiener, *The Theming of America*, 110.
15. Bornoff, *Pink Samurai*, 17.
16. Gottdiener, *The Theming of America*, 80.
17. Chris Rojek, *Ways of Escape: Modern Transformations in Leisure and Travel* (Lanham, Md.: Rowan and Littlefield, 1993), 165.
18. *Eyewitness Travel Guides Japan* (New York: DK Publishing, 2005), 289.
19. Gottdiener, *The Theming of America*, 145.

20. Gottdiener, *The Theming of America*, 115.
21. Greg Dickenson, "Joe's Rhetoric: Finding Authenticity at Starbucks," *Rhetoric Society Quarterly* 32, no. 4 (Fall 2002): 10.
22. Robert Venturi, Denise Scott Brown, and Steven Izenour, *Learning from Las Vegas* (Cambridge, Mass.: MIT Press, 1972), 53.
23. <http://www.fantasylandhotel.com/rooms/wemindex.asp>.
24. <http://www.westedmontonmall.com/newsreleases/2006/03/Frontier%20Press%20Release.pdf>. In the United States, adult-oriented theme hotels, such as the chain of Fantasy Suite hotels, offer distinctive themed rooms for customers. In many U.S. cities, hotels are themed for the benefit of customers desirous of a sexualized, fantasy experience.
25. <http://www.palmsfantasy.com>.
26. David Harris, *Key Concepts in Leisure Studies* (London: Sage, 2005), 82.
27. Sonja Foss, "Theory of Visual Rhetoric," in *Handbook of Visual Communication*, ed. Ken Smith, Sandra Moriarty, Gretchen Barbatis, and Keith Kenney (Mahwah, N.J.: Lawrence Erlbaum, 2005), 141.
28. Greg Dickinson, Brian L. Ott and Eric Aoki, "Memory and Myth at the Buffalo Bill Museum," *Western Journal of Communication* 69, no. 2 (April 2005): 88.
29. Sonja K. Foss, Karen A. Foss and Robert Trapp, *Contemporary Perspectives on Rhetoric* (Prospect Heights, Ill.: Waveland Press, 1991), 14.
30. Greg Dickinson, "Memories for Sale: Nostalgia and the Construction of Identity in Old Pasadena," *The Quarterly Journal of Speech* 83, no. 1 (February 1997): 4.
31. Carole Blair, "Contemporary U.S. Memorial Sites as Exemplars of Rhetoric's Materiality," in *Rhetorical Bodies*, ed. Jack Selzer and Sharon Crowley (Madison: University of Wisconsin Press, 1999), 19.
32. Quoted in Gottdiener, "Themed Environments," 74.
33. Gottdiener, *The Theming of America*, 158.
34. Carole Blair and Neil Michel, "Commemorating in the Theme Park Zone: Reading the Astronauts Memorial," in *At the Intersection: Cultural Studies and Rhetorical Studies*, ed. Thomas Rosteck (New York: Guilford, 1999), 32.
35. Greg Dickinson, Brian L. Ott and Eric Aoki, "Spaces of Remembering and Forgetting: The Reverent Eye/I at the Plains Indian Museum," *Communication and Critical/Cultural Studies* 3, no. 1 (March 2006): 29.
36. Paula Mathieu, "Economic Citizenship and the Rhetoric of Gourmet Coffee," *Rhetoric Review* 18, no. 1 (Autumn 1999): 115.
37. Dickinson, Ott and Aoki, "Spaces of Remembering," 35.
38. Foss, "Theory of Visual Rhetoric," 145.
39. Foss, "Theory of Visual Rhetoric," 146.
40. Dickinson, Ott and Aoki, "Spaces of Remembering," 29.
41. Renato A. Pirotta, "Popular Architecture," in *Handbook of Japanese Popular Culture*, ed. Richard Powers and Hidetoshi Kato (New York: Greenwood Press, 1989), 39. The use of theming to "clean-up" illicit areas of the city is the subject of Samuel R. Delaney, *Times Square Red, Times Square Blue* (New York: New York University Press, 2001).
42. Dodd and Richmond, *The Rough Guide to Tokyo*, 145.
43. <http://www.okada.de/archive-japansitis/love/love.html>.
44. Dickinson, Ott and Aoki, "Spaces of Remembering," 29.
45. Jean Baudrillard, *Simulations* (New York: Semiotext(e), 1983), 142.
46. Rojek, *Ways of Escape*, 160.
47. Venturi, Brown, and Izenour, *Learning from Las Vegas*.

48. Hess, *Viva Las Vegas*, 7.

49. Cited in Barbara Rubin, "Aesthetic Ideology and Urban Design," in *Common Places: Readings in American Vernacular Architecture*, ed. Dell Upton and John Michael Vlach (Athens: University of Georgia Press, 1986), 504–05.

50. Rubin, "Aesthetic Ideology and Urban Design."

51. Gottdiener, *The Theming of America*, 97.

52. Dilip Parameshwar Gaonkar, "The Idea of Rhetoric in the Rhetoric of Science," in *Rhetorical Hermeneutics: Invention and Interpretation in the Age of Science*, ed. A. G. Gross and W. M. Keithe (Albany: State University of New York Press, 1997), 26.

53. Kevin DeLuca and Jennifer Peeples, "From Public Sphere to Public Screen: Democracy, Activism, and the 'Violence' of Seattle," *Critical Studies in Media Communication* 19, no. 2 (2002): 134.

Chapter 11

How the Theme Park Gets Its Power: Lived Theming, Social Control, and the Themed Worker Self

Scott A. Lukas

> Think of Six Flags as the ultimate 3D movie. Everything we do is scripted, staged and rehearsed for the enjoyment of our guests. The parks are the stage and the scenery, and you are the actor. Just like a movie, Six Flags is fantasy. And the best way for our guests to have a great time is to believe the fantasy with themelands and your performance. They will believe!
> —Six Flags Promotional Video, 1994.[1]

One of the most confounding questions that must be applied to any themed space is whether or not theming, as an expression of both material and immaterial life, is natural? Is theming a form of culture that can take on authentic dimensions and, as such, can it impact the nature of social relationships present in everyday life? Like any form of consumer society, theming reflects deep cultural traditions, varied ideologies, and foundational qualities of life. Unfortunately, many people have been unable to accept theming as a legitimate form of culture because of the assumption that is produces stereotypical, inauthentic, and simulated reflections on people, things, cultures, places, and moments in history. Likewise, in addition to the concerns raised about the material conditions of themed spaces—including architecture, decor, and associated material culture—many critics and laypersons have expressed doubts about the behaviors that occur in their confines. Some people have taken issue with the effect of theming on human behavior. For example, criticism has been leveled against the staged nature of social interactions present in Disney theme parks.[2] Others have expressed that because sociality is predetermined in themed spaces—namely because people are acting in accordance with the narratives of the given themed space—the conditions of work produce dehumanization and routinization in workers, as well as in patrons.[3] In this chapter I am interested in exploring the inherently social dimensions of theming that are present in themed spaces. Specifically, I will focus on the relationship of theming in a now-defunct Six Flags theme park—Six Flags AstroWorld in Houston, Texas—to the dynamics of social interaction among workers, patrons, and managers. As well, I will focus on the ways in which the performance of theming, or how it is lived out by people, impacts the self, particularly as theming is recognized as a form of discipline and social control. I hope to stress that regardless of one's opinion on theming and the social relations that are a product of it, themed spaces are, inherently, highly gregarious sites of popular culture. As well, I wish to emphasize that theming is more than the materiality found in its obvious signs—architecture, signage, and decor. It is also the performative dimensions of themes that are played out by the employees and patrons of themed venues.

As this volume helps illustrate, themed spaces vary in size, thematic approach, geography, and architecture, but what all have in common is their imbrication in consumerist systems of service culture. Most themed spaces are also service spaces—they are venues in which customers pay for particular goods and services (usually connected to the particular themes of the venue), in which workers provide those goods and services (in ways consistent with the themes), and in which managers assess the overall effectiveness of the delivery of the goods and services (particularly as this delivery is determined to be in-line with or consistent with the theming). Some of the classic studies of service industry culture have illustrated the peculiar social relationships that are created in the triad of worker, patron, and customer.[4] Contrary to some popular beliefs that the service industry offers easy employment—perhaps because workers get to work among other people—it is the site of some of the most demanding jobs, especially in terms of the emotional and improvisational acumen needed by its workers. For nearly three years I worked as a training coordinator at the now-defunct Six Flags theme park, AstroWorld, located in Houston, Texas. Along with a number of other coordinators, my job involved training park employees in safety, public relations, rides operation, cleanliness, and many other aspects of park operations. Though the combination of these areas was seen by park management as a holistic order that all employees had to understand and execute equally, what was *the* most pronounced area of concern was perception, performance, and image.

Arlie Hochschild once remarked that for the actor, the illusion of performance is established in reference to professional roles, whereas in everyday life, especially the service industry, illusion "takes on meaning with reference to living persons."[5] At AstroWorld, the effective performance of theming was a top priority, and employees were expected to act effectively, even if they had no background in performance or previous work in the service industry. After some experiences interviewing employees for initial hire in the Human Resources department, I was struck with the disconnect between potential employees' perceptions of working in a theme park and the realities of the job that they might encounter during their first week of employment. Typical AstroWorld recruitment ads played on the workplace's status as a theme park to sell jobs to the Houston workforce—slogans would stress the AstroWorld job as the "dream job" or work at the park as "fun," "exciting and challenging." Management relied on the fact that the potential workforce was comprised of teenagers who had spent many of their childhood and teen years at the park, as well as the idea that a job at AstroWorld was one of the most unique ones in the city. A major selling point was the fact that the park was themed. I would teach employees that if they got tired of their jobs, they could transfer to another section of the park, and, not only would their work status change—moving from a troika to a roller coaster—but so too would their costume and performance in a new theme land or themed venue. Unfortunately, the disconnect that I mentioned earlier was a major reality for management. The excitement that a patron experienced in a themed area of the park was not necessarily replicated when that same person, years later, put on the uniform to staff that area; likewise, the positive emotions that I witnessed during new employee hiring and orientation were often quelled when employees made it out into the park—dealing with one hundred-degree temperatures, unruly and demanding patrons, and the politics of organizational culture, including sometimes difficult relations with other employees and management.

Like their non-themed counterparts, workers in the themed service industry are familiar with the demanding political, social, and existential conditions of their places of work. Added to the demands of the service culture—which typically include heavy and often intense face-to-face interactions with patrons, other workers, and sometimes demanding and unreasonable managers—there is the component of the theme, the Rosetta stone of the themed venue. During 1994 and 1995, the main years of my employment, AstroWorld had nine theme lands. Nottingham Village was based on a combination of Arthurian and Robin Hood stories, and included the roller coaster Excalibur and the sit-down restaurant the Sword and Crown. Oriental Village was the most generally themed areas, and it housed the Viper roller coaster, a log flume ride, and a number of Asian-themed shops. Mexicana included the Sky Screamer vertical drop ride and the water ride known as Tidal Wave. Western junction was a themed area based on the imagination of cowboys and the West—it featured a well-themed ride, the Greezed Lightnin' and Gabby's barbeque restaurant. Bugs Bunny Land was a themed area intended solely for children, and it included many small rides, shops, and games based on Looney Tunes characters.[6] European Village was themed according to loose associations of the Alps and European landscapes; it offered a number of spinning rides and the roller coaster Ultra Twister. USA/Coney Island was a theme land that featured one of the most famous rides in the United States—the Texas Cyclone. This area focused on a carnival atmosphere with very loose connections to Coney Island of New York. The park entrance was known as Americana Square, and its architecture, shops, and mood resembled the main street popularized by Disney theme parks.[7] In addition, one major ride—the popular Batman the Escape roller coaster—had its own theming, including a Batcave queue area. Each themed area featured attractions that were associated with the major theme, in some cases the associations were clear, in others, they were left to the patron's imagination. Each theme land had costumes that were connected to the theme, and some jobs required that employees perform in a way consistent with the costumes, theming, and symbolic associations of the area. In the 1994 *Park Operations Rides Manual*, this aspect was stressed to employees: "The Presentational Costume is instrumental in theming the park. Each section of the park will have a certain theme, and the costumes in that area will correspond to that theme."[8]

Norbert Elias once wrote of the damaging effects of civilization on human instincts, suggesting that, ultimately, our cultural forms are outpacing our biological evolution.[9] The question of the naturalness of theming that began this chapter is relevant to understanding the dynamics of social relationships within themed spaces. Thematic representations have always been a part of the lived spaces and architecture of the species—the cave paintings of Lascaux, for example, provided individuals with a sense of security, group solidarity, and fulfilled creative, aesthetic, and spiritual needs. The themed spaces that populate the contemporary world do not share with the caves of early humans the dynamics of survival; instead themed spaces like AstroWorld are places of entertainment. They are, however like the representational lived spaces of early humans, places in which people's immediate emotional and existential needs are fulfilled and in which varied and often difficult forms of social interaction take place. During my walks through the park as I conducted audits—including "Quick Strike" ones intended to catch people not playing their roles in the theme land—I commonly saw patrons and workers enjoying themselves. As unnatural as themed spaces may seem, individuals do enjoy them. In 1995, the park's mission statement reflected the propensity of people to enjoy theme parks: "To create a world of fantasy and excitement for our Guests that gives them an escape from their everyday routine."[10] During our training sessions with employees, we stressed the mission statement continually, offering to employees that they could make a patron's day, they could make someone smile, they could bring happiness to people who are in need of "escap[ing] from their everyday routine." Walking in the theme lands of AstroWorld gave the patron an opportunity to enjoy themselves in a fantasy world, while the worker was responsible for ensuring that the fantasy was effectively performed. Much of theming rests on the ability of the worker to consistently and convincingly deliver the theme. Like the patron who experiences the theme and who often internalizes it, the worker is subject to the psychological conditions that often result in a closer association of the person with the theme than might be anticipated.

The Subjectivity of Theming

The making and existence of the artifact that portrays something gives one power over that which is portrayed.
—Michael Taussig, *Mimesis and Alterity*.[11]

We don't put people in Disney. We put Disney in people.
—Disney trainer Richard Park.[12]

The work of the preeminent philosopher Michel Foucault has revolutionized the way in which we understand power and its operation in society. Foucault's work is particularly germane for comprehending the elusive networks of power that operate in the organizational culture of a theme park.[13] Foucault's concepts of biopower and governmentality emphasized that power is something which operates through people, not necessarily upon them.[14] Ultimately, these concepts addressed the control of the human species at the levels of demography, mortality, morbidity, and reproduction. Though these concepts do not map onto the theme park body in the specific areas intended by Foucault, they do relate to the manifestation of the State in the control of the individual—an "acting at a distance" in a "range of multiform tactics."[15] One of the greatest transformations of the corporation involved the movement of the mechanisms of control *into* the mind and body of the worker. As Nikolas Rose said, the "path to business success lies in engaging the employee with the goals of the company at the level of his or her subjectivity . . . the more the individual fulfills him or herself, the greater the benefit to the company."[16] Like any corporation, the theme park functions as an organization that establishes and maintains control in subtle ways, specifically, through "modes of subjectification in which individuals can be brought to work on themselves."[17] Theming is one of the primary means that is deployed to effect the subjectivities of the theme park worker and patron.

One of the selling points of a job at AstroWorld was the idea that the employee would have more fun than he or she would in another service industry position, such as the restaurant industry. We communicated the idea that the presence of the numerous theme lands themselves made the daily experience of an AstroWorld worker meaningful. Theming is not merely an architectural technology of the material world; it is a means of social interaction, a performative practice, and even an existential state that is dually manifested by workers and patrons at themed venues. For the employee, a sense of being able to perform for others in one of the theme lands in the park relegated his or her awareness of the power that was being exercised by the company mute, while the patron, believing that he or she was able to partake in an unbridled form of consumption and fantasy, was unable to analyze the consumptive powers that were being exercised by the company and the State. Theme lands produce noticeable effects on workers and customers in both material and immaterial ways. In terms of the first area, the architecture, signage, and other material expressions of a theme like Nottingham limit the possibilities of the patron—he or she can make more decisions, ultimately, than the worker, but these decisions are all constrained by the power of the theme to dictate any choices. In terms of the second area, the worker is even more conditioned by the themed landscape that governs his or her area. Certain behaviors—whether being rude to a customer, being excessive with his or her performative expressions of theming, or not paying attention to patrons—commonly resulted in the termination of the employee. Though termination codes reflected in paperwork might have read "insubordination," often, the real reason for the dismissal was the inadequacy of the worker in maintaining the theming duties assigned to him or her.

Like many jobs in the service industry, the nature of work at AstroWorld reflected an emphasis on positive customer interactions, cleanliness, knowledge of the products and services offered, and a positive attitude. Unique to the world of the theme park is the emphasis on themed performance. One book that details the adoption of Disney customer service culture outside of Disney theme parks discusses themed performance as "performance culture."[18] During my time at AstroWorld, I came to know the Six Flags corporate trainer. She was a former Disney employee and she was hired to instill Disney-type culture at the Six Flags parks; this involved not merely the customer service programs of Disney, but the specific ways in which theming and worker performance were integrated at Disney theme parks. Six Flags corporate philosophy acknowledged the accomplishments of the Disney corporation in its high standards of customer service, but it decidedly stated that it was different in two respects. First, Six Flags parks had better theming and, second, Six Flags parks stressed exciting rides and roller coasters that were not found at Disney theme parks. Of course, this philosophy was not necessarily shared on the ground. Many members of AstroWorld's middle management stressed on the fact that theming was often worked out in a shoddy or cheap manner and they often internalized the idea that AstroWorld was the "red-haired stepchild" of all Six Flags theme parks.

During Operations Department training, we focused on this tension with Disney. Disney would sometimes come up in discussions and activities, but always obliquely. Our training department learned how to focus on the differences between Six Flags and Disney, most commonly through theming. In one example we discussed the distinctiveness of Six Flags and AstroWorld by referencing the "Past, Present and Future." The past was addressed through the biographies of park employees who began their careers in entry-level positions and then moved up to high management positions; the present was acknowledged by an emphasis on the many theme lands of the park and how they related to positive experiences of patrons; and the future was the subject of new themed projects for the park, including the Mayan Mind Bender roller coaster.[19] The major emphasis of all of the training conducted by our department was that employees acted out the parts expected of them in the park. One of the stickiest issues was how to deal with the twofold situation of a diverse employee base whose personalities would sometimes not match the roles expected of them and how to achieve consistency given the many differences in theming across the park.[20] During my fieldwork in the park, I learned that regardless of the grounding that any theme provided for management, acting out that theme through the subjectivities of the worker was never an easy accomplishment.

Typically, park theming began with the material conditions of the park—architecture reflected the theme being portrayed, such as a western-styled building for the park's Western area, signage, and other elements of decor were consistent with the theme, and employees were dressed in costumes that related to each theme land. Each area of the park had distinct costumes—Mexicana section had fiesta outfits, while Western had blue jeans and western tops, Alpine had lederhosen-type dress, and Batman the Escape had mechanic outfits that resembled those of henchmen in the first few Batman films.[21] Costumes themselves would sometimes cause an employee to become upset or even leave employment at the park. Some men felt that certain costumes were too feminine and that wearing them, even for the sake of theming, was "going too far." Operations Division manuals explained to employees the value of costumes as they related to theming: "The Operations Division uses many different costumes and theming techniques to create the fantasy environment.... We must add to the fantasy everyday by wearing the proper costume."[22] In addition to the costumes, park training emphasized the need for all employees to "look the part"—certain haircuts, piercings, and other markings were forbidden. Some employees were told to cover their noticeable tattoos with bandages because they "shouldn't give off the appearance of a carnie" while on the job. Park employees were continually surveilled to ensure their compliance with dress code and grooming standards; in some cases, an infraction as minor as the wrong style of white socks could result in the employee being sent home for the day without pay.[23] Customers were also subject to codes of dress, but they generally were left unmolested unless they happened to be wearing egregious clothing, such as gang-related items or that with obscenities printed on the garment.

Beyond the materiality of theming, theme parks like AstroWorld use other means, including narrative, to coalesce the material and symbolic expressions of theming. One of the most common ways that service industry managers deal with inadequacies within the worker pool is to rely on the narratives provided by theming. As Robin Leider wrote of service culture, "by scripting interactions, employers can try to limit their reliance on the ethnomethodological competence of their workers."[24] Scripts were modalities of theming that were played out in each area of the park. In Bugs Bunny Land, employees were hand-selected to be courteous to patrons and their children, and were often chosen based on physical appearance.[25] Some employees were promoted to Certified Ride Operator (CRO) status not merely because of their mechanical competence to operate the rides, but because of their amenable personality, gregariousness, and ability to convincingly play the roles asked of them by management. During Operations training, all employees were given the specific information they needed to work in their areas, and especially highlighted were techniques aimed at successful interactions with patrons and strategies for maintaining their themed personas. We always stressed the idea of "being on stage," such as is exhibited in one park manual: "Once on property, your performance has begun!"[26] On-the-job training followed Operations training, and in it, the focus on the subjective domain of theming became more pronounced.[27] Rides leads would emphasize the nuance that was needed to work in a given area, including the visual cues, body language, specific language, and the rhetorical delivery needed for playing the part. Certain theme lands demanded different forms of employee performance—some themed venues may have required that the employee expressed a sinister, albeit faux, attitude towards customers, while others may have involved the employee displaying complete bliss, if not flightiness, in his or her presentation of themed worker self.

One of the most specific expressions of the discourse of theming was the spiel. The spiel utilized both content (such as the discussion of different aspects of the ride or the themed area), and delivery, (including performative speech, fake accents, and variation in tone, pitch, and speed of voice). On-the-job training of the sort that included instruction in park spiels was often informal; in fact, a major challenge of park training was to find employees skilled enough to complete their job duties, not to mention the perk of having employees who could deliver a spiel or a themed performance in a convincing manner. Some employees took theming too seriously and they manifested behaviors that went beyond the dictates of park training. At the Wagon Wheel, a troika, a few employees were disciplined for being "too western" to park patrons; it turned that they acted rudely to customers like a cowboy is portrayed in spaghetti Western films. At the Greezed Lightnin' roller coaster, a spiel or programmatic script was read before and after patrons experienced the ride. The spiel of the CRO was most often a source of customer satisfaction (as revealed in Guest Services surveys), but in some cases, parents expressed that some CROs took things "too far" and became aggressive, rude, or demeaning in their spiels.[28] It turned out that employees did draw on their creativity, improvisational skills, and sense of aesthetics by acting out the scripts and performances of the theme lands. Ultimately, they did so in ways that contradicted the positive service philosophies of management and the corporation.

Unfortunately, these interpretations—in some cases gleaned from popular culture like films, video games, and novels—often created tense employee-patron interactions. As I have tried to stress, theming is not merely a material condition—it is a state of performance that involves the motivations of workers and patrons alike, and it is a shaky ground on which the "Guest First" and "Gold Standard" philosophies of management often crumbled.[29] Guest First and Gold Standard were corporate programs that stressed the correlation of customer service principles and holistic park concerns, like theming. These philosophies, though meaningful to Six Flags corporate officers and to the upper management of its parks, were often not organic entities as they were realized in employees in the parks. Theming, like the anthropological concept of culture, was often an abstraction understood in the minds of corporate and park management; within the worker, however, it sometimes lacked the attention to detail and effective performance that was desired in the corporate and managerial abstractions. Theming, were it to ideally develop in the park as a non-abstraction, would resemble a stage performance or, more appropriately, a movie.

From Movies to Lived Theming

At a very basic level, theming refers to the control of perspective. As Norman Klein noted in his study of special effects and architecture, controlling perspective is an important means of achieving social control in society.[30] In the themed space, special effects abound, but their success at convincing both worker and patron rests in how they unfold through time. Theming may share with movies the features of consistency of story, unfolding narrative, and visceral effect brought on by the representational medium. While in a themed space—like the movie, or a play or literary work—the patron is expected to suspend his or her disbelief and engage in the immersive world created by the theming, and the worker is expected to deliver a consistent representation of the theme that can be appreciated by the patron.[31] One of the most common ways to achieve the suspension of disbelief needed to produce theming is through feelings and emotion. Feelings, according to Sigmund Freud, act as signal functions indicating the positionality of actors in a social setting: "from feeling we discover our own viewpoint of the world."[32] Just as the statues, painted walls, and architectural features of a Mayan-themed ride signify, so do the ways in which employees and patrons act out themed personas within the theme park. Employees, workers, and management interact in numerous ways in the theme park, but the ground on which these interactions take place is a themed one, and it is one on which social interactions are scripted like the lines of a movie screenplay.

In an AstroWorld training session known as *Train the Trainer*—in which trainers from the park's various departments were refreshed on positive training techniques—the training philosophy was always grounded in aesthetics and performance. Statements like "people are persuaded more by the depth of your conviction than by the height of your logic . . . more by your enthusiasm than any proof you can offer" emphasized the idea that rationality was not a part of either the patron's or the employee's lifeworld in the theme park; instead, theming necessitated a shared suspension of disbelief.[33] Employees were told assumptions about patrons, including the idea that they would be approaching them in emotional ways, without logic or, to reiterate, in a context almost entirely composed of the signal functions of emotions. All of our training materials included a discussion of communication, suggesting that only 10 percent of all communication was informational content, with the remaining percent being vocal quality and body language.[34] The message portrayed by these means of training was that work was emotional, as Arlie Hochschild suggests of service work, and that it was performative. The mere presence of an Asian facade in the Oriental section of the park did not guarantee that the patron would feel comfortable in his or her fantasy; inevitably, the fantasy has to be sold by the worker and he or she has to believe in it as much as the patron, or at least project that particular appearance of belief.

The senses, as they are created, maintained, and modified in the themed space, provide cues for customer, worker, and manager. As one retail themed advisor has written, themed design is "an attempt to manage emotions" by creating "contextual cues for role-playing."[35] Some critics have suggested that the way in which the emotions and senses are managed in consumer spaces produces conditions of dehumanization and rationalization and, ultimately, the worker and patron are trapped in an inauthentic world.[36] The counter to this argument is that both patrons and workers have a choice whether or not to engage the narrative spaces of the theme park—after all, they do not necessarily have to work there and they can choose to not patronize such spaces. However, this argument is somewhat shallow given the fact that the narratives, scripts, and emotions that characterize the theme park world are becoming more ubiquitous. Even outside of theme parks, people are more accustomed with staged or superficial modes of conversation and performance that take place in venues like Starbucks. Like the movie metaphor, the emphasis in AstroWorld training was on the way in which theming unfolded as a logical and consistent product within a given theme land. This involved close attention to the material dimensions of theming—including the appearance of the themed space, such as architecture—and the immaterial components, including the performances undertaken by employees in the delivery of theming and the emotions that were produced in interactions with patrons.

Like sets of a movie, the training department commonly viewed various themed venues as bounded semiotic spaces, with workers fulfilling the roles of actors. Employees were expected to act their parts consistently with the given theme. In some cases, employees were transferred from one theme land to another in order to create a "better fit" between the person and the theme land. For example, one of the theme lands in which performance was arguably more important than the materiality of theming was Bugs Bunny Land. Employees who were aggressive with children or who lost their patience with parents were immediately transferred to sections of the park that might better fit their personalities. In this way, AstroWorld training emphasized the specific subjective conditions of the worker as they connected to the theme.[37] Though many employees felt that this matching of the employee to the best-suited theme land was justifiable, some also felt that it produced what sociologists might call employee stratification.[38] Some employees believed that there were racist and sexist motivations behind the decisions to staff certain theme lands with certain employees. Interestingly, this claim parallels back to the movie industry—some have stated that the emphasis on appearance as the raison d'etre of film has produced a stratified culture in which certain people are excluded from the big screen. Further, some employees accused management of using theming—a hierarchical indicator of employee standing in the park—as a means of rewarding some employees and punishing others. Many employees were familiar with these accusations and many went so far as to suggest a hierarchy of park theming that included both theme lands and their specific components, such as rides, attractions, and forms of entertainment. In their views, appearance—as it became the unfolding narrative of theming desired by park management—was inherently hegemonic.

As I have suggested, theming is commonly conceived of as an unfolding movie, complete with plot, story line, sets, and actors. Our training department stressed two aspects of theming—first, that the employee should consciously work on acting out the theme of his or her area as conscientiously as possible; second, that the patron's experience of theming must be meaningful not just in theme lands, but between them. In a recent text written by the Disney Institute, the comparison between the cross-dissolves and edits of a film and the space and time between themed attractions and theme lands is made.[39] At AstroWorld, the metaphor of film—including references to "actors" and good, believable "performances"—was extended to most aspects of work in the park. Major park training, including a biannual event called Top Gun, named after the major motion picture, referenced the movie metaphors of Disney to an even greater degree. During Top Gun, a group called NASCO trained employees in various aspects of customer service; commonly, the group stressed the role that the employee played in the creation of believable theme lands.[40] Like other training groups inside and outside of the theme park industry, NASCO emphasized a generalized Disney discourse and suggested that it be applied to the AstroWorld setting. Because Disney's movies and theme parks have become standardized, the training discourse that is associated with these cultural products has also become the corporate norm. Though management touted the skills of NASCO trainers, many employees felt that the standardized suggestions associated with the Top Gun training did more harm to the park than good. Some employees, due to their dedication to AstroWorld, internalized theming to such a great degree that they argued with outside auditors who claimed to "know better than them." Though these individuals would typically be considered model employees, the discrepancies related to the interpretation of customer service practices and theming between them and members of NASCO created rifts in the service culture of AstroWorld. Ultimately, an employee's close dedication to the theme park culture and his or her desire to internalize or "live" a particular theme subjectively, created an ironic situation—the employee was *too focused* on the performance of theming desired by management. In a Durkheimian sense, the employee was too integrated in the themed culture of AstroWorld, similar to the circumstance of an individual being too well-integrated in a social group or in society.[41]

According to a guidebook on extending Disney theming and customer service principles to non-Disney venues, "The final phase of building a performance culture is to give employees the freedom to begin living it."[42] Many customers consider Disney theming to be well-developed, primarily because it is holistic, in everyone's proximity, and responds to all of the senses. Like Disney's theming philosophy, AstroWorld focused on creating a holistic, integrated, park-wide expression of theming. In AstroWorld's Cues to Guest Service training, a lengthy portion of the class was spent on connecting park theming to performance. One section of the class focused on "the spur of the moment" aspects of "improvisation" that were required of all employees in the park.[43] Successful theming, according to Cues to Guest Service training, was something that should happen at every moment in which a worker was in contact with patrons. A clear front/back stage dichotomy was expressed to all employees, and they were told that behavior outside of the accepted performance of the theme should not be displayed in view or earshot of patrons.[44] In their thematic personas, employees who performed for patrons were asked to improvise and to be prepared for any number of unexpected circumstances in the park. In short, employees were asked to "live theming" in the sense that it became a part of their consciousness. They were no longer individuals with personalities and desires, they were living extensions of the theme itself. As part of the environment of theming in which "everything speaks," employees, architecture, decor, and social interactions all became part of a generalized performative order of the theme.[45]

Arlie Hochschild suggested that "by taking over the levers of feeling production, by pretending deeply, [the worker] alters herself."[46] The deep acting that is a foundation of the performance of theming in a theme park is just the beginning; in fact, the end result of theming, in the minds of management philosophy, it is more akin to living. Workers, instilled with the foundations of theming—such as cowboy attitude, distinctive speech, body language, and other characteristics associated with a theme like western—take their emotional and performative acumen out into the park. As they use their skills in an aleatoric manner, these skills become innerdirected, touching their cores, their identity. Lived theming is a consequence of the "other-worldiness" of theming that, like performance, requires that all parties in the theme park reference the myriad cues of theming.[47] As patrons are impacted by the performances of employees, the effects of theming become outer-directed, affecting both patrons and other workers.[48] It is not surprising that Walt Disney, the primogeniture of the theme park, began to see his role in life as being a pedagogue not a mere entertainer.[49] What Disney realized was the powerful potential that theming could have in society, especially as it could be used to impact the lives of everyday people. Acting as the glue that holds together the theming of AstroWorld, the expressions of workers and their living of the theme established a seamless form of entertainment that parallels the cinematic effects of motion pictures. In film, the pacing of scenes, the editing of shots, and the effects of music and lighting help establish a believable text; the same can be said of theming in which workers create believable performances of the theme. This connection of theming and motion pictures is made explicit in employee training videos like the one mentioned at the beginning of the chapter. A significant remaining issue is the impact of the inner- and outer-directed personal nature of theming on the value structures of both company and society.

The Value Structure of Theming

In the late 1990s the Polynesian Resort at Walt Disney World underwent major architectural renovations; at the same time, Disney staff created a new value system that would complement the revamping of the resort theming. Disney management "studied the island cultures of the South Pacific and created new connections between traditional island values and the performance culture of the hotel."[50] According to Disney, the hotel furthered its theme by incorporating Pacific Island cultural values, including openness, honesty, courage, diversity and respect, and the "values were then linked directly to cast behaviors."[51] Disney's efforts at the Polynesian Resort reflect a growing emphasis in theming—the connection of architectural and performative aspects of themed spaces to the cultural systems of the originals that are referenced by the thematic copies. Disney's strategies suggest that corporations can use theming as more than a means of material simulation; theming can be connected directly to the values that are referenced in the originals that themed venues attempt to mimic. One of the most significant yet overlooked aspects of theming is its connection to specific cultural values of the society in which it is embedded, as well as its own value system that is produced as it is manifested in the material and immaterial means discussed in this chapter. Simultaneously, theming reflects the values of the culture that has created it and it creates values among its workers and patrons.

As I suggested in the previous section, the example of the incorporation of Disney discourse in AstroWorld training seminars was a reflection of the growth, embellishment, and standardization of Disney theming and customer service standards throughout the service and theming industries. AstroWorld management often stated that a goal of park training was the alteration of the worker. On the surface this related to the inculcation of the values of Six Flags in the worker—including punctuality, responsibility, and professionalism. At a deeper level, the goal of management included a more profound desire to *change* the worker—to act on his or her value structures. Members of management often told me that new AstroWorld workers came from tough backgrounds and that they lacked positive values and life skills. Working at the park, these workers could directly benefit from the values that were connected to Six Flags corporate philosophy as well as those associated with customer service and theming standards of the park. In this sense, management hoped that the sum of AstroWorld's values would serve to civilize the unruly worker, as well as the customer.[52]

Theming is a seemingly controllable form of consumer culture that is played out through the uncontrollable bodies of theme park workers and their patrons. Like the values that characterize the emancipatory hopes of consumerism—including individualism, cleanliness, and optimism—theming is commonly realized as a form of culture that is orderly. In many cases, however, the promised order of theming is thwarted by the realities of everyday life. In *Team Rodent*, a diatribe against the values of Disney, author Carl Hiaasen discusses the peculiarities that accompanied the opening of Disney's Animal Kingdom theme park in Orlando, Florida. In particular, he illustrates the circumstances of the unpredictability of the real animals that populate the stimulated savannahs of the park—some of them copulated in front of patrons, while others escaped or died, and a rhino was sodomized by someone with a stick.[53] What Hiaasen is pointing to is the issue of control that is endemic to any successful theme park. On the surface, theming is not messy or unpredictable—it is, by definition, a formative architectural undertaking that is carried out by controlled and predictable performances of employees, who, in turn, instill control in the patrons who populate themed spaces. As Hiaasen's analysis of Animal Kingdom illustrates, though theming strives to create orderly spaces that negate the disorders of the outside world, very often, unexpected circumstances prevail and theming fails to achieve desired forms of spatial and social control. Theming is a frustrating undertaking, especially for corporations that are grounded in the principles of predictability and control.

At AstroWorld, control was a difficult thing to achieve. The park's various themed lands supplied the necessary geographical boundaries that delimited one theme from the next. Operations and on-the-job training supplied the scripts, forms of behavior, and social patterns that were deemed appropriate for the given theme land. However, a variety of circumstances often made the spatial regulations of theming insignificant and also abated our training efforts. Employees were told to take a "flexible" attitude towards their work—even though they might be prepared to deliver the performances asked of them in their given themed work area, certain situations could never be predicted.[54] As a form of social control and form of social interaction, theming plays at the uncanny meeting of two poles—one is the demand for the worker to engage in what Hochschild denotes as "emotional labor," the other is the employee's manifested feelings and sense of self that are often at odds with the unnatural scripts, predetermined behaviors, and routinized interactions that characterize themed employment. Our training department stressed the readiness of the worker in both conveying the theme associated with the work area and in meeting the unpredictable and often difficult circumstances of their interactions with patrons. Though the worker must effectively convey the theme—including its emotional and performative aspects—there is no similar requirement of the patron to perform in kind. In fact, the patron can choose to ignore the effective portrayal of themes in the park—as was often the case at AstroWorld—or even respond with disdain for the worker, including insults.[55] The job of the theme park worker is to "enhance the customer's status," and even the best employee performance of theming could result in little or no appreciation by the patron; this is the downside of theming—commonly, it is behavior performed for the satisfaction of the self and that of the patron but which often results in neither.[56] Like many forms of consumerism that populate the social relationships of the everyday world, theming commonly produces a value structure that is based on vacuous elements. Ironically, though it is often purported to be a force that establishes orderly spatiality and predictable and hospitable sociality, theming is a commonly ambiguous cultural form.

The ambiguity of theming rests on many levels. For one, a theme is inherently a product of cultural associations that are marked more by referential slippages (différance) than solidified orders. As it is played out, and as it is further diluted in interpretative and social contexts, theming is made even less solid. At a final level, the ambiguous nature of theming is connected to the problem of assessment. Theming is not a final product—it is a moving target that unfolds, alters, and repositions. Commonly, our training department assessed theming in the following senses: (1) cleanliness, (2) perception is reality, (3) characterization of roles, (4) appearance of work areas, (5) employee moving through park (the idea of the cross-dissolve). As training coordinators, our job was to ensure that employees received the proper customer service and theming training that would hopefully guarantee success out in the park. However, management realized that effective theming was not an exact science and that means of assessment were needed to improve it. As we ourselves were trained, management often focused on idea of "making behaviors measurable," and training seminars in which we were involved included activities that asked participants to try and redefine park issues by making them measurable.[57] The problem of subjectivity and measurement was rooted in the unachievable nature of theming—though architecture and materiality could convey a theme, and though employees could be trained to perform it through their behavior, skills at social interaction, demeanor, and emotions, it was impossible to achieve because of its inherently rhizomatic nature. Unlike theming, quotidian social behavior is marked not by stasis, uniformitivity and solidity, but by liquidity, seepage, and effacement.[58] In the numerous examples of assessment at AstroWorld, management expected trainers to hold employees accountable for inaccuracies in their depictions of theming, but, ultimately, such expectations were based in an inaccurate understanding of theming as a predictable, not unpredictable, quality.

In his critical study of Disney entertainment culture, critic Henry A. Giroux writes that Disney employs a number of ideological devices in its construction of its media worldview. Innocence, normalized history, rationality, acceptance of authoritarianism, and the rejection of subversive tendencies are some of the values that Giroux suggests are found in the Disney worldview.[59] Though often overlooked, theming is directly related to values like those stressed in the Disney universe. As well, theming is often conceived as a form of socio-political emancipation—the customer is allowed to experience fantasies that are not available at home, while the worker is compensated for low salaries with the promise of being part of an exciting work environment and being able to play part of a theme. As theming becomes subjectively associated with both the worker and the consumer, the individual may be inclined to accept the values associated with it, particularly those that link choice, freedom, and identity. As Rose writes:

> Leisure has been invented as the domain of free choice *par excellence*. However constrained by external or internal factors, the modern self is institutionally required to construct a life through the exercise of choice from among alternatives.

> Every aspect of life, like every commodity, is imbued with a self-referential meaning; every choice we make is an emblem of our identity.[60]

At AstroWorld, one of the clear values that was stressed in park theming was comfort. Wherever a patron went, he or she could theoretically experience a good time—one free of stress and effort. Theming, as a conglomeration of multiple themes and entertainment possibilities, represented (to the consumer) the idea of anything goes. Of course, the "choices" that are offered by the various theme lands of a park have been deliberately conditioned. As Klein remarks, even when the choices appear to be given to the customer, he or she is subject to "form[s] of predestination, and the consumer journey acts out the illusion of free will. The consumer finished the story, but the object of the story (and the objects themselves) belongs to those who run the script."[61] Within the company, the value of comfort was also stressed in employee-employee relations. AstroWorld's "Welcome to Six Flags" training conducted by Human Resources used the analogy of the guest to relate comfort to new employees. In one exercise, new hires were asked to hypothesize how they would treat friends and family members if they were throwing a party.[62] Corporate myths, like those of Disney and Six Flags, are "unjustified beliefs, often enshrined in stories, and which influence how organisational actors understand and react to their social situation."[63] In many cases, the myths are encapsulated in seemingly innocuous and innocent material and immaterial expressions, like those identified by Giroux. Typically, customers are not encouraged to question the values that are associated with the services, products, and forms of entertainment that they receive in a theme park. As well, theme park employees are asked to accept the scripts, interactive styles, and consciousness-altering programs that are a part of the organizational structures of theming and customer service. In some cases, employees are told that, just like customers who appear to have infinite choice while in a theme park, they too can exercise decisions over their work life. Theming, as much as it is an entertainment practice, is an ideological undertaking that highlights certain values and underplays others.

As it was utilized at AstroWorld, the powerful discourse of Disney conveyed the idea of choice to our employees. In corporate training manuals like *The Disney Way*, Disney discourse is often touted as an expression of democracy. For designers and imagineers, establishing a new film, attraction, or ride begins with storyboarding and the idea of *blue sky*.[64] Blue sky refers to a symbolic canvas—a blank space on which any member of the team can brainstorm, dream, and provide ideas for the direction of the project. Though AstroWorld did not explicitly use the term *blue sky*, it did emphasize the idea of team decision making throughout the park. Because theming was an imaginative construction—after all, Mayan-themed roller coasters and the like are fantastical constructions—a corollary was that the park workers who staffed the various themed areas of the park were an intimate part of the imaginative order. Like the "cast members" of Disney parks, AstroWorld workers were asked to play their parts on the "stages" that were represented by rides, attractions, and shows. Unfortunately, many of the decisions that were promised to entry-level workers were not, in the end, available to them. Rides leads and middle management of the park called the shots, and, often, this led to some employees doubting the philosophy of imagination and shared decision making that was presented to them early in their park training. In some cases, employees did have suggestions regarding the improvement of the delivery of park theming, but these suggestions were often ignored. Arguably, had management really tapped into the imagination of theme park workers—who, after all, acted as the primary means of social interaction with patrons—park theming could have been more inventive, interactive, and enjoyable. Like the value of choice that dominates the vision of consumerism for the patron, the purported democracy of theming is unrealized. In the theme park, similar to the scripts that function as part of the flow of park rides, attractions, and entertainment, the idea of theming as a participatory, democratic, and nonhierarchical undertaking itself became a script of the corporation.

The issue of the democracy of theming and corporate structure rests on the social values in which theming is embedded. Though theme parks sometimes purport to do otherwise—as was illustrated in Disney's remolding of the Polynesian Resort in Orlando, Florida—the typical values that are promoted in theming are United States ones.[65] The prominence of capitalism, the American Dream, and assumptions about gender and race, are all products of the value structure that is promoted in theming. For many of the reasons discussed in this chapter, employees and patrons are often unwilling or unable to reflect on the ideological aspects of theming. In some instances, people are unaware of the political intentions behind a particular themed area; in others, even if they are cognizant of some motives—such as understanding the intentions of an explicitly corporate-themed venue like Batman the Escape and its numerous movie and product tie-ins—they are uninterested in critique precisely because they are enjoying the theme as pure entertainment.[66] For the patron, theme parks like AstroWorld provided entertainment that, whether understood as ideological or not, promoted situations and interactions that may have been uncommon in the outside world. Like any person seeking "an escape from their everyday routine," as our AstroWorld slogan promoted, the patron is desirous of values that may be absent in the "real" world outside the theme park. Yet, for cultural critics the very values that theming promotes result in the admonishment of people who use theme parks and their theming as sources of entertainment and personal meaning. Many critics would not apply the same criticism to people who hike in nature or who look to the outdoors as an escape from their everyday reality, possibly because "nature" still maintains some sense of the real—an unimpeded, uncontaminated, and immutable place outside of the realm of consumerism and culture. The elitism of this criticism illustrates the interesting and peculiar role that the themed space plays in social life.[67] One should be aware of the many ways in which consumerist values impede positive social realizations in themed spaces and outside them, but one should also be understanding of circumstances in which positive values can actually be instilled as a result of participation in themed spaces like AstroWorld.[68]

Like the condition of the patron in the theme park, the worker is subjected to many forms of criticism. Often, a similarly etic or outsider's view is emphasized in which critics discursively assail workers for their participation in the consumerist simulated fantasy of the theme park. Theme park workers are not simple automata who slavishly perform the themes of the park. Many of my co-workers expressed a nuanced understanding of their work conditions: some criticized management for its lack of understanding of their needs and for its emphasis on training regimens that served to transform them into lifeless beings who serviced the rides. Some even took an active role in theming by providing feedback to management. In one case, a rides lead expressed concerns about inaccuracies of symbols on the Mayan Mind Bender ride. For many AstroWorld workers, the experience of working at the park was not, as is commonly offered in media portrayals, the opportunity of a lifetime. Even though positions in themed spaces are sometimes presented as dream jobs, it is a common occurrence for the worker to emotionally detach him- or herself from the work itself.[69] In the case of emotional labor in the service industry, the example of the smile is telling. In the service industry, "smiling is separated from its usual function, which is to express a personal feeling, and attached to another one—expressing a company feeling."[70] This circumstance, in which a quotidian behavior is transformed from its typical use and context to one that serves an artificial use and business context, results in a crisis of authenticity that simultaneously confronts the worker, patron, and society itself.[71] Theming is inauthentic symbolism that is made authentic through the employee's performance of it out in the park. Some workers with whom I was associated enjoyed performances of theming, such as smiling and friendliness, and they rarely resulted in a crisis of identity. In other cases, workers were negatively affected by the ways in which theming played out through them. They became upset with customers, and themselves, and they developed cynical attitudes and often took out their frustrations on co-workers and management. They even began to internalize that because they could not handle a job that was supposed to be fun and easy, that they, themselves, were failures.[72]

As an AstroWorld trainer, I struggled with the ethical dimensions of my assessment work, as well as with the concerns that I had for general social well-being of my co-workers and patrons, which was generally complicated by the effect of theming and other forms of simulation. Theming, as a means of negotiating the social world, plays on the uneasy tension between forms of sociality and identity that are present outside the themed space and forms of sociality and identity that are mutated, reinterpreted, filtered, and recast within the themed space. Like many of my co-workers, I wrestled with the tension between the real and the unreal that developed on a daily basis—racism, sexism, and homophobia, which are purported to not be a part of the world of the theme park, often reminded workers of the creeping real that emerged in the simulated theme lands of AstroWorld. In some cases, it was difficult to establish a clear line between the real and the simulated, the authentic and the inauthentic, the theme and the non-theme. Writers have suggested that *there is* a clear demarcation between the real world outside of theme parks and the unreal world inside of theme parks, but I believe that this construction is a result of the lack of ethnographic attention that has been given to themed spaces. Were more anthropological studies of themed spaces conducted, the public would realize that themed spaces are, in many ways, no different than their non-themed counterparts of the everyday world. Such studies would also indicate that, contrary to the writings of etic critics, theme parks like AstroWorld can fulfill meaningful needs for identity, social interaction, and happiness in workers and patrons.

Epilogue: The End of AstroWorld

In October 2006, while searching the Internet for current information about AstroWorld theming, I discovered that AstroWorld had closed. I had expected to find pictures of the theme lands, albeit updated since I had worked at the park in the early 1990s, but, instead I found a note that the park had closed. I searched the Internet for signs of the park that I had known, and discovered some images that were familiar to me but now seemed surreal—the Batcave being torn down by bulldozers, the razing of the Texas Cyclone, and a photo of a now empty wasteland that looked nothing like the park that I had known. Gone were the theme lands, all of the rides and attractions, and the many memories that I, and other workers and patrons, had associated with the park. I mentioned to someone that I felt melancholy about the destruction of the park, and I could sympathize with people on the Internet who had asked the city of Houston to protect the park from demolition. It is interesting that I did not have the same reaction to the closures and demolishment of casinos on the Las Vegas Strip, but it makes sense given the fact that I worked at AstroWorld. Like other employees and patrons, I have fond memories of the park, and I am sad to learn that it is no more. Now, it is merely a product of our collective imagination. We have no more rides to hop on, no more stunt shows to watch, and no more barbeque to eat. Everything is a memory, even the theme lands. As a critic, I can bemoan the fact that theme parks promote inauthenticity in their constructions of western, Mexican, Coney Island, and other themes, but as an individual and former AstroWorld trainer I can attest to the fact that the relationships engendered at the park were very real. If the "real" happens to be themed, as is becoming more the case in all venues of everyday life, then we can only hope that the relations that emerge in themed spaces can be as meaningful as those of the symbolic caves of Lascaux. In attempting to understand places like AstroWorld, though our best intentions may tell us to focus only on the materiality of themed spaces, we must look instead to the immaterial conditions of our intimate relationships that may, ultimately, matter most.[73]

Notes

1. This video was shown to all new employees at Six Flags AstroWorld.

2. The Project on Disney, *Inside the Mouse: Work and Play at Disney World* (Durham, N.C.: Duke University Press, 1995).

3. Though not specific to themed service venues, two major sources related to dehumanization and service are George Rizter, *The McDonaldization of Society*, rev. ed. (Thousand Oaks, Calif: Pine Forge, 1996); Robin Leidner, *Fast Food, Fast Talk: Service Work and the Routinization of Everyday Life* (Berkeley: University of California Press, 1993).

4. Arlie Russell Hochschild, *The Managed Heart: Commercialization of Human Feeling* (Berkeley: University of California Press, 1983). See also Susan Benson, *Counter Cultures: Saleswomen, Managers, and Customers in American Department Stores, 1890–1940* (Urbana: University of Illinois Press, 1987).

5. Hochschild, *The Managed* Heart, 5.

6. During my employment, Six Flags was owned by Warner Brothers. The Looney Tunes characters were part of the corporate theming of the park that was undertaken in areas outside of Bugs Bunny Land.

7. For more on the associations of Disney's main street see Richard V. Francaviglia, *Main Street Revisited: Time, Space, and Image Building in Small-town America* (Iowa City: University of Iowa Press, 1996).

8. Six Flags AstroWorld, *Park Operations Rides Manual*, 1994, 7.

9. Norbert Elias, *The Civilizing Process* (Malden, Maine: Blackwell, 2000).

10. Six Flags AstroWorld, *Six Flags Employee Handbook*, 1995.

11. Michael Taussig, *Mimesis and Alterity: A Particular History of the Senses* (New York: Routledge, 1993), 13.

12. Quoted in Disney Institute, *Be Our Guest: Perfecting the Art of Customer Service* (New York: Disney Editions, 2001), 79–80.

13. Scott A. Lukas, "Signal 3: Ethnographic Experiences in the American Theme Park Industry" (PhD diss., Rice University, 1998). My dissertation develops the emphasis on the politics of the social networks at Six Flags AstroWorld.

14. Michel Foucault, *Society Must Be Defended* (New York: Picador, 2003); Michel Foucault, *Power*, ed. James D. Faubion (New York: New Press, 2000); Michel Foucault, *The History of Sexuality: An Introduction* (New York: Vintage, 1990).

15. Nikolas Rose, *Governing the Soul: The Shaping of the Private Self* (London: Routledge, 1989), 10. Michel Foucault, "Governmentality," in *Power*, ed. James D. Faubion (New York: New Press 2000), 211.

16. Rose, *Governing the Soul*, 56.

17. Paul Rabinow and Nikolas Rose, "Thoughts on the Concept of Biopower Today," <http://www.molsci.org/files/Rose_Rabinow_Biopower_Today.pdf> (15 October 2006).

18. Disney Institute, *Be Our Guest*, 32. The authors call for the "creation of location-specific *performance cultures*," and define a performance culture as "a set of behaviors, mannerisms, terms and values that are taught to new cast members as they enter their job location."

19. Six Flags AstroWorld, *Operations Manual*.

20. Another related issue is the discontinuity between the personality of the worker and that being expressed by the company. Joanne Martin, "An Alternative to Bureaucratic Impersonality and Emotional Labor: Bounded Emotionality at the Body Shop," *Administrative Science Quarterly* June 1998, <www.findarticles.com> (5 September 2006).

21. Some employees, such as Grounds Quality and Parking Lot individuals, were not a part of any theme land, and their costumes were more generic, without reference to theme. This fact often led to animosity of these employees because some felt that due to their being "left out" of the story of a particular theme land, they were less valued as employees and individuals.

22. Six Flags AstroWorld, *Operations Division Manual*, 15.

23. Hairstyle policies at Six Flags and Disney parks are very controversial. The American Civil Liberties Union was contacted in regards to hairstyle policy enforcement at Six Flags America. Many workers claim discrimination over park policies that ban "extreme" hairstyles. Avis Thomas-Lester, "At Six Flags, the Don'ts of Dos," *Washington Post*, 17 June 2006, B01.

24. Leidner, *Fast Food*, 23.

25. There were claims made by some employees that segregation occurred at the park; some argued that management did not trust some ethnic groups to perform in certain theme land, and they were relegated to less desirable positions in other theme lands. There were also claims that segregation occurred as a result of gender and sexual orientation.

26. Six Flags AstroWorld, *Entertainment Department Manual*, 1993–1994.

27. In a study of Disneyland employees, Van Maanen and Kunda indicate that on-the-job training is a form of socialization in which employees are conditioned into park culture. John van Maanen and Gideon Kunda, "Life with Tinkerbell," (part of "Real Feelings: Emotional Expression and Organizational Culture"), in *Research in Organizational Behavior* Vol. 11, ed. L.L. Cummings and Barry M. Staw (Greenwich, Conn.: JAI Press 1989), 64.

28. A similar example is related in a discussion of the early Disneyland park. Apparently, a young boy who was assigned to play Tom Sawyer on Tom Sawyer Island took his part too seriously. He had read the book and took on an aggressive persona, even attacking other kids who visited the attraction. Bill Capodagli and Lynn Jackson, *The Disney Way: Harnessing the Management Secrets of Disney in Your Company* (New York: McGraw-Hill, 1999), 133.

29. Both of these philosophies were corporate campaigns aimed at improving the levels of customer service in Six Flags parks. Both relied on a heavy use of discourse related to performance.

30. Norman Klein, *The Vatican to Vegas: A History of Special Effects* (New York: New Press, 2004).

31. During Human Resources training sessions, employees were told that service was connected to "your performance and [park] theming . . . just like in a movie or a fantasy." Six Flags AstroWorld, *Welcome to Six Flags*.

32. Hochschild, *The Managed Heart*, 77.

33. Six Flags AstroWorld, *Train the Trainer Manual*.

34. Six Flags AstroWorld, *Operations Manual—Back to the Basics*, 7. Six Flags AstroWorld, *Coordinator Training Manual*, 34.

35. Ronald P. Mendoza, "Themed Retail Design," *Where It's @*, <http://www.where-its-at.com/articles/spotlightarticles/spotlight4.html> (2 March 2004). For more on the role of stories in creating emotional labor, see David M. Boje, "Stories of the Storytelling Organization: A Postmodern Analysis of Disney as 'Tamara-Land'," *Academy of Management Journal* 38 (4): 997–1035.

36. See Scott A. Lukas,"Theming as a Sensory Phenomenon: Discovering the Senses on the Las Vegas Strip" in this volume for more on this argument. Also, Ritzer discusses this idea in depth in his work, *The McDonaldization of Society*, 131.

37. Within contemporary management philosophy, there is a new emphasis on the matching of the employee's subjectivity with the goals of the corporations. See Marcus Buckingham and Curt Coffman, *First, Break All the Rules* (New York: Simon and Schuster, 1999).

38. In a study of the dynamics of workers at Disneyland in Anaheim, California, it is noted that "where one is assigned to work in the park carries social weight." Van Maanen and Kunda,"Life with Tinkerbell," 61. For an excellent discussion of the dynamics of employees and service culture see Aviad E. Raz, *Riding the Black Ship: Japan and Tokyo Disneyland* (Cambridge, Mass.: Harvard University Asia Center, 1999).

39. Disney Institute, *Be Our Guest*, 120.

40. For more on NASCO's work in the park see, Scott A. Lukas, "An American Theme Park: Working and Riding out Fear in the Late Twentieth Century," in *Late Editions 6, Paranoia within Reason: A Casebook on Conspiracy as Explanation*, ed. George E. Marcus (Chicago: University of Chicago Press, 1999), 405–28.

41. Emile Durkheim, *Suicide* (New York: Macmillan, 1966).

42. Disney Institute, *Be Our* Guest, 98.

43. Six Flags AstroWorld, *Cues to Guest Service Manual*. The entire Cues to Guest Service program stressed the teaching of improvisational skills to employees, including how to deal with spur-of-the-moment difficulties with customers.

44. Erving Goffman, *The Presentation of Self in Everyday Life* (New York: Anchor, 1959).

45. Disney Institute, *Be Our* Guest, 33.

46. Hochschild, *The Managed Heart*, 33.

47. For more on the idea of performance as an "other-worldly" experience, see Richard Schechner, *Performance Theory* (New York: Routledge, 1988), 9.

48. Lived theming is the equivalent of a theme becoming the reality that workers and customers accept as meaningful and natural. It is akin to Baudrillard's concept of hypereality in which the copy displaces the original as the original. See Jean Baudrillard, *Simulations* (New York: Semiotext(e), 1983). In many of our training classes, as an example, we stated that employees should perform not only for the patron, but for their co-workers, who were, similar to patrons, also "guests."

49. The Project on Disney, *Inside the Mouse*, 221.

50. Disney Institute, *Be Our Guest*, 92.

51. Disney Institute, *Be Our Guest*, 92–93.

52. This project of civilizing is similar to the notions of Frederick Law Olmsted who envisioned Central Park as a project of democracy, in which it "would soothe discontent and encourage sociability.... It would discipline conduct and uplift public taste by providing a restful and decorous environment." John F. Kasson, *Amusing the Million: Coney Island at the Turn of the Century* (New York: Hill and Wang, 1978), 15. As Van Maanen and Kunda write of the socialization of Disneyland employees, the effect of the social communication of customer service principles to employees is a "penetration into the private spheres of individual thought and feeling." Van Maanen and Kunda, "Life with Tinkerbell," 68.

53. Karl Hiaasen, *Team Rodent: How Disney Devours the World* (New York: Library of Contemporary Thought, 1998). See, in particular, the section "Jungle Book," 68–83.

54. Flexibility has become a buzzword in corporate culture. Many corporate advisors, like Tom Peters, argue that companies need to be more responsive to customers and more open to employees and their idiosyncrasies. See Gary Heil, Tom Parker, and Rick Tate, *Leadership and the Customer Revolution* (New York: Von Nostrand Reinhold, 1995), 158.

For a discussion of the general impact of flexibility in culture see Emily Martin, *Flexible Bodies* (New York: Beacon, 1995).

55. This idea is developed in Hochschild's study of the situation of airline stewardesses. *The Managed Heart*, 110.

56. Hochschild, *The Managed Heart*, 139.

57. *Six Flags Academy of Excellence Leadership Summit*, 1995.

58. I attribute this conceptualization of the social to the important work of sociologist Zygmunt Bauman, including *Liquid Life* (Malden, Mass.: Polity, 2006), *Liquid Modernity* (Malden, Mass.: Polity, 2005), and *Liquid Love* (Malden, Mass.: Polity, 2003). For more on the connection of liquidity and theming, see Scott A. Lukas, "The Theming of Everyday Life: Mapping the Self, Life Politics, and Cultural Hegemony on the Las Vegas Strip," forthcoming *Community College Humanities Association Journal* (2007).

59. Henry A. Giroux, "Beyond the Politics of Innocence: Memory and Pedagogy in the 'Wonderful World of Disney,'" *Socialist Review* 23, no. 2 (1993): 79–107.

60. Rose, *Governing the Soul*, 227.

61. Klein, *The Vatican to Vegas*, 355. As Klein writes, the value of the customer finishing the theme or of the theme being intimately connected to him or her in an *individual* way is becoming a primary focus of many consumer themed spaces. For example, a 2006 brochure for Disneyland stated, "This is where . . . each person is transformed into the star of his or her own amazing story from the moment they walk through the gates."

62. Six Flags AstroWorld, *Welcome to Six Flags*. In another training, Cues to Guest Service, employees were asked to compare park theming to throwing a party for friends.

63. Andrew Brown, *Organisational Culture* (London: Pitman, 1995), 15. Similar to myth, theming commonly functions as "depoliticized speech." See Roland Barthes, *Mythologies* (New York: Hill and Wang, 1995), 142.

64. Capodagli and Jackson, *The Disney Way*, 149.

65. Stephen M. Fjellman, *Vinyl Leaves: Walt Disney World and America* (Boulder, Colo.: Westview, 1992), 29. For the classic discussion of American values, see Robin M. Williams, *American Society: A Sociological Interpretation*, 2nd ed. (New York: Alfred A. Knopf, 1964).

66. I often overheard customers poking fun at the gift shop that all people had to move through when they exited the Batman the Escape ride. In some cases, this awareness of the explicit corporate intentions of AstroWorld led them to exit the shop without purchasing any Batman-themed items.

67. For more on the problematic nature of anti-Disney theme park discourse, see Greil Marcus, "Forty Years of Overstatement: Criticism and the Disney Theme Parks," in *Designing Disney's Theme Parks: The Architecture of Reassurance*, ed. Karal Ann Marling (Paris: Flammarion, 1997), 201–207.

68. For example, though not always the case, there is sometimes a recognition of the mutuality of the other that occurs in interactions between patrons and workers. Were positive values to be promoted, such as mutual respect, the theme park could begin to resemble a space of social possibility rather than one of consumerist doom.

69. Hochschild, *The Managed Heart*, 17.

70. Hochschild, *The Managed Heart*, 127.

71. For more on the crisis of authenticity see, Charles Guignon, *On Being Authentic* (London: Routledge, 2004).

72. At AstroWorld, this circumstance of burnout resulted in 45 percent of the workforce leaving before season's end.

73. Some memories of Astroworld may be found at <http://www.astroworldpark.com/> and <http://www.sixflagshouston.com/>. Nostalgia for theme parks helps illustrate the ways in which consumer themed spaces do become meaningful in the minds of workers and patrons. Though they are dismissed by critics, themed spaces are often connected with significant memories by patrons and workers. The Internet helps establish this important dimension of the themed space and memory.

Chapter 12

Behind-the-Scenes Spaces: Promoting Production in a Landscape of Consumption

Ann Brigham

In May 2004, The Henry Ford Museum in Dearborn, Michigan, opened a new attraction, The Ford Rouge Factory Tour. Located on the grounds of the historic Rouge plant, the tour ushers visitors through the Legacy Theater, Art of Manufacturing Theater, Observation Deck, and Assembly Plant. In the months leading up to its debut, the tour's Web site touted the distinctive character and allure of this unique five-part attraction:

> GO behind the scenes inside one of the world's largest automotive complexes. EXPERIENCE a virtual reality theater adventure. SEE the world's largest living roof. WITNESS the new factory where the Ford F-150 will be made.[1]

This text's graphic emphasis on active verbs—the capitalization of GO, EXPERIENCE, SEE, and WITNESS—positions the tourist as an active participant on the move. That is, the text encourages each visitor to understand the factory tour as a dynamic encounter between sightseer and sight in which everyone plays a part. This rhetorical appeal appears in a more literal way at another tourist hot spot, the Universal Studios, Hollywood theme park. In a brochure, Universal Studios welcomes visitors to: "Step into the spotlight. Come face to face with world-famous stars! Learn movie making secrets. . . . Star in your own thriller." Its Web site also features directives to potential visitors: "Get into blockbuster thrills. Go behind-the-scenes and on the sets where movies are made. Then cast yourself in the thrilling rides, shows and attractions that bring movie action to life."[2] No matter what the choice of attraction, things happen to those who visit Universal Studios; your heart will stop on Jurassic Park: The Ride, you'll "scream through time" on Back to the Future: The Ride, and be blown out of the water by the pyrotechnics and special effects of Waterworld: A Live Sea War Spectacular.[3] Although they seem to have little in common, these two popular attractions, the factory tour and the theme park, share an appeal: the promise to transport visitors to backstage, or behind-the-scenes, spaces, in which paying tourists will not just passively consume, but actively produce, their experiences.

In what follows, I discuss these two tourist attractions in order to examine the larger phenomenon of behind-the-scenes tourism. Specifically, I explore these attractions' common enterprise of taking sightseers behind the scenes to show them how things are made. In replicating movie sets from some of Hollywood's hottest films, the Universal Studios theme park guarantees that visitors will "go deep behind the scenes" to see how movies are made.[4] The Rouge factory tour will take its visitors behind the scenes to "See where the new Ford F-150s are assembled in a new lean and flexible manufacturing plant."[5] Behind-the-scenes tours, in general, seem to operate on a shared promise of taking visitors to off-limits spaces to show them how things are made. But, as I will argue, these two backstage tours not only display modes of production, but do so in order to resurrect the figure of the active producer in a world driven by consumption. In a land where we "make a difference" and most notably "just do it," an ideology of production, and by extension, productivity, seems quintessentially American. And what better way to laud that ideology than through the active witnessing of the making of two products—the Hollywood movie and the automobile—that stand as prominent symbols of American cultural identity? But in a time when consumer culture threatens to crowd out any other vision of ourselves—that is, when the ideology of consumption is ubiquitously visible—it is those hidden behind-the-scenes spaces, sites that by definition promise to reveal insider knowledge of what is most authentic and "real," that become the ideal site for the performance of the revival of production.

The Promise of Authenticity

Behind-the-scenes tours have, of course, been around since the beginning of mass tourism. In his groundbreaking book, *The Tourist*, originally published in 1976, Dean MacCannell proposed that the figure of the tourist represented a model for "modern man in general."[6] He argued that modernity created a profound alienation in which the modern person, having lost "his attachments to the work bench, the neighborhood, the town, the family, which he once called 'his own,'" went in search of authenticity.[7] The modernistic disruption of "real life" prompted a touristic fascination with the "real life" of others.[8] According to MacCannell, sightseers, "motivated by a desire to see life as it is really lived," attempted to see the back regions of the places they visited.[9] Forays into back regions, as staged as they might be, promised to show visitors the *real* ways people lived or things worked. During this time period, then, behind-the-scenes tours showcased a sense of authenticity seemingly lost in the transition from the industrial to the modern world, when individuals felt alienated from a new social order.

MacCannell discusses this modernistic search for authenticity in relation to the European subject's desire to preserve so-called primitive cultures as symbols of a lost, or quickly disappearing, authentic way of life. In addition, across modern and industrial settings, backstage tours of work allowed modern subjects to gain a more local sense of an authentic way of life by restoring their identification with the figure of the worker and the importance of the individual's work in general. According to MacCannell, "Wherever industrial society is transformed into modern society, work is simultaneously transformed into an object of touristic curiosity . . . labor and production are being presented to sightseers in guided tours of factories and in museums of science and industry."[10] It is this focus on work as spectacle that is most relevant to the presentation of behind-the-scenes spaces at Universal Studios theme park and the Rouge plant. Although the factory tour, with its explicit and sustained focus on the magnificent history of Ford production, most obviously illustrates the labor-as-spectacle phenomenon, the theme park is unique from other amusement parks in the way that it repeatedly gives its visitors jobs to do. Both attractions' dramatizations of work and production exemplify the search for authenticity MacCannell identifies as the result of economic and cultural change, and the ensuing crisis, at the turn of the twentieth century.

However, at the turn of the twenty-first century, the meaning of the individual's alienation has shifted to reflect the different relations created by consumer capitalism and globalization, relations in which the identity of the figure of the producer faces obsolescence. These two contemporary behind-the-scenes tours emerge in an era when consumption—and not the production MacCannell analyzes—represents the organizing ideological framework for our capitalistic culture. And it is, notably, a shift that has everything to do with Ford and the auto industry.

Consuming Identities

Very briefly, the effects of the large-scale implementation of Fordist practices shaped twentieth-century material and symbolic relations between production and consumption in the United States. The labor processes made (in)famous by assembly-line production increased the efficiency and standardization of production by making uniform and compartmentalizing labor tasks, de-skilling workers, and decreasing labor value, that is, by generally disempowering workers. Since that time, in Philip Cooke's words, "workers have come to accept that if there is relatively little satisfaction to be had from the labour process itself, deprived as it is of any significant element of control, then it is in the sphere of consumption that psychological satisfactions are to be found."[11]

At the individual scale, then, consumption practices provided fulfillment and a sense of identity. But, consumption also shaped practices at a larger scale. As Mark Gottdiener argues, in the twentieth century, "it is the act of consumption that is at the base of the survival of capitalism."[12] According to Gottdiener, the issue "for the continued expansion of capital is no longer so much the problem of production," that is, "competitive profit-making through cost reduction and mass production" but the problem of consumption, of how to realize profit in the market.[13] In the twentieth century, capitalism came to depend "more on the transformation of individuals into desiring free-spending consumers than into industrial workers."[14]

In the twentieth century, mass production generated a need for mass consumption. The assembly line's "explosion of commodity production" created a culture in which people were encouraged to "purchase commodities even if they go into debt and whether or not their purchase satisfies some basic need."[15] Offering extensive credit plans to its workers and others, the Ford company, and the automobile culture it inspired, provides a prominent example of this shift to an emphasis on the material and symbolic importance of consumption. As the quintessential symbol of mass production, the automobile quickly emerged as the ultimate sign of individual consumption and individualism itself. Unlike the railroad or public transportation, the private car seemingly promised everybody the ability to go, live, and work anywhere. The automobile imbued the consumer with a sense of geographical, social, and economic mobility that epitomized American identity. This shift in the stage of capitalism moved from a system in which profit depended on "the production process, or the exploitation of labor," to one that depended on "the control of consumer desire" through advertising and other strategies that foregrounded the symbolic meanings of goods and services.[16]

Throughout the twentieth century, scholars from numerous fields have written about consumer capitalism and consumption both as a means of social reproduction and a vehicle for democratic, liberatory expression, as well as everything in between. Though scholars disagree on how, and why, consumption has become an organizing ideology, they share the perception that consumption exists as a realm of identity formation for American culture and its diverse citizens.[17] The automobile example I briefly sketched is only one instance of this consumer ideology, in which consumers value their buying behaviors and choices as "status- or identity-conferring" practices.[18] Taking their cues from buying patterns, marketers understand that people "must experience consumption as a volitional site of personal development, achievement, and self-creation, not as a place in which they are simply mapping their lives on some advertiser's template."[19]

Furthermore, as the twentieth century progressed, the "proliferation of customized products and niche markets," as well as the use of brands to "differentiate functionally equivalent products" and, I would add, services, "elevated the importance of symbolism" of commodities.[20] That is, as marketers promote seemingly identical products and services, the narratives created around and about those commodities gain increasing importance. Consumers distinguish purchases based on their symbolic meaning. In effect, we assert who we are and what we stand for through consumption. As Douglas B. Holt and Juliet B. Schor argue, even the postmodern marketplace:

> retains the idea that subjectivity is created, and naturalized, through consuming. Indeed, the commodity form continues to gain stature as the preeminent site through which people experience and express the social world, even as the worlds that are channeled through it are orchestrated less by marketers than by consumers. In this contemporary marketplace, escaping the commodity form becomes increasingly difficult. Difference, dissent, resistance, opposition—they all resurface as consumables, whether through the purchase of a black Barbie, a Working Assets telephone card, or a Patagonia organic T-shirt.[21]

Although Holt and Schor identify a consumption-saturated culture, they also find "doubts about consumer society reemerging at the end of the twentieth century."[22] They posit a range of reasons for such doubt, including increasing dissatisfaction with the inequality of wealth distribution, "the relentless commodification of all areas of social life," and the corporate vision of global consumerism, which profits from "cheap commodities based on exploiting labor and natural resources."[23]

Holt and Schor observe that there exists now a growing sense of "a better, *more authentic*, and less consumerist way to live."[24] As an opposition to consumption, production becomes the site of authenticity—again. And so we seem to have returned to MacCannell's analysis of work as the site of authenticity in the wake of modernist alienation. However, tourist experiences at the end of the twentieth century (and beginning of the twenty-first) differ from earlier examples because the contemporary ones manifest our doubts about consumer society by offering a transformation of the figure of consumer into something else.

For instance, evidence of this difference appears in certain leisure activities, where consumers use their purchasing power to buy experiences rather than commodities (something not new in twentieth-century capitalism, but more pronounced). Such leisure activities mend the splintering of the identity of the American worker by inviting consumers to use their consumption as a way to regain a sense of productivity. These touristic enterprises are marketed around the attractions of production and productivity. Archaeological tours, for example, charge large fees for vacationers to work at digs. Or, "green tours" offer paying customers the chance to make trails, build housing, count endangered birds, and other activities. In their leisure time, then, people pay for the opportunity to engage in fulfilling labor. Such tours' appeal seems to be their emphasis on meaningful activity. By positioning tourists in a larger train of events that, perhaps, couldn't succeed without their participation, these enterprises send visitors home feeling like valuable agents in a larger social order.[25] Tourist sites such as these have become the settings for performances that laud productivity in a world where our identities are overwhelmingly defined by consumption.

But how does this ideological shift away from consumption play out in tourist attractions that promote experiences behind the scenes? These performances of production and productivity emerge within, and engage with, another shift in capitalism, one from Fordism to post-Fordism. Fordism can be characterized as involving "not only the rationalization of production through the Taylorization of work processes and the introduction of assembly lines, but also of consumption (the family wage and the eight-hour day were meant to encourage workers to consume the products they made)."[26] Post-Fordism is identified with a more flexible accumulation, one defined by "niche marketing and the shift from durable goods to services and media."[27] However, as some scholars have argued, the mass production/mass consumption economy is not statistically or empirically in rapid decline. Rather, the "info-service-niche-marketed capitalism" of post-Fordism has emerged as the "image of capitalism being promoted throughout popular media," and so it has gained "ideological dominance."[28] What I want to suggest is that this ideological dominance of post-Fordism appears, however unwittingly, in recent popular cultural forms that, as a result, allow us to analyze shifting conceptions of production, consumption, and the relations between them. Take, for instance, the theme park.

Theming Production at Disneyland and Universal Studios

As Disney scholars have recounted, Walt Disney founded his theme parks after a family trip to Coney Island convinced him that such places threatened his daughters' physical and moral security. By contrast, his parks, beginning with Disneyland, restored familial wholesomeness as the structuring narrative of popular amusement. Disneyland promised a pleasure free from literal and symbolic dirt—not only trash and waste, but disorder, displays of sexuality, spontaneity, and "tough-looking" employees.[29] This mission was largely realized through the spatial design of the park, and subsequent Disney parks such as Disney World and EPCOT. The elaborate division of the theme park into on- and off-stage or front- and back-spaces premiered a vast and intricate infrastructure that concealed the unsightly aspects of the business of pleasure. Even today, while "pneumatic tubes 'whisk away refuse like magic,'" elaborate technical systems keep the inner workings of amusements hidden and quiet.[30] Disney's architectural underground sweepingly suppresses modes of production. Employees don their costumes in subterranean spaces before traveling unseen through labyrinthine tunnels in order to emerge into their appropriate part of the park. Bifurcating space into above/below, valuable/waste, visible/invisible, and public/private, the parks' architectural design defines the goal and the fruition of social reproduction as the rigorous separation of worth and waste.

With their bifurcated designs, Disney parks like Disneyland, Disney World, and EPCOT literalize spatially Marx's notion of commodity fetishism. As Alexander Wilson has also noted, the facets of production are hidden from sight—"much as productive forces are hidden in the image of the commodity"—so that we are left to revel in our role as consumers.[31] This capitalist scheme works to hide from view, and thus erase from memory, exploitative labor practices. This erasure is necessary so that individuals will buy into the system as consumers since, conceivably, in their roles as workers they would reject the system. But at theme parks like Universal Studios Hollywood, the display of behind-the-scenes spaces of production, those that Disney emphatically concealed, sells the tickets. If we accept this to be the case, why display the modes of production that dispel the trick of the commodity?

At this theme park, the revelation of modes of production functions to transform the consumer into the producer, challenging the passivity of the consumer by resurrecting consumption as an act of invention and discovery. While Disney's rigid order, automata, and de-skilling of tourists imparts a Fordist tone, Universal Studios moves theme parks into the post-Fordist age. By design, Disney parks tend to control every inch of our experience, crowding us out as producers and as imaginative participants, offering consumerism, as many Disney critics point out, as the visitor's singular activity.[32] By contrast, Universal Studios emphasizes multiple, flexible, and diverse identifications, making available at least the possibility of many more fantasy subject positions than Disneyland/Disney World. Like a characteristically post-Fordist service industry, the park capitalizes on attractions that seem to meet niche markets, emphasizing changing, heterogeneous exhibits where performative options allow customers to experience the same ride differently on repeat visits.

Universal Studios' invitations to activity and adventure exalt role-playing, performance, and audience interaction. While the narrative tightness of themed lands and audio-animatronics organizes the pleasures of Disneyland and Disney World into, perhaps, an assembly-line-like experience, live shows, stunt people, and special effects deliver Universal Studios' "amazing adventures." Disneyland maps and scripts its terrain unilaterally; visitors know what to expect in Frontierland or Tomorrowland, places where visitors will line up dutifully to meet with their favorite Disney characters—characters who will not stray from their assigned lands. Universal Studios, however, has the barest of floor plans (the place is divided into the upper and lower lots) with lots of open, "directionless" space, inviting interaction and invention. And, what occupies that space is not fixed. For instance, in order to keep pace with the latest movie sensations, Universal Studios updates and adds attractions at a higher rate than Disneyland, partly because the symbolic meaning of its attractions are not circumscribed by the thematic organization of Disney's lands. Universal Studios' amusements literally make room for diverse and changing experiences. Photo opportunities are left to the guests' imaginations and here, unlike EPCOT, no Kodak instructions direct visitors where to stand to shoot. Visitors can pose with a huge replica of JAWS or in front of a backdrop featuring the famous Hollywood sign. Seemingly less rules-bound than Disney parks, Universal Studios embraces performativity. For example, at the Hollywood Cantina—one of the park's many opportunities for alcoholic refreshment—patrons can dance with actresses costumed as Lucille Ball, an option imbued with the physical and conceptual mobility integral to the amusements. At Waterworld, one of several live shows, cast members spray unsuspecting audience members' backsides and then innocently point to other audience members as the culprits, all to the screaming delight of the show's seated fans.

The visitor-as-participant is essential to, perhaps even responsible for, Universal Studios' trademark spontaneity. This is most evident at the park's two behind-the-scenes signature attractions. During the studio tour, guests will "Journey onto the backlot and catch an inside glimpse of films and television shows currently in production." Counseled to, "Keep your eyes peeled for stars!" visitors are reminded not only that looking is, in itself, active participation, but that they might see something no one else does. This line of encouragement continues at the "Special Effects Stages" where visitors will "Witness real moviemaking secrets revealed." But here, visitors have the chance to do more than look: they might cast their lot with celebrities as they "Follow in the footsteps of Hollywood's biggest directors and stars—behind the scenes."[33] Once backstage, the lucky visitor might even go from seeing to being seen: as a live show demonstrates special effects, one lucky guest "may even get your very own starring role!"[34]

With these attractions, the back region becomes a landscape of creation that revives the prominence of the active producer, catapulting him/her to center stage. This focus on the active producer continues throughout the park. Even the lines at Universal Studios cultivate interaction. Transforming waiting into part of the fun is distracting, too, since visitors can spend half their visit standing in lines. At many theme parks, popular rides demand extensive space and strategies for organizing crowds into serpentine order. While waiting in line for most rides at Disneyland, some kind of visual stimulus entertains guests, often glimpses of people already on the ride. Some of the more recent rides provide a narrative to entertain those whom may wait up to two hours to actually board. But even those—Space Mountain, the Temple of the Forbidden Eye, and Splash Mountain come to mind—often address the visitor only with songs or as tourists, or with bald pitches for the ride's corporate sponsor. The Temple of the Forbidden Eye's narrative slogan is "Keep your eye on the globe." The Foucauldian drift of the story becomes apparent at the ride's end, where a sign announces "True Rewards Await Those Who Choose Wisely. AT&T." It is always the discipline and punishment, control and reward, narrative. Surprisingly enough, people standing in these lines overwhelmingly do keep their voices down, do not cut in front of others, swear, complain, or act out in other rude ways. However, the mingling of bodies that Walt Disney originally wanted to curtail at his family park occurs precisely because his parks are so popular. Extensive and explicit flirtation passes the time while people wait in long lines for the "real" attraction.

By comparison, the lines at Universal Studios are generally more complex, moving through various spaces and changing shape as they go. At many attractions, speakers broadcast story extensions of the movie on which the ride is based. These narratives often assign the visitors a mission. In line at Back to the Future: The Ride, visitors are told their job is to chase down Biff, the character who has stolen one of the automobile time machines. In short, you are appointed something to do when technically you are doing nothing. As you move further into the hidden, back regions, you are given a responsibility that, no matter how staged, singles you out as an individual. Waiting morphs into productivity and performance in even the most benign of rides, evident at E.T.'s Adventure, which also becomes the visitor's adventure, when a voice projected through an intercom system informs guests that their duty is to help E.T. save his planet. The narrative even tries to undercut its necessarily repetitious style with moments of apparent spontaneity. At one point in line guests receive interplanetary ID cards. Lucky patrons will hear their names announced over the speaker. In this "personalized" atmosphere, customers adopt roles as figures other than tourists. And, each visitor can repeatedly go on the same ride and produce a new experience, so that experience, rather than the commodity, is hyped as the selling point of the tourist attraction.

Of course, the draw at Universal Studios, like at other theme parks, *is* the heart-stopping roller coaster rides. The climax of Jurassic Park: The Ride, is a waterfall that drops EIGHTY-FOUR feet at a gravity-defying angle. After making the plummet in their raft, stunned, soaked, and delighted passengers disembark through the Jurassic Park store, where one glimpses the final attraction: a large-screen projection of a picture taken of each boat as it plummets down the drop. Each photo, of course, may be purchased in 5 × 7 or 8 × 10 size. Here and throughout the park, visitors are invited to buy into a vision of themselves as an odd hybrid of consumer/producer. For much of the success of the photo depends upon the visitor's actions when the camera snaps its shot. Are your hands up? Do you show a playful awareness of the camera? A fluency with handling the gravity-defying challenges of the ride? A penchant for a challenge? An adventure? In short, have you managed to make this ride your own? In inviting, if not insisting, that visitors make the attractions their own (at least to some degree), the park illustrates a particular relation between consumption and production.[35] Even though it displays some of the labor practices associated with the realm of production—and sometimes makes its visitors "work" as part of the pleasure—ultimately, Universal Studios creates the figure of the consumer as participant-producer, an identity that expresses and affirms what Miranda Joseph deems the "individualism and apparent free choice" associated with the post-Fordist marketplace.[36]

Ford's Behind-the-Scenes Tour: "The Great American Production"

The image, albeit contrived, of individual agency brings me to the Ford Rouge Factory Tour. Advertised as the "The Great American Production," the tour's title makes a double claim. First, it points to the history of the Ford automobile as a great American production. Secondly, it asserts Ford's own identity as producer of Americanism. The symbolic emphasis fits perfectly into the larger cultural phenomenon of reviving an ideology of production that I have been discussing. But Ford's assertion, and its reputation as inventor of assembly-line production, presents a problem. How does one promote—or reinvent—Fordism in a post-Fordist age? Or to put it another way, if the behind-the-scenes tour functions to revive the role of the producer in an age of consumption, how can a tour of an auto assembly plant create an identification with production that would not just return us to the alienating effects of mass production?

The Ford Rouge Factory Tour highlights the history of the Rouge plant, which originally opened in 1918, and showcases the plant's new "environmentally sound" incarnation. The visit to back regions culminates with the Assembly Plant Tour, where visitors can watch workers assemble F-150s. Although the tour celebrates modes of production—*how* Ford makes cars and trucks—this celebration is presented as only one part of a larger, all-encompassing narrative: the representation of a specific model of productivity. Discussing the damaging cultural effects of twentieth-century capitalistic developments, MacCannell observes: "It is a source of anxiety that our kind of society has the capacity to develop beyond the point where individuals can continue to have a meaningful place in it."[37] Ford's signature innovation, assembly-line production, seems a prime example of a work, and to a larger degree, a social practice that erases the individual's contribution, and thus, his or her sense of productivity. Although the Ford tour notes the sometimes brutal labor struggles in the company's history—struggles that demonstrate the lack of a meaningful place for the laborer—it shifts the emphasis away from the exploitative labor practices of mass production and replaces it with a history that defines the producer as an individual figure, not a cog in the industrial machine.

This figure is further, and repeatedly, represented as an innovator and inventor—roles that celebrate a model of productivity built on the vision, resourcefulness, perseverance, and hard work of the individual person. Not surprisingly, that figure is Henry Ford who, throughout the tour, is not portrayed as an industrialist or manager, but as an inventor. The tour introduces visitors to this focus during their bus ride to the plant when, during a video played on that ride, Bill Ford informs viewers that the Rouge plant is "where twentieth-century manufacturing was *invented*" (my emphasis). In the Legacy Theater, the first stop on the plant premises, visitors watch a film that celebrates the history of the Rouge and its innovations. The narrator introduces the Rouge factory as an "embodiment of his [Henry Ford's] dreams and ideas." Ford created not just a structure of brick and steel, but a "legacy." The plant, then, is the stuff of individual imagination and creation—and, as an embodiment of Ford, it stands as an extension of his individual self. Also in this film, the narrator claims, "it was not only cars that were being produced at Ford; new members of the middle class streamed from its gates." The film identifies the workforce, not as producers, but as a "product" of Ford's ingenuity; he changed America by, seemingly single-handedly, creating new members of the middle class.

The second theater continues the thematic focus on invention, most notably—and some would say, jarringly—with its use of an innovative virtual reality presentation. While the structure of the first theater imparted a Fordist tone—a staid shape of parallel rows of seats facing the same direction—the second theater mixes it up. The seats seem randomly placed; they are not in straight rows, and viewers can pivot and swivel, thus controlling what they look at (the screen is 360 degrees), and creating an individualized experience. This spatial design, one that emphasizes the creation of a custom-made experience, mirrors the presentation's thematic focus. Rather than project historical footage, this film embarks on a journey behind the scenes into the processes involved in the creation of the F-150 truck. And, although it goes through all of the phases of production, it emphasizes the "Art of Manufacturing." The artistic process of conception—dreams realized—takes center stage. The film opens with the drafting board, and throughout, pays a lot of attention to white-collar, middle-class work—doodling, coming up with designs, working in the offices. Here is another story of the individual as inventor, and unlike the earlier film of Henry Ford, this one invites viewers, as they turn and look rather than passively view, to move towards an identification with the figure of the inventor, or at least, that figure's sense of imagination. Perhaps this emphasis on invention is entirely appropriate in a multi-stage tour that strives to let visitors witness all of the aspects of Ford's production. But even when tourists are ushered into the plant to view the assembly room floor, their experience is still framed by this narrative. While they can look down at teams of workers on the floor, visitors also find video monitors in their lines of sight. Positioned at various places along the catwalk, each video features a different individual worker, who introduces him or herself, explains the process and often invites you to try to find him or her on the floor at work. Again, we are reminded of individual contribution.

In taking visitors behind the scenes to gain a more intimate and authentic view of the production process, the Rouge tour circumvents the exploitative practices of Fordism by focusing overwhelmingly on an ideology, not of mass production, but of individual productivity. But perhaps what is most compelling is how the tour extends this ideology to its vision of the factory itself, a vision that, in turn, successfully promotes and reinvents Fordism as a post-Fordist practice. Starting with their chaperoned, narrated journey to the factory in tour busses (no private cars are allowed), visitors approach the Rouge with a sense of awe. Once on the grounds, the physical and historical magnitude of the place is undeniable, especially since landmarks allow the visitor to both imaginatively recreate the plant's history (with help from the tour's narration) and witness its ongoing, and vibrant, operation. The tour cultivates this image during the various stages. During the Legacy Theater presentation, the factory is even personified, becoming the protagonist of the film after Henry Ford's death. Speaking of the foreign competition that might be the company's greatest contemporary challenge, the film narrator asks, "How will the mighty Rouge, which led the twentieth century, continue to be a leader in the twenty-first century?"

The image of the mighty Rouge as innovative leader—as an individual— develops into a story that champions the importance of a place-centered ideology. Such an insistence is particularly notable in this era of globalization—an age characterized by the reliance on, and proliferation of, information, services, and technology often defined by placelessness. The ubiquity of big box stores, the virtual accessibility of the globe made possible by the Internet, and simulations like the one of the Venetian hotel and casino in Las Vegas, all contribute to a sense of loss of the distinctiveness and productiveness of single places. In addition, globalization and post-Fordist business practices are characterized by the relocation and division of sites of production to places outside of the United States. The transition to a post-Fordist economy literally and symbolically depletes the U.S. of its geographical image as the unparalleled landscape of production and productivity. This has certainly been true with the auto industry. But the tour insists upon the Rouge as a timeless producer—in the bus video, Bill Ford says, "The Rouge is more than a place that makes cars and trucks; it's a place that makes history"—thus, insisting upon the primacy of place, and the ability of individual places to make their unique mark at a time when economic shifts suggest those identities are obsolete.

There is no more convincing evidence of this assertion than the factory's "Living Roof," which speaks directly to the kind of place and producer the Rouge will be in this post-Fordist age. Panels in the observation deck inform visitors that, in 1999, "Bill Ford, the great-grandson of Henry Ford, made a dramatic announcement. The Rouge would undergo a $2 million makeover to transform it into an icon of the next Industrial Revolution." Playing on its reputation as an industrial giant, the Ford company both transforms that identity and reestablishes its unwavering importance. The centerpiece of the makeover is the installation of "The Living Roof," a 10.4-acre sedum plant mat that performs multiple duties. It collects and filters storm water runoff in order to reduce the amount of water running into the Rouge River and improve water quality, insulates the assembly plant—thus, reducing heating and cooling costs—and improves air quality by trapping airborne dirt, absorbing carbon dioxide, and producing oxygen.[38]

Fitting in with its overall narrative of an ideology of production and productivity that centers on creativity and invention, this stage of the tour is entitled "*Reinventing* the Rouge: Ford's New Vision." The Living Roof reinvents not only the factory, but also the factory's relationship with the natural landscape and the relationship between the industrial and the modern. In terms of the latter, the new incarnation of the Rouge offers a classically Fordist site as the solution to dissatisfaction caused by post-Fordism's "rapid globalization of the world economy."[39] The reinvented Rouge rejects a "corporate vision of global consumerism," which profits from "cheap commodities based on exploiting labor and natural resources" to offer instead a vision of itself as a local economy that supports sustainability and "locally controlled manufacturing and retailing."[40]

In doing so, the new Rouge responds to and redirects a larger cultural anxiety about obsolescence—of labor sites, practices, and jobs. At the end of the twentieth century, globalization seems responsible for making two entities vulnerable to extinction—nature and American production. But in the case of the place-bound American industrial factory, extinction provides an opportunity for invention. As one display describes it, with "nature and industry working side-by-side," the Rouge produces nature and, as a result, becomes more productive. In the past, the Rouge factory had been thought of as literally consuming the natural environment—now, it actively produces it. Traditional oppositions collapse: nature becomes both the future of industry and the representative of technology. It is the reverse of the machine in the garden. Here the garden thrives as a result of industry.[41]

At the Rouge, then, behind-the-scenes tours function not just to show visitors off-limits sites of production, but also to reinvent the meaning and significance of production. No longer is the factory the symbol of mass production and its static, repetitive, and routine practices. Instead, this tour emphasizes the dynamism and modernity of industrial production—it is a system based on invention, novelty, and the ability to transform itself—not unlike a characteristic post-Fordist business. Finally, the tour also encourages its viewers to identify with this view by inviting the visitor to admire Henry Ford both as an exceptional visionary and as proof that one person can produce something that will change the future.

Foregrounding Production in Behind-the-Scenes Spaces

On the surface, these two tourist attractions may not seem to have much in common, but, their shared emphasis on revitalization and transformation seems to speak to concerns of our specific millennial moment. In terms of its larger cultural symbolism, contemporary backstage tours and spaces ease anxieties about the disappearing role of production by reviving it as an act of invention. In this era of globalization, behind-the-scenes attractions both articulate and allay a larger anxiety about the *individual*'s role in production. "The Great American Production" identifies a prevalent cultural vulnerability—a fear that we are no longer inventors, but only passive consumers (or servicers, even), unable to produce anything new or meaningful. However, the tour shows those fears to be unfounded. Universal Studios theme park, by definition a much more pleasure-oriented venue, celebrates spontaneous and continuous audience interaction. Perhaps the park's greatest special effect is its suggestion that its visitors are not consuming at all, but producing an experience that represents individualism and free choice.

As a final point, I want to suggest that the contemporary behind-the-scenes phenomenon, as I have described it, has an extensive range. Reality shows that take viewers behind the scenes to witness "real people" interact with each other in "authentic ways" (even if the situations are staged), or talent shows, like *American Idol*, which not only invite, but absolutely rely on, audience participation for their existence, both operate on the promise of offering their viewers an authentic experience. In addition, as with *American Idol, Rock Star,* or *Dancing with the Stars*—shows that focus on the production of something (the next lead singer for Supernova, or a new invention, for instance)—the television viewer is no longer positioned as a passive consumer of what she or he is watching, but, potentially, the producer of its outcome. The emphasis on the viewer as producer and active participant, rather than strategy in a ratings game, seems compelling enough to keep viewers watching, voting, and transforming a simulation into a production of the real.

In addition, these newer trends extend the cultural narratives apparent in the two entertainments I discussed at length, suggesting one possible future trajectory of behind-the-scenes spaces. At some point, the backstage spaces at Universal Studios and the Rouge both focus on the contributions of the "average" person, or as Ford might put it, the "everyman." Furthermore, as these spaces draw our attention to this figure, they cast him or her as a celebrity. At Universal Studios, the move is ubiquitous and explicit—advertisements promise that visitors can become "the star of the show." Elsewhere, especially on television, with reality shows that take viewers behind the scenes to witness off-camera, unscripted, or authentic situations, the narrative is increasingly structured around the promise of celebrity. The series *Average Joe* is perhaps the most transparent example of how ordinary people can, by virtue of their very ordinariness, reach celebrity status. It seems that what is most important in these narratives is both the emphasis on authenticity and the emphasis on the production of the self. That is, behind-the-scenes spaces allow the creation of stories that show the ideology of production at its most important scale—the production of the self as individual, and if you are lucky, the production of the self as celebrity.

Other kinds of behind-the-scenes tours increasingly focus on the promise of intimacy with previously off-limits activities or knowledge. More and more musical and theatrical companies offer tours and/or open rehearsals.[42] A wide range of cultural organizations are also getting into the act. There is a rapidly growing trend among aquariums, for instance, to offer behind-the-scenes tours as part of admission—some allow visitors to view the feeding spaces; one even markets a "Sleepover with Sharks." In an interesting twist, these tours transform entertainers into workers. Whether they are famous musicians or fascinating fish and mammals, these performers interest us as workers. This is the case, too, with television shows where we watch celebrities learn to sing or ballroom dance; we are encouraged to view these exploits as real people working hard to do real things. This concurrent trend may offer an antidote to the hype of the celebrity-making amusement trend, suggesting that in these times of simulation, there are still ways to get closer to the real thing. Taken together, these two behind-the-scenes trends suggest our latest cultural ambivalence towards celebrity. They simultaneous play out our desires to be discovered, to catch glimpses of celebrity voyeuristically, and to remain true to our democratic production—and celebration—of the everyday and the average as exceptional.

Notes

1. "The Henry Ford: Ford Rouge Factory Tour." <http://www.hfmgv.org/rouge/default.asp> (30 Mar. 2004). Today, over two years after the tour's opening, the Web site offers less promotional text, adding pictures of, and links to, the five parts of the tour.

2. Universal Studios Hollywood, "Universal Studios Hollywood.com—Theme Park Overview." <http://themeparks.universalstudios.com/hollywood/website/park_overview.html>, 1996 (31 July 2006). The arguments about Universal Studios theme park in this article are drawn largely from my earlier article, "Consuming Pleasures of Re/Production: Going Behind the Scenes in Spielberg's *Jurassic Park* and at Universal Studios Theme Park," *Genders* 36 (2002). <http://www.genders.org/g36/g36_brigham.html>

3. Universal Studios Hollywood, 1996.

4. "Universal Studios Amusement Park California—Studio Tour—What's Filming?" <http://themeparks.universalstudios.com/hollywood/website/st_filming.html?calendar=ush_whatsfilming&template=ush_film_tmpl.html> (31 July 2006).

5. "The Henry Ford: Ford Rouge Factory Tour," <http://www.thehenryford.org/rouge/tour.asp#assembly> (31 July 2006).

6. Dean MacCannell, *The Tourist: A New Theory of the Leisure Class* (Berkeley: University of California Press, 1999), 1.

7. MacCannell, *The Tourist*, 91.

8. MacCannell, *The Tourist*, 91.

9. MacCannell, *The Tourist*, 94. For his in-depth discussion of front and back regions, see MacCannell's chapter 5, "Staged Authenticity."

10. MacCannell, *The Tourist*, 6.

11. Philip Cooke, *Back to the Future: Modernity, Postmodernity, and Locality* (Winchester, Mass.: Unwin Hyman, 1990), 66.

12. Mark Gottdiener, *The Theming of America: Dreams, Media Fantasies, and Themed Environments* (Boulder, Colo.: Westview Press, 2001), 47.

13. Gottdiener, *The Theming of America*, 46.

14. Gottdiener, *The Theming of America*, 47.

15. Gottdiener, *The Theming of America*, 56, 11.

16. Miranda Joseph, *Against the Romance of Community* (Minneapolis: University of Minnesota Press, 2002), 41. Here, Joseph is discussing the work of theorists Jean Baudrillard, Frederic Jameson, and others.

17. For one recent and wide-ranging overview of North American perspectives on

these issues, see Juliet B. Schor and Douglas B. Holt, eds., *The Consumer Society Reader* (New York: New Press, 2000). In addition, historian Lizbeth Cohen's *A Consumers' Republic* (New York: Vintage Books, 2004) makes a compelling argument about postwar America and the rise of a Consumers' Republic, defined as "an economy, culture, and politics built around the promises of mass consumption, both in terms of material life and the more idealistic goals of greater freedom, democracy, and equality," 7.

18. I borrow this phrase from Joseph, *Against the Romance of Community*, 41.

19. Douglas B. Holt and Juliet B. Schor, "Introduction," in *The Consumer Society Reader*, ed. Juliet B. Schor and Douglas B. Holt (New York: New Press, 2000), xx.

20. Holt and Schor, "Introduction," xxi.

21. Holt and Schor, "Introduction," xxi.

22. Holt and Schor, "Introduction," vii.

23. Holt and Schor, "Introduction," vii–ix.

24. Holt and Schor, "Introduction," xii. My emphasis.

25. For more on the trend of participatory tourism see Marina Novelli, ed., *Niche Tourism: Contemporary Issues, Trends and Cases* (Amsterdam: Elsevier, 2005).

26. Joseph, *Against the Romance of Community*, 47–48.

27. Joseph, *Against the Romance of Community*, 49.

28. Joseph, *Against the Romance of Community*, 186n17. Here, Joseph is also discussing the work of David Harvey and Martyn J. Lee.

29. For more on Disney's criticism of other parks as the motivation for his own, see Margaret J. King, "Disneyland and Walt Disney World: Traditional Values in Futuristic Form," *Journal of Popular Culture* 15 (1981): 116–40, and Raymond M. Weinstein, "Disneyland and Coney Island: Reflections on the Evolution of the Modern Amusement Park," *Journal of Popular Culture* 26 (1992): 131–64.

30. Alexander Wilson, "Technological Utopias," *South Atlantic Quarterly* 92 (1993): 160.

31. Wilson, "Technological Utopias," 160.

32. See, for instance, Jane Kuenz, "It's A Small World After All: Disney and the Pleasures of Identification," *South Atlantic Quarterly* 92 (1993): 63–88; Susan Willis, "Disney World: Public Use/Private State," *South Atlantic Quarterly* 92 (1993): 119–37; and The Project on Disney, *Inside the Mouse: Work and Play at Disney World* (Durham, N.C.: Duke University Press, 1995).

33. "Universal Studios Amusement Park California—Real Moviemaking." <http://themeparks.universalstudios.com/hollywood/website/po_movie.html> (31 July 2006).

34. "Universal Studios Hollywood—Special Effects Stages." <http://themeparks.universalstudios.com/hollywood/website/attr_ses.html> (31 July 2006).

35. One example of making an attraction one's own is found in the "Flash Mountain" phenomenon. At Disney's Splash Mountain water ride, some female patrons expose their breasts to the cameras that offer keepsake photos for purchase. See <http://www.europa.com/~cabelsa/flash/> for more information. See also, Marla Dickerson, "For Disney, It's a Case of 'Unzip-A-Dee-Doo-Dah'," *Los Angeles Times*, 11 January 1997.

36. Joseph, *Against the Romance of Community*, 57. For more on the connection of individualism, choice, and consumption, see Nikolas Rose, *Governing the Soul: The Shaping of the Private Self* (London: Routledge, 1989), 227.

37. MacCannell, *The Tourist*, 15.

38. "The Henry Ford: Ford Rouge Factory Tour."

<http://www.thehenryford.org/rouge/livingroof.asp> (31 July 2006).

39. Holt and Schor, "Introduction," ix.

40. Holt and Schor, "Introduction," ix.

41. Leo Marx, *The Machine in the Garden: Technology and the Pastoral Ideal in America* (Oxford: Oxford University Press, 2000).

42. For example, for an additional fee, the popular production show *Jubilee!* at Bally's Las Vegas offers visitors a behind-the-scenes tour of the stage, dressing rooms, and other production areas associated with the stage show.

Chapter 13

The Experience of a Lifestyle

Brian Lonsway

During the 1990s, the theming of everyday life reached a new temporary apogee. The rigorous, didactic scripting of social experience, developed within the gates of the late-century theme park, began to influence the design and development of a wide range of projects for which themed design may seem a surprising goal. As with most historical developments, however, the transition was gradual, and marked with a fascinating track of convergences, repudiations, and a fair number of ostensibly radical proposals. No longer is the intensely narrated experience of space exclusive to the theme park; back-stories engineered to affect moods, organize movement, and compel engagement have moved first to the realm of retail design, then to urban redevelopment, and most recently to health and palliative care facilities. Central to all of these advances of thematic design is the commercial understanding of spatial experience, a concept recently popularized by a 1999 book in popular economics: *The Experience Economy*.[1] From the experience of shopping to the experience of dementia and the experience of death, the narrative control of an individual's experience is arguably central to commercial success. As a result, today's commercial design practices, from real estate development to urban planning and from architecture to industrial design, have responded, borrowing design techniques and spatial planning logics from the former owners of thematic experience design—the entertainment industry. When the mall becomes a Lifestyle Village; the hospital, a Lifestyle Enhancement Center; and the Alzheimer's treatment center, a Memory Care Center, there is more than nomenclature at work.

It is certainly fair to say that the intents of these changes are often beneficent, and in the case of dementia care, even noble, but the convergence of experiential concern with the commercial intents of the entertainment industry does raise some significant questions that do not appear to be addressed in any of the highly promotional literature that accompanies their advance. In particular, questions concerning the commercial origins of the so-called experience economy seem highly relevant, as they mark one of the first transitions toward the infusion of entertainment-industry models into the world beyond the theme park. The authors of *The Experience Economy* reinforce the value of entertainment to the scripted experiences central to their new economic framework, but they argue that it is not entertainment alone that will guarantee its success. Implicit in all of their arguments is the value of spatial deployment; their analysis, in fact, rests on the spatial metaphors of the stage and screen, on the spatial apparatuses of stage sets, and on the notion of everyday life as public performance. While they refrain from explicitly stating the spatiality of their venture, this is a radical gesture. Through dramaturgical metaphors (which explicitly heighten the entertainment bias of their message), their book ultimately insists on the fundamental importance of spatial experiences. Where architects, urban designers, and planners have often failed—in demonstrating a concrete value of improving spatial experience—the authors of *The Experience Economy* have succeeded. With this demonstration comes the argument that the themed experience is holy grail of the new spatially-driven economy.

In 1995, the Urban Land Institute—a Washington, D.C. international research, education, and advocacy group heavily supported by commercial real estate interests—officially declared the birth of the Urban Entertainment Destination, or UED. These projects, which use entertainment "as an anchor or as a magnet to enhance retail, hospitality, residential, or mixed-use development" were born out of the sudden rediscovery of the spatial value of entertainment, and represent one of the most important ancestors of the experience economy.[2] The strategic placement of entertainment centers in urban contexts was, of course, nothing new in the 1990s. Western cities have relied upon formalized entertainment for centuries, and the modern city has consistently incorporated theaters, arcades, sport clubs and fields, panoramas, themed restaurants, and amusement parks as a central aspect of their organization.[3] However, there apparently was something new and radical about the UED. Between 1994 and 1995 "nearly every major entertainment company has established development teams to evaluate, plan, or develop UEDs." There was more than just a bandwagon involved; the UED represented a serious investment potential, with very few precedents. Michael Wolf, a media and entertainment consultant and pop economist, called this infusion of "entertainment content" the *E-Factor*, attributing its inspiration to the fall of Soviet Communism and the end of the Cold War.[4]

> You make a missile, and the defense manufacturer gets paid, its workers get paid, a few officers get paid, and then the missile sits there in the silo gathering dust. You make a movie, on the other hand, and you can potentially release it again and again (try doing that with a missile after it's exploded). Next, it can be released on video. It can play on network television and cable and overseas. It can sell related dolls, lunch boxes, soundtrack albums. You can send it out on the Web when real-time video hits the Internet. Years from now, you can send it out again to a nostalgia-crazed marketplace.[5]

What changed, thus, between the urban entertainment of the nineteenth century and that of the late twentieth is the commercial savvy of the entertainment industry, especially as it grasped the value-added nature of these product tie-ins, including the value of spatial diversification. But if part of the reason the industries supporting the Cold War retooled themselves into entertainment machines in the 1990s was to profit from the non-physical, informated, nature of entertainment, why would entertainment developers venture into the difficult domain of territory itself? What value is to be gained from literally grounding the fluid media of entertainment content? The E-Factor, manifesting the ability for traditional—what architects call *bricks and mortar*—industries to increase their fluidity, promotes, in fact, a way to make territories themselves appear fluid in the branding strategies of an entertainment corporation. An entertainment brand that is architecturalized has the capacity to both embed itself in everyday life in a way that a mere image or product may not, and escape the static attributes of a non-branded, non-entertaining real estate investment. Alternatively, while spaces and the architecture which occupies them may just sit there—gaining or losing value from volatile local real estate markets—fluid E-Content travels virtually without borders, gaining value through a complex set of mechanisms completely separate from those which determine the values of material goods.

An ESPN Zone store, for example, is not only a sports bar. As a tourist attraction, it provides an immersive environment for Disney to promote the ESPN brand itself, which of course supports increased viewing in homes around the world. It is the Urban Entertainment Destination which laid the groundwork, as well as provided the spatial context, for the invention of ESPN Zone. An entertainment center, in addition to manifesting a brand through typical iconographic means, can easily become an accidental background in various media representations; its greater permanence than a disposable object grounds its trademarks in everyday routines; and its physically inhabitable scale opens up opportunities for immersive branding that no product can offer with the same ease. Adding entertainment content to a typically non-entertaining facility adds distinction, sets a company apart, and, according to Wolf, fills the eyeballs of millions seeking short-term, user-controlled, instantly gratifying distractions.[6] By injecting the E-Factor into bricks-and-mortar investments, companies are able to diversify their holdings, enter the global information marketplace, and make people have fun all at the same time. These are none other than the architectural implications of George Ritzer's "McDonaldization of Society" carried into the brand-happy world of late-twentieth-century marketing, with an added touch of entertaining distraction.[7]

Wolf's book was published in the same year as Joseph Pine's and James Gilmore's *The Experience Economy*, and while their point is fundamentally the same, Pine and Gilmore stress that the new economic model is not exclusively based on entertainment:

> Because so many exemplars of staged experiences come from what the popular press loosely calls the entertainment industry, it's easy to conclude that shifting up the Progression of Economic Value to stage experiences simply means adding entertainment to existing offerings. That would be a gross understatement. Remember that staging experiences is not about entertaining customers, it's about *engaging* them.[8]

With staging as their operative framework, they immediately establish the spatiality of the relationships between actor and audience, front stage and back, stage right and left, theater and everyday life, as central aspects to the presentation of commercially driven experiences. By expanding Wolf's argument, they present a more helpful analysis of the spatial drive of the entertainment economy. To the extent that the E-Factor—and here E means either Entertainment or Experience—arguably injects commercial value to an enterprise, it does so exclusively because it occurs in physical space, requires active spatial engagement by customers and employees, and locally grounds the intangible effects of a global brand. The stage—and here "all the world is a stage" is taken literally—is the grounding point for the future of the service economy. For a service exchange to engage the customer, it must be staged, and to be staged, quite simply, there must be a stage. This stage, and the provision thereof, is the space of commercial activity, of exchange, and of immersive experience. As with the theatrical metaphors of Erving Goffman, whose work is periodically cited in *The Experience Economy*, the roles played by individuals both construct, and are constructed by, the spaces in which they occur. A mature understanding of the value of the spatial context is thus powerfully implicit, while seldom acknowledged, in the experiential analysis of the new economy.

Location-Based Experience

John Hannigan, in *Fantasy City: Pleasure and Profit in the Postmodern Metropolis*, pinpoints the birth of so-called location-based entertainment ventures in response to urban redevelopment efforts as early as the 1970s.[9] Developer James Rouse's Festival Marketplace idea—initiated with Boston's Faneuil Hall in 1976 and since replicated throughout the United States—led in part to a renewed interest in redeveloping inner cities through the renovation of disused marketplaces, train stations, waterfronts, industrial areas, or old urban entertainment districts. As the Festival Marketplace evolved into the Urban Entertainment Destination in the

1980s, the business logic of Wolf's entertainment economy sets in. The synergies between real estate, broadcast media, film, and retail companies, which both Hannigan and Wolf describe, thus saw the placement of entertainment features as a crucial aspect of the success of many of these new urban ventures. The publisher of *Urban Land*, the self-promotional journal of the Urban Land Institute, offers his version of the historical evolution of the UED:

> Crystal palaces and expositions were the hallmarks of the Victorian era; legitimate theaters, vaudeville houses, and amusement parks were the stars of the 1900s and 1910s; the first motion pictures with sound were features in the movie palaces of the 1920s and 1930s; and TV and family theme parks dominated entertainment from the 1950s to 1980s. For the 1990s and the next millennium, the combination of live and participatory entertainment, innovative film applications, simulation rides (more than hard rides), and high-tech wizardry will make up urban entertainment destinations.[10]

The popular rise of this new development form suggests, as Hannigan points out, that new corporate synergies and syntheses had entered the retail development landscape. M. Christine Boyer offers a brief historical context for the Festival Marketplace-cum-Urban Entertainment Destination in her detailed examination of another of James Rouse's projects.[11] Boyer places these urban developments in the narrative imaging spectacles of the nineteenth century—the window display, the panorama, the amusement spectacle. She calls the Festival Marketplace an exercise in *picture writing*, referring implicitly to the urban imaging theories of twentieth-century planner Kevin Lynch, who saw the design of the successful urban landscape as a process of constructing sequences of clear and informative images. When commercialized, these imaging strategies are some of the most profoundly directed ways to promote well-managed and financially calculated retail narratives. In a related vein, author Norman Klein labels these outgrowths of the baroque function of the nineteenth-century spectacle *scripted spaces*, where commercialized image is turned into a didactic script for the proper occupation of space.[12]

What is architecturally significant about recent commercial forays like the UED, is that they have the effect of bringing this narrative, through the spatial metaphors of the stage and screen, to a wider variety of services and locales than previously considered. While nineteenth-century urban entertainment ventures did attempt to create entertainment destinations, they lacked the scientific retail and marketing logics of the twentieth century which commoditized the form and social program of urban entertainment. Boyer reveals that Rouse's 1983 South Street Seaport project:

> is really an outdoor advertisement that narrates a story about trade and commodities, and these narratives of adventure and conquest fill out the more intangible nostalgic desires of the consumer. This subtle form of advertising blurs the distinction between the atmospheric stage-set and the commodities on sale, for its

well-constructed historic tableau not only enhances the products on display but locks the spectator into a larger-than-life store/story.[13]

Under these new marketing and mercantilist development protocols, major parts of city centers were themed to support entertainment brands, theme park spatial logics were deployed in shopping malls and individual retail establishments, and the spatial tenets of the experience economy refigured the services of the service economy. The role of Klein's scripted space took on new prominence, as it supported not only the entertainment function of the new experiential retail landscape, but its rational-scientific logic supported the financial interests of retail developers taking great risks moving into an unknown development model. Decades of scientific research into the quantitative analysis of social space found a home in the new experience economy—as useful models for spatializing narrative, for scripting a space.[14] Patterns, landmarks, nodes, radii, mean distances, demographic distributions, and statistical models became a foundation upon which a story would unfold through the spatial movements and sensory distractions of a consumer. With entertainment conglomerates clearly in the picture, the missing link between the economic development of everyday space and the storytelling desires of media entertainers was forged.

After the Festival Marketplace model lost steam among the development community in the late 1980s—due principally to financial failures with many of the developments—the Urban Entertainment Destination, with a wave of entertainment/industry support, came in to take its place. Clearly seen by those in the industry as a part of the historical continuum of themed ventures, UEDs represented a new product line for developers that combined the humdrum urban retail center with entertainment amenities prototyped in the theme park environment. Arguably little more than outdoor shopping malls with a few entertainment-focused stores (branded theaters, arcades, stores marketing movie tie-ins, etc.), the first UEDs like the renovated Third Street Promenade in Santa Monica (opened in 1989) and Yerba Buena Gardens in San Francisco (opened in 1993) stood at the transition point of urban revitalization using entertainment industry techniques. These two developments represent an end to the era of unthemed UEDs, as new ground was broken with Universal Studio's 1993 CityWalk. This project undertook a rigorous cross-pollination of the urban pedestrian retail center model and theme park. Located on the civically unincorporated land now owned by Vivendi Corporation called Universal City, CityWalk's adjacency to the Universal Studios Hollywood Theme Park and film production facilities guaranteed its E-Factor. CityWalk, integrating ostensibly entertaining signage, themed decor in all its venues, and architectural devices borrowed from Universal's film and television set-making experience, attempts to give a feeling of urban density outside of the urban context.

It does a reasonably good job across its mere 500-meter length, mediating visitors' spatial experiences through a jumble of landmarks and spatially orienting devices. While CityWalk is in central Los Angeles (although Universal City is not, in fact, part of the city), it is quite remote from the kind of urban experience it attempts to promote. In fact, while there is no admission charge to the attraction, one cannot reach it by Los Angeles public transit, and it would present a quite challenging hike on foot, in both cases a result of Universal City's strange and exclusive public-private status. Yet, it presents the city as its predominant theme. It attempts to mimic the visual overload of an urban experience just enough to make its occupants feel the sense of excitement that an urban core is supposed to contain, but without the concomitant risks. CityWalk is architecturally modeled on a suburban strip mall first and foremost; but by taking its thematic cues—its experiential referents—from the city core, it offers a theme that is specifically relevant to contemporary everyday life (unlike the nostalgic theme of the Festival Marketplace). This theme presents city life outside of the city—a polished, organized, and secured representation.

Following CityWalk's financial success, the urban theme became more common in UEDs, even for those in dense urban environments themselves (consider the new Times Square in New York City, for example: an on-site rethemeing of Times Square itself). At the service of retail and tourist economies, CityWalk and its urban-themed progeny require the ability to provide its guests a sense of security, and so borrows urban signifiers only as appropriate. For many, especially historical themes, this has posed problems, as the technologies and systems required for such security visually intrude upon the historical theme. By thematizing the contemporary city itself, however, the potential for such intrusions is inherently eliminated. In an essay from the journal *Urban Land* in 1994, the executives of a management consulting firm describe three approaches to theming for UEDs: scripted themes, theme-enhancement, and multitheming.[15] The urban theme provides the opportunity to engage all three of these methods, combining the control of intensive scripting with the added value of theme enhancements and the commercially productive benefits of the distractions of multiple themes. For an urban theme to feel urban, for example, it must embrace differentiation within its well-managed composition ("sanitized razzmatazz" according to Hannigan), thus moving beyond the solitary, highly scripted theme into something ostensibly more loose, something multithemed.[16] Yet, the script must be maintained to provide a controlled and consistent experience.

CityWalk provides this scripting via the instrumentalization of urban markers. By storyboarding visual experiences, the center's designers, the Jerde Partnership, created experiential episodes which unfold into an urban narrative, or script, which shoppers have a proclivity to follow. And thematic enhancement is provided by overblown physical cues. The signage (of which there are more than retail establishments) first draws attention to the edgy (but secure) garishness of an urban entertainment district; the overscaled architectural details heighten one's sense of immersion; the rotunda serves as an orientational landmark, much like a grand public plaza or major intersection, and frames privileged views of either the cinema megaplex or the studio theme park. While nothing is particularly radical architecturally in all of this, what is innovative is the amalgamation of these thematic models. By combining scripted design with entertainment attraction and pedestrian retail in an urban theme, the Jerde Partnership unveiled a prototype soon to influence urban design projects around the world. As well, it placed its own practice at the helm of these developments, creating a near synonym between "urban redevelopment" and the "Jerde UED."

As a model of urban redevelopment, however, CityWalk had one major problem: it was not immersed in an urban context. While it initiated a new breed of UED, it remained a disconnected entity, reachable only by car and connected exclusively to entertainment attractions—a movie studio and a theme park. The real desire of the UED developer was to see such thematic developments refigure urban land, setting up the potential for gentrification, reinvigorating disused waterfronts as high-end shopping districts, and stimulating the return of tourists to waning downtown cores. While projects done prior to CityWalk did situate themselves in downtown centers—in addition to the Yerba Buena Center and the Third Street Promenade, Baltimore's Inner Harbor, Miami's CocoWalk, and Underground Atlanta are some of the more notable—these were less emphatically narrative, themed, or scripted. It is specifically because it was developed first as an appendage of a theme park by an entertainment company, that CityWalk represents a critical hinge between the hyper-controlled and blatantly obvious scripting in a theme park and the more subtly controlling themes that were about to unfold in urban retail developments.

Lifestyle Experience

While all this was transpiring in the world of retail, new concepts were entering the landscape of residential development. Seaside Florida, a new town concept designed by Andreas Duany and Elizabeth Plater-Zyberk in the late 1970s, placed the tenets of a new model of city design on the real estate development radar. As this town developed through the 1980s, new "new" towns were modeled on ideas that began collectively to be known as *New Urbanism*. Reston Town Center, in the already somewhat New Urbanist Reston, Virginia (founded in the 1970s), broke ground in 1990, introducing the idea of the from-scratch downtown to the real estate development portfolio. With Seaside, Reston Town Center, and Disney's completely new town development, Celebration, Florida, developers were well-prepared to consider the planning and development of complete towns as a significant part of their investments. For the retail component of these downtowns, developers were of course becoming increasingly motivated by entertainment-industry synergies. Through these trajectories, the UED began to slowly evolve into today's Lifestyle Village.[17]

An extension of the shopping center, the Lifestyle Village restyles the urban theme into one of demographic-specific consumption. It also marks a significant advance of theming into the realm of everyday life. A specific lifestyle here is the theme, with retiring baby-boomers and young well-paid suburban dwellers the targets of the villages' designers. If the theme of the city has as its referents in the forms of buildings and the image of a well-occupied sidewalk, the thematization of lifestyle incorporates fashion, desire, style, culture, and demographics. Building on the psychological-cum-marketing idea of a lifestyle, these retail concepts strive to build their narratives around the patterns of living and consuming manifest by a select group of individuals.[18] Early Lifestyle Centers of the 1980s and 1990s were, like early Urban Entertainment Destinations, simply restyled malls.[19] But since 2000, influenced by the success of New Urbanist developments which incorporate retail and residential functions, developers have begun to incorporate residential accommodations above strip-mall-like retail establishments, radically (and naively) proclaiming the discovery of an age-old, mixed-use building type: the apartment above the store.

One of the newest of these villages at the time of writing is Santana Row in San Jose, California. Built on the site of an empty old-style mall, Santana Row seeks to attract an elite clientele both to shop and live. Unlike a traditional city, where spontaneous development densities arose from commercial convenience along waterways or trade routes, or at geographically strategic areas for the protection of commerce, the thematized citoid presents an allusion to such narratives in its built form, but overwrites the mercantilist referent with a more provocative commercial conceit. Of course, the commercial location of the city is still present: it is only that the strategic land is not a waterfront but a disused mall in an up-and-coming suburb. Santana Row's narrative functions doubly—while the story may appear to be clearly about consumption (its architectural design merely adds apartments to a strip mall), it is rigorously promoted as a place to live independent of shopping. This is expressed clearly by Steve Guttman, the former CEO of Santana Row's developer, Federal Realty Investment Trust: "The parks are for people who don't necessarily shop at all. Just come and play chess, play checkers in our park with your family. Enjoy the fountains. We want people to come and get married here."[20] While the new frontier people may not have everyday grocery stores, religious establishments, or community services, they are provided many of the other amenities of a pedestrian city. Of course, for all but a few non-residents to casually play chess or checkers in Santana Row, they would have to drive in, as Santana Row is immersed in the suburban big box retail belt. The urbanity embodied in Santana Row employs the mass-mediated image of the city to immerse inhabitants into its lifestylized space of consumption—to provide, in other words, an *experience* of urbanism. Whether or not there is any urbanism provided is less relevant.

In fact, labeling it urban or not seems more academic than critically useful. While playing with programmatic relationships and forms of traditional city organization, it makes no logistical pretense of being an incorporated city—it serves an urban function for those who care, and are authorized, to engage. The lifestyle village is both aleatory city and controlled suburb or, perhaps, neither. It is its own thing—another step in the economic evolution of living, of the spaces of everyday life, scientized by commercial urban logics and scripted to suit its commercial intent. Its spatial machinations are strategically deployed: to appear secured and commoditized but also public and accessible, to appear stylistically homogeneous but also inclusive of diversity. Mostly, this is handled by its developer's maintenance of exclusively private rights: Federal Reality Investment Trust accepted no public funding, breaks, or considerations specifically because it wanted complete control.[21] Its logistical overtures toward an image of publicity thus borrow more from the ownership rights of the enclosed mall than the publicly-mediated social contract of the inner-city UED. Any potential ambiguities of agency and authority in the case of this Lifestyle Village prototype are thus simply washed away. Santana Row, in this respect, represents the commercialized extreme of the company town—the city entirely owned, managed, and policed by a private corporation. But commercialized under the pretenses of the experience economy, Santana Row attempts to thematize everyday life itself. As with Disney's town of Celebration, Florida, the very goal of Santana Row is to attract individuals both to live and shop who are of a particular financial and aesthetic type. In the case of Santana Row, the pricing of the apartments (between $2,100 and $10,000 per month), condominiums (around the $1,000,000 mark), and the content of the stores (the main grocery store is a Dean and Deluca) are clearly targeted, in the aspiration that visitor, shopper, and resident self-selection will follow suit. It is assumed that the demographically targeted tenants themselves are expected to serve as advertisements for the development and its commercial tenants.

For style to become spatial narrative through the realm of social experience, spatial and architectural techniques must corroborate commercial interests within the subtle tactics of everyday practice. No longer is decor sufficient, nor is the symbolic display of narrative intent, for these can simply be forgotten or dismissed when the themed locale is left behind. Here, the narrative textuality of a space explicitly engages the quotidian actions of its inhabitants. Where the narrative of the theme park operates primarily through its spatial artifacts, the Lifestyle Village is narratively incomplete without its styled lives. In the Disney theme park, for example, the attire and social customs of the guest are prima facie extra-thematic. But in the Lifestyle Village, they are themselves the theme. On the one hand, the value of a commercial developer's consideration of social experience can be appreciated: at least it acknowledges the experiencing body of the occupant. But when experience is scripted not to integrate into a way of living, but to hegemonically form a commercially profitable lifestyle, questions regarding the agency of experience come to the fore. How explicitly are the experience models enforced? Is there room for personal experiential autonomy?

These are the interpersonal implications of what is being called *place branding*. This marketing strategy, built on traditional brand management theories, is directed primarily at the branding of locales with high volumes of tourism or those that will potentially receive high volumes of tourism. In a recent issue of the budding discipline's official research journal *Place Branding*, Bodil Blitchfeldt draws from the brand management literature to conclude that a "place brand relies on (or supervenes) the people living at that particular place."[22] Observing that the literature in this area "focuses on marketer's efforts to *build* and/or *manage* destination images, and hence destination brands," she concerns herself with the potential to build or manage residents to conform to a place's brand.[23] While her conclusions differ platonically from many of her contemporaries—who believe in the ability to manage local residents as part of a place branding strategy—she proposes in the end what amounts perhaps to a more insidious approach of "internal branding . . . how to get the populace behind it and 'live the brand.'"[24] This is the strategy of the Lifestyle Village and, as we shall see, other more recent lifestyle-related real estate "products." Successful internal branding on this scale promotes a new form of hegemony, one seeking to eliminate so-called brand gremlins—those "people, processes and other entities that are out of alignment with the organisation's overall brand strategy."[25] By commoditizing a lifestyle, and nurturing its self-promotion on an everyday basis through savvy commercial strategy, the gremlins—"like vehicle wheels out of alignment, sand in the gears of machinery, bugs in a software program, or other recurring glitches"—can be safely accounted for.[26]

In a similar vein, Pine and Gilmore point out with unfailing double entendre: "the customer is the product."[27] The customer's transformation by an experience is what the experience economy magnate should pursue. But as well, with only services (or experiences) to offer, the "transformation elicitor" has only the customer as tangible good.[28] It is in this vein that the lifestyle villager becomes product. Their transformation, by way of styling their quotidian existence through the symbolic manipulation of their person, is the directed goal of the Lifestyle Village experience. This is architecturalized at Santana Row not only in the neo-traditional styling of its architecture and urban spaces, but even in the detailed control over the public face of its inhabitants: in certain buildings, the ground-level merchants are given the right to dress the resident's windows above their stores, either for advertising or simply to control its environmental context.[29] The spatial image of the villager's domicile is literally styled for them, curtailing self-representation beyond the merchant's brand. This harks back to architect Mies van der Rohe's battle over the window shades in his 1951 Lake Shore Drive Towers in Chicago. His dismissal of the owner's personal window shade choices as aesthetically ruinous to the artfulness of his architectural composition has now been commercially instrumentalized in Santana Row—the modernist art of the logo. In the Lifestyle Village, all dwelling and occupation is seen as advertising product: everyday life as everyday lifestyle.

From Hospitalization to Hospitality

Other developments on the lifestyle front have led to the rebranding of hospitals and medical clinics as *Lifestyle Enhancement Centers*, both a nomenclatural and narrative transformation which seemed to surface, like the themed UED, in the mid-to-late 1990s. The beneficent intent behind this rebranding is to promote the emotional and therapeutic improvement of the medical experience of a patient. Yet, in the midst of growing competition among private medical care facilities, the continued scientization of built-environment studies, and the commercial propagation of the entertainment and experience economy models, this noble intent is slowly becoming buried behind layers of thematic narrative. The year 1997 represents an important transition in this regard: East Jefferson General Hospital in Metairie, Louisiana received a "Mouscar" service award from The Walt Disney Company, delivered in full Mickey Mouse regalia; and Florida Hospital opened a radically themed Lifestyle Enhancement Center in Disney's new town of Celebration, Florida—Celebration Health. East Jefferson Hospital received the award for exemplifying "the guest relations philosophy of Walt Disney World."[30]

The Disney Institute based in Orlando teaches this philosophy to various industries, but began a specific health care training unit based on the popularity of its general courses to those in the health care industries.[31] The hospital *guests* (not patients, in accord with the Disney corporate nomenclature), are treated by first-name-only *cast members* (otherwise known as doctors and nurses) sporting the "EJ (East Jefferson) Look." "The hospital knows what its patients and neighbors think about men with hoop earrings and women with long decorated fingernails, and it instructs its people accordingly."[32] This "show" aspect (one of the Disney Institute's four cardinal principles, along with safety, courtesy, and efficiency) borrows explicitly from the spatial imaging strategies employed through the Disney theme parks, and has even had an impact on the hospital's interior design. By 1997, the hospital had painted skyscapes on its ceilings so that guests were not staring blankly at acoustic ceiling tile and fluorescent lights. None of this may seem particularly radical, nor even done with suspicious intent; enough of us have had less-than-positive hospital experiences to desire a more positive environment. Again, it is not so much the intent, but the odd fusion of entertainment industry design and management techniques with the service trades—in this case health care service— that warrants greater critical attention. Even more so than in the Lifestyle Village, the fusion here is direct and explicit: Disney's imagimarketers (that is, the marketing version of the Disney imagineer) are training service professionals to emulate the thematic model of the entertainment industry.

By the time it awarded the Mouscar award to East Jefferson Hospital, Disney was near the final steps toward opening a hospital of its own in its town of Celebration. Celebration Health, a branch of the Seventh-Day Adventist Florida Hospital, carries the theming of hospitalization yet further, building not only upon their service expertise, but their cinematic and architectural knowledge. By applying a typical theme park's organization to their Lifestyle Enhancement Center, the hospital's designers offer a unique example of the extremes of beyond-the-theme-park theming. At Disney theme parks, areas, activities, and employees are described theatrically, borrowing from the media production concepts with which the company is most familiar. Park employees are called *cast members* (as we saw emulated at East Jefferson), the functional behind-the-scenes space they occupy is considered the *back stage*, and the park areas open to the public are called *front stage* areas. Not only has this thespian terminology permeated Disney projects (including the town of Celebration itself), it forms the core, as we have seen, of Pine and Gilmore's argument for the Experience Economy. Celebration Health, then, is getting a double dose of theatricality, influenced as it is by both health care service trends studied by Pine and Gilmore and its near neighbor Walt Disney World. Routinely described in its promotional literature as a place to maintain wellness rather than a place to treat illness—"eliminate negative cues" is one of the six points of progress in the experience economy—Celebration Health employs this thematic model to defer the presence of hospitalization in favor of its hospitality.[33] The hospital cafeteria is promoted as a public amenity, and the physical therapy facility is incorporated into a day spa for community residents.[34] In order to accommodate the diversity of this functional hybridization, the designers of the hospital doubled its corridor and elevator systems so that Friday evening guests on their way from the spa to the restaurant are unlikely to encounter actual hospital patients.[35] By architecturally and commercially representing the hospital as a hybrid between hospital and leisure center, its creators constructed the problem of separately managing two clienteles. The architects, Robert A. M. Stern with NBBJ, chose to restrict the overlap of patients and club members through an architectural mediation influenced by the theatrical narrative of the theme park.

Admittedly, were the two functions to overlap in their entirety, the hybrid program perhaps could not be sustained. The Lifestyle Enhancement Center's design asserts that neither patients on gurneys waiting for treatment nor fitness buffs on their way from the spa to the restaurant would likely feel too comfortable in each other's presence. Perhaps this may be the case if they are treated typically: the ill patient a subject of an often-alienating medical practice, and the spa patron a paying client to be pampered and coddled. While Celebration Health recognizes a very positive goal—increasing the hospitality of hospitalization—in the end its thematically influenced separation of the ill and the pampered reinforces the status quo. Increasing the hospitality of the hospital by incorporating amenities merely to spatially segregate them along commercial lines (spa membership versus physio-therapy treatment, for example) seems to defeat the purported goal. If all "guests," patients, and spa members alike, were pampered equally—medically, therapeutically, and architecturally—then, perhaps, we could have a more hospitable hospital. Perhaps then, lives, as well as lifestyles, might be enhanced.

Consider furthermore, Seaside Imaging, the medical imaging center of the Hospital, which has gone to the furthest extreme of thematic narration, casting their imaging center as "A Day at the Beach."[36] Combined with the more visibly subtle architecture of the front- and back-stage double-corridor system, the Imaging Center presents itself as a faithful executor of theme park design and planning:

> From the smell of suntan lotion and ocean spray to the soothing sounds of breaking waves and seagulls, this is standard fare for Seaside Imaging. Beneath our unique sand castle lies our newest diagnostic tool, the advanced GE SIGNA twin-speed MRI, the first in central Florida.[37]

The multisensory atmosphere of the imaging department includes a boardwalk floor, barium drinks served with paper umbrellas, Adirondack waiting chairs, and Hawaiian shirts in lieu of gowns. Perhaps most visually striking is the MRI machines made into shotcrete sand castles. "I wanted to do similar [sic] to what Disney does; when you go to one of their theme parks, it affects all of your senses," claims Sally Grady, director of imaging services at Celebration Health and one of the ideologues behind the theming.[38] The MRI machines were first dressed up to improve the attendance rate of Seaside Imaging's MRI appointments. After the theming, cancellations decreased 50 percent, attesting to the increased desire to partake in the narrative experience.[39] Building on this success, the nuclear medicine waiting area doubles as a movie theater, complete with popcorn machine and theater seating. And in a historical coup loaded with gender politics, the mammography area is done up like a proper English tea room (gazebo included). MRI patients about to enter the sand castle—the imaging machine—encounter another Disney-invented technology, an audio-animatronic bear ("Buddy") upon exiting their changing cabanas which describes the MRI process. While Buddy's intent is to help comfort children who are themselves going through the process of medical imaging, the opportunity for product tie-ins has not been lost, with Buddy paraphernalia given to childhood patients as a gesture of corporate brand loyalty.[40] In Seaside Imaging, a desire for hospitality has uncritically turned into an opportunity to exemplify Disney-style theming. Undoubtedly, experiences had at this imaging center would be memorable, but do these experiences continue to perform a medical function, or have they shifted to the more fundamental branding functions of the experience economy? Are these thematic ventures designed to treat the somatic conditions of the patient, or the equally vexing ones of the brand gremlin? There is a clear value to providing some levity and distraction for a child approaching an MRI visit, or providing some serious architectural consideration of a waiting room experience. There may even be some value to the humor of a more extreme gesture like the decoration of an MRI machine as a sand castle. But to what extent does the improvement of medical experience necessarily connect with theme park theming? At what point does the narrative offer comfort and at what point does it disguise treatment or alienate the patient seeking to be more in touch with their condition?

What is most significant about these thematic efforts is their potent ability to elide obvious narratives of control. As a postmodern narrative space, the site of lifestyle enhancement revolves around the idea of branded experience. While the link between the hospital and the Walt Disney Company may on the one hand be merely geographic, the establishment of entertainment content within the town of Celebration both reinforces the Disney brand and relies on its putative positivity. Most profoundly, as with the Lifestyle Village, this is accomplished (at least apparently) through self-fulfillment rather than paternal dictate. The developers of Celebration were once frightfully concerned that the town's residents would expect Disney perfection in their everyday lives: "Those (Disney aficionados) are the people who think their kids will never get a B in school and there is never going to be a weed in their lawn when they move to Celebration."[41] But in the end, the residents have proven to be more self-policing (thematically) than Disney managers originally expected.[42] This classic form of Gramscian hegemony has led to some of the more interesting and significant thematic environments outside of the theme park. Where central control over a manifest theme has become more difficult because of the gremlins of everyday life, willing participants are happy to take on the policing role. Through the self-fulfillment of the thematic narrative, designers, developers, residents, and others are promoting a model of narrative control as a comfortable and productive model for everyday life.

While personal narrative is a powerful motivating force for an individual, the standardization and hegemonic promotion of an authorized narrative has the potential to deaden an individual's ability to construct their own everyday narrative.[43] The Disney narrative impetus has directly affected those who subscribe to the Celebration model, and they are comfortable, even exuberant, about promoting it as the authorized narrative about their town and the kinds of livelihoods and lifestyles which are acceptable within it. This appears to be the case especially when this self-constitution of narrative supports a desired experience for which the ground has already been laid. The thematization of the hospital falls into this category of self-induced narrativity—where negative cues of "illness" are reconstituted as positive cues of "leisure" through tremendous narrative work. Recall that the purported outcome of the experience economy is the transformation economy (and that "the customer is the product"), wherein economic progress is made through the instillation of the belief of personal transformation. Jeans are not "just bought," a lifestyle is approached through the *transformation* of one's attire. Likewise, an MRI exam is not "just had," a healthy lifestyle is achieved through the transformation of a guest's frame of mind through a distracting spatial experience. But, there is a point to the MRI beyond distraction, beyond entertainment.

This issue takes on even greater significance in another medical application of entertainment-based theming: Alzheimer's care. Recently refigured as *Memory Care Centers*, Alzheimer's care facilities have, since about 1990, begun to consider the advantages of non-pharmacological treatments for the care of Alzheimer's disease.[44] There are two main arguments behind this approach. First, the disease directly affects the regions of the brain theorized to be associated with environmental memory and spatial way-finding, and second, many of the neurological effects of the disease are believed to be treatable by improving the physical environment of the patient.[45] While the former argument has been part of the scientific knowledge of Alzheimer's physiological progression for some time, a number of scientific studies from the late 1980s began to investigate the relationship between the care environment and patient behavior.[46] An important study in 2003, examining thirty Alzheimer's Special Care Units—physically distinct areas of care centers specifically devoted to Alzheimer's care—presents results of positive associations between specific environmental conditions and residents' non-aggressive and non-depressive mental states.[47] As a result of these studies, a number of environmental factors, including highly visible landmarks, clear pathways, commodious social spaces, concealed exits, and a so-called residential aesthetic are heavily weighted architectural devices to improve a care environment.

To an architect, it is unsurprising that there are positive correlations between well-designed spatial environments and positive feelings. But there is well-designed and there is designed. In 1996, the Clare Bridge Senior Living Home opened in Dublin, Pennsylvania; in 1998, the Corumbene Nursing Home for the Aged opened in New Norfolk, Tasmania; and in 2001, the Village at Waveny Care Center opened in New Canaan, Connecticut, each carrying a bit more extremely the thematic environmental design of the Alzheimer's special care unit. These three centers focused on the fact that Alzheimer's sufferers, while unable to retain events in short-term memory, can recall memories of distant years. By cuing in to what we would typically call nostalgia, and understanding the value of smart environmental design on the quality of care, the designers of these three clinics looked to the same precedents as the Lifestyle Village and Lifestyle Enhancement Center: the Disney theme park "Main Street" and the CityWalk-style Urban Entertainment District.[48] The Clare Bridge simply contains a miniature indoor "town square" as its social space, rendered in carpet patterns, painted wall surfaces, and outdoor furniture, provided to offer a calming gathering space modeled on the urban environments many of the residents grew up in. The Corumbene Home takes thematic design to the next level of nostalgic immersion, building on geographically and historically specific narratives to reconstruct a traditional hop farm and farming village out of recycled oast houses (kilns used for drying hops in preparation for brewing).[49] In this latter case, the representations are not merely aesthetic: the center provides a functional oast house, and provides residents with activities emulating the tasks of a traditional hop farm. Current residents would have grown up in or around these farms, and the reconstructions as well as the specific siting of the center are meant to provide comfort in the symbolism of a distant past. Any hop farming work done at the center is nevertheless simulated: daily reenactments of work for the mental comforts of dementia sufferers. Finally, at The Village at Waveny, designers found architectural inspiration in photographs not only of mid-century downtowns but of "reproduction[s of] streets in shopping malls, Disney World, and even a casino in upstate Connecticut."[50] The central area of this facility is thus an ersatz downtown New Canaan, circa 1950, designed to comfort residents by providing familiar images from their youth. While the designers of the Waveny

Village may be the only among these three projects to explicitly admit their Disneyesque roots, there is a growing coalescence of work on environmental design for dementia with the theoretical motivations that underlay the late-twentieth-century theme park, the UED, and the Lifestyle village.

A key figure promoting these architectural developments since the early 1990s is John Ziesel. His early work in applying applied sociology to design resulted in the 1981 publication *Inquiry by Design*.[51] In it Ziesel lays out a scientific methodology for Environment-Behavior (E-B) research: to provide a verifiable method for understanding the relationship between a physical environment and the behavior which results from it. Unsurprisingly, due in no small part to his quantitative sociology background, *Inquiry by Design* is highly influenced by the scientistic strain of spatial research. A recent profile of Zeisel specifically attributes the design of one of the care centers he commissioned to "the principles of urban planner Kevin Lynch and architect Chris Alexander," two key figures in this area.[52] Since 1993, he has been the President and co-founder of Hearthstone Alzheimer Care, Ltd., a set of assisted-living centers for Alzheimer's patients, where he has been putting his design ideas to the test. In practice, Zeisel's main influences in the design arena appear to be the urban planner Kevin Lynch and the cognitive scientist Donald Norman. From Lynch, Zeisel borrows the idea of environmental images, and from Norman, the idea of "natural mappings" to form his theory of the "naturally mapped environment." In so doing, he constructs a more scientifically grounded and controlling version of Lynch's theories than the urban planner ever intended: "A naturally mapped environment doesn't have to be read, it speaks for itself . . . you always know exactly where you are going, either because you see it or you have only one choice."[53] By extrapolating Norman's argument of natural mappings from *The Design of Everyday Things* to the scale of the environment, Zeisel makes the critical (and I believe, ethically problematic) assumption that what may be good for the object is good for the environment.[54] Donald Norman's classic example is the door. He argues:

> There is not much you can do to a door: you can open it or shut it. . . . A door poses only two essential questions: In which direction does it move? On which side should one work it? The answers should be given by the design, without any need for symbols, certainly without any need for trial and error.[55]

While I respect the argument for thoughtfully designed objects, I imagine a world designed by Norman's standards to be phenomenally unstimulating. Nothing requires curiosity, as it is so clearly designed as to avoid study. Object interaction decisions fundamentally disappear, as there is no longer any ambiguity to the way something may be used. But even if every object in the world were designed along these lines, we would still have the freedoms of spatial ambiguity. The mere assembly of the multitudes of things in the world, at different scales, used for different purposes, by different individuals and cultures, would create the opportunity for the ambiguities and complexities of everyday life that make for the social diversity and heterogeneity that keeps us thinking. But a naturally mapped environment, an environment which always "speaks for itself," where you "have only one choice," removes even this. It is an environment of complete narrative control—the environment presents only one theme, that is chosen or authorized by its designers. Alternative inhabitations, while not impossible, are severely curtailed, if not through direct proscription, then simply by being intrinsically dismissed as unthematic anomalies.

What makes the study of environments deployed for the care and support of Alzheimer's sufferers challenging is that the argument for environmental control is quite ethically persuasive. In lieu of physically restraining patients or sedating their behavior, providing the patient with a range of smartly designed, controlled spatial freedoms seems not only more humane but outright liberative. Spatial proscription in this case is not so much a means of control, but of a small dose of liberation from a debilitating disease. The question nonetheless remains whether such spatial controls need to be accomplished through entertainment industry scripting. Consider the other side of such scripting: the explicit construction of an other, a so-called brand gremlin or thematic anomaly that results from a strictly controlled narrative environment. The 1950s downtown of New Canaan Connecticut was most assuredly not race or gender inclusive. One simply needs to ask about those who would not be comforted by images of a Rockwellian (Norman, that is, not David) pre-civil-rights era downtown to question the inclusiveness of a standardized narrative.[56] The white middle-class designers of this white middle-class design narrowly focused on the narrative elements borrowed from mass-media representations of an idyllic town (and even representations of such representations). By reifying one particular image of, or better, one particular point of view, upon the American mid-twentieth century main street as a palliative instrument, they have demographically located medical treatment for dementia sufferers. The same mid-century-barbershop which a European American patient would find comforting, an African American might find distasteful because it was "Whites Only," or an Irish American, because of the "No Irish Need Apply" sign which likely appeared in its window. What happens as generations pass? Will they renovate Waveny's simulated main street, then board it up, or suburbanize it and put in a Wal-Mart? Or will there be Alzheimer's special care units for ethnic minorities, modeled on places of comfort which might be outside the Norman Rockwell image of the United States? To use Disney's Main Street, U.S.A. or Foxwoods Resort Casino—the casino in upstate Connecticut referred to by Waveny's design team—as design motivation for a terminal care clinic is not to merely replicate aesthetic decor, but to replicate the spatialization of control, and the social and political implications thereof. Within the context of a medical care facility, borrowing from Disney and borrowing from geriatric psychiatry seem altogether different. The former entails an engagement with spatial practices that are not about medical support or recovery, but about consumption and subservience along class and racial lines. A special issue of the *Journal of Architectural and Planning Research* devoted to therapeutic environments, for example, goes to great pains to stress the use of the word *consumers* to describe center owners and architects (*intermediate consumers*) and patients (*end consumers*).[57] While the consumerization of medical care is rapidly advancing, not all special care units are following the thematic trend; recall that the general principles laid out by medical researchers (including Zeisel) do not call explicitly for thematic decor. No clear data are nevertheless available on how pervasive the theming of hospitals or dementia care centers may be. What appears to be clear, however, is the medical literature's support of the evolution from the experience economy to the transformation economy.

What is perhaps most enlightening about the confluence of the experience economy, its thematic design logic, and dementia treatment is the commentary it provides on the very spatial qualities of theming itself. It took nearly fifty years after the opening of Disneyland to have a scientific researcher describe the themed environment (specifically, the naturally mapped environment) as "being [so] self-evident, [that] it compensates for neurological losses."[58] Narrative theming, as either leisure fantasy or medical treatment, is asserted to have a specifically palliative function. Whether there are actual neurological losses involved in a trip to Disneyland or the local Lifestyle Village is another story, but there seems nothing particularly surprising that at least the emulation of such loss may be at play. Participation in a spatial narrative does require the suspension of some belief, and it does seem reasonable to say that this suspension is mostly a suspension of some version of short-term memory. Entering the gates of a theme park, immersing yourself in an interiorized casino complex, or leaving your car behind in a suburban Lifestyle Village entails a temporary immersion in a story that has nothing to do with what is beyond its architectural boundaries.

These forms of entertainment, leisure, and consumption are escapes, where a neurological function is deferred at the service of enjoyment. Ostensibly, this is done at the service of liberation from other constraints on everyday life. The textualized thematic environment, from theme park to Alzheimer's clinic, employs these deferrals to script a set of constraints on our spatial behavior. Deferred memories—the recollection of the space "outside" the themed environment or of what activity took place just moments before—are blended, and the pursuit of any "true" meanings becomes hopeless. The control mechanism of narrative theming is, in a way, exposed. Its symbolic manipulations of the spatial environment are no less strategically deployed than in the theme park, but we are given access to it as we witness, potentially, the onset of cancer in the case of the imaging center, or dementia in the case of the Alzheimer's special care unit. We are, in witnessing the environmentally medicated "other," witnessing ourselves, equally environmentally medicated, albeit for other ends. Whether meandering at Disneyland, along CityWalk, through Santana Row, in Seaside Imaging, or at the Waveny Village, we are partaking in a contemporary form of architecturally institutionalized leisure—a profoundly radical kind of spatial landscape which may require new tactics of inhabitation, new theories toward dwelling, and new attitudes toward illness.

Notes

1. Joseph B. Pine, II and James H. Gilmore, *The Experience Economy: Work Is Theatre and Every Business a Stage* (Boston: Harvard Business School Press, 1999).
2. Michael D. Beyard and Michael S. Rubin, "A New Industry Emerges," *Urban Land* 54, no. 8 (1995): 6.
3. John Hannigan, *Fantasy City: Pleasure and Profit in the Postmodern Metropolis* (London: Routledge, 1998). M. Christine Boyer, "Cities for Sale: Merchandising History at South Street Seaport," in *Variations on a Theme Park: The New American City and the End of Public Space*, ed. Michael Sorkin (New York: Hill and Wang, 1992), 181–204. Norman Klein, *The Vatican to Vegas: A History of Special Effects* (New York: New Press, 2004).
4. Michael J. Wolf, *The Entertainment Economy: How Mega-Media Forces Are Transforming Our Lives* (New York: Random House, 1999), 50.
5. Wolf, *The Entertainment* Economy, 6.
6. Wolf, *The Entertainment Economy*, 16, 30–48.
7. George Ritzer, *The Mcdonaldization of Society*, 2nd ed. (Thousand Oaks, Calif: Pine Forge, 2000).
8. Pine and Gilmore, *The Experience Economy*, 30
9. Hannigan, *Fantasy City*, 51–54.
10. Frank H Spink, "From the Publisher," *Urban Land Supplement: Urban Entertainment Destinations* (1995): 4.
11. Boyer, "Cities for Sale."
12. Klein, *The Vatican to Vegas*.
13. Boyer, "Cities for Sale," 202.
14. The scientization of spatial theory has a rich and complex history that cannot be easily addressed in an essay of this scope. I will explore the many disciplinary confluences which have contributed to this effort in a forthcoming book-length work.
15. Michael S. Rubin, Robert J. Gorman, and Michael H. Lawry, "Entertainment Returns to Gotham," *Urban Land* 53, no. 8 (1994): 64.
16. Hannigan, *Fantasy City*, 67.
17. It appears that the term *lifestyle village* has been adopted for two quite different architectural functions. Throughout North America, the term refers to the mixed retail/residential form described here. Throughout Australia and New Zealand, the term has come to refer to a certain style of retirement community, based more on the model of a resort than a geriatric residence.
18. The word *lifestyle* has an interesting history. The *Oxford English Dictionary* outlines its etymological origin in the early-twentieth-century work of psychologist Alfred Adler, referring to a "person's basic character as established early in childhood which governs his reactions and behaviour." The OED pinpoints the evolution to the contemporary, more commercial notion in the 1970s. *The Online Oxford English Dictionary*, <http://www.oed.com/> (14 August 2006).
19. William L. Hamilton, "Five Rooms, Gucci View," *New York Times*, 21 February 2002, F1, F6.
20. Thuy Vu, "Santana Row: Grand Opening," reported by Thuy Vu. KGO-TV San Jose, California, Channel 7, ABC affiliate (7 November 2002).
21. Sharon Simonson, "Utopian Santana Row Model Is Flawed, Its Developers Say," *Silicon Valley/San Jose Business Journal*, 17 September 2004.

22. Bodil Stilling Blichfeldt, "Unmanageable Place Brands?" *Place Branding* 1, no. 4 (2005): 394.
23. Blichfeldt, "Unmanageable Place Brands?," 395.
24. Blichfeldt, "Unmanageable Place Brands?,"399.
25. P. H. Farquhar, "Editorial: Uncovering Brand Gremlins and Other Hidden Perils," *Journal of Brand Management* 10, no. 6 (2003): 368–92.
26. Farquhar, "Editorial," 389.
27. Pine and Gilmore, *The Experience Economy*, 163.
28. Pine and Gilmore, *The Experience Economy*, 181.
29. Hamilton, "Five Rooms, Gucci View," F6
30. J. Duncan Moore, Jr., "A Mickey Mouse Operation: Louisiana Hospital Learns Customer Service Lessons from Disney," *Modern Healthcare*, 14 April 1997, 62.
31. Moore, "A Mickey Mouse Operation," 63.
32. Moore, "A Mickey Mouse Operation," 64.
33. Pine and Gilmore, *The Experience Economy*, 55.
34. Michael Lassell, *Celebration: The Story of a Town* (New York: Roundtable Press, 2004), 67. Tanya Ott, "When Mickey Mouse Meets Medicine," Radio Broadcast: *Marketplace*, 9 November 1998. Celebration Fitness, "The Fitness Centre and Day Spa at Florida Hospital Celebration Health," <http://www.celebrationfitness.com/> (5 June 2006).
35. Ott, "When Mickey Mouse Meets Medicine."
36. Seaside Imaging, *Seaside Imaging Radio Commercial: "A Day at the Beach,"* <http://www.celebrationhealth.com/chstory/imaging_center/index.html> (14 August 2006).
37. Seaside Imaging, *Seaside Imaging Radio Commercial*.
38. Danielle Cohen, "Seaside Imaging Program Adds Up," *Decisions in Imaging Economics*, October (2005), <http://www.imagingeconomics.com/library/200510-09.asp> (23 February 2006).
39. Florida Hospital, "Make Your Next MRI Scan a Day at the Beach," *Partners in Health*, May, 2001.
40. Cohen, "Seaside Imaging Program Adds Up."
41. Douglas Frantz and Catherine Collins, *Celebration U.S.A.: Living in Disney's Brave New Town* (New York: Owl Books, 2000).
42. Many of these are documented in Michael Lassell's *Celebration: The Story of a Town*, albeit with a pro-Disney slant. Andrew Ross's *Celebration Chronicles: Life, Liberty, and the Pursuit of Property Values in Disney's New Town (New York: Ballantine Books, 1999)* also describes a number of these, from a more critical point of view.
43. This theme has been central to a number of writers on everyday space, from Henri Lefebvre, most notably in *The Production of Space* (Oxford: Blackwell, 1991), and Michel de Certeau, in *The Practice of Everyday Life* (Berkeley: University of California Press, 1988).
44. J. R. Zeisel and P. Raia, "Non-Pharmacological Coordinated Treatment for Alzheimer's Disease," *Neurobiology of Aging* 21 (2000): 80.
45. John Zeisel, "Environmental Design Effects on Alzheimer Symptoms in Long Term Care Residences," *World Hospitals and Health Services* 36, no. 3 (2000): 27–31.
46. Julia Frank, *Alzheimer's Disease: The Silent Epidemic* (Minneapolis, Minn.: Lerner Publishing Group, 1985). M.P. Lawton, "Environmental Approaches to Research and Treatment of Alzheimer's Disease," in *Alzheimer's Disease Treatment and Family Stress: Directions for Research*, ed. E. Light and B.D. Lebowitz (Rockville, Md.: U.S. Dept. of Health and Human Services, Government Document #89–1569, 1989).

47. J. N. M. Zeisel et al., "Environmental Correlates to Behavioral Health Outcomes in Alzheimer's Special Care Units," *Gerontologist* 43 (2003): 697.

48. Deborah Baldwin, "Main Street as Memory Lane," *New York Times*, 10 January 2002, F1, F7. Richard V. Francaviglia, *Main Street Revisited: Time, Space, and Image Building in Small-town America* (Iowa City: University of Iowa Press, 1996).

49. Ian Falconer, "You Must Remember This," *Nest, a Magazine of Interiors*, no. 14 (2001): 86–95.

50. Baldwin, "Main Street as Memory Lane."

51. John Zeisel, *Inquiry by Design: Tools for Environment-Behavior Research* (Monterey, Calif.: Brooks/Cole Publishing Company, 1981).

52. Jonathan Shaw, "Healing by Design," *Harvard Magazine* 1998.

53. Shaw, "Healing by Design."

54. Donald A. Norman, *The Design of Everyday Things* (New York: Basic Books, 2002).

55. Norman, *The Design of Everyday Things*, 3.

56. David Rockwell is the founder and CEO of The Rockwell Group, one of the leading design and architectural consulting firms for the entertainment industry. See <http://www.rockwellgroup.com/> for more information.

57. Mardelle McCuskey Shepley and Molly McCormick, "How This Issue Came About," *Journal of Architectural and Planning Research* 20, no. 1 (2003): 1–3.

58. John Zeisel, "Environmental Design Effects," 28.

Chapter 14

Themed Environments and Virtual Spaces: Video Games, Violent Play, and Digital Enemies

Talmadge Wright

Themed environments derive a major part of their attractiveness from what Russell Nye termed *riskless risk*.[1] These are urban entertainment destinations that offer an intense emotional experience without threat, accompanied by reference to an authentic experience. The creation of faux authenticity in themed designs is an attempt to mediate the desire for authenticity—real-life contact with diverse populations and societies, with the guarantee of safety provided by a heavily controlled and designed world. Themed environments depend upon a specific limited narrative using film conventions, stereotypes, and fantasy constructions in order to be successful. This is especially the case in the example of Disney productions, but occurs in other themed productions as well.

Not a simulation of something real or an exaggerated spectacle, themed commercial environments are examples of a limited set of representations chosen by the developer to give physical form to a fantasy that is expected to communicate to the consumer what an experience might be like, not what the experience actually is; a hint is offered, but, only a hint. Therefore, authenticity, like the proverbial horizon, is always receding, never quite in one's grasp. What is experienced are environments not with the rich complexity of everyday lived symbols, but with only a few symbols or icons that communicate a stripped-down version of a real experience, a safe experience, free from the fear of real challenges to one's bodily or psychological safety. What is considered safe is clearly a product of the perception of risk, where risk is associated with one's class, gender, racial/ethnic status, and geographic location.[2] Themed environments then are places designed to invoke the fantasy of realistic understandings but not the complex engagement typical of real-life settings. But of course, why should they, since the principle reason for such themed developments is to generate profit by offering the customer an experience that allows one to continue life as before. In many cases this means reducing social, cultural, and political conflict to simple safe platitudes or moral homilies.

Earlier holiday environments like the local carnival and later place-based attractions like Coney Island provided places for America's working and middle classes to occupy a space of pleasure and play.[3] Within these early middle- and working-class commercial venues, entertainment was often provided by freak shows, stereotypical and often racist treatment of foreign cultures, and dioramas depicting Biblical scenes of abandon. Because of the intense and diverse social character of these spaces, class and racial conflicts could hardly be avoided, leaving many middle-class consumers fleeing the working-class space of carnivals for the safe theme parks of Disney where behavior could be safely regulated. The advent of the Disney theme parks would sanitize many of these images for middle-class sensibilities and repackage them as historical and fantasy themes removed from the crude depictions of early carnival images. Fantasies of moral uplift were blended with emotional release.[4] Hollywood films, in turn, provided the narrative material for the new theme parks and generated new commercialized fantasies.

This intersection of the film industry and theme park commercialization continues today in developments as diverse as designs for urban redevelopments, gated communities, and themed restaurants. However, the emergence of computer technology has provided the means for a new application of entertainment both in the home and in the workplace—a virtual themed environment. Used extensively in the development of high-end graphics for film as well as in military simulations and video games, digital technology has created new worlds within which the theme park experience can be extended from its prior physical locations into the virtual landscapes of gaming spaces. Game spaces as "evocative spaces," according to Henry Jenkins, share many aspects of the theme park's environmental storytelling, allowing for the evoking of preexisting story associations, a ground upon which stories may be played out, provide information about particular stories, and "provide resources for emergent narratives."[5] Digital technology allows for the graphic representation of these stories, standard or otherwise, through player involvement that draws the player deeper into the story than would otherwise be possible through film. However, the paucity of complex narratives, partly a result of the limitations of game technology, and the repetition of standardized or formulaic scripts that revolve around particular story genres (a marketing decision), reinforces a limited imaginary.[6]

According to James Gee, video games represent cultural models as "stories or images of experience that people can tell themselves or simulate in their minds, stories and images that represent what they take to be 'normal' or 'typical' cases or situations."[7] While cultural models will vary between societies, what they provide are a set of predefined scripts for constructing what is to be feared and what is to be embraced or simply who is the enemy and who is the friend. What is imagined by game developers and fans as the enemy is conditioned in part by the imagination that emerges from the historical treatment of power relationships within the given society. This imaginary is also reinforced by market considerations since one of the primary purposes in developing games as a product is to reinforce audience identification which has already been conditioned by prior media products. Game producers do not wish to radically challenge such identification in ways that might turn away an audience. Mainstream audience identification depends upon reproducing already understood artistic or aesthetic conventions that emerge from stories established in the public's consciousness, via social institutions (family, church, school, media, and politics). Taking chances on risky or politically radical scripts or radical game innovations is less likely where success is not assured by past market behavior. This is especially the case in the film, theme park, and game industries where development budgets have expanded from the early years of simple programs to complex special effects and celebrity power requiring millions in development and marketing costs. Themed environments, whether they are the physical spaces of theme parks, the film world of Hollywood blockbusters, or the virtual landscapes of digital game play, all depend upon conventional representations that work to reproduce already existing images, scripts, or fantasies of power. Very rarely do they contest those conventions.

As trite as it might sound, it bears repeating that video games are not movies or theme parks. The ability to render lush three-dimensional worlds on a two-dimensional screen and to be able to move around within that world from various angles of viewing expands audience engagement with that world and draws one into the game story. In film production the camera moves over the surface of a set, highlighting the changing stage on which actors perform. A film is watched from a given set position determined by the director and cannot be changed.[8] The film experience demands that one watches and suspends, at least momentarily, the question of what is behind the set. In theme parks a similar engagement occurs where one is directed physically through carefully arranged physical barriers to move in the patterns expected by the theme designer—one cannot simply wander through a door backstage without being rapidly escorted out. More physically engaging than watching a film, the theme park still reduces the experience to one engineered by the designer.

Game designers—through their control of game map development, artificial intelligence, and game graphics—work in a similar manner to film directors. They can direct and control the movement of the player through that virtual space by the placing of map objects that restrict movement and visual or aural cues which encourage the player to move in one direction over another. However, unlike traversing theme parks or watching films, game fans can modify an established game engine to generate completely new game "mods" which, while changing the objects in game maps, the visuals, and aural cues, can extend the life of the original game and provide new material for innovative storytelling and game play. Game engines have even functioned as material for the creation of new movies called *machinima* that explore a diversity of topics. This also demonstrates that fan involvement in game development and even playing the game itself can offer the possibility of self-reflection and new forms of learning.[9] The meanings that game players make of their experience come not only from their interactions with already established scripts chosen by the developer and the state of artificial intelligence of the computer-controlled characters, but also emerge from their personal and social understandings of those scripted representations. This is even more the case for online multiplayer games, such as *World of Warcraft*. While the developer's skills can set the background for the game, game meanings are much more a product of player-to-player interaction.

The interactive quality of game play as opposed to passive film viewing changes the experience of represented space and the meaning of the landscapes presented to the player. Whether or not a game is designed from a third-person, first-person, or a linear-scroll perspective, the involvement of the player in changing the view of the landscape produces a quite different experience of space than having that viewpoint changed by the film director. In the case of adventure games, such as *Syberia* or *Myst* which have extensive puzzle solving components, movement is rendered in a series of static images through which one clicks and moves the character. In action, sports, and role-playing games, the virtual environments allow one the freedom to move in 360 degrees, giving one a sense of spatial depth and creating a greater sense of immediate involvement, facilitating game flow. While adventure games are highly dependent upon spatial puzzle solving and story narratives, action and war games depend more upon the sophistication of game play that require both strategy and tactics to succeed. Role-playing games, like *Dungeon Siege,* and online games like *EverQuest,* depend more heavily upon game play and narrative—not to mention the erotics of managing in-game resources, leveling up, and dealing with the complexity of player interactions.[10]

Each game genre—role playing, action, adventure, first-person shooter—similar to different film genres, contains a set of themed environments built from artistic or film conventions combined with carefully orchestrated game play options. Fantasy games most often include avatars (the virtual representation of the user) built around elves, half-giants, dwarfs, monsters, and other fantasy characters—in essence the fantasy world inherited from science fiction and writers such as J. R. R. Tolkien and Edgar Rice Burroughs. First-person shooter games, especially those involving police or military themes, draw heavily from the narratives and film scripts of Tom Clancy and World War II documentaries or war movies.

Similar to theme park rides, game worlds work to move the player between virtual spaces which may be cramped and spaces which open up into large vistas. This spatial rhythm is well known in the game design industry as one method of keeping player interest in the game. For example, transitions between surface landscapes and descent into a hidden dungeon or darkened cave increase player attraction by emphasizing contrasting environments. Film directors plot similar transitions when moving a script along. In video games such transitions, however, are often limited by the character of the game engine, unlike film. For example, the environments in the game *Doom 3* by ID Software are confined to mostly interior cramped spaces of a Martian research base, a function, in part of the limitations of the game engine. On the other hand, Novalogic's game engine renders large, open spaces more easily than closed interior spaces. One can easily see this in games like *Delta Force Extreme* or *Delta Force: Black Hawk Down*. Similarly, the artificial intelligence employed in animating game characters is limited by both the power of the game engine and the power of the player's computer to run the program. Another factor in constructing themed environments in virtual space is the limitations of the technology of representation. The recent popularity of the *Grand Theft Auto* series is less about the stereotypical portraits of thug life, and more about the innovative game play—the freedom of movement offered in the completion of tasks and the ability to move around a game map without linear scripting. That freedom of movement means that games do not have to be confined to a linear script—they can move in quite different directions allowing the player to directly influence the outcome of the game.

Taking a subset of video games—first-person shooter games (FPS)—we can ask, how do themed environments manifest themselves within this genre? What constitutes these landscapes of virtual conflict where engaging with enemy forces is the modus operandi? Game developers rely upon conventions of what landscapes look like, especially where realism is expected; for example, *Medal of Honor*, *Call of Duty* and *Brothers in Arms*, to mention a few of the World War II shooter games. The treatment of such landscapes is dependent upon the stories to be told. Hence a game which attempts to recreate World War II combat is most likely to develop landscapes, weapons, and avatars which closely correspond to what consumers expect from World War II images—images that are conditioned by World War II films and documentaries. A good example of this is the Omaha Beach assault in *Medal of Honor: Allied Assault* where the game landscapes and game play worked to match images of Omaha Beach established in documentaries and in the movie *Saving Private Ryan*.[11] Another example is fighting to liberate Stalingrad from the Nazis in the game *Call of Duty* using landscape conventions taken from movies like *Enemy at the Gates*. For fantasy landscapes or science fiction environments, more latitude is allowed for aesthetic conventions, such as in the game *Half-Life 2*, *Doom 3*, *Quake 4*, *Unreal II*, and *Halo*. There is a dialogic relationship between video games, theme parks, and movies—a trend marked by the remaking of video games (*Resident Evil*, *DOOM*) and theme park rides into movies (*Pirates of the Caribbean*).[12] Many action movies, such as *The Matrix*, *The Godfather*, *Scarface*, and others, have already made their way into the virtual environment—a recycling of useful scripts.

Due to the limitations of game technology, the complex narratives easily evoked in film are more difficult to replicate, especially where the quality of game play is considered more important than textual narrative, as is typical in multiplayer online games. Rather, a spatial narrative or spatial story, as discussed by Henry Jenkins, is privileged in both the aesthetics of a game's look and in the balance of forces within the game action as it is played. It is a game's aesthetics that generate the atmosphere necessary to establish a themed environment, but it is not the determining factor in the meaning of the game.

Realism, Advertising, and Virtual Themed Environments

The realistic quality of a game's aesthetic is the subject of intense debate between developers and game fans. For example, it is the concern over the quality of this aesthetic—the issue of what and how realistic a game should be—that forms the foundation for disagreements among players on the presence of advertising in games. While game players work to keep their virtual play separate from their everyday real lives, it is advertisers, marketing departments, and others who are working hard to occupy a space—a literal space that collapses fantasy and reality—within games to sell their products. In *Ghost Recon: Advanced Warfighter*, a building in the center of a virtual Mexico City is adorned with the Nokia brand name. Ad placements within games have accelerated as advertisers realize that the demographic of 18–24 male viewers has migrated from television watching to video game playing. Massive Inc., one of the largest in-game advertisers, and now being acquired by Microsoft, is working to establish an ad system that will be integrated into forty different video games.[13]

How game players will react to this attempt to market products in-game and how that marketing is accomplished will change the virtual themed environments established by game artists. While players approach these virtual themed environments as play spaces—ones free of consumerism and selling that characterizes real life—it is clear that business interests approach these same environments as vehicles for making money, that is, a work environment. Of course, one can find exceptions to this in the brisk market trading that goes on between players for virtual weapons in such online multiplayer role-playing games as *EverQuest*, where virtual weapons are given actual monetary value and may even be purchased over the Internet by those players who do not want to put the time in to play the game, to level up their character. The clash between these two approaches in virtual space becomes obvious when advertisers push to make their ads not simply part of the landscape, but *the* landscape. Of course, product placement and excessive advertisements are not new to the world of theme parks. Many theme parks, like Six Flags, use recognizable, copyrighted characters (such as the Looney Tunes) throughout their spaces.

Virtual Themed Environments and Cultural Models

Themed environments in virtual space can be arranged along a continuum between landscapes designed without a real-world location reference, such as many fantasy landscapes in role-playing games, to those virtual landscapes which attempt to reproduce faithfully the terrain of a real-life environment. The latter is best represented in games attempting to recreate an authentic look. In the game *Brothers in Arms: Road to Hill 30*, the development team of Gearbox Software went to the Normandy coast of France to photograph the actual settings of World War II battles and matched them with authentic military battle reports in order to recreate how buildings and terrain looked during the 1940s. Getting the look of the game correct and the accuracy of the weapons, uniforms, and landscape features was of paramount importance to the development team. Within the horror game genre, such as *The Suffering: Ties that Bind* by Midway Games, we can see an attempt to faithfully replicate a prison environment. As one of the only African American main characters seen in action video games, Torque plays the role of a male prisoner incarcerated in a fictional virtual island prison called Abbott State Penitentiary for murdering his family. However, as the narrative unfolds through a series of flashbacks, triggered at different parts during the game, the player acquires a more complex understanding of both the avatar's emotional torment and of the nature of the murders. The antihero is freed from the prison by demons from hell and then has to battle his way across the island fighting symbolic representations from monsters representing dead prison guards and inmates to surrealistic figures in chains that represent the past history of slavery. The original game disc also contained a DVD featuring the model for the game landscape—the Eastern State Penitentiary, located outside of Philadelphia and built in the early 1800s as a Quaker experiment in prison reform. The themed environment of a virtual prison was accompanied by an educational DVD that detailed how game developers drew inspiration for the virtual landscape.

Other shooter games, like the Tom Clancy series from Ubisoft and Red Storm Entertainment, *Ghost Recon, Ghost Recon: Advanced Warfighter, Splinter Cell* and the *Rainbow Six* series, feature contemporary settings from the former Soviet Republic of Georgia, Iraq, Cuba, Columbia, and Mexico City, as well as other locations. In the newest *Ghost Recon: Advanced Warfighter*, game fighting takes place in the heart of Mexico City, with U.S. military operatives working to take down a military general who has arranged a coup against the elected government of Mexico. In other games like *Conflict Desert Storm I* and *II*, the first Gulf War is presented as a cartoon version of U.S. special operatives destroying key military installations in Iraq. This role-based shooter game set in the sands of the Middle East contains a strong jingoist and nativist orientation. At the end of the game, the commander's John Wayne-styled voice praises the team for a job well done in taking out SCUD launchers, killing Iraqis, and completing the mission. In the game sequel the player battles her way through various settings including a sarin gas factory and the destruction of huge artillery guns. Both of these are imagined distortions of the real Gulf War conducted in 1991—a projected imaginary of conservative political forces within the United States. What is imagined are threats and paranoid fears inflated by long-standing political forces which work to further reinforce a view of Middle Easterners as dangerous and anti-American. These stereotypes of Middle Easterners have a long history in the United States and are common in contemporary action films and biased television news. The cultural model from which these games derive is one based on American exceptionalism, individualism, and a nativist and jingoist reactionary view that sees all opposition to United States authority as inherently subversive.[14] Opposed to this American cultural model, the game *Under Ash,* created by the Syrian publishing house Dar Al-Fikr, presents a Palestinian named Ahmed who can throw stones to fight Israeli soldiers and settlers but who must reach the Al-Aqsa mosque in Jerusalem where he helps injured Palestinians, looks for weapons, and attacks only those figures not considered civilians. As Gee expresses, the game's cultural model assumes that all settlers are advanced guards of an occupation.[15] Because game development and game audiences are expanding worldwide, we can expect more diverse cultural models in video games. This increased diversity will work to make these virtual themed landscapes more interesting and will also allow for an expanded imaginary in how we understand unfamiliar people and places.

What is important to understand about these types of virtual themed environments is not just the literal aesthetic look, the story line, or even the stereotypical enemies which abound, but, rather the quality and nature of the game play that players bring to the game. The popularity of online battles between game players has progressed from the simple death matches of the early *Doom* and *Quake* games to the more complex social characteristics of the first-person shooter game *Counter-Strike,* and now to the struggles between players in *Battlefield 2.* While it is tempting to judge video games and those who play them by the simple presentation of stereotypical narratives and images, such a literal reading of game content ignores exactly what players do within a game and how they make sense of those narratives.

Playing *Counter-Strike*: Making Sense of Virtual Killing

Counter-Strike is a team based first-person online multiplayer shooter game in which players assume the roles of either counterterrorists or terrorists, and using an elaborate array of virtual weapons purchased through an in-game reward system, seek to either plant or defuse bombs, keep or rescue hostages, and defend or attack important persons.[16] Created by Minh Le as a modification for the game *Half-Life* that could be downloaded for free, the success of the game prompted a retail release by Valve Software in 2000. It is still one of the most popular online, shooter games. Between January 2001 and June 2002, I worked with a team of researchers exploring, through participant observation and open interviews, the meaning that playing *Counter-Strike* held for game players. During the course of our study we noted that at any one time, there were between three and eight thousand servers running the game worldwide with approximately twenty-three to twenty-five thousand players online at the same time.[17]

To understand FPS virtual game worlds as themed environments, it would be helpful to focus on the types of emotions that are aroused in playing within these landscapes. In many ways playing within a virtual game world mirrors those emotions that are found in theme park rides and other types of entertainment found in themed venues—most often, laughter and exhilaration. Anxiety and nervousness were also mentioned, but laughter was the most common emotion described by game players. In a theme park, the thrill of exploring new environments is accompanied by the bodily thrill of the amusement park ride. Similarly, the tension of outsmarting one's opponents in a multiplayer game, of successfully using the virtual landscape to compete, increases the pleasure of the game, albeit without the physical sensations of a theme park ride. The ability to produce such emotions is dependent upon the degree of realism within the game, or how well the player can identify with the game action and setting. Game players will often discuss this as the distinction between game aesthetics or narrative and game play.

In the public debate over the question of the relationship between fantasy and real violence—a point of anxiety to many concerned citizens—the virtual sandbox is thought to have political implications in supporting an ideological view of one sort or another. Our study found that relationship to be much more complicated than expected. Just as one goes to a theme park to be entertained and not lectured to, game players expect to play, not give or receive sermons on political ideology.[18] However, they are also aware of their own political perspectives, but they most often want to keep that separate from the world of play and fun. Nonetheless, the politics of the game did intrude several times following September 11th in both the comments of online players, the names they gave themselves, and in their choice of game characters. Running throughout these debates on virtual killing is the always shifting distinction between fantasy/play and reality/work, between realism and realistic depictions of violence and gunplay.

Performative Skill, Laughter, and Gunplay

Playing video games requires a particular degree of performative skill and interactive competency, not just hand-eye coordination, but tactical thinking, patience and the ability to assess situations quickly while under stress. The emotions produced by enacting these performative skills range from nervousness, frustration, pride, and pleasure, to anxiety and laughter. However, of all the emotions generated by *Counter-Strike* game play, laughter seems to be the one most favored. This may not be the case with single player games where emotions are generated through the complex interaction of elaborate scripting, performative skill, and complex lighting and sound schemes; note the nervous tensions which build when playing through the darkened, virtual blood-soaked corridors of the horror/sci-fi game *F.E.A.R.* by Monolith Productions. In multiplayer games, the focus moves from the sequences of game advancements and puzzle solving to one of individual player skill on display for other human players who are more than likely to comment on one's level of proficiency or lack thereof. In this context laughter becomes a response to the real interaction of game players with each other, mediated via the game. The themed environments merely provide a backdrop for the larger story of player vs. player interaction. However, if these environments are not carefully constructed to facilitate "good" game play, they will be judged as inferior, such as "bad game maps."

The game players with whom I talked mentioned both feeling elated and laughing throughout the game, unless the game slowed down or became boring due to a string of battles losses or incompetent playing, a failure of game balance. This was usually precipitated by player behavior that contradicted expected responses, such as backing off a building and falling to one's virtual death or failing to anticipate an opponent's move leading to an embarrassing death, usually by a knife, as opposed to a gun. As Mick states:

> Usually when somebody is just completely unaware. Caught off guard . . . usually, I'm not laughing if I'm the one that does something funny, you know. But . . . if I see somebody who clearly walks backward into his demise. Usually the biggest laugh though is when one of the other guys types or writes or says something really funny.

Playing with cartoon-like violence and finding oneself in an unanticipated position is often grounds for laughter. The specific game map one is playing will often lead to specific humorous situations. This is especially true given the sound effects in the game. On a game map called *Highrise*, featuring an uncompleted skyscraper, one runs the risk of falling off the edge if not careful. In more than one game I witnessed that players would deliberately throw themselves off the edge just to laugh at the screams on the way down. Daryl commented that when playing on this map he would hear the sound effects of someone falling off the level and would laugh at their mistake and how the player falling would sound like a Disney character. The players understand this form of humor as slapstick comedy. The virtual environment also provides the context for slapstick humor in the form of "surprise kills." As Bryson points out:

> Well, usually those sort of surprise kills, that's when you laugh the most often. Or when somebody is trying to diffuse a bomb and they blow [up] and you see their body flying across. Those are all funny moments . . . but, I suppose I would explain it in terms of slapstick comedy. I mean, obviously, you see people get hurt and fall down in a comic situation all the time, and you laugh, like Kramer and *Seinfeld*. Or Homer and *The Simpsons*. And you don't think, oh, my gosh, is he

okay? It's horrible, right? But, it's just sort of the surprise of seeing a pratfall. It just so happens it's a pratfall of somebody getting killed. But, I think, the parallels are the same there.

The "riskless risk" of the game world can allow players to engage in virtual behavior that appears antisocial, playing with that which is forbidden in real life. However, in theme parks such behavior is limited to mental fantasies while the body obeys the dictates of the ride designer: keep your hands inside the moving vehicle, do not step out of the ride until stopped, and so forth. Safety is guaranteed through rigid controls on body behavior and well-engineered spaces. In the virtual world such safety is guaranteed as a result of the action occurring on a computer screen, quite removed from the physical body. Unlike theme park attractions which are tightly controlled in a carefully designed experience, the spaces of themed virtual environments provide expanded opportunities for player behavior that can violate expected comportment—for example, team killing and cheating. However, in both virtual worlds and theme parks humor can spring from the surprises that wait when turning a virtual corner or taking a fast twirl in the latest theme park ride.

The playful tension of the hunt is countered by the limitations of human awareness, a source of laughter, since making mistakes contradicts the commonsense assumptions of professional counterterrorism behavior promoted by the game's design. On a game map called *Dune*, Bruce used the themed environment to take advantage of an opponent who was not aware of where he was:

[I] probably laugh most often whenever something funny happens to another player [when] something unexpected happens to them. Because you can tell that they had no idea that was coming . . . it's usually laughing at other people. . . . I laughed really hard last night because when I was playing the *Dune* map, David, his character was down at the bottom of the dune next to a dune buggy. And I was up at the top of a dune quite a ways away. He was shooting at me. And I turned to look at him. And, he didn't know it, but he was actually hiding behind two gas canisters. And so I started shooting at them. And, they blew up and sent him flying . . . just straight up. And I heard David [say], "what the hell happened?" . . . and that was funny. We kind of laughed about that later.

This form of slapstick comedy has historically directed its attention against the powerful while the grotesque remains a subversive force within the culture at large. In so far as games like *Counter-Strike* and other shooter games provide the themed environments for such comedic moments, they can also elucidate a particular antiauthoritarian moment which contravenes the dominant context of the game, such as fighting terrorists. This type of humor is rooted in the body, virtual or otherwise, and its performance. Historically, vaudeville, as opposed to theater with its emphasis on elite literary themes, was anchored in corporeal performance, a performance which all could understand. In this sense the humor expressed in *Counter-Strike* is very close to the world of vaudeville. While the game is set up with particular rules, such as defusing bombs, or planting them, rescuing hostages or keeping them from the counter-terrorists—for which one is awarded so many points for successful accomplishment—violating these rules is almost always a basis for humor. This is especially true when the game engine fails to fully function as it is supposed to. As Bruce says:

> The one thing that I think is funny, I think this is a good example of this, is it's always funny, not always, but almost always funny whenever a counterterrorist is supposed to be rescuing hostages. And the hostages, it seems like about a third of the time, they get hung up and they can't follow the person. Either because they get hung up behind a box or who knows. Sometimes they float in the air five feet up and you have no idea why they can't follow you. It's always funny whenever the counterterrorist shoots the people—the hostages they're supposed to rescue—just out of frustration. It's not, they're not playing their part. So, the answer to that is usually . . . "screw you, I'll just shoot you!"

Players, especially new players, will often do things that, particularly to a seasoned game player, seem foolish, leading to very comical situations. Often such players, criticized as "newbies," are met with refrains from other players about their lack of skill. One's own game behavior—as well as observing the futile attempts of others to throw virtual grenades that reflect back and kill one's self—is also grounds for laughter. When this lack of performative skill is present in many members of a team, other players will often chime in with a note of derision. Tony says he laughs all the time while playing *Counter-Strike*:

> [It's funny] when grenades explode in your hand or you toss [them] against a wall and [they] come back to you and you die. And, you know, when I see people kill themselves with grenades or even shooting, I think that's the unrealistic part about video games is when the bullets hit the wall but they kill you because they bounce back sometimes . . . I guess that could happen in real life but the chances of that are just so slim and killing you no less; that's funny I think.

The pleasures of performative skill and the unexpected surprises that emerge in multiplayer gaming make up one of the foundational elements of why multiplayer video games remain attractive. But, the other element that needs consideration is the attraction of virtual violent imagery—the pleasures of the grotesque.[19] It is important to understand that grotesque pleasure does not extend to everyday life where bodily threats are directly connected to harm, but, are an essential part of fantasy life. The character of video games as virtual themed environments allows for the safe engagement of grotesque imagery and violent transgressions within an environment of "riskless risk."[20] It is precisely the elaboration of the grotesque in fantasy which gives us the ability to reflect upon the stable state of our everyday lives. The fantastic quality of the grotesque is in contrast to realistic depictions of violence which are usually much less dramatic and more disturbing. For developers and game players alike, a game that is realistic may also be the least fun to play. Developers have to balance their attempt to create realistic effects with game play to ensure a player's continued interest in the game. In traditional themed spaces, including theme parks, restaurants, and casinos, visitors are nurtured with cut-rate food deals, packaged hotel accommodations, and safe surroundings in which their fantasies may be engaged. Game developers attempt to perform the same dance in designing game spaces and game play that will give the player enough excitement without being either too difficult or too easy—to stay engaged.

Realism and the Grotesque Character of Virtual Violence

The graphic character of *Counter-Strike* violence calls forth the meaning of realism in representations of death and injury. One gamer, Daryl, is concerned about too much realism and too much detail in graphic representation—especially those realistic representations of the human face which allow one to feel some empathy with the game character. And yet he also recognizes the humor in grotesque forms of violent representations:

Daryl: I wouldn't want too much, too much detail in certain things.

Interviewer: You wouldn't want like, legs, limbs flying all over? You know because they do that in the real *Half-Life* version when you ax a person, they explode into body parts and organs.

Daryl: Actually, I can see that as funny too, to a certain extent. I guess, because I could imagine like, well I was there, you know, and Mick's arm flew off and hit me in the head or something. No, I can see that as being funny. There's something . . . special about human facial expression that just might . . . bother me a little.

Interviewer: Too personal?

Daryl: Yeah . . . but I think that is why everybody looks fairly generic, most of them, a lot of them you know, like the guy has the beard, sunglasses, masks . . . there's nobody that's got a perfectly open face and I imagine they did that on purpose. . . . So, yeah, I wouldn't want to see . . . the trickle of blood coming out of . . . I think . . . that would remind me that this actually happens for real. . . . You want a certain level of reality. . . . I would want to draw a distinction between . . . . something that's real, something that's fake, and something that's kind of virtual and this . . . partakes of something of reality, but there's no way to get confused with that.

On the other hand Frank, a younger player, enjoyed the graphic character of grotesque virtual violence because in his eyes it is so "unreal" that it is funny. It is the very unreal character of the action and graphics in FPS games like *Quake* and *Quake II* which strike this player as funnier than *Counter-Strike*. Frank comments:

> Okay, I laughed the most in *Quake II*. There's a certain mod for it called *Weapons of Destruction* . . . it's . . . a mod like *Counter-Strike*'s a mod of *Half-life*. But in this [mod] you have rockets that when they hit someone they burst into flames, or you have a bazooka that when it hits it bursts into flames; the weapons are a little more destructive and I just laughed my ass off. It's just so funny. Because everything is so quick and you can do so many different (things).

Bruce likes the fact that the graphics in *Counter-Strike* are not terribly realistic. The crudeness of the representation allows him to maintain a safe distance from the graphic nature of virtual violence. Similarly, in the entertainment world of the theme park, some people prefer older rides that, though more rickety and less themed, may be seen as more focused on the experience than the realism of thematic representation. Bruce mentions of video game graphics:

> I think that if they were really photographically realistic, it would be disturbing to me. It would be a disgusting game. I don't want to see [where] in the game you shoot someone and you see blocks of red pixels. And that's supposed to be blood. But, it doesn't look [like] . . . his head exploded or anything like that.

This ambivalence over consuming graphic representations of virtual violence speaks to a broader concern, and that is the need to maintain the separation between the fantasy virtual world created by the computer program and the real world of everyday life. And, in fact, this separation—or "it's only a game" talk—is most important because it defines the boundaries of what is considered both morally acceptable by the players as well as that which distinguishes pathological from normal behavior. As graphics become more realistic, the concern grows over when this line will be crossed. Increased game realism means adjusting the boundaries between what is fantasy and what is reality. This adjustment is quite normal: we all make these adjustments as we grow older and learn to make distinctions between meaning and intent in social action and social representations. As the concern over violent virtual representations grows so do strategies used by game players to render those representations "safe." The ritual license to engage in transgressive behavior like the virtual violence of most shooter games is carefully circumscribed within an appropriate place removed from real everyday concerns of power and coercion, even if they do creep in online player behavior. The distinction between, for example, shooting a real gun and a virtual gun is made constantly by game players. Members of the game focus group commented:

> So something we have all pointed to is this involvement, regardless of the activity that takes place, chess or football or whatever. There is the same kind of immersion in whatever you are doing. And of course nobody makes the argument that this kind of involvement leads to any kind of violence. And so it's merely the structure of the play at work here that happens to be connected with violent images, but I take it that you can also give an analysis of those images much like you would of a text, right? It takes place within certain parameters; in this case a

16- or 17-inch screen. There are certain rules that you play by and these are simply the rules of this game. You know that for the same reason that we don't throw yellow flags in the grocery store when someone cuts in front of us, those are not the rules of that place.... We understand that there is a context here and that there are rules within this context and we are going to play within this context and that entails a certain amount of immersion. And there is no reason to think that we would take the context of this act of play and juxtapose it or tie it into another situation. Or at least the onus would be on the person who argued this.

Counter-Strike is a game, just like any other video or computer game, and should not be confused with any realistic portraits of violence, terrorism, or war. It is not truly realistic, but does mimic some of the characteristics of realism simply to increase game immersion and enable player identification. The minimal plot of the battles is simply generic Manichean contests and circumstances of antagonist/protagonist, not to be taken too seriously or literally by the players, unlike the real life and death struggles produced by real warfare. Avatar death is always accompanied by a virtual resurrection in the next round of combat, a fact which allows for riskless risk taking. You always have a second, third, and fourth chance. This playing with death and combat imagery is a characteristic which, in novels, is carried by the language and narrative of the text, but, which in computer games, similar to the architecture used in traditional themed spaces, is carried by the graphics, sound, and the workings of the game engine. As Bruce points out:

> *Counter-Strike* is a game. And the forces are not real. And, sure it can look realistic, but, it's a game. No one gets hurt. As a game, I mean it's a virtual game. It's not even a game like football where there really is force occurring and people can get hurt. Yeah, if I thought even for a second that the characters I was playing against were really people or whatever, it just, it would no longer be a game. But, I know I can throw a grenade at them and that's just part of the game and there's nothing real about it. That's just the objective.... I don't associate virtual reality or virtual games, the forces in virtual games, with real force; it doesn't affect me at all.

While the grotesque may be allowed to exist in the play world of virtual gaming, it is met with horror under the real conditions of war and street violence. This is just as true of those who play computer games as it is for the general public. Markus perhaps says it the best in the following quote, drawing careful distinctions between fictional virtual violence and the real violence in the Middle East:

> Like, the stuff in the news... people die, people suffer, people are maimed and ... there was a pizza shop in Israel that was blown [up] just recently, and when I was there... I went there. I mean they showed the picture, and I've been there, I've eaten there, my friends were there and a letter was sent to me by my Rabbi ... I don't know how much more different you can get between real life, towers falling down or bombs going off, and a bunch of people sitting around basically

in the dark hitting keys on keyboards—you know hooting and hollering and having fun . . . they're more than worlds apart, I would say.

Virtual Themed Environments: Slippages between Real and Fantasy Violence

Given the efforts game players exert to maintain a strict separation between real and fantasy violence, it is most interesting to look at those cases where slippage occurs between the fantasy virtual environment and everyday life. Real violence and crimes can exist side by side with the fantasy world, often separated by the narratives we tell ourselves about how the world is supposed to work. In Chan's account of his experience in playing *Counter-Strike* in Taiwan, this separation breaks down:

> Subconsciously you know that Americans are always the counterterrorists, and you know Arabs and Irish radicals are the terrorists. But that almost . . . entices me to be terrorists more often . . . play the underdog. . . . In Taiwan, many people who come . . . we have a huge . . . Mafia, gang problem, sort of like in Chicago, but it's kind of . . . different. . . . They sell drugs and . . . like the Triads in Asia and stuff like that; a lot of people I know are in these too, but a lot of them come and play. And so, actually a lot of the gangster guys would play as terrorists; they would only play if they could play as terrorists . . . the way I found this out was [be]cause we were sitting in a row and one guy was really good and I wanted him to . . . join our team. And it was obvious he was in a gang, like, you could kind of tell who was in a gang, and who's not. And then, he was just like, "I don't play counterterrorist[s]" . . . he kind of knew, he like wanted to kill . . . cops . . . in his virtual fight.

This slippage between real life and the fantasy of virtual violence was revealed when just after September 11th, all of the game players I worked with decided to call it quits for a few weeks. In their eyes it did not seem appropriate to play a violent video game after experiencing the largest attack on American soil since Pearl Harbor.[21] When the players finally returned to the game about a month later, the talk was centered around which character not to play, usually the terrorist. On the other hand the younger game player relished playing either role as a defiant rejection of the imposed slippage between virtual fantasy and real events. The continuous effort needed to maintain the distinction between fantasy and reality can be easily exhausted when real violence intrudes and fear accompanied by anxiety replaces humor, satire, and pleasure.

Yet, even with the above slippage between real and fictional violence, there is the strong determination to maintain the boundaries between what is real and what is fantasy, even as politicians and major corporate advertising and marketing firms work hard to break down these distinctions that gamers themselves make. The virtual themed environments of game play provide a safe haven, removed from the horrors of everyday real-life violence—a safe distraction from our own feelings of mortality and a place to exert fantasies of superheroism and competency denied us in real life. Much like traditional themed spaces that also often feature death and violence in a subdued context, virtual violence plays on a distinction between the real violence of everyday life and that of the computer screen.[22] Bryson emphasized the importance of the difference between real and virtual violence and the impact virtual violence may have on any real-life desire to harm another:

> It would never occur to me in a million years to actually pick up a Steyr Aug [assault rifle] and, you know, shoot somebody between the eyes with it. It wouldn't even occur to me to even buy a gun. I'm generally opposed to gun ownership in [the] home. I just think it's just dangerous and more trouble than it's worth. But, I recognize that this is a fantasy. This is role-playing, you know.

This last quote points to the fact that play and instrumental actions are quite different in both intent and result. Simulators designed for military or commercial training may have some of the graphic features that games have, but, their purposes are far different.[23] Military simulations are not performed for fun, but for perfecting a science of killing. While the military employs extensive computer simulators in tank training as well as small group tactics, the goal is to instill a particular type of reaction, a particular type of thinking which can perfect those skills necessary to control a real battlefield. Playing *Counter-Strike* or any other military style game designed for play is but a thin shadow of real military simulators. To equate the two is to confuse reality with virtual fantasy.[24] One explanation for why this confusion seems more common in adults than in children has to do with a greater realization of death and mortality with age, the responsibilities of keeping others safe, and the final inability to stave off the loss of loved ones and ultimately of ourselves. Fantasy, games, religious ritual, indeed, most of our symbolic reality are manifestations of terror management that allow us to get along with the task of living in the knowledge that we and all that we love will ultimately die. In virtual games, our avatar can always be born anew, no matter how horrific the game death. Play is not simply a practice for life's activities, but an engagement in repetitions and rituals that reaffirm our unique and collective presence in the world, virtual or otherwise.

The Social Complexity of Virtual Themed Environments

What is important to recognize is how these violent virtual themed environments provide a venue for playing out complex social interactions between game players as well as a venue for private fantasies—a phenomenon which Erving Goffman would have easily recognized in his analysis of team performance.[25] The fact that this complexity flies in the face of conventional wisdom about video games reveals the flawed character of media effects research.[26] In our study forty-three separate subject categories alone emerged when we analyzed the discourse of FPS game players. The social complexity of talk between players in what appear to be simple shooter games demonstrates that the virtual violent themed environments of FPS video games cannot be examined merely by looking at game content. Just as traditional theme parks cannot be merely understood as reflections of themed architecture alone, video games must be viewed as complex combinations of thematic space, player interaction, and game play. The pleasure of play in violent virtual themed environments is not just the pleasure of the grotesque or the enactment of jingoist or stereotypical assumptions about others. It is about the ability to play with your own demons as well as the demons of others—an ability which can form the basis for critical self-reflection as easily as it can reinforce our worst prejudices. The fact that violent virtual themed environments are primarily occupied by young men—who through trash talk and other online behaviors seek to demonstrate their ability to dominate another, male or female—raises questions about the reproduction of gendered stereotypes in player behavior.[27] However as much we may wish to critique such attitudes of gender, we should not assume that these behaviors can be mapped easily on the everyday life of game players. It is just not that literal or simple. Video games are a tool for pleasure, subject to a multiplicity of uses. Importantly, the issue comes back to the wisdom of the user. Following Douglas Kellner and the sociology of culture literature, I would suggest that a fruitful avenue for studying video games, violent virtual themed environments, and society is one which incorporates a critical analysis of game content, an examination of the political economy of the industry, and an in-depth examination of audience response.[28]

Virtual themed environments can create a safe context for an emotional identification with a socially designated other as easily as they can discourage identification with stereotypes of racist and sexist images. They can hint at the risk of unsafe environments in the comfort of our homes. There are times when we can laugh at the most grotesque excesses of video game violence and yet at other times we can be stunned into sadness by identifying with virtual victims or what their context means to us metaphorically. What does this tell us about the future of virtual themed environments? Clearly, the immersion provided by interactions within virtual environments and between players will expand, along with graphic/audio realism, and emotional identification, violent or otherwise, as game spatial narratives become more sophisticated. Game narratives and themed environments will become more diverse, encompassing both non-Western as well as Western themes, providing artists opportunities to fashion virtual environments of historical situations with diverse endings. Ethical decisions will be incorporated in the path a player chooses leading to greater complexity of both game play and game understanding—a process we can see in the early years with games like Ion Storm Inc.'s *Deus Ex*. We can also expect virtual themed environments to reflect a broader array of environments, not simply wrecked, war-torn landscapes, fantasy worlds, or lush desert islands. Players will be able to reproduce their likeness in the virtual world by mapping their real-world features onto game avatars, features which can be recognized by other players. Such immersion and porting of real-life features into virtual life will also expand the possibilities for social contact and play.[29] Last, while virtual themed environments remain a commercial environment, there is nothing written which says they have to remain this way. It is entirely possible to imagine a virtual public nonprofit world emerging, as predicted by William Gibson and the other writers of cyberpunk literature, in the future which will encompass much more than playing games—much more about playing life with real-life effects.[30] Better that we learn to play with the building elements of such a world in order to grasp how they can help us or hurt us. The choice will be ours.

Notes

I am grateful to Dr. Henry Jenkins (Director, Comparative Media Studies Program at MIT) for his initial reading of the chapter and his excellent feedback.

1. Quoted in John Hannigan, *Fantasy City: Pleasure and Profit in the Postmodern Metropolis* (New York: Routledge, 1998), 71–74. See also Mark Gottdiener, *The Theming of America* (Boulder, Colo.: Westview, 2001); and Robert P. Gephart, Jr., "Safe Risk in Las Vegas," M@n@gement 4 (3): 141–58.

2. Deborah Lupton, *Risk and Sociocultural Theory: New Directions and Perspectives* (Cambridge: Cambridge University Press, 1999). See also the work of Ulrich Beck, *Risk Society: Towards a New Modernity* (London: Sage, 1992).

3. Gary S. Cross and John K. Walton, *The Playful Crowd: Pleasure Places in the Twentieth Century* (New York: Columbia University Press, 2005).

4. Cross and Walton, *The Playful Crowd*, 171.

5. Henry Jenkins, "Game Design as Narrative Architecture," in *The Game Design Reader: A Rules of Play Anthology*, ed. Katie Salen and Eric Zimmerman (Cambridge, Mass.: MIT Press, 2006), 670–89. See page 676–77 for quotes from Don Carson on Walt Disney's imagineering and the development of environmental storytelling. Jenkins usefully refutes the extreme positions of ludologists who privilege game play as well as those advocating a simple narrative reading of games. He wisely understands that games are about both narrative and game play, calling for an expanded definition—a spatial definition of video games.

6. "It is only insofar as the radical imagination of the psyche seeps through the successive layers of the social armor, which covers and penetrate it up to an unfathomable limit-point, and which constitute the individual, that the singular human being can have, in return, an independent action on society." Cornelius Castoriadis, *Philosophy, Politics, Autonomy: Essays in Political Philosophy* (New York: Oxford University Press, 1991), 146. Castoriadis believes that this capacity is extremely unusual in any society. Rebellion and transgression are the most common form in which the individual can manifest itself against the "bundles of roles" it is expected to play. But where this social capacity exists, a "true individuation of the individual" is possible—the radical imaginary of the "singular psyche" can then create new social ways of expressing itself in a public manner which are both original and contribute to changing the world. Fantasies or stories of such a radical imaginary can provide

powerful scripts for the film/game industry; ones that can move beyond the standard stories of rebellion and fighting with an imagined enemy.

7. James Paul Gee, *What Video Games Have to Teach Us about Learning and Literacy* (New York: Palgrave Macmillan, 2003), 146.

8. With new DVD technology, it is possible for consumers to alter some aspects of the director's decisions, including the viewing angles and the assemblage of scenes. In the film *Final Destination 3*, viewers can select a version of the film that allows them to choose the destiny of the characters.

9. Sandvoss discusses fandom as a form of self-reflection using media. It can be used to understand game players' attractions to the games they play and the virtual environments they choose to frequently inhabit. Sandvoss draws upon Herbert Marcuse's notion of surplus repression in modern society and that fantasy in media is one way that players can produce "a libidinal cathexis that overcomes divisions between the erotic, cultural, social, technological and economic." Cornel Sandvoss, *Fans: The Mirror of Consumption* (Malden, Mass.: Polity Press, 2005), 121. On a different note the increasing dominance of console over PC games means a decline in the production of independent mods and a tighter control of game technology by game companies.

10. The themed environments of computer games can only be enjoyed if there is both performative skill and interactive competency on the part of the player. The ability to project oneself into the game is essential, as it is for any form of entertainment. In Fine's excellent study of Dungeons and Dragons players, he discusses the importance of game play, how playing encourages engrossment, and allows for player identification with the game figures. Gary A. Fine, *Shared Fantasy: Role Playing Games as Social Worlds* (Chicago: University of Chicago Press, 1983), 3. He understands that fantasy gaming has three sets of rules built from commonsense reality, gaming rules, and the content of the game fantasy. Game players then "enact different persona on each of these three levels." Rule-based play within video games means that pleasure is derived from both the enactment of those rules and the attempt to break them. See also the work of Jasper Juul, *Half-Real: Video Games between Real Rules and Fictional Worlds* (Cambridge, Mass.: MIT Press, 2005), 76 and Steven Poole, *Trigger Happy: Videogames and the Entertainment Revolution* (New York: Arcade Publishing, 2000), 168–72.

11. See Geoff King and Tanya Krzywinska, "Introduction: Cinema/Videogames/Interfaces," in *Screenplay: Cinema/Videogames/Interfaces*, ed. Geoff King and Tanya Krzywinska (London: Wallflower Press, 2002), 13–14.

12. See Scott A. Lukas, "Remakes as a Question of Medium," in *Fear, Cultural Anxiety, and Transformation: Horror, Science Fiction, and Fantasy Films Remade*, ed. John Marmysz and Scott A. Lukas (Lanham, Md.: Lexington Books, forthcoming).

13. Chris Morris, "Pepperoni, Anchovies and Dragon's Tail: Advertising Prepares to Make Its Biggest Push into the Video Game World," *CNN Money*, 18 February 2005, 2. See also, David F. Smith, "Branding Iron: Virtual Billboards Get Bigger in Games," *Computer Gaming World*, Issue 248 (February 2005): 26–7 and *Reuters News Service*, "Advertisers Explore Virtual Video Game Frontier," *New York Times*, 9 December 2005.

14. For example, in the game *Rainbow Six: Lockdown* the inequalities of underdevelopment and protests against such inequalities, violent or otherwise, are immediately dismissed and equated with terrorism as part of the game setup. The in-game text reads in the second mission, "Global Liberation Front. They blame the problems of the Third World on the developed nations. The GLF wants third world debt forgiven, an end to military occupation, and a better life for everyone. Or else they start killing random civilians." Other

comments in the game are: "There are indications that the GLF is going to attack at the World Bank Conference in Amsterdam. We believe they plan to take hostages and execute them. You're going to be at the conference, disguised as a news crew." The fact that fictional news reporters were actually used by members of Al Qaeda to penetrate the Northern Alliance in Afghanistan and kill the Alliance's leader Ahmed Shah Massoud completely reverses the fictional text of *Rainbow Six*. Disguising spies and military operatives as news reporters in real life has the real-world effect of getting legitimate reporters killed.

15. Gee, *What Video Games Have to Teach*, 148–49. Christian video games have now entered the market with early titles like *Catechumen* and *Ominous Horizons*. In the newest Christian video game, a strategy game called *Eternal Forces*, a virtual army takes on the forces of the Antichrist, presented as United Nations Peacekeepers. The game is set in New York city and features cries of "Praise the Lord!" whenever an enemy is dispatched. The game, based on Rev. Timothy LaHaye and Jerry Jenkins, *Left Behind: Eternal Forces*, speaks to the dominionists' version of evangelical Christianity which advocates world domination by Christians and the coming of the Rapture. See Zack Pelta-Heller, "Kids Kill in Violent Christian Videogame," *AlterNet*, 21 July 2006, <http://www.alternet.org/story/38873/> (27 October 2006).

16. The ability to play either as a terrorist or as a counter-terrorist allows one to see different sides of a scenario. In the game *America's Army*, developed by the U.S. Army as a recruiting tool, this taking the side of the other is absent. All players play as U.S. soldiers and all enemy figures are presented as the terrorist other. The absence of blood in America's Army was a conscious decision. According to Col Wardynaski, the developer, "We don't want to use violence as an entertainment vehicle." Brian Kennedy, "Uncle Sam Wants You (To Play this Game)," *New York Times*, 11 July 2002, E6.

17. My team and I engaged in participant observation with a small group of *Counter-Strike* players at a medium-size Midwestern university in the United States. Game play occurred on a weekly basis for a three-hour session at a time and employed a LAN (local area network) setup most of the time. Occasionally, outside players would be allowed into the gaming sessions. Prior to this we had played *Counter-Strike* on fifty different servers for seventy hours, recording the text files of in-game chats from which we observed very specific patterns of social interaction. See Talmadge Wright, Paul Breidenbach, and Eric Boria, "Creative Player Actions in FPS Online Video Games: Playing Counter-Strike," *Game Studies: The International Journal of Computer Game Research* 2, no. 2 (2002). <http://www.gamestudies.org>. The data from that initial research was incorporated into an open-ended questionnaire that we administered in extensive one- to two-hour interviews with twenty-three game players both on campus and off campus, including the ones we played with at the university. We also conducted a single focus group session with a small group of five game players who we had played with at the university and examined game publications and game Web sites.

18. Yet, given the overt militarist ideology of many shooter games, especially ones which involve combat in a virtual Middle East, it is not surprising that the ideology of games would come under fire. What is interesting is the extent with which some game players contest the political assumptions of these games. For example, Joseph DeLappe created an anti-war protest within the game *America's Army* by making a public memorial for those U.S. soldiers who have died in Iraq. His Web site is <http://www.unr.edu/art/delappe.html>. His work started in March 2006 by using the online game *America's Army*. After logging into the game he would manually type in, through the in-game chat function, the name, rank and date of death of each service person who has died to date in Iraq. And then he would

just stand within the game waiting to get killed: "I enter the game using my login name, 'dead-in-iraq' and proceed to type the names using the game's text messaging system. As is my usual practice when creating such an intervention, I am a neutral visitor as I do not participate in the proscribed mayhem. Rather, I stand in the position and type until I am killed. Upon being re-incarnated [sic] I continue to type." As of May 5, 2006 he had typed in over 250 names and will keep doing so until the end of the war.

   19. The grotesque—a term standing for ugliness, the strange and bizarre, and those unreal behaviors and appearances which disturbed the social order—emerged during the Romantic era in Europe. Most often these traits were associated with those who were marginalized in society, confined to the lower classes and looked down upon with scorn by social elites. The grotesque hence became a badge of honor for the dispossessed whom were able to make use of its conventions to disrupt established hierarchies and subvert the Kantian sublime. In fact, it is precisely the understanding of Kant's dynamic sublime which best mirrors the pleasure that accrues from playing violent games. The symbolic inversion of the social order practiced by lower-status social classes and employed in figures like the joker or trickster is developed most thoroughly in the carnivalesque discussed by Bahktin in his comments on Rabelais. See Mikhail Bakhtin, *Rabelais and His World* (Cambridge Mass.: MIT Press, 1968). The grotesque has often been accompanied by the joker, the trickster, and the fool with the ascension of comedy. Subverting the dominant moral order through joking, word play, parody, imitation, and symbolic performances, is in fact, one of the standard forms of social resistance to hierarchies exerted by the powerful. All of these are present in actual gamer behavior and are also reflected in traditional themed spaces.

   20. Gerard Jones discusses the need for individuals to play with their demons, to have the imaginary space to grapple with their monsters in either video games, books, or other forms that represent our fears and anxieties. Gerard Jones, *Killing Monsters: Why Children Need Fantasy, Superheroes, and Make-Believe Violence* (New York: Basic Books, 2002). The assumption that contemporary entertainment is more violent than in the past is contradicted by the historical record: Harold Schechter, *Savage Pastime: A Cultural History of Violent Entertainment* (New York: St. Martin's, 2005). Also see, Jeffrey H. Goldstein, *Why We Watch: The Attractions of Violent Entertainment* (New York: Oxford University Press, 1998). Theme parks have also traditionally represented spaces that allow patrons to escape everyday life by exploring the fears and anxieties of life in safe, sanitized contexts.

   21. Since September 11th, it is clear that some of the hijackers did practice, in fact, using computer games. However, they were not violent games like *Counter-Strike* but flight simulator games produced by Microsoft for flying 757 airplanes. This anxiety was expressed to me frequently after September 11th and only faded slowly over the several months after the incident. The game sessions I attended were interrupted for about two weeks and then resumed their normal schedule. The real world intruded within the online sessions as players chose online names that reflected the headlines. "Osama Your Mama" was a favorite online name to adopt at the time, and later "Osama Bin Forgotten."

   22. Scott A. Lukas, "The Theme Park and the Figure of Death," *InterCulture* 2 (May 2005), <http://www.fsu.edu/~proghum/interculture/The%20Theme%20Park%20and%20the%20Figure%20of%20Death.htm> (1 October 2006).

   23. For more on the connection of the military to gaming simulation, see J.C. Herz, *Joystick Nation: How Videogames Ate Our Quarters, Won Our Hearts, and Rewired Our Minds* (Boston: Little, Brown and Company, 1997), 197–213.

24. An interesting film dealing with the connections of real military violence and military and non-military training simulations is *Game Over: Gender, Race and Violence in Video Games*, produced by the Media Education Foundation. See <http://www.mediaed.org/videos/MediaGenderAndDiversity/GameOver>. However, the video remains flawed in its lack of treatment of game player understandings. The didactic quality of the film reproduces the standard assumptions about media effects which remain unproven and represents elite criticism of a popular media.

25. Erving Goffman, *The Presentation of Self in Everyday Life* (New York: Doubleday, 1959), 82–83. Also see Erving Goffman, *Interaction Ritual*, (New York: Random House, 1967). Goffman's analysis of the symbolic action of teamwork is very helpful in looking at game player dynamics. Playing games as a way of increasing worker productivity is now being explored by corporate America. Employees at JotSpot in Silicon Valley are regularly encouraged to play video games at work as a way to increase worker productivity. This is being replicated at other Silicon Valley firms. Gaming is viewed as a team-building activity. Jessica Guynn, "Making Gaming Pay Off," *San Francisco Chronicle*, 23 July 2006, F1–4. Complex simulations based on modifications of the video game *Sim City* can allow players to examine the impact city planners have on lived spaces and the decisions they make that may transform how cities will look in forty years. See Ben Sutherland, "The Real Sim City," *BBC News*, 6 July 2006, <http://news.bbc.co.uk/2/hi/technology/5105534.stm> (20 October 2006).

26. The media effects literature is a minefield few would like to walk through. However, John Springhall reveals the manner in which such debates have resonated historically about youth culture in general. John Springhall, *Youth, Popular Culture and Moral Panics: Penny Gaffs to Gangsta-Rap, 1820–1996* (New York: St. Martin's, 1998). See also: Martin Barker and Julian Petley, eds., *Ill Effects: The Media/Violence Debate* (New York: Routledge, 2001); Jonathan Freedman, *Media Violence and Its Effect on Aggression: Assessing the Scientific Evidence* (Toronto: University of Toronto Press, 2002); Karen Sternheimer, *It's Not the Media: The Truth about Pop Culture's Influence on Children* (Boulder, Colo.: Westview, 2003); Andrea Millwood Hargrave and Sonia Livingstone, *Harm and Offense: A Review of the Evidence* (Bristol, UK: Intellect Books, 2006); and David Buckingham, *After the Death of Childhood: Growing Up in the Age of Electronic Media.* (London: Polity Press, 2000).

27. See the work of: John Beynon, *Masculinities and Culture* (Philadelphia: Open University Press, 2002), 66–68 on being tough and homophobic; Justine Cassell and Henry Jenkins, eds., *From Barbie to Mortal Kombat: Gender and Computer Games* (Cambridge, Mass.: MIT Press, 1999); Lori Kendall, *Hanging Out in the Virtual Pub: Masculinities and Relationships Online* (Berkeley: University of California Press, 2002); Michael A. Messner, *Power at Play: Sports and the Problem of Masculinity* (Boston: Beacon Press, 1992); Donna Eder, Catherine Colleen Evans, and Stephen Parker, *School Talk: Gender and Adolescent Culture* (New Brunswick, N.J.: Rutgers University Press, 2001); Sue Morris, "Shoot First, Ask Questions Later: Ethnographic Research in an Online Computer Gaming Community," *Media International Australia*, 110 (2004): 31–41. Social relations of gender dominance and subordination do not end in cyberspace, but, rather are carried over from the everyday lives of game players who bring those attitudes and behaviors into the playing of the game. Just as these behaviors are predicated upon an unconscious working out of gender power, they can also be contested both in the violent virtual themed landscapes as well as in the real world of everyday life.

28. Douglas Kellner, "Cultural Studies, Multi-culturalism and Media Culture," in *Gender, Race and Class in Media*, ed. Gail Dines and Jean M. Humez (Thousand Oaks, Calif.: Sage, 1994), 5–17. Kellner outlines the necessary parameters of a cultural studies analysis that moves beyond a simple examination of a medium's content. We often forget that what people do with media texts, games, film, or television is just as important, if not more so, than the stereotypes such texts display.

29. See Johan Huizinga, *Homo Ludens: A Study of the Play Element in Culture* (New York: Beacon Press, 1971); Roger Caillois and Meyer Barash, *Man, Play and Games* (Chicago: University of Chicago Press, 2001); Brian Sutton-Smith, *The Ambiguity of Play* (Cambridge, Mass.: Harvard University Press, 1997).

30. Scott Bukatman, *Terminal Identity: The Virtual Subject in Post-Modern Science Fiction* (Durham, N.C.: Duke University Press, 1993).

Chapter 15

A Politics of Reverence and Irreverence: Social Discourse on Theming Controversies

Scott A. Lukas

In 2006 a restaurant opening in Mumbai, India attracted international attention. The eatery, known as Hitler's Cross, featured the red, black, and white colors of the Nazis, a portrait of Adolf Hitler near the door, and a swastika adorning the prominent signage next to the words, "From Small Bites to Mega Joys."[1] According to the restaurant's owner, "We wanted to be different. This is one name that will stay in people's minds. We are not promoting Hitler. But we want to tell people we are different in the way he was different." The establishment's manager added, "This place is not about wars or crimes, but where people come to relax and enjoy a meal."[2] The international outrage—including major stories on CNN, MSNBC, postings on blogs, and numerous Internet reports—eventually resulted in major alterations at the eatery. The restaurant owners finally responded to public outrage and renamed the place The Cross and removed references to Hitler and Nazism.[3] The Hitler's Cross incident highlights two aspects of the continuing evolution of themed spaces. The first is the wide range of subjects, persons, and events that are possible sources for thematic representations, and the second is the public's interest in themed spaces, especially its concern for the contextual and representational nature of the given themed space. In this chapter I will focus on the controversies related to themed spaces and how these controversies suggest a new critical understanding of theming at levels of content and representation.

By their nature, themed spaces are places that play through the dichotomy of exclusion/inclusion. Since theming is a stereotype—an approximation of place, time, event, culture, or person—there are limitations as to what can be included in a space to constitute a particular theme. Theming is always a limited inclusion. Similarly, because theming cannot cover all aspects of the original nor cannot give complete nuance in its re-presented form, some elements have to be excluded from the thematic space. Theming is always a pronounced exclusion. Theming, as an ideological construction of space, is best understood at the intersection of the representational dichotomy of inclusion/exclusion and public notions of reverence and irreverence. Very often, themed spaces are critiqued as simply "getting it wrong."[4] Such discourse is inherently limited, for as I will illustrate through a number of case studies, themed spaces are culturally complex products; they are much more than the "bad copies" that sometimes define them in the public discourse. Theming, itself, is a discourse—it is commentary about culture, history, social values, events, people, and places that is realized in architectural, material, and performative means. The many types of themed spaces, including restaurants, bars, casinos, and theme parks, have dealt with a myriad of topics. In the past, the more generic and safe forms of theming like western venues and tropical island places were accepted; in part this was because of their less political nature and in part because of their less-developed architectural approach to space. In today's more competitive consumer world, a controversially-themed venue is becoming the norm.

In this chapter I will focus on the ways in which certain themed spaces have been interpreted by critics, workers, patrons, and others and emphasize the issues at stake in the contestation of themed spaces—extant, extinct, and never-realized. The first section will offer a consideration of the reasons why heightened social discourse emerges around themed spaces and how it played out in venues like the Holy Land Experience and the failed Disney's America theme park. Next, I will address the concept of dark theming or the relationship of death, the gothic, disasters, and tragedy to theming, particularly the fine line that exists between acceptable theming of death and tragedy and that which is deemed inappropriate by the public. Included as my examples are Holocaust museums, the failed Crash Cafe, prison- and disaster-themed restaurants and bars, a planned but unrealized National Rifle Association restaurant and entertainment complex, the failed Dracula World theme park in Romania, and the small war theme park in the United Kingdom known as Eden Camp. The chapter then focuses on circumstances in which theming takes on a postmodern dimension, often emphasizing aspects of excess, kitsch, and the carnivalesque. The issue of retheming is considered as a means of mediating controversies related to theming. Conceptually focused venues like the Paranoia Cafe in Japan, the Martun restaurant in Taiwan, Bonbon Land of Denmark, the Time and Library hotels of New York City, and York England's Jorvik are discussed. Finally, I consider how the controversies related to theming and the associated social discourse impact the future of themed spaces.

Social Discourse on Theming

> We're a theme park. Nothing more.
> —Splendid China theme park spokesperson[5]

As an anthropologist who studies theming, I am often surprised with individuals who fail to see the cultural logic implicit in themed spaces. For many visitors to theme parks, themed restaurants, and casinos, participation in the given venue is not merely a form of slavish consumerism, and for workers at these venues their status is more than acting out a predestined part in a thematic script established by hegemonic designers and managers. An important realization of the anthropology of theming is that behavior associated with these spaces is as culturally meaningful as behavior occurring outside of themed spaces. As well, the anthropologist must consider the nuanced ways in which individuals interpret, respond to, and alter their behaviors as a result of visiting or working in themed venues, and the effect of those sources of criticism of theming that appear in newspapers and on the Internet. During a trip to Euro Disney outside of Paris in 2004, I had a conversation with a former Walt Disney World employee. His understanding of Disney corporate history included connections to current and past projects at the theme park, and he demonstrated both in-depth knowledge of theming technologies and personal appreciation of them. During my years as a trainer at Six Flags AstroWorld, I was often surprised that patrons would openly comment on aspects of theming that appeared cheap or irregular to them, and I once overheard a conversation between two rides managers who critiqued the inaccuracy of the glyphs of the Mayan Mind Bender roller coaster.[6] A realization that I have gained from my anthropological research is that theming is culturally significant, particularly in the ways in which it is interpreted and acted on by individuals. In the contemporary world, more workers in themed spaces are aware of the history behind the themes in which they work, and many are even aware of the ideological dimensions of themed spaces. Similarly, patrons—in part due to the rise of theme park shows on stations like Discovery and due to the many tip and insider sites on the Internet—enter a themed space with a much greater knowledge of its workings than patrons of the past.

Like other forms of discourse, discourse on theming reflects the cultural, ideological, and personal struggles of the outside world, but this discourse is heightened due to the immediate and manifested realities of architecture, signage, decor, and performance that make up the themed space. The cultural anthropologist Victor Turner once remarked that "symbols instigate social action."[7] His acknowledgement of the power of symbols to motivate people to respond in varied and personal ways can be applied to the domain of the themed space. There are many examples of social controversies arising in the world of art, often due to the tensions between aesthetics and politics.[8] Andres Serrano's *Piss Christ*, Scott Tyler's *What Is the Proper Way to Display an American Flag?*, the photographic work of Robert Mapplethorpe, and the *Sensation* exhibit at the Brooklyn Museum of Art, are just a few of the works and exhibitions that have incited the public to react to powerful and highly controversial symbols.[9] Museums have also been sites of public contestation. As architectural spaces that often combine immersive technology that is designed to engage patrons at heightened levels, museums—especially those dealing with political issues like the Holocaust (Museum of Tolerance) and specific cultural groups (National Museum of the American Indian), or difficult periods of history (Imperial War museums in the United Kingdom)—may heighten the public's understanding of cultural and representational issues. When the Smithsonian's Air and Space Museum announced plans for an exhibition on the Enola Gay and atomic power, to be called *Crossroads*, members of the public responded in outrage. Interestingly, some critics complained that the exhibition would present the Japanese as victims, while others claimed that it glorified the atomic bomb.[10] Like the discourse surrounding contemporary themed spaces, the public outrage over museum exhibitions reflects a range of political positions and representational understandings.

Many museums, like Air and Space, are thematic in that they organize exhibitions around a common theme—in this case, airpower, spacecraft, and associated technology—but themed spaces are generally considered to be less educational, more focused on entertainment due to the manner in which themes are developed, and involved in selling specific commodities and services. The controversies related to thematic museums emphasize that the public is often willing to comment on proposed or current designs of exhibitions, especially when the issue associated with the exhibition is already present in public discourse. I argue that the engagement with these spaces is also increased by the availability of new and more immediate channels of technology, such as newspaper and the Internet. In some cases, the public's commentary on theming may be limited to a bad experience at a themed venue. While working at AstroWorld, I overheard complaints that were levelled against the park that certain theme lands looked "cheesy." Patrons may also connect the effectiveness of theming to the overall value of the experience at the venue. In other cases, members of the public respond in surprisingly detailed manners and offer commentary on themed spaces that rivals the discourse of cultural critics, architects, and designers.[11] Very often this commentary is present on the Internet in blogs and Web sites that reflect the public's increasing knowledge of tourist and consumer sites. In some cases there is a disconnect between public discourse on themed spaces and the discourse present and emanating from those who visit the spaces.

In 2005 I began ethnographic research at the Holy Land Experience, a messianic Jewish theme park in Orlando, Florida.[12] Prior to my visit, I had conducted extensive reviews of the criticisms of the park reflected on the Internet and in newspapers. One issue that has emerged in Jewish communities is the park's avocation of Messianic Judaism—a tradition that promotes the existence of Jesus as the Messiah. Additionally, much attention has been given to the park's policy against hiring charismatic or Pentecostal Christians and its policy against "disruptive behavior" such as speaking in tongues.¹³ Trying to discover interpretations beyond the public discourse about the park, I wanted to understand how theming played out on the ground, in the experiences of visitors. Like any themed space, the Holy Land Experience establishes architecture, decor, performance, material culture, food, and all other aspects as a unified discourse. Theming acts as a holistic cultural order that allows the patron to step outside the predominant cultural orders outside the park. At the front gate centurions greet me with "Shalom." Contrary to other parks, the Holy Land creates its space through a pronounced progression. Due to the timing and schedule of shows, visitors end up moving through the park in an order—a narrative that connects the various events, shows, and exhibits as a unified whole. During a visit to one of the gift shops, an attendant tells me not to miss the crucifixion, "except if it rains," she says. After an hour or so in the park, I was immediately struck by my inability to define the Holy Land Experience. It was not like a traditional themed venue due to the predominant narrative that is carried throughout the park. It had museal elements like the Scriptorium, a display of historic Bibles, and interactive events, and because of the overwhelming effect of religiosity, it resembled an interactive site of worship.¹⁴ Overall, it was controversial—it presented elements that typically would not be found in other themed venues, and it did so in a very serious manner.

Theming itself, as it governed the semiotic order of displays, the menus at the restaurants, the particular items in giftshops, and the performative utterances of actors, spoke to the cultural interests of patrons and workers at the park. Unlike some themed spaces in which a more open order governs the park—in which people from varied backgrounds can interact with the spaces—the Holy Land Experience deliberately focuses its theming on a specific ideological project.¹⁵ It is for this reason that criticism of the park has little effect on those who visit and enjoy the venue. At one point during my visit, I was taken with the level of connection that patrons felt with the narratives of the place. Near the end of the Scriptorium, I was with a Baptist couple from North Carolina. They spotted me taking copious notes in a less than inconspicuous notebook, and the woman asked me, "Are you a journalist?" I responded that I "am an anthropologist" and that "I study theme parks." She smiled and resumed singing a psalm with the pre-recorded soundtrack. After I left the Holy Land Experience I had the reflection that I had just visited one of the best-themed venues that I had ever seen, and, yet, I could not connect to the theming in the way of the couple from North Carolina. Some people will never visit the park because of the various controversies, while others, like the Baptist couple, will find theme parks like the Holy Land to be an alternative to secular, consumerist, and mainstream themed venues.

Regardless of the controversies that surrounded the opening of the Holy Land Experience, and that persist in the present, the park remains open in 2007. A project that attracted even more attention and complete disdain by the public was Disney's Civil War theme park. Disney's America was planned for one hundred acres of land in Virginia, a few miles from the sacred Manassas National Battlefield Park.

Unlike previous parks that have been criticized for whitewashing history, Disney's America would have included a World War II airfield, Ellis Island, a steel mill, a state fair, a family farm, a Civil War fort, an Indian village, and many themed areas. From the onset, what distinguished the Disney park was the plan to deal with difficult and dark moments of American history. Said Michael Eisner and Vice President Robert Weis, "We will show you the Civil War with all its racial conflict. . . . We want to make you feel what it was like to be a slave or what it was like to escape through the underground railroad."[16] From the beginning, Disney's America was doomed to fail. Groups of historians, archaeologists, concerned citizens, politicians, and media celebrities assembled on both sides to debate the plan.[17] Historians took issue with the historical narratives being deployed by Disney, while archaeologists worried about cultural resources and the preservation of local sites; others took a view of Manassas as a sacred site at which the legacy of the Civil War and its victims should be remembered solemnly, not through a thematic enterprise.[18] Many of these debates took place on e-mail and in journalism, and this fact allowed parties on both sides of the debate to gain more support for their causes.

In large part, the controversies related to Disney's America illustrate the peculiar relationship of themed spaces to the public imagination.[19] Even though themed spaces, particularly theme parks, remain incredibly popular forms of public entertainment, the public refuses to allow certain events or cultural ideas to be represented in some forms. One historian wrote that Disney's America would "mock a theme as momentous as slavery," and that "[no] combination of branding irons, slave ships or slave cabins, shackles, chained black people in their wretched coffles, or treks through the Underground Railroad could begin to define such a stupendous experience . . . to present even the most squalid sights would be to cheaply romanticize suffering."[20] Much of the discussion of Disney's Civil War theme park seemed to emphasize the inappropriate connection of the content of Civil War history to the themed materiality of the proposed theme lands, attractions, and narratives. What is interesting and telling about the park and its relationship to the discourse on theming is how, unlike the many films dealing with the Civil War and the darkness of the United States' past, so many are unwilling to accept the idea of a Civil War–themed park. The privileging of certain representational forms for such depictions—including film, nonfiction, and fictional texts, and some museum spaces—suggests that the technology of theming itself is often the inciter of the controversy. It is conceivable that in the case of the Holy Land Experience and Disney's America that less objection would have been raised with the projects had they not been themed spaces but museums and heritage centers.

Dark Theming

As geographer Yi-Fu Tuan has written, "Spaces act as boundaries against innumerable forces—of evil, contagion and fear."[21] It is understandable that lived spaces, even non-themed ones, bespeak of values, circumstances, and events that are uncomfortable, but what seems surprising is that themed consumerist spaces have begun to take on these issues. Typically, entertainment has meant that the consumer wishes to escape the disturbing events that are portrayed on the news and in the newspaper, but more consumers are now interested in engaging these dark topics in personal and interactive senses. A growing trend of both museums and themed spaces involves the portrayal of dark, disturbing, and tragic events of human history. This general trend, including tourism in non-themed spaces, is denoted by John Lennon and Malcolm Foley as *dark tourism*. In dark tourism, any site of disaster, tragedy or death "becomes a tourism resource to be exploited like any other."[22] Themed spaces also reflect this movement to "representing the unrepresentable."[23] Some museal spaces, like the Museum of Tolerance in Los Angeles and the National Holocaust Museum in Washington, D.C., utilize the technologies familiar to themed spaces—video screens, interactive displays, recreated landscapes and spaces—to put the visitor in a different psychological mood. At the Museum of Tolerance visitors complete the museum in a concrete chamber that resembles a concentration camp gas chamber while images of Nazi atrocities are projected on concrete walls. At the National Holocaust Museum visitors receive replica photo identification cards that simulate the personal tragedies of all those who perished, and some who survived, in the Holocaust. In the case of representations of horrific human events of the past, including the Holocaust and other genocides, the politics of inclusion/exclusion are at full force. Recent controversies have developed about the lack of discussion of groups, such as the Armenians, in the Museum of Tolerance located in Los Angeles.[24] What is instructive is how dark tourism has been extended to themed spaces. Themed spaces that have a dark dimension to them differ from Holocaust museums or spaces where tragedy has occurred in the past, such as Daley Plaza in Dallas, Texas. Themed spaces use the symbolism of death, concepts of destruction, or intimations of tragedy, as a means of creating their unique spaces, with markedly differing success.[25]

In terms of the discourse related to theming, there is a heightened awareness of certain topics, events, or persons that should not be addressed in thematic representations; yet, the line between acceptable and unacceptable themed death is often difficult to ascertain. Spaces themed around death or tragedy—by their nature of being less clearly defined as heritage sites of real death or depictions of real death, and being between education and entertainment—invite discourse that is at once personal and uncomfortable. Recently, prisons have become the subject of themed spaces, especially in Japan. One chain of prison-themed restaurants, Alcatraz, features restaurants with jailers (servers) in skimpy outfits and toilet paper napkins for the tables, while Prison Restaurant offers handcuffs, footcuffs, chains, and prison-themed dishes.[26] Though prisons are dark, disturbing places that signify the existential outskirts of any society, many patrons seem to enjoy eating and being entertained in such spaces. This was not the case with all prison-themed venues, but many enjoy popularity. Much like the Hitler's Cross restaurant of India,

Taipei's the Jail was forced to alter its theming as a result of offensive referencing of the past. At the Jail, customers eat shackled in cells among the prison-themed decor of the eatery. A series of photos of prisoners at Nazi concentration camps and a sign above the restrooms reading "Gas Chamber" sparked outrage and led to the removal of the items.[27]

The darkness of prison-themed restaurants may reflect our desire to meditate on the disturbing and seedy side of our lives or the desire of restaurant owners to use a controversial theme to attract more customers. Disasters, human or natural, are particularly interesting when they are narrated by a themed space. In Tokyo, the Taitanic [sic] bar uses shipwrecks, life vests, and video images of the Titanic to produce a space that references the Titanic and other ship disasters of the past.[28] Perhaps the most infamous example of disaster theming is the Crash Cafe—a Baltimore restaurant planned by Patrick Turner. The restaurant was to have been "born from destruction," with cars and motorcycles wrapped around poles, a DC-3 airplane fuselage busting through the front wall, and numerous video screens depicting train collisions and airplane disasters. Prior to September 11th, one widow of an airplane crash victim spoke out against the planned cafe: "This is horrible," she said. "This is worse than the dark side of humor. He [Turner] has no idea what an air crash endures on [sic] people. To turn it into some entertainment eatery, he is morally bankrupt."[29] Crash Cafe was never built, and this is understandable given the traumatic associations of airplanes and terrorism following September 11th. Interestingly, films like *United 93* and *World Trade Center* were not met with the same protest as the Crash Cafe. Perhaps it is the medium of representation that impacts the public's reception of a controversial site. In the case of a feature film, it seems more organic and affects the viewer in a more sober way. In contrast, a themed space, like a restaurant or theme park, requires that the patron take on a more active role in the representations. Instead of viewing a film and reflecting on it personally, the patron must also take part in a corporeal experience of walking in a restaurant, ordering off the menu, visually inspecting the architecture and decor, and partaking in the environment in a multisensory way.

Violence has a contradictory role in themed spaces. In some cases it is promoted, perhaps to a muted degree, in other cases it is presented in the open. Like death and disaster, it is clear that the public's awareness of certain cultural topics has an effect on the possibility of a new themed space opening or the longevity of one already in operation. In 2000 the National Rifle Association announced plans to open an NRA-themed restaurant and entertainment complex in Times Square. The proposed restaurant was to have featured wild game dishes, mineral water, and a virtual arcade and entertainment center for the outdoor enthusiast. No real guns would have been present at the venue, only simulated ones in virtual reality games. When the plans for the NRA Sports Blast were made public, citizens came out against the plan, as well as expressed support for it. Some complained that the restaurant would glorify violence, guns, and killing, while others said that it brought the wrong image to New York City—a city that is already associated with real violence in the streets.³⁰ Some Internet sites ran parodies of the NRA concept while others offered critical editorials. It is telling to think about the intersection of a group that some Americans consider to be extreme and an architectural approach that others consider to be outrageous. Groups like the Coalition to Stop Gun Violence used the already marked image of the NRA, coupled with a heightened sensitivity that people have to certain forms of entertainment (theming), to stage a more public protest against both the NRA and the NRASports Blast. Theming is a semiotic construction that is completely mutable—for some it is an apt means of attracting the attention needed to compete with other entertainment venues, especially in a saturated entertainment market like Times Square. For others, it is a form of simulation that should be reserved to light topics, not heavy ones like guns and politics. Because the NRA venue was an architectural product in a renown area of New York City, the public responded in ways that acknowledged the site's architectural presence. Because they are present, more so than non-architectural forms of popular culture, themed sites like the NRASports Blast invite a form of public participation in them that discursively parallels the interactivity that is found in the places themselves.

As the NRASports Blast illustrates, the mere association of certain themes with consumer spaces can incite public outrage. The controversy surrounding Dracula World, a theme park planned for Sighisoara, Romania, was even more pronounced. Like the discourse related to the NRA themed space, the discussion of Dracula World was marked by political, organizational, and personal verities, and, similar to the defeat of Disney's America, the decision to not build the Dracula theme park was based on opposition from multiple concerns. Dracula has loose associations with the real figure Vlad the Impaler and the fictional character from the Bram Stoker novel, and many of Sighisoara, including Tourism Minister Dan Matei-Agathon, saw the gothic and popular associations as a way to bring more tourism and development to the community.³¹ Much like the ways in which Six Flags theme parks used the Looney Tunes characters and Warner Brothers movies like Batman as concepts around which to theme rides, attractions, and restaurants, planners of Dracula World used the mythical figure of Dracula to create themed space. Rides and attractions would have had a gothic flair, theme lands would have connected to the Dracula legend, food would have included "blood pudding" and "dish of brains," and the park would have featured a vampirology institute.³² When these plans emerged, the planners were beset with complaints from all political sides. Prince Charles, who has a keen interest in architectural theory and history, opposed the park on environmental reasons, saying the park "[would] ultimately destroy [Sighisoara's] character."³³ Cultural agencies, like UNESCO, echoed the Prince's argument and spoke out against the park's potential impact on the environment and cultural heritage sites, while religious groups, including the Romanian Orthodox Church, complained that the "Dracula myth has nothing to do with the Romanian people or its history" and that the country should have no part of "entertainment and games based on cruelty, horror, occultism and vampirism."³⁴ In some cases, gothic themes can be toned down as in the case of Kavon, a gothic-themed restaurant in Australia that is geared towards children, but it is telling that the Dracula park was seen as too extreme by some. It could also be that the residents of Sighisoara feared that the thematic associations developed within the park would create an unfavorable connection between their community and the Dracula legend.[35]

Dark theming is not always considered negative by the public. Some European themed spaces and heritage museums that deal with tragic topics have been wholly accepted by the public. This reflects the fact that themed spaces, though universal cultural phenomena, must be understood as discursive products of the cultures in which they reside. In 2004 I visited a war theme park named Eden Camp. Eden Camp is situated a few miles outside of the northern English town of York. During World War II, the site was known as Prisoner of War Camp No. 83 and it was actually used as a POW camp. Today it is a war theme park/heritage site that focuses on the dynamics of the Second World War. The site has won numerous awards as the country's top attraction and it claims to be the "Only Modern History Theme Museum of Its Type in the World."[36] The park includes a number of military vehicles that are scattered around the parameter; on the inside is a series of thirty huts, each reflecting a different aspect of the war. One focuses on the rise of Hitler, others on the prisoner of war experience, civil defense, women and the war, and numerous battles. In some cases certain huts involve technological devices and effects to immerse the visitor in an experience. The gift shop includes small scent bottles that variously read, "Take a trip back in time, smell the aroma of a U-Boat at sea" and "Take a trip back in time, smell the aroma of a bombed street," while the mess hall—known as the *Prisoner's Canteen*—includes themed appetizers and entrees like Chicken Piece Convey, POW Quarter Pounder, and Churchill's Pie. Eden Camp reminded me that theming, as a cultural discourse, is embedded in the particularities of the culture in which it resides. Some critics have mistakenly analyzed all theming as result of the same presumably western narrative. In fact, even the seemingly homogenous Disney model of theming is reinterpreted and modified by designers, workers, and patrons as it is transmitted to non-western venues. In the case of Eden Camp and other war-themed sites, such as the Imperial War Museums, the fact that the British experienced the Blitz, an attack on the home front, results in a much darker themed product.[37] Themed projects like Eden Camp, aside from being controversial, can also be instructive.

Postmodern and Excess Theming

Edward Chappell denotes a themed experience as:

> One in which an element—often lifted from past or present reality—is projected out of proportion. The theme is borrowed from a different time or place and is

promiscuously spread across new settings with minimal concern given to its role in the historical context or as a component in a larger social or political setting.[38]

Some themed spaces invite controversy because of the contexts that they invoke with their theme, others are surprising because of the way in which they create theme, such as through their use of design, architecture, or the representational associations that they create between specific things. As Chappell reminds, the public is often unable to accept a representation that is "projected out of proportion" or that associates too loosely between the original and the re-presented form. Depending on the interpreter's background, the reaction to a themed space may be one of indifference, of appreciation, or disdain. No themed space, whether a complex project like Disney's America or a smaller themed restaurant like Scotland's gothic Frankenstein 1818, is interpreted by the patron in the same way.[39] For one person theming may represent a modernist mode of representation—it attempts to connect one thing, place, event, or culture to the present using architecture and other means of material culture. For another person, theming may come to signify a postmodern project—it makes connections that are nonlinear, often simplifies the associations with the past or with the other place being represented, and it deals with topics or issues that are best suited to other means of representation. Retheming is one example of an increasing postmodern trend in the theming industry.

In some cases, the social controversy related to theming can be abated when a space is rethemed. Retheming refers to the transformation of an existing themed space into a new one, often for the purpose of revitalizing the venue. In 2006 Caesars Lake Tahoe casino, following a transfer of ownership, became the MontBleu. The move was from an explicit Roman theme to an ambiguous theme of blue as a synecdoche of Lake Tahoe.[40] For some Caesars represented a masculinist theme, for others it represented a theme that had grown old and tired. In the same year, the Aladdin resort in Las Vegas, representative of an unpopular Arabian theme, began the transition to the Planet Hollywood Hotel and Casino.[41] In both cases retheming took place, in part, as the result of corporate decisions, but the public's perceptions of the theme did play a role in the decisions. In the late 1990s, the MGM Grand in Las Vegas underwent a major thematic transformation. The casino entrance that featured a lion's mouth was removed due to associations with bad luck. At the same time, the MGM removed a *Wizard of Oz* diorama and replaced the area with more slot machines. Though the MGM lion is still referenced in 2006 at various locations across the casino, the MGM has eschewed the childlike associations of Oz and lions for a more sleek, refined, and adult-oriented movie theme, "The City of Entertainment." A similar retheming has occurred at the Treasure Island (T. I.) in Las Vegas—the childish pirate theme has been replaced with racy connotations of pirates, including a recast outdoor show, and the renaming of the casino as the T. I.

Retheming indicates a discursive shift in the theming industry. The previous cases illustrate that marketing efforts, changing demographics, slumping profits, and public interests can necessitate retheming. Retheming, at a basic level, has a purely aesthetic function—changes of theme are undertaken to make consumers reaware of the themed space. In some instances, retheming has occurred for explicit political reasons. In the 1990s the famous Pirates of the Caribbean ride was altered due to public concerns over some of the situations and associated narratives on the ride.[42] The circumstance of pirate men chasing women was altered to a subtler version. Oakwood Theme Park of Wales rethemed its Voodoo Mansion ride as Spooky 3D due in part to the controversial connotation of voodoo and religion. With architecture, decor, and technologies already in place, a venue can be rethemed when a controversy arises over the narrative governing its attractions. Retheming indicates a postmodern shift in the theming industry, for whether it is for marketing reasons or in response to a controversial ride narrative or an unfamiliar cultural theme like voodoo, retheming allows an attraction to be remodelled along an entirely new narrative line or to be completely altered as a new theme. In some cases, venues like the MontBleu casino in Lake Tahoe, California, due to the transition involved in their retheming, reveal a theming palimpsest—a situation in which themes from different eras are visible in the same spaces.

In some cases, theming takes on an unexpected dimension merely due to the type of space that is themed. Stargate Dental, a Florida *Star Trek*-themed dental office, attracts attention because it is a dental office.[43] Unlike restaurants, dental offices are not spaces that are typically associated with theming. The Impala condominium structure in New York City is themed according to the animal the impala—not a typically popular animal in the public imagination. The structure includes indoor animal photos and fourteen life-size sculptures of impalas.[44] Another postmodern approach to themed space design involves the combination of themed elements that do not seem to fit together. An example is the defunct Virtual World in San Diego, California. Virtual world offered a combination of Victorian and hi-tech computer theming.[45] In part due to transformations of the conception of the home—including more experimentation with themed decor like that addressed in the introduction to this volume—structures such as Stargate Dental and the Impala may eventually be received by the public as less dramatic. Themed spaces can also take on a postmodern dimension when theming reaches an eclectic and nearly incomprehensible level. In San Luis Obispo, California, the Madonna Inn features over one hundred variously themed hotel rooms. Some of the rooms have a local theme, while others are more ambiguous, such as Cloud Nine and Country Gentleman. Many reference specific exotic locations like Matterhorn, Old English, Old Mexico, and Holland Dutch.[46] The combination of less defined themed rooms including those that reference a concept, and traditional themed rooms, like those referencing a place or time, illustrates how some venues use the very concept of theme as a semiotic attraction. The emphasis is not on any specific theme or a set of themes, but on the idea of theme itself. In this way, theming has become a conceptual, self-referencing category in popular culture.

The Time Hotel in New York City is a conceptual themed venue. There are references to the concept of time, including a large timepiece in the lobby and hallway runners decorated with clocks, but the main thematic element at the hotel is color. According to the hotel's Web site, "The Time's design eschews convention." Guests are oriented to their stay through one of the three primary colors—red, blue, and yellow—and each is asked "to truly experience a color: see it, feel it, taste it, smell it and live it." Another ironic themed space is the Library hotel in New York City. The Library uses the book as a thematic association and carries it throughout the space. Included are rooms that are themed according to the Dewey decimal system, such as erotic literature, world culture, the paranormal, dinosaurs, money, and many others. Like the Madonna Inn, the Library emphasizes an eclectic array of themes within its rooms, but the overarching theme provided by the Dewey decimal system and books dictates the design of rooms.[47] Another postmodern space, the Paranoia Cafe in Japan, features hardcore music, gothic interior, hundreds of eyes that cover the walls and ceiling, and drinks with names like "suicide lover" and "enigma of unconsciousness."[48] Unlike some of the controversial spaces discussed previously in this chapter, these conceptually themed venues provide the patron with a themed experience without the political baggage. Because it deliberately eschews realism in its representational modes and provides a less specific narrative of association and, often, no original to speak of, a conceptually themed space, even like the Paranoia Cafe and its focus on uncanny and gothic elements, is received by the public as less controversial.

The emphasis on excess is another example of postmodern theming. In this case, a space is themed in accord with a topic that is associated in some cultures with what Georges Bataille denotes as the "low."[49] Often, the low emphasizes bodily processes or themes that are avoided, such as excrement, bodily fluids, and certain acts like urination and defecation. The Martun restaurant in Kaohsiung, Taiwan develops a theme based on the toilet, including seats that are commodes and serving bowls that are shaped liked toilets.[50] Bonbon Land of Holme Olstrup, Denmark has become famous with some tourists for its portrayals of farting, anal, breast, and other body part humor. There is a clear precedent for these excessive representations that may seem to be bawdy or offensive in the contemporary world. The early theme parks of Coney Island, including Dreamland, Luna Park and Steeplechase Park, featured rides, attractions, and performances that look nothing like the sanitized theme lands of contemporary theme parks. Many of Coney Island's amusement parks featured raucous entertainment, edgy attractions like midgets who would smack men with canes and blow up the dresses of women with compressed air, and rides like Hell Gate that featured a dark and sinister theme.[51] At Bonbon Land there are depictions of animals defecating, a dog fart roller coaster, a seagull defecating in the mouth of an alligator, vomiting rodents, a dog with excrement on the ground next to it, rides that involve patrons exiting outside the buttocks of an insect.[52] Excess theming, like that of the Martun restaurant and Bonbon Land, reflects what Bakhtin discussed as the carnivalesque.[53] It is important to note that excess-centered theming may become the norm in more cultures. In United States popular culture, there is a growing genre of the low in television, video games, and movies. Shows like *Beavis and Butthead*, *South Park*, and *Jackass*, and films like *Borat*, focus on defecation, flatulence, and non-politically correct interpretations of popular culture. Though a few theme parks have featured these "low" themes—including some Paramount theme parks' Wayne's World theme lands, complete with associations with vomit—this trend is still to take hold in the United States. When the low does creep into themed venues, it often is associated with sexism. For example, the biker-themed restaurant Twisted Spoke in Chicago, Illinois features a "Smut & Eggs" event that allows customers to dine while they watch pornographic films.[54]

As theming becomes more postmodern, a question that lingers is whether the legitimation of themed spaces is a product of the discursive debates that characterize the controversies described in this chapter or if it is a result of the representational medium (theming) and its ability to convey a narrative about a particular thing, person, time, or event? Or, is it both of them? Perhaps the most interesting development in theming is a result not of the representational medium but the imagination related to theming. Some have written of the conceptual value of theming as it allows for the categorization of memes or ideas into distinct conceptual spaces, much like the use of space in Greek rhetoric and the method of loci.[55] Theming as a technology of geography, architecture, material culture, and performativity will be increasingly realized as a virtual or narrative technology. As Talmadge Wright expresses in this volume, theming is already moving towards the realm of the virtual, and many contemporary themed attractions utilize some form of virtuality in their spaces creating hybrid theming. As well, there is an abundance of Web sites that focus on themed spaces. Some are advertising sites associated with the purveyors of themed venues, but many are fan sites and those of patrons and workers who wish to offer their commentary on theming. Many of these sites include in-depth reviews of themed spaces, including photos, commentary, and discussion of the most minute details of the spaces. The combination of new virtual technologies, hybrid virtual approaches, and the plethora of Web sites focused on theming will produce a new level of discourse on theming itself.

However, the most postmodern of all themed spaces are the conceptual ones of the mind—the spaces that are never realized, perhaps because they are too eclectic or ridiculous. As part of my dissertation research on United States theme parks, I suggested the development of a conceptual theme park known as the "Sacrificial Economy." This avant-garde theme park utilized theming as a means of referencing the sacrificial or profane aspects of the United States cultural economy. The theming technologies included non-linear and performative means of representation, and theme lands were nontraditional, including an Exxon Valdez/human-induced disaster area, a themed restaurant that emphasized diners' connection with the processes that produced their foods, and a serial killer themed playland for children.[56] Interestingly, a similar though more subdued idea was conceived by musical artists Laurie Anderson, Peter Gabriel, and Brian Eno. The park, known as *Real World*, was to have featured nontraditional theming and attractions. Visitors would have been greeted by sixty-foot-high working tornadoes, and one ride, The River of Life, would have taken patrons through seven stages of life in small boats, complete with visual and olfactory technologies. The section for the adolescent stage would have been designed by controversial filmmaker John Waters, and the conclusion of the ride involved the patrons being swept into a large "(gene) pool where they could reincarnate in any way they wished."[57] Unfortunately, the Real World park was not conceived, perhaps because its approach to theming and entertainment would have been too postmodern for the public.[58] Even in video games like *Sim Theme Park* and *Roller Coaster Tycoon*, in which one could imagine producing postmodern theme lands, there is an emphasis on creating theme parks that resemble, both architecturally and conceptually, the theme parks that are most familiar to us.

The Future of Theming

A result of the meditation on the real and imagined theme spaces, and of the continued interest in theming due in part to controversial themed spaces, is the formation of a thematic economy. This economy is found at the intersection of themed spaces (copies of originals) and their original spaces (the places from which designers draw inspiration for themed spaces). Of course, even original spaces are no longer immune from the effects of consumerist development and the use of theming techniques in their own environments. As well, in many cases they draw on stereotypes or representations of originals that are many times removed in a semiotic sense. A western-themed space may reference an actual event of the past, real people or actual places, but it may also just be an amalgam of ideas of what is western in the minds of designers. As a theme like western is produced in more and more venues, it becomes part of a larger economy of theming. This economy contains all of the thematic formations like western, tropical and others, and it, as an order of culture, effects all other future representations of theming and their reception in the public. Certain types of themes may fit outside the margins of the economy, such as the many controversial examples of theming discussed in this chapter. Because of the intersection of this representational economy and the sociopolitical foundations of the given society, certain spaces are forced to retheme or even close their doors. Some conceptually edgy places like Dracula World, Disney's America, and Crash Cafe are never even built. The social discourse that reflects the controversies over themed spaces is itself a telling illustration of the representational and political limits of society.

As evidenced by the Wynn resort in Las Vegas, more companies may move towards general theming instead of increasing the nuance of representation in theming. Also, to avoid the political controversies that marked Hitler's Cross, Disney's

America, Dracula Park, Splendid China, and the Holy Land Experience, more designers may emphasize apolitical and non-cultural themes. The techno and space-themed Mars 2112 in New York City is an example of a themed restaurant that uses theming in an apolitical and consumerist vein.[59] Conceptual spaces, like the Time and Library hotels in New York City, may also be an option for depolicitizing theming. Perhaps if the public were to learn from the past controversies related to themed spaces, they would understand architect Daniel Liebeskind who, himself embroiled in a conceptual battle over the reconstruction of the site of the World Trade Center, suggested that his architectural goal for that site was "not to re-create the past, but to reinterpret it."[60] Themed spaces are often criticized for representational issues that are beyond the intentions of their designers, and people often seem unwilling to accept them simply because they are themed spaces.

One question that remains is what is the social role of the themed space in society? Is it merely an entertainment venue or does it offer educational opportunities for visitors? More museual spaces have embraced theming technologies to attract visitors, while themed spaces have begun to incorporate the narrative and interpretive approaches of museums, involving much more detailing of spaces than in the past. Jorvik, a Viking-themed entertainment complex in York, England eschews traditional typologies. Like a museum, the venue features displays of Viking culture, but more like a heritage center it offers souvenirs for purchase that are crafted by skilled individuals dressed in historic garments, and like a theme park it features a Pirates of the Caribbean-style ride that takes visitors on a ride through Viking history, ending in a gift shop where visitors can purchase numerous trinkets, including smells of the Viking latrine and other items.[61] Jorvik also encourages visitors to visit the nearby Archaeological Resource Center to learn more about archaeology and Viking history, and in this sense, it does more than a typical themed space in that it stresses a pedagogical project. It encourages visitors to look beyond the immediate theme and to use its re-presentational technologies as an extension to other reflections of the Viking theme. Jorvik does more than signify the distinction between museums, heritage centers, and themed spaces, it helps us to recognize that these very representational and conceptual distinctions are breaking down and that, ironically, some museums—because they have taken on the technologies formerly reserved for themed spaces—may lose their vital role as the pedagogical purveyor of the State. Similarly, some themed spaces—because they have begun to take on the educational roles formerly reserved for museums—actually may serve a more important function in society than simply entertaining the masses. Themed spaces, perhaps especially the controversial and postmodern ones, may educate us in ways previously unrealized.

Theming, by its very nature, invites irony and political uncertainty. At the Beijing, China restaurants Intellectual Youngster Restaurant and Elder Intellectual Youngster Restaurant patrons wear straw huts amid pictures of Chairman Mao and photos from the Cultural Revolution. Flickering oil lamps light the place as people sip bowls of porridge and focus on memories of politics and exile.[62] The past is often seen as unmasterable, uncomfortable, and even unthinkable, and in many ways, themed spaces, like their museal counterparts, play on the unmasterable past and the unthinkable present and the difficult cultural times and places that cannot be reconciled.[63] The public discomfort that is produced by controversial theming, and sometimes even conventional, may reveal deep sutures in the structure of society. Perhaps the representational remove that theming provides gives the public an opportunity to consider ideas that may escape its grasp otherwise. Some people may be unwilling to confront difficult topics like slavery, genocide, and social oppression in texts and even films, and it may be the space of representation that is given by theming that allows the public to more deeply consider the troubled past. Theming may also enlighten all of us about ourselves and force us to ask questions that cannot emerge in so-called serious spaces of representation. A danger is also found in the same technology that may educate the public, and this is the problem of relegating important social issues to contexts that are still defined by entertainment, not education. Restaurants like the Intellectual Youngster Restaurant may symbolically reference the difficulty of Mao and the Cultural Revolution, but they may also encourage visitors to accept the past in a tongue-in-cheek manner, without critical reflection. After all, how political is one likely to be while he or she is nibbling on a hamburger? The discomfort and outrage that resulted in the cancellation of Dracula Park and Disney's America suggests that as much as themed spaces are often dismissed as mere places of entertainment and folly they are, in fact, incredibly significant places that have made indelible marks on the public's imagination. Perhaps it is the themed space, ironically, that may provide suggestions for social change and opportunities for cultural critique in an American society that seems more and more apolitical.

Notes

1. Krittivas Mukherjee, "Outrage Over Indian Restaurant Named After Hitler, *Scotsman*, 22 August 2006, <http://thescotsman.scotsman.com/international.cfm?id=1231542006> (15 September 2006).

2. Reuters, "India's Hitler-themed Restaurant Draws Fire," *MSNBC*, 21 August 2006, <http://www.msnbc.msn.com/id/14121008/> (5 December 2005).

3. Monica Chadha, "Climb Down by 'Hitler' Restaurant," *BBC News*, 24 August 2006, <http://news.bbc.co.uk/1/hi/world/south_asia/5275866.stm> (9 September 2006). One of the owners stated that "We have decided to change the name of our restaurant and remove all signs and articles associated with Hitler and Nazism in and around it."

4. Mark Schatzker, "Historical Fiction: How Do Medieval-Themed Restaurants Get It Wrong?, *Slate*, 6 October 2004, <http://www.slate.com/id/2107363/> (24 May 2006). Schatzker discusses what he believes are the top reasons that medieval themed restaurants are inaccurate.

5. A representative responding to claims of propaganda and historical revisionism at Splendid China theme park. Robert H. Brown, "Florida Splendid China," Florida's Lost Tourist Attractions, <http://www.lostparks.com/china.html> (25 September 2006).

6. Interestingly, one of the managers went so far as to check the accuracy of the glyphs in research texts.

7. Victor Turner, *The Forest of Symbols: Aspects of Ndembu Ritual* (Ithaca, N.Y.: Cornell University Press, 1986), 36.

8. Andreas Huyssen, *After the Great Divide* (Bloomington: Indiana University Press, 1986), 7.

9. For further discussions of these aesthetic controversies see Carol Becker, *Zones of Contention: Essays on Art, Institutions, Gender, and Anxiety* (Albany: State University of New York Press, 1996).

10. For more on the *Crossroads* controversy see Steve C. Dubin, *Displays of Power: Memory and Amnesia in the American Museum* (New York: New York University Press, 1999), 186–226; Charles T. O'Reilly and William A. Rooney, *The Enola Gay and the Smithsonian Institution* (Jefferson, N.C.: McFarland, 2005).

11. I refer to these individuals as *watchers*. They are motivated by a passion to understand, interpret, comment on, and act for the improvement of the themed spaces through which they travel. See Scott A. Lukas, "Signal 3: Ethnographic Experiences in the American Theme Park Industry" (PhD diss., Rice University, 1998) and Marla Dickerson, "Self-Styled Keepers of the Magic Kingdom," *Los Angeles Times*, 12 September 1996, A1, 24.

12. Thank you to Holy Land's Executive Secretary Barbara Lowery for providing tickets to the park and additional information related to my research visit.

13. Eric Tiansay, "Biblical Theme Park Garners New Critics," *Beliefnet*, 21 March 2001, <http://www.beliefnet.com/story/70/story_7086_1.html> (8 March 2004).

14. There has been some controversy related to the park's status—is it a theme park, a museum, a place of religious worship? Is it eligible for nonprofit tax-exempt status? According to the park's founder, Marvin Rosenthal, "We're not in the entertainment business. We're not in the museum business. . . . This is designed to communicate the truths of the word of God." In my view, the park fits none of these categories—it is a thematic hybrid of museum, theme park, and place of worship. Perhaps like other places, it reflects a new trend of hybrid theming venues. Associated Press, "Controversial Christian Theme Park to Open in Orlando," *CNN*, 22 January 2001, <http://archives.cnn.com/2001/TRAVEL/NEWS/02/05/christian.themeparkt/index.html> (23 January 2001).

15. In a related religious topic, some people believe that religious restaurants not only fulfill a marketable demographic niche, but they provide an opportunity for the devout to come together and share experiences. In this sense they are not merely themed spaces but they are venues that meet personal, social, and existential needs deeper than consumerism. Cherise Williams, "Christian-Themed Restaurant Offers More than Just Dinner," *The Virginian-Pilot*, 15 July 2003, <http://web-lexis-nexis.com> (8 April 2004). The particular restaurant discussed in this article is called Testimonies.

16. Mike Wallace, *Mickey Mouse History and Other Essays on American Memory* (Philadelphia: Temple University Press, 1996), 164. Later, Disney backed off from statements that the park would be dark, instead it would celebrate America and would leave the visitor "with a smile on your face." Wallace, *Mickey Mouse History*, 167. Interestingly, a park that closed in the 1960s, Freedomland, featured a Civil War-themed ride in one of its

theme lands. See <http://ourworld.compuserve.com/homepages/robfriedman/> for more information.

17. The debate even included a Senate hearing. *Potential Impact of Disney's America Project on Manassas National Battlefield Park*, Hearing Before the Subcommittee on Public Lands, National Parks and Forests of the Committee on Energy and Natural Resources, United States Senate, 21 June 1994, U.S. Government Printing Office, 1994.

18. For more on the political coalitions involved in the debate see Nick Kotz and Rudy Abramson, "The Battle to Stop Disney's America," *COSMOS Journal*, <http://www.cosmos-club.org/web/journals/1997/disney.html> (10 September 2006). As in any major debate about local development, some of the voices focused on the negative impacts that the park would have on traffic, living conditions, sprawl, etc. I do not see this aspect of the debate as relating to the peculiarity of the themed space form. As Mike Wallace wrote of Disney's America, the location of the themed space can also result in social outcry. In the cases of both the Disney park and Dracula park, severe criticism was raised with the demographic, social, and geographic effects on the surrounding area. Wallace, *Mickey Mouse* History, 165. Another interpretation of the controversy is that sacred space was being disturbed in the plans to build the Disney park. For a detailed discussion of the role of American sacred spaces in public life, see David Chidester and Edward T. Linenthal, "Introduction," in *American Sacred Space*, ed. David Chidester and Edward T. Linenthal (Bloomington: Indiana University Press, 1995), 1–42.

19. Another park that was involved in significant cultural controversy was Florida's Splendid China. Splendid China closed in 2003 as a result of continued protests by Tibetan Buddhists and others who were concerned with the ideological focus of the park. Although I did not have the space to deal with Splendid China in this chapter, I consider it to be a social controversy on the same scale as Disney's America.

20. Mike Wallace, *Mickey Mouse* History, 165.

21. Yi-Fu Tuan, *Landscapes of Fear* (New York: Pantheon, 1979).

22. John Lennon and Malcolm Foley, *Dark Tourism* (London: Continuum, 2000), 9-10. A new trend in dark tourism is the visiting of former sites of death and genocide. See Denis D. Gray, "Atrocity or Theme Park?: Cambodia's 'Genocide Trail' Attracting Tourists and Criticism," *MSNBC*, 16 August 2006, <http://www.msnbc.msn.com/id/14363744/> (25 August 2006). Some have called dark tourism a "form of virtual nostalgia in which the traveler vicariously visits the tragedy's scene." Peter E. Tarlow, "Dark Tourism: The Appealing 'Dark' Side of Tourism and More," in *Niche Tourism: Contemporary Issues, Trends and Cases*, ed. Marina Novelli (Amsterdam: Elsevier, 2005), 52.

23. Mark Gottdiener, *The Theming of America: American Dreams, Media Fantasies, and Themed Environments*, 2nd ed. (Boulder, Colo.: Westview, 2001), 138–42. As Huyssen has suggested, the Holocaust may simultaneously enable a powerful memory of the tragic past and block any such representation "by insisting on the absolute incommensurability of the Holocaust with any other historical case." Andreas Huyssen, *Present Pasts: Urban Palimpsests and the Politics of Memory* (Stanford, Calif.: Stanford University Press, 2003), 99.

24. Christopher Reynolds, "Armenians Seek Place in Museum," *Little Armenia*, 3 February 2003, <http://www.littlearmenia.com/html/los_angeles_armenians_seek_place_in_museum.asp> (8 March 2004). For more on the Holocaust's representation in tourist venues, see Griselda Pollock, "Holocaust Tourism: Being There, Looking Back and the Ethics of Spatial Memory," in *Visual Culture and Tourism*, ed. David Crouch and Nina Lübbren

(Oxford: Berg, 2003), 175–89.

25. Scott A. Lukas, "The Theme Park and the Figure of Death," *InterCulture* 2 (May 2005), <http://www.fsu.edu/~proghum/interculture/The%20Theme%20Park%20and%20the%20 Figure%20of%20Death.htm> (1 October 2006). A related topic that I deal with in another article is the way in which themed spaces relate to tragedies that occur on their premises. An example is the relationship of Las Vegas to 911 and Al Qaeda. See Scott A. Lukas, "The Theming of Everyday Life: Mapping the Self, Life Politics, and Cultural Hegemony on the Las Vegas Strip," *Community College Humanities Association Journal*, forthcoming, 2007.

26. Matt Wilce, "Eating Out: Don't Eat the Scenery," *Metropolis: Tokyo Eating Out*, <http://metropolis.co.jp/tokyofooddrinks/388/tokyofooddrinksinc.htm> (10 August 2006). Chain Cool Restaurant is a prison-themed restaurant in Beijing, China. Zhen Xueyuan, "Themed Restaurants Flourish in China," *Market News Express*, <http://www.tdctrade.com/mne/food/food011204.htm> (10 March 2004).

27. Taipei Times, "Taipei Restaurant Removes Offending Décor," *Taiwan Headlines*, 21 January 2000, <http://www.taiwanheadlines.gov.tw/20000121/20000121s1.html> (10 September 2006).

28. Sam Johnson et al., "Feature: I Have a Theme," *Metropolis*, <http://metropolis.co.jp/tokyofeaturestoriesarchive349/308/tokyofeaturestoriesinc.htm> (1 October 2006). There are also examples of cruise ships engaging in homage to the Titanic disaster. Some offer menus and music that replicate those on the night of the Titanic disaster.

29. Michael Janofsky, "Mixing Mayhem and Fun Upsets a Neighborhood," *Baltimore Journal*, 13 February 1999. For more on the restaurant see, Dennis Blank and Robert Mc-Natt, "A Seat Near the Hindenburg, Please," *Business Week*, 15 March 1999, 8; Gregg Cebrzynski, "Crash Cafe Gets Ready to Explode onto Dining Scene," *Nation's Restaurant News*, 1 March 1999, <http://www.findarticles.com> (20 March 2004); Dan Rodricks, "Crash Cafe Has No Place in Our Strange New World," *Baltimore Sun*, 21 September 2001, <http://www.baltimoresun.com> (20 March 2004). The Crash Cafe would have also featured servers/stunt persons who would have accidentally fallen off of balconies in the restaurant. Robin Lee Allen, "Theme Restaurant to Die For?: Crash Cafe Idea Offers Lesson in Bad Taste," *Nation's Restaurant News* 32, no. 15.

30. See Deborah Feyerick, "NRA Plans Theme Store for Times Square," *CNN*, 19 May 2000, <http://archives.cnn.com/2000/FOOD/news/05/19/nra.restaurant/index.html> (2 October 2006); Julian E. Barnes, "Giuliani Doubts NRA Arcade in Times Square would Survive," *New York Times*, 23 May 2000, <http://www.csgv.org/news/headlines/nyt5_23_00.cfm> (2 October 2006); Alec Applebaum, "Burgers and Bullets: Will the NRA's New Big Apple Eatery ever Make it off the Ground?," *Salon.com*, 7 June 2000, <http://archive.salon.com/business/feature/2000/06/07/nracafe/index.html> (2 October 2006). Interestingly, other restaurants of the past have used guns, including servers who brandished gangster violin cases at their tables, to theme their spaces. Robert Klara, "Familiar Themes," *Restaurant Business* 100, no. 10. See also Stephen Michaelides, "What Goes Around, Comes Around," *Restaurant Hospitality* 94, no. 78: 152.

31. See Penny Young, "DraculaWorld," *History Today*, February 2003, <http://www.findarticles.com> (10 March 2004); Robert R. Thompson, "Dracula's Revenge," *PopMatters*, 7 August 2002,

<http://www.popmatters.com/columns/thompson/020807.shtml> (17 September 2006).

32. Piers Moore Ede, "Dracula Lives, But His Theme Park Sucks," *E: The Environmental Magazine*, September – October 2002, <http://www.findarticles.com> (10 March 2004). Mark Andress, "The New Curse of Dracula?" *BusinessWeek*, 19 November 2001, <http://www.businessweek.com/magazine/content/01_47/b3758126.htm> (1 October 2006).

33. BBC, "Prince Opposes Dracula Park," *BBC News*, 6 May 2002, <http://news.bbc.co.uk/2/hi/europe/1971271.stm> (4 September 2006).

34. World Heritage Committee, "United Nations Educational, Scientific and Cultural Organization—Convention Concerning the Protection of the World Cultural and Natural Heritage," Budapest, Hungary, 24–29 June 2002, <http://whc.unesco.org/pg.cfm?cid=31&id_site=902> Jonathan Luxmoore, "Churches Want to Drive a Stake in Transylvania's Dracula Park," *Christianity Today*, 30 November 2001, <http://www.christianitytoday.com/ct/2001/148/53.0.html> (19 September 2006).

35. For more see <http://www.kavon.com.au/>. In terms of the point about associations between Sighisoara and Dracula, I am reminded of the common contentions that residents of Orlando, Florida have when the topic of Disney comes up. Some are offended by the association of their community with Walt Disney World theme parks. Additionally, some extreme forms of theming have their influence in other forms of representation, including movies and video games. In the Rob Zombie film *House of 1000 Corpses*, the director parodies both slasher films and theme park rides in a scene that features a theme park ride that journeys through the history of mass murder. As part of a 2006 Halloween celebration, Universal Studios Hollywood opened its Bates Motel—the house used in numerous horror films, including *Psycho*—as a living theme park ride in which patrons walked through a house of horrors.

36. Eden Camp, *Eden Camp: The People's War, 1939–45* (Leicester, England: The Print House, 2004). For on Eden Camp see <http://www.edencamp.co.uk>.

37. To contrast with the dark and apologetic approach to war is the National Museum of American History's *The Price of Freedom: Americans at War* exhibition in Washington, D.C. The narrative reflects a neoconservative, unapologetic understanding of war. Other nations are demonized, while the U.S. is always presented as the reluctant warrior. At the end of the exhibition the visitor is shown a steel girder from the World Trade Center and an adjacent display on the war in Iraq. For more discussion of how a Disney park is introduced into a non-American culture, and the cultural reinterpretations that occur, see Andrew Lainsbury, *Once Upon an American Dream: The Story of Euro Disneyland* (Lawrence: University Press of Kansas, 2000) and Aviad E. Raz, *Riding the Black Ship: Japan and Tokyo Disneyland* (Cambridge, Mass.: Harvard University Asia Center, 1999).

38. Edward A. Chappell, "The Museum and the Joy Ride: Williamsburg Landscapes and the Spectre of Theme Parks," in *Theme Park Landscapes: Antecedents and Variations*, ed. Terence Young and Robert Riley (Washington, D.C.: Dumbarton Oaks Research Library and Collection, 2002), 122.

39. For more on the theming of Frankenstein 1818, see Scott A. Lukas, "Fragments of The World Thinking Me, or How the Digital Facilitates Human Separation," *International Journal of Baudrillard Studies* 3, no. 2 (July 2006). For the restaurant's site, <http://www.frankenstein-pub.co.uk/>.

40. William Ferchland, "Themes Used Widely to Boost Business," *Tahoe Daily Tribune*, 27 April 2006, A1, A8.

41. Ron Fortune, "Desert Passage Soon Passé: Aladdin Mall Undertakes 'De-theming,'" *Gaming Today*, <http://www.gamingtoday.com> (4 April 2006).

42. Clarence Page, "Sink Disney's New PC Pirates," *Chicago Tribune*, 8 January 1997, Section 1, 15.

43. See <http://www.stargatedental.com/about.htm>.

44. Real Estate Weekly, "Impala Opens in the East 70's: Themed Condominium, Manhattan, New York," *Real Estate Weekly*, 11 October 2000, <http://www.findarticles.com> (2 October 2006).

45. Francisco Asensio Carver, *Theme and Amusement Parks* (New York: Arco, 1997), 62–3.

46. For more examples of the specific themed rooms see <http://www.madonnainn.com/>. Another hotel, the Pelican in Miami Beach, Florida, offers a psychedelic room and a best whorehouse room. See Rafer Guzman, "Hotel Offers Kids a Room with a Logo," *Wall Street Journal*, 6 October 1999, F1.

47. For more on the Time see <http://www.thetimeny.com/>, and for more on the Library, see <http://libraryhotel.com/>. For an article on the Library Hotel, see Interior Design, "Modern Classic," *Interior Design* 72, no. 8: 230–33.

48. Wilce, "Eating Out."

49. Denis Hollier, *Against Architecture: The Writings of Georges Bataille* (Cambridge, Mass.: MIT Press, 1992), 102–104.

50. Reuters, "Taiwan Bowled Over by Toilet-theme Restaurant," *MSNBC*, 30 June 2005, <http://www.msnbc.msn.com/id/8417691/> (2 July 2005). Thanks to Michael Holtzclaw of Central Oregon Community College for locating this source. The trend also seems to have taken hold in China. The Press Trust of India, "Toilet-Themed Restaurants Attract Trendy Young People in China," *The Press Trust of India*, 21 August 2006.

51. Edo McCullough, *Good Old Coney Island: A Sentimental Journey into the Past* (New York: Fordham University Press, 2000); Rem Koolhaas, *Delirious New York* (New York: Monacelli Press, 1994).

52. Pictures are available at <http://www.themeparkreview.com/europe2005/bonbonland/bonbonland1.htm>.

53. Mikhail Bakhtin, *Rabelais and His World* (Bloomington: Indiana University Press, 1984).

54. Nation's Restaurant News, "Targeting Those with Thirsty Appetites," *Nation's Restaurant News* 40, no. 40: 16. The Twisted Spoke Web site is <http://www.twistedspoke.com/smuteggs.html>.

55. Steven Pace, "Web Sites as Theme Parks: An Exercise In Lateral Thinking," <http://www.csu.edu.au/OZCHI99/short_papers/Pace.doc> (10 September 2006).

56. Scott A. Lukas, "Signal 3: Ethnographic Experiences in the American Theme Park Industry" (PhD diss., Rice University, 1998). Scott A. Lukas, "An American Theme Park: Working and Riding Out Fear in the Late Twentieth Century." In *Late Editions 6, Paranoia within Reason: A Casebook on Conspiracy as Explanation*, ed. George E. Marcus (Chicago: University of Chicago Press, 1999), 405–28.

57. The park was not merely conceptual, according to a site associated with Brian Eno, one that is unfortunately now down, the three artists met and produced drawings and large maps of the theme park. Brian Eno, "REAL WORLD." *Voyager Web site*, <http://www.voyagerco.com/LA/theme/tpark.html> (10 March 1998). For a current Web site see Anon., "A Real World Experience Park: Peter Gabriel and Brian Eno Talk about

Future Possibilities," <http://music.hyperreal.org/artists/brian_eno/realworld-txt.html> (10 October 2006).

58. Years ago, I came across a proposal for a new Arizona theme park known as "Anasazi Motion Picture Studio Theme Park." Like Real World, this park was never built, and also like Real World, it featured more conceptual and surreal theming. Theme lands focused on Native Americans, nature, aliens and UFOs, and the whole park emphasized elements not typically found in a theme park, like archaeological excursions, crystal seminars, animal totemism, UFO encounters, and nature walks. One of the rides, known as "WAR," would have featured clips and recreations of major wars of the past and would have asked patrons to reflect on the tragedy of human conflict.

59. Ed Rubinstein, "Mars 2112 to Beam Restaurantgoers into the 22nd Century," *Nation's Restaurant News* 32, no. 29: 158–59.

60. Daniel Liebeskind, *Breaking Ground: An Immigrant's Journey from Poland to Ground Zero* (New York: Riverhead Books, 2004), 46.

61. For more on Jorvik see <http://www.jorvik-viking-centre.co.uk/>. For discussions of the trend involving museums appropriating the techniques of theming see Margaret J. King, "Theme Park Thesis," *Museum News* 69, no. 5: 60–62; Margaret J. King, "The Theme Park Experience: What Museums Can Learn from Mickey Mouse," *The Futurist* 25, no. 6: 24–31.

62. Zhen Xueyuan, "Themed Restaurants Flourish in China," *Market News Express*, <http://www.tdctrade.com/mne/food/food011204.htm> (10 March 2004).

63. For more on this theme in history see Charles S. Maier, *The Unmasterable Past: History, Holocaust, and German National Identity* (Cambridge: Harvard University Press, 2003).

Key Terms

anti-theming. The avoidance of explicit theming (such as at Bally's casino in Las Vegas) or the underproduction of it (such as at the Wynn casino in Las Vegas).

archetheme. A common theme that is found in multiple themed spaces, regardless of the specific theme of the venue. For example, gender, water, branding, etc.

dark theming. The use of previously taboo themes like violence, death, and genocide to provocatively organize a space in a thematic way.

hybrid theming. A combination of virtual and traditional physical theming, often through the use of immersive technologies that allow patrons to interact with the elements of the themed space.

lived theming. The movement of the material elements of theming into the realm of the immaterial. It refers to situations in which workers or patrons of themed spaces psychologically take on the characteristics, values, or attitudes that are connoted by the particular themes of the venues.

microtheming. The use of minute details and nuance to create theming effects. Commonly it includes attention to detail at a microscopic level, such as the creation of patina on a themed wall.

performative theming. The use of specific modes of performance—including costumed actors, singing and speaking performers with accents, and people who replicate another place, time, or event—to create an authentic sense of a theme.

retheming. The transformation of a venue from one theme to a new one, often of a radically contrasting nature to the original.

theming. The use of an overarching theme, such as western, to create a holistic and integrated spatial organization of a consumer venue.

theming complex. The overall extent of theming development that is created throughout a venue, including architecture, decor, signage and the performances of costumed workers.

theming palimpsest. The existence of multiple and often contradictory themes within one theming venue.

theming vistas. The various points of visual and spatial interest that are created in a themed space. For example, at the New York–New York casino in Las Vegas, patrons move from a recreated New York village to a section featuring a roller coaster.

virtual theming. The creation of theming effects that occurs in nontraditional spaces, such as in virtual reality simulations and video game environments.

Selected Bibliography

Adams, Judith A. *The American Amusement Park Industry.* Boston: Twayne, 1991.
Adler, Jerry and Maggie Malone. "Theme Cities." *Newsweek*, 11 September 1995.
Amusement Business. "Theming Plays Major Role in Popularity of Coasters." *Amusement Business* 106, no. 20: 22–25.
Anderson, Grace. "Entertainment Architecture." *Architectural Record* September 1989: 65–71.
Anderton, Frances. "The World According to Disney." *Architectural Record* September 1988.
Angelo, Bonnie and Stacy Perman. "Hungry for Theme Dining." *Time* 148, no. 5.
Apfel, Ira. "Magic-Theme Restaurants Conjure Up Spellbinding Sales." *Restaurants USA*, February 1998.
Arndorfer, Jim. "McSploitation." Pp. 173–81 in *Boob Jubilee: The Cultural Politics of the New Economy*, edited by Thomas Frank and David Mulcahey. New York: W.W. Norton, 2003.
Atkinson, Connie Zeanah. "Whose New Orleans?: Music's Place in the Packaging of New Orleans for Tourism." Pp. 171–82 in *Tourists and Tourism: A Reader*, edited by Sharon Bohn Gmelch. Long Grove, Ill.: Waveland, 2004.
Bagli, Charles V. "Novelty Gone, Theme Restaurants are Tumbling." *New York Times*, 27 December 1998: 1.
Baldwin, Deborah. "Main Street as Memory Lane." *New York Times*, 10 January 2002, F1, F7.
Balides, Constance. "Jurassic Post-Fordism: Tall Tales of Economics in the Theme Park." *Screen* 41, no. 2 (2000): 139–60.
Ball, Edward. "To Theme or Not to Theme: Disneyfication without Guilt." Pp. 31–37 in *The Once and Future Park*, edited by Deborah Karasov and Steve Waryan. New York: Princeton Architectural Press, 1993.
Barron, Kelly. "Theme Players." *Forbes* 163, no. 6 (22 March 1999): 52.
BBC. "Theme Park for Vegetable Lovers." *BBC News*, 3 January 2002. <http://news.bbc.co.uk/1/hi/england/1741350.stm> (11 February 2005).
Beardsworth, Alan and Alan Bryman. "The Wild Animal in Late Modernity: The Case of the Disneyization of Zoos." *Tourist Studies* 1, no. 1: 83–104

———. "Late Modernity and the Dynamics of Quasification: The Case of the Themed Restaurant." *Sociological Reviews* 1999: 228–57.
Beeton, Sue. *Film-induced Tourism*. Clevedon, UK: Channel View, 2005.
Bégout, Bruce. *Zeropolis: The Experience of Las Vegas*. London: Reaktion Books, 2003.
Bell, Claudia and John Lyall. *The Accelerated Sublime: Landscape, Tourism, and Identity*. Westport, Conn.: Praeger, 2002.
Blair, Carole and Neil Michel. "Commemorating in the Theme Park Zone: Reading the Astronauts Memorial." In *At the Intersection: Cultural Studies and Rhetorical Studies*, edited by Thomas Rosteck. New York: Guilford, 1999.
Bradley Joseph Beck, "From Brand to Architecture." MA thesis. University of Cincinnati, 2003.
Braithwaite, David. *Fairground Architecture: The World of Amusement Parks, Carnivals, and Fairs*. New York: Frederick A. Praeger, 1968.
Brannen, Mary Yoko. "Bwana Mickey: Constructing Cultural Consumption at Tokyo Disneyland." Pp. 216–34 in *Remade in Japan*, edited by Joseph Tobin. New Haven, Conn.: Yale University Press, 1992.
Brigham, Ann. "Consuming Pleasures of Re/Production: Going Behind the Scenes in Spielberg's *Jurassic Park* and at Universal Studios Theme Park." *Genders* 36 (2002). <http://www.genders.org/g36/g36_brigham.html> (7 October 2006).
Brumback, Nancy. "Museum Piece?" *Restaurant Business* 99, no. 24.
———. "Theme Song." *Restaurant Business* 103, no. 13: 42–43.
Bryman, Alan. "The Disneyization of Society." *The Sociological Review* 1999: 25–47.
———. "McDonald's as a Disneyized Institution." *American Behavioral Scientist* 47, no. 2: 154–67.
Buchanan, Chris. "The Long Road to Riches." *Mail & Guardian Friday*, 30 June–6 July 2000, 3.
Bukatman, Scott. "There's Always Tomorrowland: Disney and the Hypercinematic Experience." *October* 57: 55–78.
Burka, Madeleine. "Evolution, Not Revolution: Theme Restaurants Come of Age." *Restaurants USA*, December 1999.
Burnside, Mary Wade. "Halloween Theming Growing Trend In Europe, Asia." *Amusement Business* 114, no. 9.
Business Wire. "Airline to Middle-earth Scores a Flying Hat-Trick with New Lord of the Rings 747: The Return of Aragorn and Legolas." *Los Angeles Times*, 17 November 2003. <http://web.lexis-nexis.com> (8 April 2004).
Carr, Adrian. "Understanding the 'Imago' Las Vegas: Taking our Lead from Homer's Parable of the Oarsmen." *M@n@gement* 4, no. 3: 122–40, <http://www.dmsp.dauphine.fr/management/PapersMgmt/43Carr.pdf> (7 July 2007).
Carver, Francisco Asensio. *Theme and Amusement Parks*. New York: Arco, 1997.
Cashill, R. "Architecture/Themed Entertainment: The Jekyll and Hyde Club." *Entertainment Technology Communications* 30, no. 2: 44–7.
Cass, Jeffrey. "Egypt on Steroids: Luxor Las Vegas and Postmodern Orientalism." Pp. 241–64 in *Architecture and Tourism: Perception, Performance, and Place*, edited by D. Medina Lasansky. Oxford: Berg, 2004.
Cass, Jeffrey and Dion Dennis. "Ground Zero: Las Vegas' Luxor." *CTHEORY* 19(3), Event-scene 32, 6 November 1996.
Chamish, Barry. "Bible-Themed Park Fares Well in Land of Political Instability." *Amusement Business* 106, no. 43: 45.

Chang, T. C. "Theming Cities, Taming Places: Insights from Singapore." *Geografiska Analer: Series B, Human Geography* 82, no. 1.
Chaplin, Sarah. "Heterotopia Deserta: Las Vegas and Other Spaces." Pp. 340–61 in *Designing Cities: Critical Readings in Urban Design*, edited by Alexander R. Cuthbert. Oxford: Blackwell, 2003.
———. "Authenticity and Otherness: The New Japanese Theme Park." Pp. 77–79 in *Architectural Design: Consuming Architecture*, edited by Maggie Toy. West Sussex, UK: John Wiley and Sons, 1998.
Chappell, Edward A. "The Museum and the Joy Ride: Williamsburg Landscapes and the Spectre of Theme Parks." Pp. 119–56 in *Theme Park Landscapes: Antecedents and Variations*, edited by Terence Young and Robert Riley. Washington, D.C.: Dumbarton Oaks Research Library and Collection, 2002.
Chase, John. "The Garret, the Boardroom, and the Amusement Park." *Journal of Architectural Education* 47, no. 2: 75–87.
Chung, Yea Sun. "Identification of Economic Value Drivers Impacting Operational Cash Flows in the Casual Theme Restaurant Industry." MA Thesis. Virginia Polytechnic Institute and State University.
Cicora, Elaine T. "Your Place or Mayan?" *New Times*, Cleveland Scene, 25 October 2006.
Clanton, Brett. "Hollywood's Out, Carnival's In: Restaurant Gets New Theme." *New Orleans City Business* 21, no. 32: 7.
Coates, Nigel. *Guide to Ecstacity*. London: Laurence King, 2003.
Collins, Larry K. and Lorna Collins. *31 Months in Japan: The Building of a Theme Park*. Lincoln, Neb.: iUniverse, 2005.
Cooper, Marc. "Searching for Sin City and Finding Disney in the Desert." Pp. 325–50 in *Literary Las Vegas*, edited by Mike Tronnes. New York: Henry Holt, 1995.
Dale, Crispin and Neil Robinson. "The Theming of Tourism Education: A Three-domain Approach." *International Journal of Contemporary Hospitality Management* 13, 1: 30–35.
Davies, Paul. "The Algiers Motel." Pp. 97–108 in *Stripping Las Vegas: A Contextual Review of Casino Resort Architecture*, edited by Karin Jaschke and Silke Ötsch. Germany: University of Weimar Press, 2003.
———. "Sites of Vicarious Consumption: Hollywood's Living (Room) History." Pp. 72–5 in *Architectural Design: Consuming Architecture*, edited by Maggie Toy. West Sussex, UK: John Wiley and Sons, 1998.
———. "New York, New York: Las Vegas' Latest Hotel Takes Theming to New Heights." *Blueprint* no. 134 (Dec. 1996): 20–22.
Davis, Susan G. *Spectacular Nature: Corporate Culture and the Sea World Experience*. Berkeley: University of California Press, 1997.
———."The Theme Park: Global Industry and Cultural Form." *Media Culture and Society* 18: 399–422.
Delany, Samuel R. *Times Square Red, Times Square Blue*. New York: New York University Press, 1999.
Dennett, Andrea Stulman. "A Postmodern Look at EPCOT's American Adventure." *Journal of American Culture* 12, no. 1: 47–53.
Dickenson, Greg. "Joe's Rhetoric: Finding Authenticity at Starbucks." *Rhetoric Society Quarterly* 32, no. 4 (Fall 2002): 5–27.
———. "Memories for Sale: Nostalgia and the Construction of Identity in Old Pasadena." *The Quarterly Journal of Speech* 83, no. 1 (February1997): 1–27.

Dickerson, Marla. "Self-Styled Keepers of the Magic Kingdom." *Los Angeles Times*, 12 September 1996, A1, 24.
Dodsworth, Clark. "Theme Parks in the Digital Age." *Animation World Magazine* 3.9 (December 1998), <www.awn.com/mag/issue3.9/3.9pages/3.9dodsworthtech.html> (7 July 2007).
Doss, Erika. "Making Imagination Safe in the 1950s: Disneyland's Fantasy Art and Architecture." Pp. 179–90 in *Designing Disney's Theme Parks: The Architecture of Reassurance*, edited by Karal Ann Marling. Paris: Flammarion, 1997.
Dunlop, Beth. *Building a Dream: The Art of Disney Architecture*. New York: Harry N. Abrams, 1996.
Dutton, Barbara. "Pirates, Primates and Pyramids: To Compete with Area Attractions, Regional Waterparks Look into Theming to Set Them Apart." *Parks and Recreation* 39, no. 11: 84–88.
Ebster, Claus. "The Role of Authenticity in Ethnic Theme Restaurants." *Journal of Foodservice Business Research* 7, no. 2: 41–52.
Eco, Umberto. "Travels in Hyperreality." Pp. 3–58 in *Travels in Hyperreality*. San Diego: Harcourt Brace Jovanovich, 1986.
Edensor, Tim and Uma Kothan. "Sweetening Colonialism: A Mauritian Themed Resort." Pp. 189–206 in *Architecture and Tourism: Perception, Performance, and Place*, edited by D. Medina Lasansky. Oxford: Berg, 2004.
Emmons, Natasha. "New Library's Design Taps Park Theming Talent." *Amusement Business* 114, no. 7.
Enders, Deborah G. "Are Thrills Giving Way to Shared Emotional Experiences?: High Tech or High Touch." *Amusement Business* 105, no. 37: 32.
Ferchland, William. "Themes Used Widely to Boost Business." *Tahoe Daily Tribune*, 27 April 2006, A1, A8.
Findlay, John M. *Magic Lands: Western Cityscapes and American Culture after 1940*. Berkeley: University of California Press, 1993.
Firat, A. Fuat. "The Meanings and Messages of Las Vegas: The Present of our Future." *M@n@gement* 4, no. 3: 101–20, <http://www.dmsp.dauphine.fr/management/PapersMgmt/43Firat.pdf> (7 July 2007).
Fjellman, Stephen M. *Vinyl Leaves: Walt Disney World and America*. Boulder, Colo.: Westview, 1992.
Forgetta, John. "Architect Brings Art to the Table." *Daily Variety* 270, no. 5.
Fortune, Ron. "Desert Passage Soon Passé: Aladdin Mall Undertakes 'De-theming.'" *Gaming Today*, <http://www.gamingtoday.com> (4 April 2006).
Fox, William L. *In the Desert of Desire: Las Vegas and the Culture of Spectacle*. Reno: University of Nevada Press, 2005.
———. *Driving by Memory*. Albuquerque: University of New Mexico Press, 1999.
Francaviglia, Richard V. *Main Street Revisited: Time, Space, and Image Building in Small-town America*. Iowa City: University of Iowa Press, 1996.
———. "Main Street U.S.A.: A Comparison/Contrast of Streetscapes in Disneyland and Walt Disney World." *Journal of Popular Culture* 15, no. 1: 141–56.
Franci, Giovanna. *Dreaming of Italy: Las Vegas and the Virtual Grand Tour*. Reno: University of Nevada Press, 2005.
Frantz, Douglas and Catherine Collins. *Celebration U.S.A.: Living in Disney's Brave New Town*. New York: Owl Books, 2000.

Frenkel, Stephen, Judy Walton, and Dirk Andersen. "Bavarian Leavenworth and the Symbolic Economy of a Theme Town." *Geographical Review* 90, no. 4 (October 2000): 559–84.
Friedman, Bill. "Casino Design and its Impact on Player Behavior." Pp. 69–86 in *Stripping Las Vegas: A Contextual Review of Casino Resort Architecture*, edited by Karin Jaschke and Silke Ötsch. Germany: University of Weimar Press, 2003.
———. *Designing Casinos to Dominate the Competition*. Reno, Nev.: Institute for the Study of Gambling and Commercial Gaming, 2000.
Gegax, T. Trent. "Booming Amusement Parks: The Theme Is Extreme." *Newsweek*, March 30, 1998, 12.
Gill, Patrick. "Themed Restaurant Chains are Catching On." *The Moscow Times*, 15 October 2002. <http://web.lexis-nexis.com> (8 April 2004).
Goldberger, Paul. "From English Pub to Chinese Pagoda: EPCOT's Eerie but Endearing Sameness." *New York Times*, 3 February 1985.
Gottdiener, Mark. *The Theming of America: American Dreams, Media Fantasies, and Themed Environments*. 2nd ed. Boulder, Colo.: Westview, 2001.
———. *Life in the Air: Surviving the New Culture of Air Travel*. Lanham, Md.: Rowman and Littlefield, 2000.
———. "Consumption of Space and Spaces of Consumption." Pp. 12–15 in *Architectural Design: Consuming Architecture*, edited by Maggie Toy. West Sussex, UK: John Wiley and Sons, 1998.
———. "Themed Environments of Everyday Life: Restaurants and Malls." In *The Postmodern Presence*, edited by Arthur Asa Berger. Walnut Creek, Calif.: AltaMira, 1998.
Grech, Daniel. "An Eatery that Links Its Ware with Software." *Business News New Jersey*, 5 May 1997, 26–27.
Guier, Cindy Stooksbury. "Themed Experience Right in Style." *Amusement Business* 111, no. 37 (13 September 1999): 9–10.
———. "Theming Usage Varies, but Can Be Critical to Success." *Amusement Business* 111, no. 37 (13 September 1999): 10–12.
Guzman, Rafer. "Hotel Offers Kids a Room with a Logo." *Wall Street Journal*, 6 October 1999, F1.
Hall, Martin and Pia Bombardella. "Las Vegas in Africa." *Journal of Social Archaeology* 5, no. 1: 5–24.
Hamilton, Carolyn. *Terrific Majesty: The Powers of Shaka Zulu and the Limits of Historical Invention*. Cambridge: Harvard University Press, 1998, 168–205.
Handler, Richard and Eric Gable. *The New History in an Old Museum: Creating the Past in Colonial Williamsburg*. Durham, N.C.: Duke University Press, 1997.
Hannigan, John. *Fantasy City: Pleasure and Profit in the Postmodern Metropolis*. London: Routledge, 1998.
Hansen, Zia. "Interview with Zia Hansen from Avery Brooks and Associates, Interior Architects." Pp. 87–90 in *Stripping Las Vegas: A Contextual Review of Casino Resort Architecture*, edited by Karin Jaschke and Silke Ötsch. Germany: University of Weimar Press, 2003.
Harris, Neil. "Expository Expositions: Preparing for the Theme Parks." Pp. 19–28 in *Designing Disney's Theme Parks: The Architecture of Reassurance*, edited by Karal Ann Marling. Paris: Flammarion, 1997.
Harvey, Penelope. *Hybrids of Modernity: Anthropology, the Nation State and the Universal Exhibition*. London: Routledge, 1996.

Heller, Alfred. *World's Fairs and the End of Progress.* Corte Madera, Calif.: World's Fair Inc., 1999.
Henderson, Justin. *Casino Design: Resorts, Hotels, and Themed Entertainment Spaces.* Gloucester, Mass.: Rockport, 1999.
Hermanson, Scott. "Truer than Life: Disney's Animal Kingdom." Pp. 199–230 in *Rethinking Disney: Private Control, Public Dimensions,* edited by Mike Budd and Max H. Kirsch. Middletown, Conn.: Wesleyan University Press, 2005.
Herwig, Oliver and Florian Holzherr. *Dream Worlds: Architecture and Entertainment.* Munich: Prestel, 2006.
Hess, Alan. "Beautiful Chaos: The Latest Collision of New and Old on the Strip Is Not Always Pretty, but Effective." *Las Vegas Life,* November 1999, 42–44.
———. *Viva Las Vegas: After-hours Architecture.* San Francisco: Chronicle Books, 1993.
Hiaasen, Carl. *Team Rodent: How Disney Devours the World.* New York: Ballantine Publishing Group, 1998.
Hickey, Dave. "Real Fakery." Pp. 66–67 in *Spectacle,* edited by David Rockwell. New York: Phaidon, 2006.
Higgs, Eric and Jennifer Cypher, "Manufacturing Natural Heritage: Disney's Wilderness Lodge." *Tourism Development: The Theming of Vernacular Settings* 104: 1–12, Center for Environmental Design Research, International Association for the Study of Traditional Environments, Traditional Dwellings and Settlements, Working Paper Series. Berkeley: University of California.
Hollands, Robert and Paul Chatterton. "Producing Nightlife in the New Urban Entertainment Economy: Corporatization, Branding and Market Segmentation." *International Journal of Urban and Regional Research* 27, no. 2 (June 2003): 361–85.
Holtorf, Cornelius J. *From Stonehenge to Las Vegas: Archaeology as Popular Culture.* Walnut Creek, Calif.: Altamira, 2005.
Hong, Michael. "Interview with Michael Hong from The Jerde Partnership." Pp. 91–96 in *Stripping Las Vegas: A Contextual Review of Casino Resort Architecture,* edited by Karin Jaschke and Silke Ötsch. Germany: University of Weimar Press, 2003.
Interior Design. "Modern Classic." *Interior Design* 72, no. 8: 230–33.
Isozaki, Arata. "Theme Park." *The South Atlantic Quarterly* 92, no. 1 (1993).
Ives, David. "Welcome to World World." *New York Times Magazine,* 17 December 1995, 100.
Jakle, John A. and Keith A. Sculle. "Concept Restaurants." Pp. 277–95 in *Fast Food: Roadside Restaurants in the Automobile Age.* Baltimore, Md.: Johns Hopkins University Press, 1999.
Jaschke, Karin. "Casinos Inside Out." Pp. 109–32 in *Stripping Las Vegas: A Contextual Review of Casino Resort Architecture,* edited by Karin Jaschke and Silke Ötsch. Germany: University of Weimar Press, 2003.
Jaspistos. "Competition: Themed Eating." *Spectator,* 13 November 2004, <http://www.spectator.co.uk/archive/diversions/12828/themed-eating.thtml> (7 July 2007).
Jencks, Charles "Ersatz in LA." *Architectural Design* 43, no. 9: 596–601.
———. *The Language of Post-modern Architecture.* 4th ed. New York: Rizzoli, 1984.
Jerde, Jon. "Capturing the Leisure Zeitgeist: Creating Places to Be." Pp. 69–71 in *Architectural Design: Consuming Architecture,* edited by Maggie Toy. West Sussex, UK: John Wiley and Sons, 1998.

Johnson, David M. "Disney World as Structure and Symbol: Re-creation of the American Experience." *Journal of Popular Culture* 15, no. 1: 157–65.
Judd, Dennis R. and Susan S. Feinstein, eds. *The Tourist City*. New Haven, Conn.: Yale University Press, 1999.
Kaplan, Mike. *Theme Restaurants*. Glen Cove, N.Y.: Pbc Intl, 1998.
Kasson, John F. *Amusing the Million: Coney Island at the Turn of the Century*. New York: Hill and Wang, 1978.
Kaufman, Leslie. "Our New Theme Song." *Newsweek*, 22 June 1998.
Kazakina, Katya. "Eastern Bloc Party." *New York Times*, 25 June 2000.
Keating, Sheila. "One-track Mind." *The Times* (London), 4 May 2002. <http://web.lexis-nexis.com> (8 April 2004).
King, Margaret J. "'Disneyfication'? Some Pros and Cons of Theme Parks. 'Never Land' or Tomorrowland?" *Museum* 43, no. 1 (1991): 6.
———. "Disneyland and Walt Disney World: Traditional Values in Futuristic Form." *Journal of Popular Culture* 15 (1981): 116–40.
Kirsner, Scott. "Are You Experienced?: From Anheuser-Busch's Exclusive Tropical Paradise to VW's 3-D Marketing Brandland, the Personalized Theme Park Is Here." *Wired* 8.07 (July 2000), <http://www.wired.com/wired/archive/8.07/themeparks.html> (7 July 2007).
———. "Experience Required." *Fast Company* 39 (September 2000), <http://www.fastcompany.com/online/39/experiencereq.html> (7 July 2007).
Klara, Robert. "Familiar Themes." *Restaurant Business* 100, no. 10.
Klein, Norman. *The Vatican to Vegas: A History of Special Effects*. New York: New Press, 2004.
———. "Scripting Las Vegas: Noir Naïfs, Junking Up, and the New Strip." Pp. 17–29 in *The Grit beneath the Glitter: Tales from the Real Las Vegas*, edited by Hal K. Rothman and Mike Davis. Berkeley: University of California Press, 2002.
———. "Scripted Spaces: Navigating the Consumer Built City." Pp. 80–83 in *Architectural Design: Consuming Architecture*, edited by Maggie Toy. West Sussex, UK: John Wiley and Sons, 1998.
Knight, Cher Krause. "Beyond the Neon Billboard: Sidewalk Spectacle and Public Art in Las Vegas." *Journal of American and Comparative Cultures* 25, no. 1/2 (Spring 2002): 9–13.
Koolhaas, Rem. *Delirious New York*. New York: Montacelli Press, 1994.
Koolhaas, Rem and Hans Ulrich Obrist. "Re-learning from Las Vegas." Interview with Denise Scott Brown and Robert Venturi. Pp. 150–57 in *Content*, edited by Rem Koolhaas. Köln: Taschen, 2004.
Kornfeld, Alana B. Elias and Valerie Reiss. "WWBD?" *Newsweek*, 14 August 2006.
Kotler, Philip, Donald Haider, and Irving Rein. *Marketing Places*. New York: Free Press, 2002.
Kozinets, Robert V. et al. "Themed Flagship Brand Stores in the New Millennium: Theory, Practice, Prospects." *Journal of Retailing* 78, no. 1 (Spring 2002): 17–29.
Kroker, Arthur and Marilouise Kroker. "Treasure Island at the Mirage," "Las Vegas Theme Park," "Luminous Luxor Las Vegas," Pp. 94–97, 103, in *Hacking the Future*. New York: St. Martin's, 1996.
Kuenz, Jane. "It's a Small World after All: Disney and the Pleasures of Identification." *South Atlantic Quarterly* 92, no. 1: 63–88.
La Gallienne, Richard. "Human Need of Coney Island." *Cosmopolitan* 39 (July): 239–46.

Lainsbury, Andrew. *Once Upon an American Dream: The Story of Euro Disneyland.* Lawrence: University Press of Kansas, 2000.
Lankauskas, Gediminas. "Sensuous (Re)Collections: The Sight and Taste of Socialism at Grūtas Statue Park, Lithuania." *Senses and Society* 1, no. 1: 27–52.
Lasansky, D. Medina. "Tourist Geographies: Remapping Old Havana." Pp. 165–88 in *Architecture and Tourism: Perception, Performance, and Place*, edited by D. Medina Lasansky. Oxford: Berg, 2004.
Lennon, John and Malcolm Foley. *Dark Tourism.* London: Continuum, 2000.
Lowenthal, David. "The Past as a Theme Park." Pp. 11–23 in *Theme Park Landscapes: Antecedents and Variations*, edited by Terence Young and Robert Riley. Washington, D.C.: Dumbarton Oaks Research Library and Collection, 2002.
Lukas, Scott A. *Theme Park.* London: Reaktion, forthcoming.
———. "The Theming of Everyday Life: Mapping the Self, Life Politics, and Cultural Hegemony on the Las Vegas Strip." *Community College Humanities Association Journal* (2007), forthcoming.
———. "The Theme Park and the Figure of Death." *InterCulture* 2 (May 2005). <http://www.fsu.edu/~proghum/interculture/The%20Theme%20Park%20and%20the%20Figure%20of%20Death.htm> (1 October 2006).
———. "An American Theme Park: Working and Riding Out Fear in the Late Twentieth Century." Pp. 405–28 in *Late Editions 6, Paranoia within Reason: A Casebook on Conspiracy as Explanation*, edited by George E. Marcus. Chicago: University of Chicago Press, 1999.
MacCannell, Dean. "A Semiotic of Attraction." Pp. 109–33 in *The Tourist: A New Theory of the Leisure Class.* New York: Shocken Books, 1989.
———. "Staged Authenticity." Pp. 91–107 in *The Tourist: A New Theory of the Leisure Class.* New York: Shocken Books, 1989.
MacLaurin, Donald J. and Tanya L. MacLaurin. "Customer Perceptions of Singapore's Theme Restaurants." *Cornell Hotel and Restaurant Administration Quarterly* 41, no. 3.
Magnet, Shoshana. "Playing at Colonization: Interpreting Imaginary Landscapes in the Video Game *Tropico.*" *Journal of Communication Inquiry* 30, no. 2: 142–62.
Malamud, Margaret. "As the Romans Did? Theming Ancient Rome in Contemporary Las Vegas." *Arion* 6, no. 2 (1998): 11–39.
———. "Pyramids in Las Vegas and in Outer Space: Ancient Egypt in Twentieth-Century American Architecture and Film." *Journal of Popular Culture* 34, no. 1: 31–47.
Marling, Karal Ann. "Imagineering the Disney Theme Parks." Pp. 29–177 in *Designing Disney's Theme Parks: The Architecture of Reassurance*, edited by Karal Ann Marling. Paris: Flammarion, 1997.
McCarthy, Anna. "Brand Identity at NikeTown." Pp. 410–14 in *Signs of Life in the USA: Readings on Popular Culture for Writer*, edited by Sonia Maasik and Jack Solomon. 4th ed. Boston: Bedfords/St. Martin's, 2003.
McCombie, Mel. "Art Appreciation at Caesars Palace." Pp. 53–64 in *Popular Culture: Production and Consumption*, edited by Denise D. Bielby and C. Lee Harrington. London: Blackwell, 2000.
McDowell, Bill. "Bread and Circuses: The Theme Restaurant Revolution." *Restaurants and Institutions* 105, no. 11: 50–72.

Mechling, Elizabeth Walker and Jay Mechling. "The Sale of Two Cities: A Semiotic Comparison of Disneyland with Marriott's Great America." *Journal of Popular Culture* Summer 1981: 166–79.

Mendoza, Ronald P. "Themed Retail Design." *Where It's @*, <http://www.where-its-at.com/articles/spotlightarticles/spotlight4.html> (2 March 2004).

Michaelides, Stephen. "What Goes Around, Comes Around." *Restaurant Hospitality* 94, no. 78: 152.

Mikunda, Christian. *Brand Lands, Hot Spots and Cool Spaces: Welcome to the Third Place and the Total Marketing Experience*. London: Kogan Page, 2004.

Miller, Julie. "San Francisco Follows Theme Trend on Vegas Strip." *Hotel and Motel Management* 212, no. 14: 7.

Miller, Ross. "Euro Disneyland and the Image of America." *Progressive Architecture* October 1990.

Mintz, Lawrence. "In a Sense Abroad: Theme Parks and Simulated Tourism." Pp. 183–92 in *Tourists and Tourism: A Reader*, edited by Sharon Bohn Gmelch. Long Grove, Ill.: Waveland, 2004.

Mitchell, Patricia B. "Theme and Decor: How Important to Restaurants?" *Register and Bee* (Danville, Virginia), 7 April 1991. <http://www.foodhistory.com/foodnotes/road/theme.htm> (7 July 2007).

Mitrasinovic, Miodrag. *Total Landscape, Theme Parks, Public Space*. Burlington, Vt.: Ashgate, 2006.

Moore, Alexander. "Walt Disney's World: Bounded Ritual Space and the Playful Pilgrimage Center." *Anthropological Quarterly* 53: 207–18.

Moore, J. Duncan, "A Mickey Mouse Operation: Louisiana Hospital Learns Customer Service Lessons from Disney." *Modern Healthcare*, 14 April 1997, 62.

Morris, Brian. "Architectures of Entertainment." Pp. 205–19 in *Virtual Globalization: Virtual Spaces/Tourist Spaces*, edited by David Holmes. London: Routledge, 2001.

Munarriz, Rick Aristotle. "Theme Restaurants Battle Extinction." *The Motley Fool*, February 28, 2006, <http://www.fool.com/investing/high-growth/2006/02/28/theme-restaurants-battle-extinction.aspx> (7 July 2007).

Muto, Shoichi. *Las Vegas: 16 Hotel & Casinos, 5 Theme Restaurants*. Tokyo: Shotenkenchiku-sha, 1997.

Nelson, Steve. "Walt Disney's EPCOT and the World's Fair Performance Tradition." *The Drama Review* 30: 106–46.

Newman, Morris. "The Strip Meets the Flaming Volcano." *Progressive Architecture* February 1995: 82–86.

New York Metro. "Create a New York City Theme Restaurant." *New York Metro* <http://www.newyorkmetro.com/nymetro/news/people/columns/intelligencer/thecompetition/10431/index.html> (3 October 2006).

Ockman, Joan and Saloman Frausto, eds. *Architourism*. Munich: Prestel, 2005.

Onosko, Tim. *Fun Land U.S.A.* New York: Arno.

Opel, Andy and Jason Smith. "Zootycoon: Capitalism, Nature, and the Pursuit of Happiness." *Ethics and the Environment* 9, no. 2: 103–20.

Ostwald, Michael J. "Identity Tourism, Virtuality and the Theme Park." Pp. 192–204 in *Virtual Globalization: Virtual Spaces/Tourist Spaces*, edited by David Holmes. London: Routledge, 2001.

Ötsch, Silke. "Earning from Las Vegas." Pp. 133–52 in *Stripping Las Vegas: A Contextual Review of Casino Resort Architecture*, edited by Karin Jaschke and Silke Ötsch. Germany: University of Weimar Press, 2003.
Paneri, M. R. "Is Themed Architecture Legitimate?" <http://www.watg.com/> (23 February 2000).
Paradis, Thomas. "Theming, Tourism, and Fantasy City." Pp. 195–209 in *A Companion to Tourism*, edited by Alan A. Lew, Allan M. Williams, and Colin Michael Hall. London: Blackwell, 2004.
———. *Theme Town: A Geography of Landscape and Community in Flagstaff, Arizona*. Lincoln, Neb.: iUniverse, 2003.
———. "The Political Economy of Theme Development in Small Urban Places: The Case of Roswell, New Mexico." *Tourism Geographies* 4, no. 1 (2002): 24–43.
Paterson, Mark W. D. *Consumption and Everyday Life*. London: Routledge, 2006
Pegler, Martin M. *Theme Restaurant Design: Entertainment and Fun Dining*. Retail Reporting Corp, 1997.
Penner, Barbara. "Doing It Right: Postwar Honeymoon Resorts in the Pocono Mountains." Pp. 207–26 in *Architecture and Tourism: Perception, Performance, and Place*, edited by D. Medina Lasansky. Oxford: Berg, 2004.
Philips, Deborah. "Narrativised Spaces: The Functions of Story in the Theme Park." Pp. 91–108 in *Leisure/Tourism Geographies: Practices and Geographical Knowledge*, edited by David Crouch. London: Routledge, 1999.
Pine, Joseph B. II and James H. Gilmore. *The Experience Economy: Work Is Theatre and Every Business a Stage*. Boston: Harvard Business School Press, 1999.
Pinoniemi, Lynn. "Theming Parks: Creating Memorable Playgrounds by Building on a Theme." *Parks and Recreation* November 2003.
Postrel, Virginia. *The Substance of Style*. New York: Harper Collins, 2003.
Potteiger, Matthew and Jamie Purington. *Landscape Narratives: Design Practices for Telling Stories*. New York: John Wiley and Sons, 1998.
Project on Disney, The. *Inside the Mouse: Work and Play at Disney World*. Durham, N.C.: Duke University Press, 1995.
Raz, Aviad E. *Riding the Black Ship: Japan and Tokyo Disneyland*. Cambridge: Harvard University Asia Center, 1999.
Real, Michael R. "The Disney Universe: Morality Play." Pp. 46–89 in *Mass-Mediated Culture*. Englewood Cliffs, N.J.: Prentice-Hall, 1977.
Rinella, Heidi Knapp. "Heavy Roman Theming Makes Way for Truly Upscale Restaurants." *Las Vegas Review Journal*, 6 August 2006.
Ritzer, George. *Enchanting a Disenchanted World: Revolutionizing the Means of Consumption*. Thousand Oaks, Calif.: Pine Forge, 2005.
Ritzer, George, and Todd Stillman. "The Modern Las Vegas Casino-Hotel: The Paradigmatic New Means of Consumption." *M@n@gement* 4, no. 3: 83–99, <http://www.dmsp.dauphine.fr/management/PapersMgmt/43Ritzer.pdf> (7 July 2007).
Roost, Frank. "Synergy City: How Times Square and Celebration Are Integrated into Disney's Marketing Cycle." Pp. 261–98 in *Rethinking Disney: Private Control, Public Dimensions*, edited by Mike Budd and Max H. Kirsch. Middletown, Conn.: Wesleyan University Press, 2005.
Ross, Andrew. *The Celebration Chronicles: Life, Liberty, and the Pursuit of Property Values in Disney's New Town*. New York: Ballantine Books, 1999.

Rubin, Barbara. "Aesthetic Ideology and Urban Design." *Annals of the Association of American Geographers* 69, no. 3 (1979): 339–61.
Rubin, Michael S., Robert J. Gorman, and Michael H. Lawry. "Entertainment Returns to Gotham." *Urban Land* 53, no. 8 (1994): 64.
Rubinstein, Ed. "Mars 2112 to Beam Restaurantgoers into the 22nd Century." *Nation's Restaurant News* 32, no. 29: 158–59.
Rugare, Steven. "The Advent of America at EPCOT Center." Pp. 103–12 in *Cartographies: Poststructuralism and the Mapping of Bodies and Spaces*, edited by Rosalyn Diprose and Robyn Ferrell. Australia: Allen and Unwin, 1991
Rugoff, Ralph. "Honey, I Shrunk the City." Pp. 25–29 in *Circus Americanus*. London: Verso.
Russell, Deborah. "New Restaurant Brings Bit of Nashville to L.A." *Billboard*, 3 September 1994.
Russell, James S. "Theming vs. Design." *Architectural Record* 185, no. 3: 90–93.
Rutes, Walter A., Richard H. Penner, and Lawrence Adams. *Hotel Design, Planning, and Development*. New York: W. W. Norton and Company, 2001.
Sally, Lynn. "Fantasy Lands and Kinesthetic Thrills: Sensorial Consumption, the Shock of Modernity, and Spectacle as Total-Body Experience at Coney Island." *Senses and Society* 1, no. 3 (November, 2006): 293–309.
———. *Fighting the Flames: The Spectacular Performance of Fire at Coney Island*. New York: Routledge, 2006.
Salvail, Andre. "Fashion Cafe Goes Out of Style in N.O." *New Orleans City Business* 19, no. 4: 1–3.
Schatzker, Mark. "Historical Fiction: How Do Medieval-Themed Restaurants Get It Wrong?" *Slate*, 6 October 2004, <http://www.slate.com/id/2107363/> (24 May 2006).
Schenker, Heath. "Pleasure Gardens, Theme Parks, and the Picturesque." Pp. 69–89 in *Theme Park Landscapes: Antecedents and Variations*, edited by Terence Young and Robert Riley. Washington, D.C.: Dumbarton Oaks Research Library and Collection, 2002.
Schmitt, Bernd H. and Alex Simonson. *Marketing Aesthetics: The Strategic Marketing of Brands, Identity, and Image*. New York: Free Press, 1997.
Schwartz, David G. *Suburban Xanadu: The Casino Resort on the Las Vegas Strip and Beyond*. New York: Routledge, 2003.
Schwartz, Nelson D. "How Investors Got 86ed by Theme Restaurants." *Fortune* 137, no. 4.
Shaw, Gareth and Allan M. Williams. *Tourism and Tourism Spaces*. London: Sage, 2004
———. "Theming the Landscape." Pp. 207–10 in *Critical Issues in Tourism: A Geographical Perspective*. London: Blackwell, 2002.
Sherry, John F. et al. "Being in the Zone: Staging Retail Theater at ESPN Zone Chicago." *Journal of Contemporary Ethnography* 30, no. 4: 465–510.
Shields, Rob. "Architecture as a Good" P. 95 in *Architectural Design: Consuming Architecture*, edited by Maggie Toy. West Sussex, UK: John Wiley and Sons, 1998.
Shu, Jianping. "A Study of the Landscaped Environments in Urban Resort Hotels as an Inducement for Secondary Commercial Activities: Three Case Studies in Las Vegas." MA thesis, University of Nevada, Las Vegas, 1997.
Siano, Joseph. "A 'Star Trek' Voyage Lands in Las Vegas." *New York Times*, 25 January 1998, Section 5, 3.

Siegel, Greg. "Disneyfication, the Stadium, and the Politics of Ambiance." Pp. 299–324 in *Rethinking Disney: Private Control, Public Dimensions*, edited by Mike Budd and Max H. Kirsch. Middletown, Conn.: Wesleyan University Press, 2005.

Solnit, Rebecca. "Las Vegas, or the Longest Distance between Two Points." Pp. 277–91 in *Wanderlust: A History of Walking*. New York: Penguin, 2001.

Sorkin, Michael. "See You in Disneyland." Pp. 205–32 in *Variations on a Theme Park*, edited by Michael Sorkin. New York: Noonday, 1992.

Specialty Retail. "Why Theme Restaurants Fail (and How They Succeed)." *Specialty Retail* (March 1999). <http://www.specialtyretail.net/issues/march99/restmain.htm> (1 October 2006).

Statesman. "Durga in Themeland." *The Statesman* (India), 2 October 2006.

Steinglass, Matt. "Why a Casino that Looks Like a Tuscan Village Is One of South Africa's Most Democratic Public Spaces." *Metropolis* October 2002, < http://www.metropolismag.com/html/content_1002/per/index.html> (7 July 2007).

Stern, Jane and Michael Stern. "When the Theme's the Thing." *Gourmet* 56, no. 11: 152–55.

Stern, Robert Am. "The Pop and the Popular at Disney." *Architectural Design* 67, nos. 7/8: 20–23.

Tao, I. M., Yasuhiko Taguchi, and Takeshi Saito. *American Theme Restaurants*. Tokyo: Shotenkenchiku Sha, 1999.

Thorns, David C. "Theme Parks" and "Theme Parks—History and Development." Pp. 138-40 in *The Transformation of Cities: Urban Theory and Urban Cities*. New York: Palgrave Macmillan, 2002.

Tuan, Yi-Fu. *Topophilia: A Study of Environmental Perception, Attitudes, and Values*. New York: Columbia University Press, 1990.

Tuan, Yi-Fu and Steven D. Hoelscher. "Disneyland: Its Place in World Culture." Pp. 191–200 in *Designing Disney's Theme Parks: The Architecture of Reassurance*, edited by Karal Ann Marling. Paris: Flammarion, 1997.

Tyson, James L. "Eat Fast, before the Crocodile Snaps Its Jaw." *Christian Science Monitor*, 13 May 1996.

USA Today. "Come for the French Chateau, but Stay for the Racin.'" *USA Today*, 22 October 2004, 11D.

Van Maanen, John and Gideon Kunda. "Life with Tinkerbell," (part of "Real Feelings: Emotional Expression and Organizational Culture"). In *Research in Organizational Behavior* 11, edited by L.L. Cummings and Barry M. Staw. Greenwich, Conn.: JAI Press 1989.

Venturi, Robert and Denise Scott Brown, "Constructing Decoration." Pp. 64–65 in *Spectacle*, edited by David Rockwell. New York: Phaidon, 2006.

Venturi, Robert, Denise Scott Brown, and Steven Izenour. *Learning From Las Vegas: The Forgotten Symbolism of Architectural Form*. Cambridge: MIT Press, 1993.

Waddell, Ray. Waddell, Ray, "Themed Restaurants Seek Country Club Atmosphere." *Amusement Business* 107, no. 22.

———. "From Simple to Elaborate, Theming Discussed During WWA Symposium." *Amusement Business* 110, no. 42: 2–4.

Walker, Derek. "Architecture and Themeing." *Architectural Design* 52, nos. 9/10: 28–31.

Wanhill, Stephen. "Creating Themed Entertainment Attractions: A Nordic Perspective." *Scandinavian Journal of Hospitality and Tourism* 2, no. 2: 123–44.

Wardle, Kelly. "Dream A Little Theme." *Special Events Magazine* August, 2005.

Warren, Stacy. "Saying No to Disney: Disney's Demise in Four American Cities." Pp. 231–60 in *Rethinking Disney: Private Control, Public Dimensions*, edited by Mike Budd and Max H. Kirsch. Middletown, Conn.: Wesleyan University Press, 2005.

———. "Cultural Contestation at Disneyland Paris." Pp. 109–25 in *Leisure/Tourism Geographies: Practices and Geographical Knowledge*, edited by David Crouch. London: Routledge, 1999.

Wasserman, Louis. *Merchandising Architecture: Architectural Implications and Applications of Amusement Themeparks*. Sheboygan, Wis.: privately printed, 1978.

Williams, Michael. "Disney's California Adventure Theme Park: Rhetorical Shape of a California Dream." *Lore* 3, no. 1: 61–70. <http://www-rohan.sdsu.edu/dept/drwswebb/lore/3_1/williams.pdf>

Williams, Michael Ann and Larry Morrisey. "Constructions of Tradition: Vernacular Architecture, Country Music, and Auto-Ethnography." In *People, Power, Places: Perspectives in Vernacular Architecture* 8. Knoxville: University of Tennessee Press, 2000.

Willis, G.E. "Army Hits Hole in One with New Restaurant Concept." *Army Times* 57, no. 48: 24–25.

Willis, Susan. "Disney's Bestiary." Pp. 53–74 in *Rethinking Disney: Private Control, Public Dimensions*, edited by Mike Budd and Max H. Kirsch. Middletown, Conn.: Wesleyan University Press, 2005.

Wilson, Alexander. "The Betrayal of the Future: Walt Disney's EPCOT Center." Pp. 118–28 in *Disney Discourse: Producing the Magic Kingdom*, edited by Eric Smoodin. New York: Routledge, 1994.

———. *The Culture of Nature*. Cambridge: Blackwell, 1992.

Wong, Kevin K. F. "Strategic Theming in Theme Park Marketing." *Journal of Vacation Marketing* 5, no. 4: 319–32.

Wynn, Steve. "Reinventing Vegas." Pp. 62–63 in *Spectacle*, edited by David Rockwell. New York: Phaidon, 2006.

Young, Renee. "Merchant of Vegas: New $1.2 Billion Las Vegas Hotel Gambles on the Beauty, Romance and Visionary Spirit of Venice." *Building Design and Construction* 40, no. 9 (Sept. 1999): 32–36.

Young, Terence. "Grounding the Myth—Theme Park Landscapes in an Era of Commerce and Nationalism." Pp. 1–10 in *Theme Park Landscapes: Antecedents and Variations*, edited by Terence Young and Robert Riley. Washington, D.C.: Dumbarton Oaks Research Library and Collection, 2002.

Zukin, Sharon. "Disney World: The Power of Facade/The Facade of Power." Pp. 217–50 in *Landscapes of Power: From Detroit to Disney World*. Berkeley: University of California Press, 1991.

Index

9 to 5, 24

Abbott State Penitentiary, 253
"Above Us Only Sky," 154, 158
absent genuine, 118
abstraction, 172, 190
Acapulco club, 142
acting, 183, 192, 193, 207; deep, 194
"acting at a distance," 13, 187
advertising, 44, 210, 220, 252, 262, 284
aesthetics, 89, 113, 120, 122, 123, 127, 130, 140, 141, 143, 145, 149, 163, 170, 175, 240, 249, 252, 254, 255
African National Congress, 115
The African Queen, 10, 116
A. G. Edwards Building, 66
agency, 16, 216
agriculture, 139
Ain Diab, 137–50
airplanes, 278
airports, themed, 60, 97, 153–63; as social destinations, 157; as themes, 161
air show, 155, 159
air travel, 105
Aladdin Resort and Casino, 76, 85, 89, 90n5, 281; Desert Passage, 89
alcohol, 89
Alexander, Chris, 241
alienation, 208, 209
allegory, 9, 11, 24, 27, 34

Allison, Gerald, 115, 116, 124, 125
allusion, 119, 121, 128, 169, 170
Al Qaeda, 267n14, 290n2
Al Quds, 146
Alzheimer's disease, 16, 225, 239, 240, 241, 242, 243
ambiance, 7, 77, 80, 120, 127
ambivalence, 221
American Dream, 141, 148, 199
American Idol, 15, 220
Americana, 9, 141, 143, 145, 149, 208
Americanism, 216
America's Army, 267n16, 267n18
Amtrak, 67, 68
Anasazi Motion Picture Studio Theme Park, 293n58
Anderson, Laurie, 285
animals, 66, 84, 125, 126, 196, 220, 282, 283. *See also* nature
Anne of Green Gables, 176
anthropocentricism, 121
anthropology, 2, 76, 80, 89–90, 105, 108, 112n36, 145, 146, 148, 189, 201, 255, 267n17, 273, 284
anti-Americanism, 254
anti-social behavior, 257
anti-theming, 3, 295
apartheid, 114, 115, 122
Applebee's, 18, 21n56
The Apprentice, 50

311

arcades, 155
Arc de Triomphe, 101
Archaeological Resource Center, 286
archaeology, 2, 14, 108, 116, 117, 121, 124–25, 127, 128, 211, 276
archetheme, 7, 78–9, 80, 82, 86, 295
archetype, 117
architectural firms, 59, 60, 110n17, 118, 274. *See also* Gensler Entertainment; Jerde, Jon; NBBJ; Wimberly Allison Tong and Goo (WATG)
architecture, 3, 14, 61, 78, 80, 81, 84, 86, 87, 88, 99, 100, 102, 103, 108, 116, 117, 124, 125, 137, 138, 139, 140, 141, 142, 143, 169, 171, 186, 191, 192, 197, 226, 227, 237, 264, 273, 274, 275, 279, 282; and benches, 62, 66; and ceilings, 76; and columns, 128; and design features, 175; and exterior features, 77, 89, 97, 121, 138, 140, 231, 235; and fixtures, 76; and floors, 76, 80; Floridian style of, 138, 142; and fountains, 85, 99, 101; and furniture, 78, 102; and interiors, 75, 76, 82, 89, 97, 169, 176, 240; and lighting, 78, 86, 119; and scenery, 114; and statues, 126, 158, 159, 160, 161, 169. *See also* decor
Arizona Historical Society, 69
Arizona State Historic Preservation Office (SHPO), 68
Armenians, 277
art deco, 156, 162
artifacts, 104, 106, 107, 108
artificial intelligence (A.I.), 249, 251
artificiality, 170
assembly line, 209, 210, 212, 213, 216
AT&T, 214
AT&SF Depot, 67, 68–69
Atchison, Topeka and Santa Fe Railway (AT&SF), 63, 68
Atlanta, Georgia, 232
Atlantic Ocean, 145
Atlantis, 116, 121, 131n13
audience response, 249, 264
audio-animatronics, 213
auditing, 186, 197
Augé, Marc, 153

aura of pastness, 117, 120, 128
Aureole, 93n36
Austin, J. L., 48–49, 50
Australia, 126, 280
authenticity, 4, 5, 6, 7, 8, 18, 22n60, 22n63, 23, 24, 25, 26, 27, 28, 29, 30, 31, 32, 33, 34, 35, 76, 81, 82, 104, 105–6, 117, 118, 124, 129, 169, 183, 200, 208, 209, 211, 220, 247, 253
authoritarianism, 197
autobiography, 23, 24, 28
automobile, 4, 7, 27, 30, 102, 141
avant-garde, 284
avatar, 250, 253, 261, 263, 265
Average Joe, 220

Bachelard, Gaston, 50
Backdraft, 39
back-spaces, 212, 213, 214
Back to the Future, the Ride, 208, 215
Back Where I Came From, 26
Bakhtin, Mikhail, 18n4, 268n19, 283
Ball, Lucille, 214
Bally's Las Vegas, 77, 85, 223
Banham, Reyner, 163
Bantu Authorities Act, 114
bantustans, 114
Baptists, 275
Barbie, 211
"The Bargain Store," 34
Barnum and Bailey, 43
baroque, 169, 229
Barthes, Roland, 205n63
Bataille, Georges, 283
Bates Motel, 291n35
Batman, 189, 279
Batman, the Escape, 186, 199
Baudrillard, Jean, 8, 142, 153, 163, 177
Bauman, Zygmunt, 205n58
beach resorts, 11, 44, 115, 127, 137, 138, 139, 142, 143, 144, 146, 156, 238
Beardsworth, Alan, 135n117
The Beatles, 154, 158, 159
Beavis and Butthead, 284
Bednarek, Janet Daly, 154
behind-the-scenes spaces, 7, 11, 13, 15, 16, 207–21, 223, 237
Beijing, China, 99, 100, 101, 102, 107, 286

Beijing World Park, 100, 101
Bellagio Hotel and Casino, 76, 77, 78, 79, 80, 81, 84, 85, 87; the Conservatory, 81, 84
belonging, 154, 158
benchmarking, 30
Benjamin, Walter, 3, 92n30, 98
Berlin, Germany, 155
Berman, Marshall, 47
The Best Little Whorehouse in Texas, 24
bevertainment, 79
Bible, 31, 248, 275
billboards. *See* signage
Bingham, Neil, 156
Bin Laden, Osama, 268n21
biographical simulation, 5, 12, 188
biopower, 187
Blair, Carole, 174
Blair, Cherie, 157
Blitchfeldt, Bodil, 235
The Blitz, 280
Bloch, Ernst, 83
blogs, 271, 274
blue sky, 198
Blue Velvet, 23
BNSF Railway Corporation. *See* Burlington Northern Railroad
the body, 7, 11, 77, 78–80, 82, 83, 85, 86, 87, 159, 195, 247, 255, 257, 258, 278
body language, 78, 194
Boeing Airport, 156
Bonbon Land, 272, 283
Bophuthatswana, 114, 125
Borat, 284
Bornoff, Nicholas, 169
Borough Park, 44
Boston, Massachusetts, 228, 232
Boulevard Corniche, 143, 144, 145
Bourdieu, Pierre, 87
boutique spaces, 21n37, 72, 176
box store, 218
Boyer, M. Christine, 60, 229
brand gremlins, 235, 239
branding, 5, 15, 92n28, 102, 162, 163, 227, 228, 230, 234, 238, 252. *See also* place branding; rebranding
Branson, Missouri, 36n33
bricks and mortar, 227

bricolage, 32, 169
The Bridge of Time, 127
Brik's Bar, 140
Brooklyn Museum of Art, 273
brothels, 170
Brothers in Arms, 251, 253
Brown, Denise Scott, 178
The Brown Derby, 19n5
Brown, Lancelot "Capability," 120
Bryman, Alan, 135n117
Buddy (the bear), 238
buffet, 81, 85, 93n39
Bugs Bunny Land, 189, 192
Bunn, David, 128
Burbank, California, 156
Burger King, 157
burlesque, 169
Burlington Northern Railroad, 68
Burroughs, Edgar Rice, 250
bushveld, 126
Butler, Judith, 48
Buyi village, 107

Caesar, Julius, 81
Caesars Lake Tahoe, 281
Caesars Palace, 55n62, 76, 78, 80, 81; Forum Shops, 76, 86
Call of Duty, 251
camp, 31
Cape Town, South Africa, 129
capital accumulation, 105, 106, 107
capitalism, 47, 60, 88, 94n52, 94n54, 99, 105, 106, 107, 108, 113, 114, 125, 128, 199, 209, 210, 211, 212, 213, 216
carnival, 248
carnivalesque, 42, 272, 283
Carson, Johnny, 26
Casablanca, 11, 137–50
casinos, 72, 75–90, 114, 129, 131n13, 240
Cass, Jeffrey, 124
Castaways, 84
cast members. *See* employees
Castoriadis, Cornelius, 265n6
cathedrals, 77
Cavern Club, 159
Celebration, Florida, 6, 16, 97, 232, 234, 236–39

Celebration Health, 236, 237
celebrity, 12, 207, 214, 220, 221
Centennial Park, 4
Central Park, 204n52
Certified Ride Operator (CRO), 189, 190
chains. *See* franchises
chamber of commerce, 67, 70
Champs-Élysées, 101
Chaplin, Sarah, 130
Chappell, Edward, 280
Charles De Gaulle airport, 158
Charles, Prince of Wales, 279
Chengdu World Park, 100, 101
Chicago, Illinois, 235, 262, 284
China, 9, 97–109
Chinese Ethnic Culture Park, 9, 99, 102, 103, 106, 107, 108
choice, 15, 197, 198, 199, 215
Christians, 142, 267n15, 288n15
cinder, 51
cinema, 10, 155, 190, 191, 192, 193, 194, 208, 214, 215, 226, 238, 247, 249, 250, 251, 254, 276, 278, 282, 284
Circus Circus Las Vegas, 85
Cirque du Soleil, 85
cities, themed, 5, 6, 16, 18, 59, 71, 228, 231
The City of Entertainment, 281–82
city planning, 6, 57–72, 140, 142, 226, 238, 269n25
CityWalk. *See* Universal Studios CityWalk
civic pride, 155, 159, 163
civil society, 98
Civil War, 275, 276, 288n16
civility, 195, 204n52, 214
Clancy, Tom, 250, 253
Clare Bridge Senior Living Home, 240
class. *See* social class
Classen, Constance, 87
cleanliness, 44, 88, 98, 106, 195, 212, 268n20
climate, 104
clothing. *See* costumes
Club of Clubs, 138
Club Miami, 138
Club Tahiti, 146
CNN, 271
Coca-Cola, 18, 71

CocoWalk, 232
codes of dress, 78, 189. *See also* grooming
cognition, 2, 4, 14, 16, 31, 77. *See also* psychology
Cold War, 226, 226
collage, 58, 59
colonialism, 2, 10, 27, 28, 113, 119, 122, 123, 124, 128, 130, 142
color, 45, 121, 141, 143, 146, 175, 240, 271, 283
Columbia, 253
comedy, 255, 256, 257, 258, 262, 268n19, 278, 283
comfort, 198
commercialism, 34
commodity form, 211, 213
communication. *See* language
Communism, 226
concealment, 105
Coney Island, 6, 7, 19n5, 39–52, 144, 186, 201, 212, 248, 283. *See also* Dreamland; Luna Park; Steeplechase Park
conflation, 117
Conflict Desert Storm I, II, 254
conformity, 177
consumer authenticity, 7, 8, 81
consumption, 2, 3, 9, 15, 58, 59, 60, 61, 71, 72, 75, 85, 94n54, 97, 98, 99, 102, 104, 105, 106, 107, 108, 118, 128, 138, 139, 141, 142, 150, 157, 169, 187, 195, 198, 199, 208, 209, 210, 211, 212, 213, 215, 219, 230, 232, 243, 247, 252, 265, 272, 273, 274, 277, 285, 286
contagion, 276
contradiction, 119
control, 122, 238
convention and visitors bureau, 58, 67, 68, 70
conventionality, 169
Cooke, Philip, 209
copies. *See* simulation
copyright, 252
corporation, 98, 187, 214
corporatization, 18, 32
corporeality. *See* the body
Corumbene Nursing Home, 240
Cosgrove, Denis, 155

costumes, 9, 105, 106, 107, 108, 111n27, 118, 119, 129, 144, 162, 185, 186, 189, 212
counterfeit, 12, 153, 247, 261, 272. *See also* inauthenticity
Counter-Strike, 16, 254–63, 267n17
country music, 26, 27–9
countrypolitan, 29
country style, 27
Cracker Barrel, 5
craftspeople, 29, 104, 119, 124, 129
Crash Cafe, 17, 272, 278, 285, 290n29
Crawford, Margaret, "163"
Crazy Girls, 79
"Create a New York City Theme Restaurant," 20n18
creative destruction, 47–48
criticism, 89, 95n58, 129, 157, 178, 183, 184, 199, 200, 205n67, 213, 264, 272, 273, 274, 275, 286, 287
Croft, Lara, 130
crossover, 24, 25, 26, 28, 29
cross-promotion. *See* synergy
Crossroads, 274
crowd, 78, 81
cruise ships, themed, 290n28
Cuba, 253
Cues to Guest Service, 194
culture, 76, 80, 98, 100, 103, 114, 128, 129, 150, 167, 186, 190, 210, 248, 272
culture industry, 15, 114, 141, 143
culture shock, 88
cultural anxiety, 52
cultural displays, 106
cultural heritage, 117, 276, 279
cultural markers, 105
cultural métissage, 144, 150
cultural models, 249
cultural products, 272
cultural resource management, 276, 278–79
Cultural Revolution, 286
cultural salvage, 104
cultural understanding, 103, 275
Curtis, Wayne, 82
customers, 76, 79, 85, 86, 87, 88, 89, 94n54, 102, 103, 105, 107, 108, 116, 117, 118, 128, 170, 174, 175, 184, 186, 189, 191, 192, 194, 196, 198, 201, 207, 236, 273; as active producers/participants, 208, 214, 215, 220, 228; and role in theming, 193, 198, 205n61, 215, 278
customer service, 193, 195, 236
CVB. *See* convention and visitors bureau
cybernetics, 77
cyberpunk, 265

The Daily Sun, 63, 64, 65, 67, 68, 69, 70
Daley Plaza, 277
Dallas, Texas, 277
Dancing with the Stars, 220
Dar Al-Fikr, 254
dark theming, 17, 272, 276–80, 295
dark tourism, 277
Dean and Delucca, 234
Dearborn, Michigan, 207
death, 256, 261, 263, 268n22, 272, 277, 278, 279
decor, 11, 76, 77, 78, 80, 83, 86, 87, 123, 128, 171, 183, 189, 234, 273, 275, 278, 282
defecation, 283, 284
dehumanization, 88, 89, 94n51, 184, 192, 202n1
de Klerk, F. W., 115
DeLappe, Joseph, 267n18
Deleuze, Gilles, 143
Delmont, Elizabeth, 122
Delphi, 121
Delta Force, 251
democracy, 10, 87, 198, 199, 210, 221
demography, 138, 139, 142, 187, 230, 232, 252, 281
Denmark, 272, 283
Dennis, Dion, 124
dental offices. *See* Stargate Dental
Department of Transportation's Child Development Center, 4
Derrida, Jacques, 51
The Design of Everyday Things, 241
desire, 3, 123, 177
destination brands. *See* place branding
destruction, 47, 48
Deus Ex, 264

Dewey decimal system, 283
dhjellaba, 144
Diamond, Elin, 49, 50
différance, 197
disaster, 1, 39, 40, 42, 46, 47, 48, 50, 51, 116, 124, 127, 272, 278, 284
discipline, 106, 107, 184
Discovery Channel, 273
discourse, 2, 272, 273, 274, 275, 276, 284
Disney, 5, 6, 8, 9, 11, 15, 16, 78, 83, 84, 97, 106, 115, 116, 129, 130, 184, 187, 188, 193, 195, 197, 212, 213, 214, 227, 232, 234, 236, 237, 238, 239, 242, 247, 248, 256, 275, 276, 280
Disney discourse, 195, 198, 236, 239
Disney Institute, 193, 236
Disneyland, 8, 11, 26, 99, 106, 125, 169, 213, 243
Disneyland Paris, 33, 137, 273
Disney–MGM Studios, 15
Disney, Walt, 4, 6, 11, 20n32, 194, 212
The Disney Way, 198
Disney World. *See* Walt Disney World
Disney's America, 17, 272, 275, 276, 279, 281, 285, 286, 287, 289n17, 289n18
Disney's Animal Kingdom, 104, 196
dissatisfaction, 211
distinctiveness, 82, 168
documentary, 5, 25, 251
Dollywood, 5, 6, 11, 23–35, 87
Dom Perignon, 86
Donaldson, Andrew, 115
Doncaster Robin Hood Airport, 158
Dongguan, China, 101
Doom, 251, 254
Downtown Business Alliance, 65
downtown development, 6, 58, 60, 61, 64, 70, 72
downtown growth coalitions, 57, 58, 59, 61, 62, 64, 70, 71, 72
Dracula, 279, 280, 291n35
Dracula World (Park), 17, 272, 279, 280, 285, 286, 287, 289n18
Dreamland, 39, 43, 44, 45, 46, 283
dreamscape, 177
drugs, 262
Duany, Andreas, 232

Dublin, Pennsylvania, 240
Dubrow, Jessica, 122
Duffy, Jack, 67
Dundy, Elmer, 41, 43
dungeon, 251
Dungeon Siege, 250
Dungeons and Dragons, 266n10
Dune, 257
Dunes Las Vegas, 84
DVD (Digital Video Disc), 253, 266n8

East Jefferson General Hospital, 236
Eastern State Penitentiary, 253
eating. *See* food
eBay, 31
eclecticism, 15, 75, 77, 163, 282
Ecochard, Michel, 139
E-Content, 227
Eden Camp, 272, 280
editing, 130
editorials. *See* journalism
education, 98
Edy's Ice Cream, 18
E-Factor, 226, 227, 228, 230
efficiency, 108, 209, 236
Eiffel Tower, 80, 88, 101
Eisner, Michael, 276
Elder Intellectual Youngster Restaurant, 286
electricity, 40, 41, 45, 155, 156
elemental performativity, 6, 40, 48, 50, 51
the elements, 6, 40, 48, 50, 51
Elias, Norbert, 186,
elites, 44, 61, 70, 125, 138, 140, 142, 143, 146, 148, 149, 233, 234
El Morocco, 19n5
emotional labor, 88, 89, 196, 200
emotions, 42, 191, 192, 196, 197, 247, 248, 255, 256, 264. *See also* place, emotional attachment to
employees, 78, 79, 84, 85, 86, 87, 88, 89, 94n54, 102, 106, 184, 186, 187, 188, 189, 191, 193, 194, 195, 196, 198, 199, 200, 201, 209, 228, 236, 237, 273; and appearance, 193; and alteration, 195; and ideas about theming, 199; and insubordination, 188, 192
engineering as style, 145

England, 120
Enemy at the Gates, 251
Eno, Brian, 285, 292n57
Enola Gay, 274
entertainment, 15, 42, 59, 81, 84, 87, 107, 120, 122, 130, 141, 167, 193, 220, 227, 228, 229, 236, 242, 247, 248, 260, 275, 277, 278, 279, 287
environment, 219
Environment-Behavior (E-B), 241
environmentalism, 216
EPCOT, 9, 212, 214
erotic, 10, 124, 128
escapism, 124, 130, 169, 171, 199, 243
ESPN Zone, 15, 16, 227
essence of Africa, 2, 10, 118, 123, 124, 125, 126, 128, 129
essentialism, 117, 118, 123, 129
Estonia, 13
E.T.'s Adventure, 215
Eternal Forces, 267n15
ethics, 242, 264
ethnic minority, 102, 103, 104, 105, 106, 107, 108, 110n9, 114
ethnicity, 9, 10, 11, 27, 28, 33, 45, 46, 72, 83, 87, 98, 99, 103, 104, 105, 106, 108, 114, 122, 123, 124, 128, 137, 139, 142, 143, 192, 199, 200, 242, 248, 253, 264, 276
ethnology, 18, 105
Euro Disneyland. *See* Disneyland Paris
Europe, 14, 99, 114, 119, 120, 122, 123, 126, 139, 141, 143, 144, 155, 280
European Capital of Culture, 162
EverQuest, 250, 252
evocation, 121, 248
evolution, 2, 186
Excalibur roller coaster, 185
Excalibur Hotel Casino, 1, 81, 85, 87; Tournament of Kings, 85
exceptionalism, 221, 254
excess, 76, 83, 86, 167, 212, 268n19, 272, 283, 284
exchange value, 61, 67
excrement. *See* defecation
exclusivity. *See* segregation
exhibits, 106, 107
exile, 286

existential issues, 185, 187, 277
exoticism, 10, 106, 113, 115, 117, 123, 125, 126, 127, 129, 141, 143, 145, 149, 163, 172, 178
experience, 7, 225, 226, 228, 233, 235, 238, 247
experience economy, 12, 15
The Experience Economy, 225, 226, 228
experimental tourism, 94n48
exploration, 124, 127
Exxon Valdez, 284
Eyewitness Travel Guides Japan, 171

fake. *See* inauthenticity
Faneuil Hall, 228
fantasy, 5, 25, 60, 83, 116, 117, 118, 126, 129, 143, 167, 171, 172, 173, 174, 177, 180n24, 186, 187, 189, 192, 198, 200, 247, 248, 249, 255, 257, 258, 260, 262, 262, 263, 264, 265n6
fantasy city, 59, 60, 71, 72, 95n60
Fantasy City, 228
Fantasyland Hotel, 172, 173
Fantasy Suite, 180n24
fauna. *See* animals
fear, 122, 247, 268n20, 276
F.E.A.R., 256
Federal Realty Investment Trust, 233, 234
feelings. *See* emotions
Feldman, Allen, 83
feminization, 122, 176
festival marketplaces, 60, 228, 229, 230, 231
fiction, 49, 50, 116, 117, 118, 123, 124, 129, 135n117
Final Destination 3, 266n8
Fighting the Flames, 39, 40, 43, 44, 45, 46, 47, 48, 49, 50, 51, 52
film. *See* cinema
Findlay, John, 106
fire, 50, 51, 52
Fire and Flames, 39, 40, 42, 43, 44, 46, 47, 48, 49, 50, 51, 52
first-person shooter games (FPS), 250, 251, 255, 264
Fjellman, Stephen, 94n54
Flagstaff, Arizona, 6, 57–72
flexibility, 75, 108, 196, 204n54, 212, 213

flora. *See* plants
flow. *See* pedestrianism
fluidity, 227
Foley, Malcolm, 277
food, 80, 81, 82, 85, 86, 87, 93n39, 102, 107, 108, 129, 214, 278, 279, 284, 286
Forbidden City, 103
forced perspective, 89
Ford, Bill, 216, 218
Ford Corporation, 15, 209, 210, 217, 220
Ford F-150, 207, 208, 216, 217
Ford, Henry, 216, 217, 218, 219
Fordism, 143, 209, 212, 213, 216, 217, 218
Ford Rogue Factory Tour, 15, 207–21
formalism, 121
Foss, Sonja, 173, 175
Foster, Norman, 157
Foucault, Michel, 187, 214
Foxwoods Resort Casino, 242
Frankenmuth, Michigan, 5
Frankenstein 1818, 281, 291n39
France, 125, 139, 140, 142, 253
franchises, 71
Frankfurt School, 141
freak show, 248
Freedomland, 289n16
free speech, 89
freeway. *See* roads
French Riviera, 140
Freud, Sigmund, 191
Friedman, Bill, 90n7
Fry's Electronics, 3, 22n56
functional space, 9, 106, 157
future, 219
Fu Yuehong, 101

Gabby's, 185
Gabriel, Peter, 285
Galena, Illinois, 58
Galveston, Texas, 39
gambling, 83, 114, 115
gangs, 262
gardens, 14, 86, 99, 119, 121, 219
Gare du Nord, 88
gated community, 248
Gatlinburg, Tennessee, 30, 31, 32, 33, 35

gaze, 10, 119, 122, 123, 128
Gearbox Software, 253
Gee, James, 248, 254
gender, 7, 10, 11, 26, 54n50, 79, 80, 86, 87, 88, 89, 91n16, 98, 99, 114, 122, 123, 125, 137, 144, 146, 147, 148, 150, 192, 199, 200, 238, 248, 264, 269n27, 281, 284. *See also* sexuality
generation, 98, 147, 148
Gensler Entertainment, 5
gentrification, 177, 232
geology, 66
geopolitics, 138
George Best Belfast City Airport, 158
George Bush Houston International Airport, 158
George Orthlieb (pool), 140, 141
Georgia, 253
Germany, 125
Ghost Recon, 252, 253
Gibson, William, 36n41, 265
Giddens, Anthony, 105
Gilley's saloon, 80
Gilmore, James, 228, 235, 237
Gilpin, William, 120, 121
Giroux, Henry A., 197, 198
Gladiator, 130
globalization, 9, 28, 71, 98, 102, 209, 211, 218, 219, 227
glocalism, 163
glossolalia, 275
The Godfather, 251
Goffman, Erving, 144, 228, 263, 269n25
Golden Resources Mall, 101
Gold Reef City, 129
Gold Standard, 190
Googie style, 143
Gordon, Alastair, 156
gothic spaces, 272, 279, 280, 281, 283
Gottdiener, Mark, 3, 14, 24, 33, 59–60, 109n4, 157, 169, 171, 174, 178, 210
government, 58; de facto, 9, 108
governmentality, 187
Grady, Sally, 238
Gramsci, Antonio, 239
Grand Canyon National Park, 61, 61, 66, 67, 90n4
Grand Ole Opry, 27

Grand Theft Auto, 251
Great American Production, 219
Great Wall of China, 103, 107
Great World, 100
Great Zimbabwe, 117, 125, 128
Greenblatt, Stephen, 8
green spaces. *See* parks
green tours, 211
Greezed Lightnin', 185, 190
grooming, 189, 203n23. *See also* codes of dress
grotesque, 258, 261, 264, 268n19
growth machine, 58, 61
Grūtas Statue Park, 13
Guest First, 190
guest relations. *See* customer service
guests. *See* customers
Gulf War, 254
guns. *See* weapons
Guttman, Steve, 233

habitus, 87
Haggard, Rider, 128
hairstyle. *See* grooming
Half-Life, 251, 254, 259, 260
Hall, Martin, 117, 127, 128
Hall, Stuart, 124
Halloween, 291n35
Halo, 251
Hamburg Fuhlsbüttel, 154, 155
Han, 103, 104, 106, 107, 108
Hannigan, John, 59, 60, 71, 95n60, 228, 229, 231
happiness, 201
Hard Rock, 97, 170
Hard Rock Hotel and Casino, 81
Harrah's Las Vegas Hotel and Casino, 82
Harvey, David, 139
Hawaii, 27, 125
Hayles, Katherine N., 159
healthcare. *See* hospitals
Hearthstone Alzheimer Care, Ltd., 241
"Heartsong," 23, 33
hegemony, 10, 28, 98, 120, 123, 124, 128, 143, 239, 249
Heidegger, Martin, 143
Hell Gate, 283
Hello Kitty, 170, 171, 176

Hendrix, Jimi, 81
Henry Ford Museum, 207
heritage. *See* history
heritage center, 276, 277, 280, 286
Heritage Square, 65–66, 69
heterogeneity, 213
Hiaasen, Carl, 196
hidden spaces, 105
Highrise, 256
Hilton, Paris, 50
historians, 105, 276
historic preservation, 57, 60, 70, 71, 276
history, 28, 30, 31, 33, 35, 59, 60, 61, 66, 68, 69, 99, 103, 113, 115, 117, 122, 127, 128, 129, 137, 138, 139, 159, 170, 207, 240, 253, 264, 272, 276, 279, 287
Hitler, Adolf, 10, 271, 280
Hitler's Cross, 10, 17, 271, 277, 285
Hochschild, Arlie, 184, 191, 194, 196
Holiday Inn, 170
Holiday Inn Family Suites Resort, 18
holism, 184, 193, 275
Hollywood, 125, 141, 214, 248
Hollywood Cantina, 214
The Holocaust, 13, 48, 272, 274, 277, 289n23, 289n24. *See also* National Holocaust Museum
Holt, Douglas B., 211
Holy Land Experience, 13, 17, 112n34, 272, 274, 275, 276, 286, 288n12, 288n14
homelands. *See* bantustans
homeowner association, 98
homes, themed, 4
homophobia, 200
Hong Kong, 102
Hong Kong International Airport, 157
Hooters, 177
Hooters Casino Hotel, 79
hospitals, themed, 16, 225, 236, 237, 239, 243
hotels, themed, 12, 165n27, 167–79, 180n24, 195, 282, 292n46
House of 1000 Corpses, 291n35
Houston, Texas, 184, 185
Howes, David, 87, 88, 94n52, 94n54
human resources, 185, 198

humor. *See* comedy
Hungarian Hero Plaza, 101
Huyssen, Andreas, 289n23
hybrid spaces, 237
hybrid theming, 16, 284, 295
hygiene. *See* cleanliness
hyperreality, 8, 130, 135n117, 204n48
hypotyposis, 7

ID Software, 251
identity, 16, 59, 98, 113, 119, 129, 143, 150, 163, 179, 197, 198, 200, 201, 209, 210, 218
ideology, 10, 11, 13, 46, 79, 87, 89, 108, 113, 114, 122, 123, 124, 128, 129, 178, 183, 197, 198, 199, 208, 209, 210, 212, 216, 217, 218, 220, 255, 267n18, 272, 273, 275
imagination, 117, 118, 120, 127, 129, 130, 170, 171, 172, 174, 175, 201, 213, 217, 248, 284, 287
imagineering, 97, 108, 265n5
imaginimarketers, 236
IMAX, 101
immersion, 7, 8, 16, 80, 83, 119, 128, 169, 177, 231, 243, 249, 259, 261
immigration, 45, 46, 52, 99
Imperial Palace, 83, 87
Imperial War museums, 274, 280
imperialism, 113, 114
imponderability, 80
The Impala, 4, 282
improvisation, 14, 190, 194, 204n43
inauthenticity, 177, 178, 179, 200, 201, 259, 272, 280–81, 287n4. *See also* counterfeit
Ion Storm, 264
India, 10, 17. *See also* Mumbai, India
Indiana Jones, 10, 116, 125, 130
individualism, 15, 195, 210, 215, 216, 217, 218, 219, 254, 265n6
information, 15, 105, 107, 108, 227
Inner Harbor, 232
Inquiry by Design, 241
instrumental logic, 106, 113, 119
intangibility, 117
Intellectual Youngster Restaurant, 286
interactivity, 16, 80, 207, 213, 275, 277, 279
Internet, 3, 19, 23, 30, 31, 98, 158, 162, 207, 218, 227, 252, 267n18, 271, 273, 274, 276, 279, 283, 284
intimacy, 85, 86
invention, 216, 217, 218, 219, 220
investment, 162
Iraq, 253, 291n37
Irish, 262
irony, 31, 32, 90
Isozaki, Arata, 117
Israel, 261
Italy, 125
Izenour, Steven, 178

Jackass, 284
The Jail, 278
Jakle, John A., 155
Jameson, Fredric, 31–32
Japan, 1, 12, 167–79, 274, 277
Jencks, Charles, 178
Jenkins, Henry, 248, 252, 265
Jensen, Joli, 27, 28
Jeppensen Airport, 157
Jerde, Jon, 110n17, 231, 232
Jersey airport, 156
Jesus, 274
Jews, 142, 146, 274
JFK Airport, 158
Johannesburg, South Africa, 115, 129
Johnson, Barbara, 49, 50
Johnstown, Pennsylvania, 39
John Wayne Airport, 158
"Jolene," 26
Joplin, Janis, 81
Jorvik Viking Center, 16, 272, 286, 293n61
Joseph, Miranda, 215
Journal of Architectural and Planning Research, 242
journalism, 275, 279. *See also* newspapers
Jubilee!, 223
junctural zone, 163
Jurassic Park, the Ride, 208, 215

Kant, Immanuel, 268n19
karaoke, 169
Kavon, 280
Kellner, Douglas, 264, 270n28

Kent, William, 120
Kerzner, Sol, 114, 115, 116, 125
kinetics, 79, 85, 93n36, 154, 160
King, Margaret, 117
King Solomon's Mines, 128
kinship, 12, 168
kitsch, 32, 122, 128, 170, 272
Klein, Norman, 191, 198, 229, 230
Knight, Cher Krause, 86
Knight, Phil, 4
knowledge. *See* information
Kodak picture spot, 214
Kon Tiki, 142
Koolhaas, Rem, 41, 46, 47, 48
KwaZulu, 129

labor, 209, 210, 211, 216, 219, 220
Lair, John, 25
Lake Shore Drive Towers, 235
Lake Tahoe, Nevada, 90, 281, 282
landscape gardening, 120
landscape painting, 120, 128
language, 49, 77, 80, 149, 191, 275
Laprade, Albert, 140
La Reserve, 140
Lash, Scott, 105
Las Vegas, Nevada, 3, 6, 7, 11, 16, 32, 55n62, 58, 71, 75–90, 97, 101, 104, 115, 118, 129, 137, 172, 173, 201, 281, 286, 290n25
Lascaux, 14, 186, 201
Leavenworth, Washington, 5
Le Corbusier, 156
Lefebvre, Henri, 109n3, 113, 138
Legacy Theater, 216, 218
Leidner, Robin, 189
Le, Minh, 254
Lennon, John (musician), 9, 12, 157, 158, 159, 160
Lennon, John (author), 277
Leonardo Da Vinci Airport, 158
Levy, Andre, 146
Library hotel, 272, 283, 286
Lido, 140, 141
Liebeskind, Daniel, 286
lifestyle, 235, 237, 239, 240
Lifestyle Enhancement Center, 225, 236, 237, 240
Lifestyle Village, 225, 232, 234, 235, 236, 239, 240, 243, 244n17
liminality, 28, 52, 119
linear-scroll perspective, 250
liquidity, 14, 21, 21n40, 47, 197, 205n58
literature, 2, 190, 276, 283
Lithuania, 13
lived theming, 8, 14, 75, 184, 193, 194, 204n48, 295
Liverpool, England, 161
Liverpool John Lennon Airport, 5, 9, 12, 153–63
Liverpool swagger, 160
living roof, 207, 218–19
Lloyd, Justine, 163
Local Area Network (LAN), 267n17
Löfgren, Orvar, 169
Logan, John, 58
logging industry, 69
logo, 235
Looney Tunes, 202n6, 252, 279
Lorde, Audre, 138
Lorrain, Claude, 121
Los Angeles, California, 8, 13, 26, 230, 231, 277
The Lost City, 2, 8, 10, 113–30; and the Legend of, 116, 124, 129
The Lost Garden, 126
The Lost Village, 129
Louvin, Charlie, 27
love hotels (*rabu hoteru*), 12, 167–79
the low, 283, 284
Lowell Observatory, 66, 67
Lowenthal, David, 9, 14, 16–17, 126, 129
luck, 281
Luna Park, 39, 41, 42, 43, 44, 45, 46, 283
Luxor Las Vegas, 78, 82, 83, 91n13, 124, 125; and the Ra Nightclub, 82
Lynch, Kevin, 241

MacCannell, Dean, 208, 209, 216
the machine, 156, 157
machinima, 250
Madison, Indiana, 58
Madonna Inn, 282, 283, 292n46
Madrid Barajas airport, 159
Mafia, 262
magical third, 150n16

main street, 11, 26, 57, 58, 72, 240, 242
Main Street Flagstaff Foundation, 58, 61, 63, 64, 65, 66, 67, 68, 70
Mall of America, 97, 169
Malinowski, Bronislaw, 2, 80
malls, 60, 61, 71, 97, 100, 101, 230, 232, 233, 240
management, 85, 89, 94n54, 105, 184, 185, 188, 189, 191, 192, 193, 194, 195, 197, 199, 200, 235; and disconnection with organization, 185
Manassas National Battlefield Park, 276
Manassas, Virginia, 17, 275
Manchester, England, 159
Manchester United, 158, 159
Mandalay Bay Hotel and Casino, 80, 83, 84, 85
Mandela, Nelson, 115
Manhattan. *See* New York City, New York
mansion, 155
manufacturing, 207
Mapplethorpe, Robert, 273
maps, 122, 123, 128, 139, 249, 250
Mapungubwe, 125
market, 59, 99, 108, 215, 227, 249, 252; and niche, 210, 212, 213
marketing, 159, 229, 248, 262
Marriott Hotels, 162
Mars 2112, 286
Martun restaurant, 272, 283
Marx, Karl, 47, 88, 213
masculinity, 176, 264, 269n27, 281
Maslow, Abraham, 3
Massive Inc., 252
Massumi, Brian, 33
Matei-Agathon, Dan, 279
The Matrix, 251
Mayan Mind Bender, 188, 200, 273
Mayle, Peter, 171
McAdams, Chief Henry W., 42
McAdoo, Commissioner William, 44
McCallum, Miss Ernestine, 43
McCarran International Airport, 97
McDonaldization, 94n51, 202n1, 227–28
McDonalds, 17, 157, 170
Mda, L., 126
measurement, 197
Medal of Honor, 251

media, 58, 99, 212, 227, 229, 230, 249, 269n26
media effects, 263, 269n26
mediators, 153, 163
memes, 284
memory, 13, 24, 25, 26, 34, 35, 114, 117, 118, 129, 206n73, 238, 240
Memory Care Center, 225, 239
Mersey Estuary, 159
Mersey Partnership, 161
Merseyside region, 158
Metairie, Louisiana, 236
metaphor, 23, 30, 34, 162, 174, 193, 226
method of loci, 284
metonym, 118, 157
metropolis, 50, 57, 58, 59, 60, 70
Mexico, 142
Mexico City, Mexico, 252, 253
MGM Grand, 84, 86, 89, 281; and Studio 54, 86
Miami Beach (Morocco), 142
Miami, Florida, 232
Miao village, 107
Mickey Mouse, 236
Microsoft, 252
microtheming, 7, 76, 77, 78, 84, 295
Middle East, 254, 261, 267n18
midway, 45
Midway Games, 253
military, 248, 250, 253, 261, 269n24, 280
Mills, Stephen, 18
mine shaft, 127
miniatures, 240
Minute Maid, 18
Mirage Hotel and Casino, 55n62, 77, 81, 83
mission statements, 186
Mitrasinovic, Miodrag, 119
mixed-use spaces, 226
mobility, 210
models, 153
modernism, 33, 40, 47, 48, 51 138, 140, 141, 142, 143, 149, 208, 218, 219
"mods" (video games), 250
Mohegan Sun, 131n13
Molotch, Harvey, 58
Monolith Productions, 256
Monster House, 4

MontBleu, 281, 282
Monte Carlo Hotel and Casino, 87
Morocco. *See* Casablanca
Morrisey, Larry, 25, 27, 30, 33, 34, 35
mosque, 125, 254
motorcycles, 4
Moulin Rouge (Las Vegas), 84
Mount Elden Pueblo, 70
Mount Pelée, 39
Mount Vesuvius, 39
Mouscar Award, 236
movement. *See* kinetics
MRI, 16, 238, 239
MSNBC, 271
MTV, 173
multiculturalism, 18
multi-referentiality, 14
multitheming, 231
Mumbai, India, 17, 271, 277. *See also* India
Murphy, Tom, 158
Museum of Northern Arizona, 67
Museum of Tolerance, 13, 274, 277
museums, 13, 16, 21n49, 58, 81, 89, 92n25, 110n9, 209, 272, 274, 276, 277, 280, 286, 287
music, 2, 27, 29, 82
Muslims, 140, 142, 146
Myst, 250
myth, 8, 9, 113, 114, 115, 117, 123, 124, 125, 127, 128, 205n63; corporate, 198

narrative, 9, 11, 12, 13, 28, 81, 82, 86, 87, 89, 92n22, 113, 114, 119, 121, 127, 128, 129, 184, 189, 198, 211, 212, 215, 216, 217, 220, 225, 229, 230, 233, 236, 237, 239, 242, 243, 248, 249, 250, 252, 254, 255, 261, 264, 275, 276, 280, 284
NASCO, 193
Nash, Alanna, 26, 29
nation, 8–11, 45, 46, 98, 103, 108, 129, 138
nationalism, 115, 210
National Holocaust Museum, 277. *See also* The Holocaust
National Museum for American History, 291n37

National Museum of the American Indian, 274
National Olympic Center, 102, 103
National Park Service, 30
National Rifle Association, 278, 279. *See also* NRA SportsBlast
national security, 98
National Trust for Historic Preservation, 70, 74n25
Native Americans, 124
nativism. *See* ethnicity
naturalism, 121
nature, 10, 28, 77, 80, 81, 84, 91n9, 103, 104, 114, 116, 119, 120, 121, 122, 125, 130, 146; and simulation, 76, 83. *See also* animals; plants
Nazism, 10, 271, 277
NBBJ, 237
neoconservativism, 254, 291n37
neocosmopolitianism, 140, 141
neoliberalization, 99, 102
networking, 148
New Canaan, Connecticut, 240, 242
The New Frontier Hotel Casino, 80, 84
New Harvest, 27
New Norfolk, Tasmania, 240
newspapers, 59, 274. *See also* journalism
new urbanism, 232, 233
New World, 100
New York City, New York, 4, 42, 44, 46, 47, 97, 231, 272, 278, 279, 282, 286
New York–New York Hotel and Casino, 76, 83, 85, 89
New Zealand, 66
Nike, 4, 71, 92n28
Nochlin, Linda, 123
Nokia, 252
nomadism, 161
nonplaces, 60, 153, 161
non-theming, 77
Norman, Donald, 241
Normandy Coast, France, 253
Normandy Farms, 4
normative space, 98, 99
norms, 147, 149, 177. *See also* values
North Africa, 125. *See also* Casablanca
Northern Arizona University, 61, 67
nostalgia, 10, 31, 84, 120, 124, 127, 130,

206n73, 231, 240, 289n22
no-tell motels, 170
Novalogic, 251
NRA SportsBlast, 17, 272, 278, 279, 290n30. *See also* National Rifle Association
Nye, Russell, 247

Oakwood Theme Park, 282
oast house, 240
objects. *See* artifacts
obsolescence, 209, 219
Occupation Museum, 13
The Old Summer Palace, 99
Old Two Spot, 69–70
Olmsted, Frederick Law, 204n52
Omaha Beach, 251
Ono, Yoko, 154, 157, 158
orderliness, 145
organizational culture, 185, 187
organizational stories, 203n35
Orientalism, 123
Orlando, Florida, 13, 18, 196, 199, 236, 274
the Other, 122, 123
overdetermination, 167

Pacific Islands, 142, 195
Page, Max, 47, 48
Palace Gardens, 115, 127
Palace Hotel, 115, 126
Palace Museum, 107
Palestinians, 254
Palms Las Vegas, 89, 173
Pan-American Exposition, 41
panorama, 120, 123, 126, 128, 229
Paramount, 284
Paranoia Cafe, 272, 283
paranormal, 283
Paris, France, 88, 101, 273
Paris Las Vegas, 76, 79, 80, 83, 85, 87, 88
Park, Richard, 187
parks, 155
Parthenon, 60
Parton, Dolly, 4, 5, 11, 23–35
Parton, Willadeene, 24
pastiche, 59, 163
Patagonia, 211

pathology. *See* psychology
patients, 16, 236, 237
patina, 83, 127
Patraka, Vivian, 48
patriotism, 66, 87, 254
patrons. *See* customers
Pearl Harbor, 262
Pearl, Minnie, 27
Pearman, Hugh, 155
pedagogy, 7, 45, 86, 106, 250, 277, 280, 286
pedestrianism, 62, 64, 71, 72, 106, 126, 143, 144, 233
Pentecostals, 274
Pentagon, 101
perception, 184
performance, 3, 9, 29, 46, 48, 49, 50, 51, 80, 81, 82, 86, 100, 101, 102, 103, 104, 105, 106, 107, 108, 123, 184, 186, 190, 192, 194, 196, 208, 212, 214, 215, 236, 257, 275
performance culture, 188, 193, 202n18
performative theming, 75, 76, 77, 78, 295
personality. *See* psychology
personalization, 12, 215, 260
personal transformation, 239
perspective, control of, 191
Peterson, Richard, 29
Peters, Tom, 204n54
Philadelphia, Pennsylvania, 253
Phoenix, Arizona, 97
Phoenix Sky Harbor International Airport, 97
photography, 160, 213, 215, 240, 253, 273, 284
picnolepsy, 111n33
picturesque, 113, 114, 116, 117, 119, 120, 121, 122, 123, 126, 127, 128, 130
picture writing, 229
Pigeon Forge, Tennessee, 5, 24, 26, 30, 31, 32, 33, 35
Pine, Joseph, 228, 235, 237
Pirates of the Caribbean, 251, 282, 286
Piss Christ, 273
place, emotional attachment to, 17, 61, 70
place branding, 234, 235. *See also* branding
Place Branding, 235

place-making, 122
Planet Hollywood, 3, 97, 170
Planet Hollywood Hotel and Casino, 89, 90n5, 281
plants, 66, 84, 101, 103, 104, 121, 125, 126. See also nature
plaques. See signage
Plater-Zyberk, Elizabeth, 232
Plato, 9
pluralism, 144
poetry, 120
political correctness, 284
political economy, 57, 58, 61, 67
politics, 8, 9, 13, 17, 61, 63, 64, 66, 89, 98, 115, 138, 154, 185, 199, 248, 254, 255, 274, 283, 286, 287
Polynesian Resort (Disney), 195, 199
polysemy, 14
Pontiac, Illinois, 58
pools. See swimming pools
population. See demography
pornography, 115, 175, 284
postcolonialism, 122
Post-Fordism, 212, 213, 215, 216, 217, 218, 219
Postmetropolis, 59
postmodernism, 12, 14, 17, 23, 32, 33, 57, 58, 59, 60, 61, 66, 72, 119, 129, 142, 172, 178, 238, 272, 280, 281, 282, 283, 284, 285, 286
Postmodern Metropolis, 59
Postrel, Virginia, 81
poststructuralism, 50
power. See hegemony
pratfall, 257
predictability, 196
Premier Parks, 5
presentation of self, 144
Pretoria, South Africa, 115
The Price of Freedom: Americans at War, 291n37
primitive, 10, 116, 123, 124, 209
Prison Restaurant, 278
Prisoner's Canteen, 280
prisons, 1, 253, 277, 278
privacy, 170, 171, 177
privatization, 60, 72, 141, 142
production, 4, 16, 58, 59, 105, 107, 208, 209, 210, 211, 212, 213, 216, 218, 219
Promotion of Bantu Self-Government Act, 114
pseudo-events, 119
Psycho, 291n35
psychology, 1, 5, 7, 14, 17, 87, 90, 186, 192, 210, 248, 260, 265n6, 277. See also cognition
public commentary, 3, 272, 274, 276, 280, 281, 284, 287
public space, 141, 142, 157
purity, 45
puzzles, 250

Qiang, 107
Quake, Quake II, 251, 254, 259
Queen Elizabeth, 158
Queen Mary, 175
queering, 172
queue line, 11, 214
Quick Strike, 186

Rabelais and His World, 268n19
rabu hoteru. See love hotels
race. See ethnicity
racism. See ethnicity
radio, 25
railroad, 61, 63, 68, 69, 70, 156, 278
Rainbow Six, 253, 266n14
Rainforest Cafe, 1, 89, 170
rational-scientific logic, 230
rationalization, 88, 89, 192
the real, 50, 200, 208, 209, 221, 247, 251, 260, 262, 264
real estate, 62, 225, 226, 229, 233, 235
reality television, 15, 220
Real World (theme park), 285, 292n57, 293n58
reassurance, 83
rebranding, 154, 158, 159, 161, 236. See also branding
redevelopment, 61, 64, 70, 71, 72, 228, 232, 248
referentiality, 118, 124
reflexive accumulation, 105, 106
regionalism, 29
Register, Woody, 42

reincarnation, 285
relations. *See* social relations
relaxation, 111n23
Relic Hunter, 130
religion, 13, 100, 137, 140, 142, 146, 186, 263, 275, 280, 288n15
remaking, 251
representation, 17, 271, 272, 274, 276, 277, 281, 283, 284, 285, 286, 287
"representing the unrepresentable," 277
The Republic, 9
research, 2, 230, 241
Resident Evil, 251
resonance and wonder, 8, 91n11
restaurants, themed, 3, 18, 19n5, 22n63, 60, 71, 82, 107, 163, 226, 248, 271, 278, 279, 280, 287, 287n4
Reston, Virginia, 232
retheming, 17, 281–82, 296
rhetoric, 48, 49, 81, 122, 167, 172, 174, 175, 176, 178, 179, 190, 207, 284; visual, 173, 174, 175
Rhinestone, 24
rhizome, 197
rides, 28, 29, 32, 39, 40, 41, 42, 85, 101, 119, 127, 185, 189, 190, 191, 207, 214, 215, 229, 250, 255, 257, 260, 273, 279, 285
rights, 108
Rio Hotel and Casino, 79, 85, 89; and Carnival World Buffet, 85
risk, 99, 247, 248, 249, 257, 258
Ritzer, George, 227
The River of Life, 28
Riviera Hotel and Casino, 79, 89
roads, 67
Roadside America, 30, 31, 32–33
road trip, 30
Robben Island, 129
Robertson, Kent, 71
Roche Noire, 139
Rockies, 157
Rock Star, 220
Rockwell, David, 242
Rockwell, Norman, 242
rococo, 169
role-playing, 192, 213, 250, 253, 263
role-playing games, 266n10

roller coaster. *See* rides
Roller Coaster Tycoon, 285
Rolling Stone, 158
Roman baths, 16
Romanian Orthodox Church, 280
romanticism, 117, 119, 123, 124, 125, 126, 127, 128
Rose, Nikolas, 187, 197
Roswell, New Mexico, 58
Rouse, James, 228, 229
Route 66, 70
routinization, 184, 196
rudeness, 188
ruins, 115, 116, 117, 119, 120, 121, 126, 127, 128
rule-based play, 266n10
Rydell, Robert, 45
ryokan, 168, 169

S&M, 3, 169, 170, 172
sacred sites, 276
sacrifice, 284
Safeco Field, 97
safety, 41, 43, 44, 68, 98, 99, 163, 186, 231, 236, 247, 248, 257, 258, 260
San Diego, California, 282
Sandvoss, Cornel, 266n9
San Francisco, California, 46, 230
San Francisco Exhibition, 90n4
San Jose, California. *See* Santana Row
San Luis Obispo, California, 282
San Remo, 79
Sanrio, 176. *See also* Hello Kitty
Santa Monica, California, 230, 235
Santana Row, 16, 233, 234, 243
Saving Private Ryan, 251
Scarface, 251
schedules. *See* time
Schivelbusch, Wolfgang, 155
Schmitt, Bernd, 12
Schor, Juliet B., 211
science and technology studies (STS), 153
Scotland, 281
scripted themes, 231
Scriptorium, 275
scripts, 71, 82, 118, 183, 189, 190, 198, 199, 226, 229, 230, 232, 234, 242, 249, 250, 251, 273

Sealey, Jeanne, 27
Seaside, Florida, 6, 232
Seaside Imaging, 237, 243
Seattle, Washington, 97
Second Life, 21n50
security. *See* safety
Sedgwick, Eve, 48
segregation, 11, 33, 122, 137, 139, 142, 143, 144, 146, 147, 192, 237, 242
Seinfeld, 256
self, 184, 196, 220
semiotics, 7, 9, 14, 82, 90, 113, 122, 142, 149, 169, 170, 171, 178, 192, 214, 275, 285
Sensation exhibit, 273
the senses, 6, 32, 53n2, 75–90, 192, 193; and aurality, 84, 86, 94n48; simultaneous use of, 77, 78, 82, 85, 89, 238, 278; and smell, 83, 85, 86, 94n48, 280, 285; and taste, 85, 86, 93n38, 178; and touch, 83, 85, 89; and vision, 77, 78, 82, 83, 89, 122. *See also* rhetoric, visual
sensuality, 86, 88, 143, 154, 169
sentimentality, 122
September 11th, 255, 262, 268n21, 278
Seremetakis, C. Nadia, 88
serial killers, 284
Serrano, Andres, 273
service industry, 75, 184, 187, 188, 200, 230, 231
Seventh-Day Adventist, 236
sexism. *See* gender
sexuality, 12, 48, 167, 168, 169, 170, 172, 173, 174, 177, 212. *See also* gender
Shakaland, 129
Shanghai, China, 100
Sheba, Queen of, 128
Shenzhen, China, 100, 101
Shepherd, Jean, 27
Shona, 115
shopping malls. *See* malls
Sichuan Province, 107
Sidi Belyout, 139
Siegfried and Roy, 83
Sighisoara, Romania, 17, 272, 279, 280, 291n35
signage, 9, 11, 75, 78, 79, 80, 81, 87, 103, 121, 126, 127, 129, 143, 187, 231, 271, 273
Silver Dollar City, 26
Sim City, 269n25
Sim Theme Park, 285
Simonson, Alex, 12
The Simpsons, 256
simulacrum. *See* simulation
simulation, 8, 9, 24, 29, 59, 89, 100, 114, 115, 118, 122, 124, 129, 130, 138, 153, 154, 157, 159, 167, 172, 178, 195, 218, 220, 221, 247, 248, 263, 278, 285
Sin City (South Africa), 115
Siren Show, 82
Six Flags, 76, 78, 183–201, 252, 279
Six Flags AstroWorld, 8, 10, 13, 183–201, 273, 274
Six Flags Over Texas, 1
Sky Screamer, 185
slavery, 253, 276, 287
sleaze, 177
slot machines, 77, 80, 84, 86
smile, 200
Smith, Patti, 26
Smith, Paul, 154
Smithsonian Air and Space Museum, 274
Smoky Mountains, 24, 25, 26, 30, 33
Smoky Mountains National Park, 23, 24, 25, 30
Smut & Eggs, 284
social change, 209, 212, 218
social class, 10, 28, 44, 45, 47, 51, 58, 72, 87, 98, 99, 102, 104, 114, 123, 137, 138, 139, 141, 142, 144, 147, 150, 217, 242, 248, 268n19
social control, 86, 98, 102, 184, 187, 191, 196
social engineering, 108
social institutions, 249
socialism, 98, 100
socialization, 203n27
social relations, 7, 16, 81, 85, 86, 87, 88, 89, 93n37, 93n38, 102, 144, 145, 146, 176, 178, 183, 184, 185, 186, 197, 198, 200, 201, 265
social reproduction, 210
sociology of culture, 264

Soja, Edward, 30, 58
solitude, 82, 83, 120, 121
Solvang, California, 5
South Africa, 8, 10, 113–30
South China Mall, 101
Southern California, 106
Southernism, 33
South Park, 284
South Street Seaport, 229
souvenirs, 158, 160, 280, 286
Soviet Union, 226, 253
space, categories of, 97
spatial narrative, 230, 252
speaking in tongues. *See* glossolalia
special effects, 7, 127, 208, 249
Special Improvement District (SID), 62, 63, 64, 65
specialty shops. *See* boutique spaces
spectacle, 42, 43, 45, 46, 47, 50, 51, 59, 60, 85, 118, 122, 123, 155, 162, 178, 179, 209, 247
speech act theory, 48
speed. *See* time
Speke, 155, 156, 161, 162
spiel, 190
spirituality. *See* religion
Space Mountain, 214
Splash Mountain, 214
Splendid China (Shenzhen, China), 99
Splendid China (Orlando, Florida), 273, 286, 289n19
Splinter Cell, 253
Spooky 3D, 282
sports, 147, 173
sports venues, 60, 71, 97, 226
sprawl, 139, 289n18
St. Mark's Square, 86
stage (metaphor of), 16, 76, 98, 105, 183, 190, 194, 198, 226, 228, 237, 238, 249
Stalingrad, Russia, 251
Stalin World. *See* Grūtas Statue Park
standardization, 209, 219, 239, 248
Starbucks, 82–83, 92n28, 157, 172, 192
Stargate Dental, 4, 282
Star Trek, 4, 282
Starways restaurant, 162
the State, 88, 187

state-enabling legislation, 59, 62, 63, 64, 70
Statue of Liberty, 169
Steelman, Paul, 118
Steeplechase Park, 41, 43, 44, 283
Stendhal's syndrome, 32, 36n41
stereotype, 10, 114, 116, 118, 126, 127, 128, 183, 248, 251, 254, 264, 272
Stern, Robert A. M., 237
Stewart, Susan, 34
Stoker, Bram, 279
Stone Forest Industries, 69
"Stop Dreaming. Start Living," 173
story. *See* narrative
storyboarding, 198, 231
Straight Talk, 24
strategic planning, 138
stratification. *See* segregation
Stratosphere Hotel Casino, 78, 85
Streetmosphere, 86
The Strip. *See* Las Vegas, Nevada
strip mall, 32
subjectivity, 3, 9, 12, 13, 15, 61, 80, 89, 120, 121, 175, 187, 192, 194, 197, 198, 204n37, 211
sublime, 32, 33, 77, 91n9, 91n11, 120, 127, 130n2, 268n19
The Suffering: Ties that Bind, 16, 253
suicide, 283
Sun Beach, 138, 142
Sun City, 114, 115, 122
Sun International, 118
Sunset Crater, 67
Supernova, 220
surveillance, 102, 189
surveys, 190
suspension of disbelief, 191, 243
swimming pools, 140, 141, 145
Sword and Crown, 185
Syberia, 250
symbols, 2, 5, 14, 60, 108, 117, 159, 167, 168, 169, 174, 179, 200, 210, 211, 213, 219, 240, 247, 263, 273, 274
synergy, 18, 98, 101, 199, 227, 229
synesthesia, 81
Syria, 254

Tahiti Beach, 138

Tahiti Plage, 138, 142
Taitanic [sic], 278
Taiwan, 102, 262, 272, 278, 283
Taj Mahal, 67, 125
taming, 122
Tao, 86
Tarzan, 10, 116, 130, 131n17
taste, 122, 143
Taussig, Michael, 91n21, 187
Taylorism, 14, 212
team performance, 263
Team Rodent, 195
technology, 9, 25, 40, 41, 42, 50, 51, 149, 219, 248, 252, 274, 287
Tel-Avi, 146
television, 25, 59, 102, 145, 220, 230, 252, 254, 273, 284
Temple of the Forbidden Eye, 214
terrorism, 254, 257, 262, 263, 266n14, 267n16, 268n21
Texas Cyclone, 185, 201
text, 113, 121, 176
"That's Hot," 50
theater, 43, 51, 52, 100, 123, 155, 220, 228, 237, 257
thematic economy, 285
theme enhancement, 231
theme lands, 11, 185, 186, 187, 188, 193, 196, 201
theme parks, 60, 97, 100, 108, 115, 117, 119, 209
themes, 90n2; 117; African, 117, 118, 172; airpower, 274; Arabian, 75, 90n5, 172; Arthurian, 75, 81, 185; Asian, 185, 191; automobile, 172, 208, 209, 210, 215, 217, 218; Buddhist, 18, 93n41; carnival, 75; cartoons, 171, 172; circus, 75; cities, 80; conflicting, 77; dinosaurs, 283; Egyptian 4, 15, 16, 75, 79, 82, 83; English, 282; European/Alps, 185, 282; French/Parisian, 75, 79, 117; high-tech, 282; Hollywood, 59, 172, 208, 249; idiosyncratic, 76; Irish, 75; Italian, 75, 76, 79, 81, 121, 129, 171, 172, 174, 281; jungle, 171; local, 6, 58, 157, 163, 240; maritime/sea, 156, 168, 175; Mayan, 3, 18, 131n13, 188, 191, 198; Mediterranean, 75; Mexican, 185, 282; money, 283; music, 75, 84, 88; as national identity, 137, 138, 179; New Orleans, 75; pirates, 75, 79, 82, 171, 281, 282; Polynesian 15, 138, 172; popular culture, 59; prisons, 171, 277, 278; railroad, 69–70; science fiction, 3, 16, 75, 169, 171, 250, 251, 256; Southwest, 4; spacecraft, 274; Spanish, 16; sports, 21n37, 59, 71, 75, 173; style 145; toilet, 283, 292n50; tropical, 16, 75, 79, 83, 127, 272, 285; typology, 113; urban, 231, 234; Venetian, 16, 83, 101, 169, 218; Victorian, 282; western, 3, 15, 16, 33, 75, 79–80, 100, 171, 185, 189, 190, 194, 272, 285; the world, 100, 283
themescapes, 119
theme town. *See* cities, themed.
theming; adult-oriented, 40, 281, 282; as aggressive, 188, 190, 203n28; ambiguity of, 14, 89, 197, 241, 282; changing, 42, 43; cheap or shoddy, 76, 188, 274; childlike, 281, 284; conceptual, 41, 272, 282, 285, 286; consistency of, 184, 186; and controversy, 3, 13, 17, 271, 272, 274, 275, 282, 283, 284, 285, 286, 287; as culturally meaningful, 273; defined, 1, 2, 18n3, 98, 117, 118, 272, 281, 291n40, 296; emerging, 4; as emulation, 154; as exclusion/inclusion, 272; familiarity of, 75, 88, 117, 170; as internalization of, 186; naturalness of, 186; personalization of, 78, 81, 84, 88, 94n57, 239; proportions, 281; rewarding, 192; as shorthand, 117; stretching of, 169; surreal, 293n58; ubiquity of, 3, 15; versus everyday life, 172, 177, 178, 179, 186, 199, 201, 227, 228, 239, 243, 252, 260, 262, 263, 268n20. *See also* airports, themed; cities, themed; cruise ships, themed; homes, themed; hospitals, themed; hotels, themed; restaurants, themed; scripted themes; theme lands; theme parks; themes.
theming complex, 7, 76, 77, 80, 296

theming palimpsest, 282, 296
theming vistas, 81, 88, 107, 119, 121, 126, 296
The Theming of America, 3, 60
therapy, 242–43
Third Street Promenade, 230, 232
Thompson, Frederic, 41, 42, 43
three-dimensional spaces, 80, 183, 249
thrill, 207
T. I. *See* Treasure Island Las Vegas
Tibet, 104
Tidal Wave, 185
Tilyou, George, 41
time, 32, 79, 107, 108, 109, 119, 128, 176, 275, 283
Time Hotel, 272, 283, 286
Times Square, 97, 231, 278, 279
Tiananmen Square, 103
Titanic, 1, 278, 290n28
Tokyo Disneyland, 168
Tokyo Disney Sea, 168
Tokyo, Japan, 278
Tolkien, J. R. R., 250
Tomorrowland, 213
The Tonight Show, 26
Top Gun, 193
topography, 33
Toulier, Bernard, 154
tourism, 30, 31, 32, 33, 58, 59, 61, 67, 70, 72, 94n48, 102, 104, 107, 108, 115, 118, 122, 123, 125, 128, 145, 146, 208, 209, 211, 212, 213, 215, 231, 232, 234, 274, 277
The Tourist, 208
tower, 45, 156
The Towering Inferno, 39
training, 76, 78, 105, 184, 186, 188, 189, 191, 193, 194, 195, 198, 200; on-the-job, 190, 196, 203n27; Operations, 189, 196; Train the Trainer, 191; Welcome to Six Flags, 198
transgression, 173, 258, 260
transportation, 51, 61, 156, 231
Treasure Island Las Vegas, 79, 82, 281
triad, of worker, patron and management, 184, 191
Trip to the Moon, 41
Tristram Shandy, 24

Tropicana (Morocco), 142
Tropicana Hotel and Casino, 80
Trumbull, Douglas, 7
Trump, Donald, 50
Tuan, Yi-Fu, 8–9, 77, 276
Turkey, 125
Turner, Patrick, 278
Turner, Victor, 14, 17, 273
Twisted Spoke, 284
Tyler, (Dred) Scott, 273

UEDs. *See* Urban Entertainment Destinations
ultra lounge, 86
Ultra Twister, 185
Under Ash, 254
Underground Atlanta, 232
Underground Railroad, 276
UNESCO, 279, 291n34
uniforms. *See* costumes
United 93, 278
United Kingdom, 125, 154, 158, 272, 274
United States Army, 267n16
Universal, 71
Universal Studios, 5, 15, 207, 208, 209, 213, 214, 215, 219, 220, 230, 291n35
Universal Studios CityWalk, 16, 230, 231, 240, 243
Unreal, 251
Urban Entertainment Destinations, 15, 226, 227, 228, 229, 230, 231, 232, 233, 234, 236, 241
Urban Land, 231
Urban Land Institute, 226, 229
urbanism, 42, 43, 44, 46, 48, 50, 51, 52, 57, 58, 59, 60, 72, 73n14, 100, 103, 120, 138, 229, 231, 232, 233, 248
urban/rural continuum, 103
urban village, 99, 103
urine, 283
Urry, John, 5, 105, 117
use value, 61
utilitarianism, 141, 158
utopia, 118

Vagamundo, 159
Valley of Waves, 115, 127
values, 195–201, 272, 277. *See also* norms

Valve Software, 254
vampires. *See* Dracula
Van der Rohe, Mies, 235
vaudeville, 257
Venetian Resort Hotel Casino, 76, 79, 80, 81, 83, 87, 104
Venturi, Robert, 32, 172, 178
vernacular culture, 31
Versailles, 125
Verwoerd, H. F., 114
ViaCom, 71
vice, 176
Victoria and Alfred Waterfront, 129
video, 277, 278
video games, 16–17, 190, 247–65, 284; design, 249, 250, 252, 254; game engine, 251, 261; game play, 256, 258–59; player interactions in, 250, 263, 264, 265
Vikings, 286
Village at Waveny Care, 240, 242, 243
violence, 90, 255, 256, 259, 260, 261, 262, 263, 264, 266n14, 278, 279
Viper, 185
Virilio, Paul, 111n33, 153
virtual reality, 16, 59, 217, 248, 252, 257, 259, 260, 261, 263, 264, 278, 282
virtual theming, 7, 16, 248, 252, 253, 254, 256, 263, 264, 284, 296
Virtual World, 282
visitor center. *See* convention and visitors bureau
visual modes, 77, 119, 120, 121, 123, 126, 129, 155. *See also* rhetoric, visual
Vivendi, 230
Vlad III the Impaler, 279
volcano, 127
vomit, 283, 284
Voodoo Mansion, 282
voyeurism, 221

Wagoner, Porter, 25
Wagon Wheel, 190
Waldrep, Shelton, 118
Wales, 282
Wallace, Mike, 289n18
Wal-Mart, 67, 242
Walt Disney World, 94n54, 124, 195, 213, 214, 237, 240, 273, 291n35
Walnut Canyon, 67, 70
Warhol, Andy, 26
Warner Brothers, 279
Washington, D.C., 226, 277, 291n37
watchers, 288n11
water, 80, 85, 99, 101, 116, 120, 121, 126, 127, 208, 220
waterpark, 115, 127
Waters, John, 285
Water World, 214
Watson, Patrick, 115
Wayne, John, 253
Wayne's World, 284
weapons, 252, 253, 254, 256, 260, 261, 263, 278, 279, 290n30
Weapons of Destruction, 260
Weis, Robert, 276
Weisten, Stephen, 42, 45
welfare, 98
West Edmonton Mall, 97, 172
westerncentrism, 101, 280
What Is the Proper Way to Display an American Flag?, 273
The White City, 44, 45, 46
White Limozeen, 27
wilderness, 121, 122, 127
Williams, Michael Ann, 25, 27, 30, 33, 34, 35
Willis, Susan, 106
Wilson, Alexander, 213
Wimberly Allison Tong and Goo (WATG), 115, 117, 118, 125, 131n13
Window on the World, 100, 101
Wisconsin Dells, 36n33
wish image, 154
Wizard of Oz, 281
Wolf, Michael, 226, 227, 228, 229
Woolton, Lord, 161
work. *See* labor
workers. *See* employees
Working Assets, 211
"The World in a Shopping Mall," 163
World of Warcraft, 250
World's Columbian Exposition 3, 10, 44, 45
world's fairs, 18, 40, 44, 90n4
World Trade Center, 286, 291n37

World Trade Center (film), 278
worldview, 197
World War II, 251, 253, 276, 280
Wuptaki, 67
Wynn Las Vegas, 76, 78, 81, 87, 285

York, England, 16, 272, 280, 286
Young, Terence, 9
"You're Fired!," 50

A Year in Provence, 171
Yerba Buena Gardens, 230, 232

Zedong, Mao, 286
Ziesel, John, 241, 243
Žižek, Slavoj, 5
Zombie, Rob, 291n35
zoning, 60, 62

Contributors

Peter Adey is lecturer in cultural geography at Keele University in the United Kingdom. Peter's work revolves around the links between space, time, and mobility, and much of his empirical research has focused upon airport geographies, security, and surveillance, and the development of aviation in Britain. His most recent articles include: "If Mobility Is Everything then It Is Nothing: Towards a Relational Politics of (Im)mobilities" (*Mobilities*, no.1: 75–94) and "Airports and Air-mindedness: Spacing, Timing and Using Liverpool Airport, 1929–1939" (*Social and Cultural Geography* 7, no. 3: 343–63). He is currently preparing a monograph on aviation culture.

Ann Brigham is associate professor of English and women's and gender studies at Roosevelt University. Her scholarship focuses on productions of geographic space and scale in literary and cultural forms and has been published in the journals *Genders* and *Modern Fiction Studies* as well as edited a number of collections. Coeditor of *Making Worlds: Gender, Metaphor, Materiality* (1998), she is currently writing a book on shifting representations of social and spatial mobility in twentieth-century American road narratives. Although her longtime interest in tourist sites has taken a scholarly turn, the thrill of riding roller coasters (front row, of course) remains.

Derek Foster received his Ph.D. in communication from Carleton University. He is an assistant professor in the Department of Communications, Popular Culture, and Film at Brock University (St. Catharines, Ontario, Canada). His research interests focus on rhetorical analyses of media. Media, in this context, range from mass media to new media, to unconventional media such as architecture and public art. His research into visual rhetoric attempts to "mine the gap" between mass communication and speech communication. To this end, he has published on such subjects as newspaper constructions of controversial social issues, reality television, environmental protests, and online culture. And yes, he has stayed in a number of Japanese love hotels.

Melissa Jane Hardie lectures English and cultural studies at the University of Sydney, with a special interest in affect theory and the vernacular landscape. Her recent work includes an article on "repulsive modernism" in the *Journal of Modern Literature* and a monograph called *Shame Became Famous: Rhetoric of Disclosure in Public Life, 1989–2001*.

Brian Lonsway is associate professor of architecture at Syracuse University. An architectural theorist and technology researcher, Brian's work concerns the history and contemporary context of technological mediations of space. He has lectured and written on issues concerning the spatiality of computing, the architectural theory of data, and the post-structuralist semiotics of contemporary design practice. He is completing his first book, *Making Leisure Work: Architecture and the Entertainment Economy*, which will appear in 2008.

Scott A. Lukas received his Ph.D. in cultural anthropology from Rice University. He is currently chair of the Anthropology/Sociology Department at Lake Tahoe College and taught previously at Valparaiso University. In 2003 he was selected winner of the Hayward Award for Excellence in Education in the state of California and, in 2005, the recipient of the national McGraw-Hill Award for Excellence in Undergraduate Teaching of Anthropology by the American Anthropological Association. He is the founder of the Gender Ads Project (www.genderads.com), and he has participated in three National Endowment for the Humanities seminars, including "Terror and Culture: Revisiting Hannah Arendt's Origins of Totalitarianism" at Stanford University, "American Cities and Public Spaces" at the Library of Congress, and "Human Rights in Conflict: Interdisciplinary Perspectives" at the CUNY Graduate School. He is currently completing the volume *Fear, Cultural Anxiety, and Transformation: Horror, Science Fiction, and Fantasy Films Remade* (coedited with John Marmysz, Lexington Books, 2008), as well as *Theme Park* (Reaktion Books, 2008).

Bahíyyih Maroon received her Ph.D. in architectural anthropology. Currently she is working on structural incarnations of CIAM 10's "Housing for the Many." She recently completed work on the Herzog & de Meuron de Young Museum in San Francisco. Her writing has appeared in several publications including *The Cell Phone Reader* and *Shock and Awe: War on Words*. She is currently at work on a monograph, *Technogenic Turns*, examining the convergence of culture, architecture, and new communication technologies.

Contributors

Thomas W. Paradis is associate professor of geography at Northern Arizona University at Flagstaff. In 2005 he became the director of academic assessment for NAU, given his interests in geographic education and student learning. His research interests include urban political economy, nonmetropolitan growth, downtown revitalization, historic preservation, neo-traditional design, and cultural landscape studies—all of which inform his research on themed landscapes of downtown business districts. His first book *Theme Town: A Geography of Landscape and Community in Flagstaff, Arizona* (2003), focused primarily on Flagstaff's downtown redevelopment and architecture. Tom is currently serving as Series Editor for a ten-book set by Greenwood Press, *Homes Through American History*, and is also writing its 1860–1880 volume on domestic architecture. Tom still teaches his two favorite courses, Urban Design and Preservation, and the capstone course for geography majors, Field Analysis.

Hai Ren is an assistant professor of East Asian studies and anthropology at the University of Arizona. His research focuses on comparative popular culture, everyday life, and inventive politics. He is the guest editor of "Neo-liberal Governmentality: Technologies of the Self & Governmental Conduct," a special issue of the online journal *Rhizomes*.

Lynn Sally received her Ph.D. at New York University. She is an assistant professor at Metropolitan College of New York. Her area of specialty is nineteenth-century American popular culture. Her interest in themed spaces began when she took a course on world's fairs in graduate school and continued through the research of her dissertation. Her book based on her dissertation, *Fighting the Flames: The Spectacular Performance of Fire at Coney Island*, is published by Routledge Press (2006). She has published articles and reviews in *The Journal of Popular Culture* and *Senses and Society* as well as an encyclopedia entry forthcoming in the *Encyclopedia of American Material Culture*. She is currently developing a book-length project that examines burlesque and the display of female bodies at world's fairs.

Jeanne van Eeden is an associate professor in the Department of Visual Arts, University of Pretoria, South Africa, where she teaches art history and visual culture. She is particularly interested in the role of the entertainment economy in postcolonial South Africa as well as in issues concerning identity, spatiality, gender, and representation in contemporary visual culture. She has published articles and presented conference papers that deal with these topics, is the coeditor of the book *South Africa Visual Culture* (Van Schaik, 2005), and assistant editor of the South African journal, *Image & Text*. Her interest in theming and entertainment landscapes stems from her doctoral thesis on the Lost City theme park in South Africa.

Talmadge Wright is an associate professor of sociology at Loyola University Chicago. His current work includes the study of players of first-person shooter games and the meanings they derive from their play. He has published and presented papers on players of the game *Counter-Strike* and is working on developing a sociology of video games which transcends the limited debates over media effects. In addition, he is also working on the relationship between modern digital play, consumer culture, and the production of gendered relationships. Another aspect of his work focuses on the issue of fantasy violence in modern society, mass media, and the role of the military and game industry. His prior work has been in the area of popular culture and themed architecture, homelessness, housing, urban social and political inequality, and social movements for justice.

Made in the USA
Middletown, DE
18 February 2015